Young Children with Special Needs

Nancy H. Fallen
Virginia Commonwealth University

with **Jill E. McGovern**
College of Charleston

CHARLES E. MERRILL PUBLISHING COMPANY
A Bell & Howell Company
Columbus Toronto London Sydney

to our mothers
Belva Byrd Herr
and
June Cottrill McGovern

Published by
Charles E. Merrill Publishing Company
A Bell & Howell Company
Columbus, Ohio 43216

This book was set in Caledonia and Optima.
The Production Editor was Linda Hillis.
The cover was prepared by Will Chenoweth
with illustration by Ann Michaels.

International Standard Book Number:
0-675-8382-6

Library of Congress Catalog Card Number:
77-94237

1 2 3 4 5 6 7 8—82 81 80 79 78
PRINTED IN THE UNITED STATES OF AMERICA

Foreword

Children with special needs are found everywhere—in well-to-do families and those struggling in poverty, in the homes of young couples who are just embarking on the challenges of parenthood, and in those of middle-aged parents completing their childbearing years. They come from every race and ethnic group.

As with other minority groups which work to remove barriers to full participation in our culture, seeking both the joys and responsibilities of membership, the parents and friends of these special children have begun to work together to obtain their acceptance as members of our society. Because this group does cut across socioeconomic and racial lines, it has become a potent lobby influencing the passage of legislation. The Education for All Handicapped Children Act, passed by Congress in 1975, mandates access to appropriate educational opportunities and the development of an individualized educational plan for each child, which is acceptable to parents and involves the many professional groups which are needed.

At the same time, there has been a growing awareness that the first months and years of life are critical. At this time of rapid growth, the organism is most responsive to favorable conditions and most likely to be damaged by unfavorable circumstances. Whereas some years ago parents were encouraged simply to enjoy their baby and wait until school years to begin to cultivate the child's mind, today there is a sense of urgency to expose babies and young children to rich and varied experiences. There is mounting evidence that the baby who is cared for by lively and loving people, who see to it that challenging and interesting things occur, develops more fully than the child who lacks an enriched environment.

This book becomes available at a most auspicious time with respect to these two trends. Interest in bringing the child with special needs into the same educational system available to other children, combined with the sense of urgency to reach and teach children when they are very young, creates the milieu out of which this book emerges. It is addressed to all of the professional groups who work with special children and their families in the schools and in the home of the child.

Dr. Nancy Fallen and her colleagues use a basic child development approach, viewing the specialness of the child as but one facet of a developmental pattern which is understandable and predictable, given our current knowledge of the way children grow and the forces which shape their behavior. Specialized techniques, when recommended, flow from a body of knowledge which applies to all children. These techniques are not exotic or mysterious; they are an imaginative application of tried and true, almost commonsensical, ideas which can be applied to all.

The authors believe that an early start in formulating and implementing an educational plan can help keep the child with special needs moving forward at an optimum rate, not further handicapped by delay in the application of skills and knowledge currently available. However, the book expresses a general approach which can enhance the effectiveness of anyone working with children. The theme might be stated: All children are special, and special children are, first of all, children.

This book will enable educators and others who work with young children to join the parents and lawmakers in meeting their common objectives of educating all young handicapped children.

Laura L. Dittmann, Ph.D.
Institute for Child Study
University of Maryland

Preface

Most textbooks are written in response to some kind of need. *Young Children with Special Needs* is not an exception. In fact, it was conceived in answer to a multifaceted need, but its existence is more closely related to evolution than it is to birth.

The need for a textbook dealing with the unique problems of young handicapped children and their parents became apparent when I became the content coordinator of a video series, *Young Children with Special Needs* (now distributed by Charles E. Merrill Publishing Company). Research for the film content revealed the startling fact that while much valuable information from programs and funded projects across the nation was being disseminated in professional journals, a comprehensive overview of this area in special education had not been published.

Because there was no appropriate book to adopt, the need to create one became apparent to me. For assistance I turned to colleagues at Virginia Commonwealth University and to strategic agencies concerned with the problems of young handicapped children and their families. Their contributions are essential portions of the present text.

In spite of major organizational and editorial changes since its beginning, the purpose of the book has remained unchanged. The overall objective of its creation is to provide a resource to students that will help to answer fundamental questions concerning the needs of the handicapped child, birth through five, and their families.

The first four chapters are addressed to the different kinds of handicapping conditions, the legal aspects of education for young handicapped children, and fundamental considerations relative to identification and educational intervention strategies. The next five chapters deal with problems and educational approaches to the developmental areas of motor, language, cognition, self-help, and emotional/social adjustment. Because play provides a natural environment for skill development in all areas, a chapter has been directed to its importance and appropriate instructional methods. The last two chapters point out the responsibilities of professionals in building effective parent/professional relationships. The importance of understanding family problems associated with living with a handicapped child and knowing the resources available to parents and professionals is emphasized.

The glossary has been included to assist the student with terminology used not only in this book, but also in related literature. The appendices provide a reference to available resources.

The content of the book embraces the thinking of many individuals as indicated by the references to existing literature. The chapters of the contributing authors have brought together the talents of professionals in various disciplines concerned with handicapping conditions in early childhood. While some of this work has disappeared in organizational changes, the underlying thoughts remain. Their contributions to the foundations of this book are gratefully acknowledged and appreciated.

A contribution of great magnitude is that of parents and their handicapped children who have been my teachers for many years. What they have provided is called REALITY. My appreciation goes far beyond the power of words.

Special expressions of gratitude are in order for the assistance provided by the talented Jill McGovern, Anita S. Fallen, and the people at Merrill, Tom Hutchinson, Vicki Knight, and Linda Hillis.

Contents

1

Introduction

Early childhood–special education is a newly emerging field of education which addresses the needs of children from birth to age 6, who, because of some exceptionality, require special educational services to maximize their potential. The trend to merge early childhood education and special education is based on several widely held educational principles. One universally accepted proposition in education is that the first 6 years of a child's life are the most critical ones for establishing the foundation or mental set for later learning. Another generally recognized educational practice is that those children identified as exceptional or special need educational services, in addition to or in place of the regular educational program. These special educational services have generally been provided for children, at the earliest, in the kindergarten or first grade of school. Thus, until recently, exceptional children received few, if any, educational services during the most important years for learning, the first 6 years of their lives. Early childhood–special education, however, attempts to meet the special needs of young children in a more effective manner. This text has as its focus the same area of concern: *young children with special needs.*

Chapter 1 presents an overview of the field of special education as it relates to the needs of young children through a discussion of the following topics:

This chapter was written by **Jill E. McGovern.** It includes material from *David A. Draper* on conditions which may lead to disabilities. Information on litigation and legislation affecting exceptional children was contributed by *Richard S. Vacca.*

1. Definitions of disability, handicap, and impairment, and their educational implications.
2. The need for labeling and the problems with it.
3. Categories of exceptionality: developmental disabilities (mental retardation, cerebral palsy, autism, and multiple handicaps); sensory disabilities (hearing impairment and visual impairment); physical disabilities (orthopedic impairment and other health impairment); language disabilities (speech impairment and learning disabilities); and behavioral disabilities.
4. Legislation including P.L. 94-142 (the Education for All Handicapped Children Act) and litigation related to early childhood–special education.

Definitions of Terms

Among special educators, there is some consensus about terms related to the field, but at the same time, there is little agreement about standard definitions and use of these terms. It seems appropriate, therefore, to define specific terms as they will be employed within this book.

Special education refers to "that additional service, over and above the regular school program, that is provided for an exceptional child to assist in the development of his potentialities and/or the amelioration of his disabilities" (Kirk, 1972, p. 37).

Exceptional child refers to "the child who deviates from the average or normal child . . . to such an extent that he requires a modification of school practices, or special educational services, in order to develop to his maximum capacity" (Kirk, 1972, p. 4). The child's exceptionality may be giftedness, mental retardation, cerebral palsy, autism, multiple handicaps, hearing impairment, visual impairment, physical impairment, speech impairment, learning disabilities, or behavioral disabilities. Exceptional children other than those who are gifted are considered handicapped.

Special child is commonly used as a synonym for exceptional child. Since this text considers all exceptionalities except giftedness, the term *special child* may be interchanged with *exceptional child* or *handicapped child* to refer to a child with any exceptionality other than giftedness.

Disability is defined as an incapacity in one or more aspects of development that may be classified according to the categories of exceptionality addressed in this book: developmental disabilities (mental retardation, cerebral palsy, epilepsy, autism, and multiple handicaps), sensory disabilities (hearing impairment and visual impairment), physical disabilities (orthopedic impairment and other health impairments), language disabilities (speech impairment and learning disabilities), and behavioral disabilities.

Impairment is defined as damage, injury or incapacity. It is used as a synonym for disability. Neither term, *disability* nor *impairment*, necessarily implies that the incapacitating condition is an insurmountable impediment to learning.

Handicap is defined as a physical, mental, sensory, linguistic, or emotional deficiency that prevents normal achievement. The term implies that learning is impeded to such a significant degree that an individual's potential is minimized.

Labeling

The preceding definitions are based on the assumption that it is appropriate to categorize and to label exceptional individuals by their disabilities and deficiencies. The issue of labeling remains an unresolved one in the special education field. There are two widely held positions in the debate over labeling.

Arguments Against Labeling. One argument made against labeling is that it stigmatizes (Telford & Sawrey, 1977). Terms such as *developmental disabilities* seem to give a negative emphasis to the individual's impairment. Once a term is applied to an individual, it is difficult to disassociate him from the label. A second point against the practice of labeling is that it may become a self-fulfilling prophecy. An individual may behave according to what he believes is expected of him as determined by the label, whether it is accurately applied or not. A third argument in opposition to labeling is that such a practice of delimiting categories discriminates against those individuals who do not fall neatly into the classifications. An individual who is outside the categorical limits may be denied special services which he needs. A final reason for not labeling is that it seems to be more important to concentrate on the prevention and treatment of all exceptionalities rather than to expend energies on locating, identifying, and placing exceptional persons in categories.

Arguments for Labeling. One major justification for labeling is that it is helpful as well as necessary to identify clusters of symptoms that convey specific meanings to all persons working with the exceptional person. Labeling is a kind of shorthand that quickly transmits key information and enables professionals to provide appropriate treatment. Another reason for labeling is created by administrative and legal requirements. In many cases an exceptional person may qualify for special services only after he has been identified through some diagnostic procedure as fitting one of the prescribed categories. This practice of labeling for administrative purposes has recently been given increased support by the enactment of P.L. 94-142, the Education for All Handicapped Children Act. This federal law requires school districts to locate, diagnose, and label exceptional children according to clearly delineated guidelines and classifications. Unless children are so identified, and meet the requirements for the labels, they may not be served in special educational programs under this law. Federal and state monies are available only for those exceptional children who *do* fit into the specific classifications.

A final point in favor of labeling is that each category provides a focal point around which community support may be rallied. Voluntary organizations composed of interested parents, laypersons, and professionals often capitalize on the unique needs of one exceptionality to gain further support, to promote

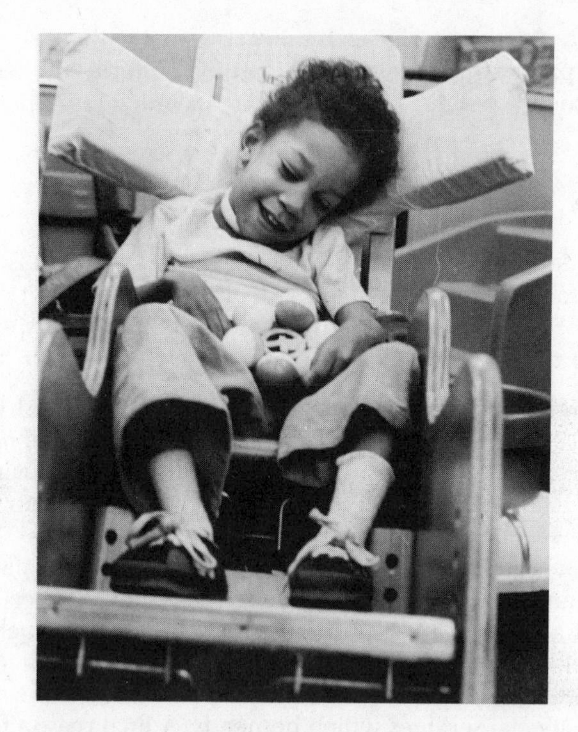

Labeling the exceptional child at this point in the development of special education is justifiable in order to provide the most effective treatment.

beneficial legislation, and to provide direction for planning and programming. Eliminating categorical labels may diffuse the interest and involvement of such groups (Telford & Sawrey, 1977).

The Need to Label. The cases for and against labeling both represent sound and valid arguments. While it is not our intention to advocate stigmatizing an exceptional child by using a label, it is felt that labeling, at this point in the development of special education, is justifiable in order to provide the most effective treatment. The use of categories and labels as defined by P.L. 94-142 will insure, as never before, that the needs of young, special children will be met, and it is to that end that this book is also committed.

Developmental Disabilities

The Developmental Disabled Assistance and Bill of Rights Act, P.L. 94-103, defines a *developmental disability* as a disability attributable to mental retardation, cerebral palsy, epilepsy, autism, or any other conditions closely related to mental retardation. The disability must originate before age 18, must be expected to continue indefinitely, and must constitute a substantial handicap to the individual in order to be classified as a developmental disability. The five specific developmental disabilities will be discussed in terms of definition, characteristics, etiology or cause, prevalence, and significance. For a listing of organizational support groups for all developmental disabilities, see Appendix A.

Mental Retardation

Definition. Mental retardation, as defined by the American Association on Mental Deficiency (AAMD), "refers to significantly subaverage general intellectual functioning existing concurrently with deficits in adaptive behavior, and manifested during the developmental period" (Grossman, 1973). This definition describes the individual in terms of his present functioning, without reference to the etiology or curability of his mental retardation. The phrase "subaverage general intellectual functioning" refers to a certain range of intellectual ability which may be divided into several levels of functioning:

Mild or Educable Mentally Retarded	51-70 IQ
Moderate or Trainable Mentally Retarded	25-50 IQ
Severe and Profound or Custodial Mentally Retarded	Below 24 IQ

The AAMD advocates the use of the terms *mild, moderate, severe,* and *profound* to indicate the various degrees of subnormality. These terms remove some of the negative connotations associated with previously used terms like *feeble-minded, moron, imbecile,* and *idiot.* The designations *educable, trainable,* and *custodial* are used for administrative and educational purposes. Other systems of classifications, like those of the American Psychiatric Association and the National Association for Retarded Citizens, use different terms but the IQ levels generally correspond to the ones presented.

In the AAMD definition, "adaptive behavior" is defined as "the effectiveness or degree with which the individual meets the standards of personal independence and social responsibility expected of his age and cultural group" (Grossman, 1973). Examples of adaptive behavior are sensorimotor skills, communication skills, self-help skills, academic skills, social skills, and later in adolescence and adulthood, vocational skills (Telford & Sawrey, 1977). The mentally retarded person exhibits deficits in one or more of these skill areas.

Characteristics. The characteristics of the mentally retarded vary depending on the level of retardation; generally, the more profound the retardation, the less competency in intellectual functioning and in adaptive behavior. Table 1 summarizes the developmental characteristics of the mentally retarded according to the different degrees of mental retardation.

Etiology. Even though there are more than a hundred identified causes of mental retardation, the exact causes of the majority of cases are unknown. The known etiologies of mental retardation may be classified into two broad categories: *genetic* causes and *environmental* causes.

1. Genetic Causes. Mental retardation caused by a single defective dominant gene occurs rarely (Telford & Sawrey, 1977). The likelihood of the defective dominant gene being transmitted to the next generation is limited, primarily because the characteristics of this kind of mental retardation include sterility.

Table 1
Developmental Characteristics of Mentally Retarded Persons

Degrees of Mental Retardation	Preschool Age 0–5 Maturation and Development	School Age 6–20 Training and Education	Adult 21 and Over Social and Vocational Adequacy
Mild	Can develop social and communication skills; minimal retardation in sensorimotor areas; often not distinguished from normal until later age.	Can learn academic skills up to approximately sixth grade level by late teens. Can be guided toward social conformity. "Educable."	Can usually achieve social and vocational skills adequate to minimum self-support but may need guidance and assistance when under unusual social or economic stress.
Moderate	Can talk or learn to communicate; poor social awareness; fair motor development; profits from training in self-help; can be managed with moderate supervision.	Can profit from training in social and occupational skills; unlikely to progress beyond second grade level in academic subjects; may learn to travel alone in familiar places.	May achieve self-maintenance in unskilled or semiskilled work under sheltered conditions; needs supervision and guidance when under mild social or economic stress.
Severe	Poor motor development; speech is minimal; generally unable to profit from training in self-help; little or no communication skills.	Can talk or learn to communicate; can be trained in elemental health habits; profits from systematic habit training.	May contribute partially to self-maintenance under complete supervision; can develop self-protection skills to a minimal useful level in controlled environment.
Profound	Gross retardation; minimal capacity for functioning in sensorimotor areas; needs nursing care.	Some motor development present; may respond to minimal or limited training in self-help.	Some motor and speech development; may achieve very limited self-care; needs nursing care.

Note: From *Resources in Maryland for the Developmentally Disabled*. Baltimore: Developmental Disabilities Council of Maryland, 1975.

Mental retardation caused by a single recessive gene occurs more frequently than dominant gene mental retardation. Single gene mental retardation may be classified into three general types: biochemical abnormalities, endocrine or gland disorders, and cranial abnormalities. One biochemical abnormality, galactosemia, may be detected by urine tests and, if detected early, may be treated effectively with a galactose-free or lactose-free diet. Abnormal protein, or amino acid, metabolism results in phenylketonuria (PKU), which if untreated causes severe mental retardation. The condition may be detected by blood and urine tests, and normal development may occur if the child is placed on a diet low in the amino acid *phenylalanine.* One condition involving defective fat, or lipoid, metabolism, *amaurotic familial idiocy,* has two forms, depending on the age of onset. The infantile form, known as *Tay-Sachs disease,* has an early onset while the juvenile form may manifest itself later, in the 3- to 10-year age span; both forms involve a deterioration of general functioning and result in early death. Tay-Sachs disease may be prevented through genetic counseling and family planning.

Among the endocrine disorders associated with mental retardation are cretinism, certain types of thyroid conditions and diabetes, sexual infantilism, and dwarfism. *Cretinism,* also known as *hypothyroidism,* is caused by a dysfunction of the thyroid, which results in irreversible central nervous system damage. The extent of hypothyroidism directly affects the degree of mental retardation. Early detection coupled with thyroid treatment can prevent the more severe symptoms (Telford & Sawrey, 1977).

Cranial abnormalities resulting in mental retardation are acrocephaly, anencephaly, and microcephaly. Acrocephalics and anencephalics seldom survive for any length of time, and microcephalics are severely mentally retarded. One other kind of cranial abnormality is hydrocephaly, which is not genetically but rather environmentally caused. Early alleviation of the excessive fluids in the brain prevents enlargement of the cranium as well as mental retardation.

Most *chromosomal abnormalities* result in embryonic or fetal death and spontaneous abortion. Of the surviving newborns with chromosomal aberrations, most are identified as having *Down's syndrome,* or *mongolism.* This group is the largest single category of the severely mentally retarded.

As many as 50 characteristics have been associated with Down's syndrome but this number may be reduced to a few significant signs: (1) a flattened skull; (2) abnormally upturned nostrils; (3) abnormal toe spacing, particularly between the first and second toes; (4) disproportionate shortness of the fifth finger; (5) inwardly curving fifth finger; (6) a fifth finger with only one crease instead of the normal two; (7) short, squared hands; (8) epicanthic fold at the inner corners of the eye; (9) large fissured tongue; (10) presence of the simian crease (a single crease across the palm of the hand); (11) abnormally undeveloped ear; (12) ear close to the head; and (13) abnormal heart (Telford & Sawrey, 1977, pp. 286–287). In addition, most individuals with Down's syndrome are severely mentally retarded.

Down's syndrome may be detected through genetic counseling and amniocentesis, a process by which amniotic fluid containing cells from the fetus is extracted from the pregnant woman and analyzed for chromosomal aberrations. Besides Down's syndrome (sometimes referred to as trisomy 21), trisomy 13 and trisomy 18 may be identified with this technique.

2. Environmental Causes. A greater percentage of mental retardation is caused by environmental factors than by genetic ones. Mental retardation may be caused during prenatal development by malnutrition, infections, toxic agents, radiation, blood incompatibility, and stress. During the perinatal period, anoxia, birth trauma, low birth weight, and prematurity may result in mental retardation. Accidents causing brain

injury, diseases and infections, lead poisoning, malnutrition, and environmental deprivation may produce mental retardation in the postnatal period. All of these possible causes of mental retardation were discussed earlier in this chapter.

Prevalence. The incidence of mental retardation is determined, to a certain extent, by the definition used to classify mentally retarded persons and the age at which the individual is identified as mentally retarded. Estimates range from 1% (Dunn, 1973) to 3% (Mayo, 1962; Telford & Sawrey, 1977). Table 2 illustrates three points: (1) relatively few infants and preschool children are identified as mentally retarded; (2) the percentage of children identified as mentally retarded increases significantly during the school-age period; and (3) the percentage of adults diagnosed as mentally retarded decreases sharply after the school-age period. The significance of the figures reported in Table 2 is that mentally retarded infants and preschool children are not identified and therefore the critical years for learning are wasted. P.L. 94-142, which mandates early identification and special educational services during the preschool years, should change the previous practices so that the special needs of young mentally retarded children will be met.

Significance. The incidence of mental retardation needs to be considered in terms of prevention and treatment. Even though the genetic causes of mental retardation represent a small percentage of all causes, they may be prevented through genetic counseling prior to conception, through amniocentesis during the prenatal period, or through the use of screening measures such as blood and urine analyses for the newborn. Genetic counseling, for example, would enable a couple, both carriers of the recessive gene causing Tay-Sachs disease, to make an informed decision about family planning. Amniocentesis would detect chromosomal aberrations in the developing fetus and allow the woman to terminate the pregnancy. Routine screening of newborns would discover inborn errors of metabolism, such as galactosemia and PKU, and endocrine dis-

Table 2

Incidence of Mental Retardation and Chronological Age

Age in Years	Number per 100 of the General Population
0–4	.07
5–9	1.18
10–14	4.36
15–19	3.02
20–29	.76
30–39	.82
40–49	.74
50–59	.45
60+	.22

Note: Adapted from *The Exceptional Individual* by C. W. Telford and J. M. Sawrey. Englewood Cliffs, N. J.: Prentice-Hall, 1977, p. 240. Reprinted by permission of Prentice-Hall, Inc.

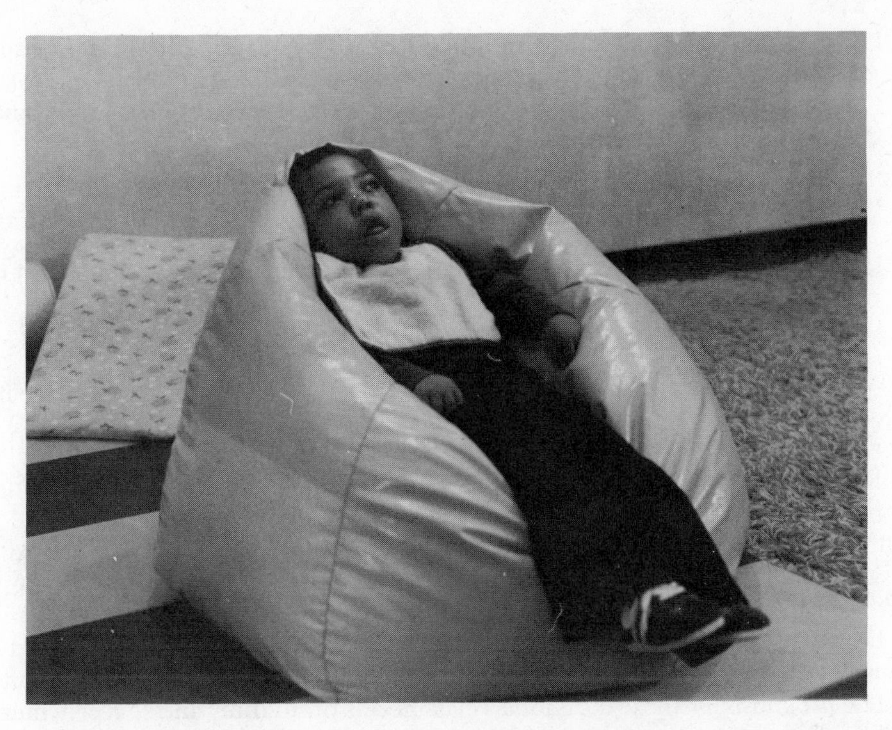

Through early identification and special educational services, the unique needs of young handicapped children can be met.

orders such as cretinism. Immediate treatment with medication or diet modification would prevent mental retardation.

Mental retardation caused by environmental factors could be eliminated or at least reduced in a number of instances if some of the following preventive measures were practiced:

1. Adequate medical care prior to and throughout pregnancy to minimize the risk of undetected and untreated infections and diseases as well as of premature births.
2. Genetic counseling, particularly if the family history indicates the possibility of aberrations or if the mother is over 35.
3. Adequate nutrition for the pregnant woman as well as for the infant.
4. Immunization against rubella for all women before conception.
5. Elimination of toxic agents like drugs, alcohol, and cigarettes during pregnancy.
6. Limitation of radiation exposure for both parents prior to conception and for the mother during pregnancy.
7. Determination of possible incompatible blood factors.
8. Reduction of stressful situations during pregnancy.
9. Thorough medical examination of newborns, including screening of blood and urine for endocrine and metabolic disorders.
10. Immunization against childhood diseases.

11. Adequate safety practices to prevent accidents causing brain injury and ingestion of harmful substances like lead-based paint.
12. Adequate postnatal health and social services to provide preventive health care and education.
13. Family planning information and techniques.
14. Training to prepare parents for their role as the primary educators of their children.
15. A stimulating, supportive environment for the child from the moment of birth.
16. Continued research into the causes of mental retardation.

When mental retardation does occur, appropriate treatment may minimize its effects and enable the mentally retarded to lead independent and productive lives. To be most effective, treatment must begin from the moment the child is diagnosed as mentally retarded or is judged to be at risk for mental retardation. A child living in a deprived environment would be considered at risk for cultural or environmental mental retardation. For example, it has been suggested that approximately 50% of an individual's intellectual development takes place between conception and age 4 and about 30% between ages 4 and 8. Intervention during these first key years may minimize the effects of mental retardation and maximize the individual's potential, whatever its limitations.

The prognosis for those individuals classified as profoundly and severely mentally retarded is somewhat limited, but with early intervention and treatment, a degree of independence may be achieved. Techniques such as behavior modification may be employed to develop self-help skills, basic language skills, and social skills in the individual. It has also been demonstrated that severely mentally retarded persons may be trained to perform simple tasks (Gold, 1973) so that within an appropriate setting, such as a sheltered workshop, they may become productive members of society.

For those individuals classified as moderately and mildly retarded, early intervention and treatment will enable them to benefit from regular educational programs with the support of special education and to learn to function as independent, productive individuals. To achieve this end, two educational practices have been initiated. One practice, early childhood–special education, advocates educational intervention as early as possible for those children diagnosed as mentally retarded. Infant stimulation programs such as Home Start and the Milwaukee Project (Trotter, 1976) are examples of this kind of approach. The other practice, mainstreaming or normalization, places the mentally retarded child in the regular educational program for as much of his instruction as possible. These two trends are not necessarily mutually exclusive. In fact, it is hoped that more widespread adoption of early childhood–special education practices with young mentally retarded children will result in more mainstreaming of school-age mentally retarded children.

Cerebral Palsy

Definition. The United Cerebral Palsy Research and Educational Foundation (1958) has defined cerebral palsy as "a group of conditions, usually originating in childhood, characterized by paralysis, weakness, incoordination or any other aberration of motor function caused by pathology of the motor control center of the brain. In addition to such motor dysfunction, cerebral palsy may include learning difficulties, psychological problems, sensory defects, convulsive and behavioral disorders of organic origin" (p. 1).

Characteristics. The characteristics of cerebral palsy are classified in five basic ways: (1) according to type; (2) according to number of limbs involved; (3) according to time of onset; (4) according to degree of involvement; and (5) according to the extent and nature of the brain damage (Stephen, 1958).

There are three main types of cerebral palsy: spastic, athetoid, and ataxic. With *spasticity,* the normal balance between the antagonistic muscles and the suppressors in the brain is absent. The result is jerky, uncontrolled movements with spasmodic muscle contraction instead of smooth, controlled movements. *Athetosis* is characterized by uncontrollable, jerky, slow, twisting movements. When the muscles of the mouth and throat are involved, speech is labored and drooling may occur. Attempts to increase control and excited reactions to lack of control often compound the situation and lead to further spasticity and tension. *Ataxia* is distinguished by a lack of balance and muscle coordination. The ataxic's gait is awkward, and his posture is uncontrolled.

In addition to these three distinct types of cerebral palsy, many cases of cerebral palsy are mixed with a combination of two or more types. The mixed types are due to damage in more than one area of the brain.

The number of limbs involved is the second way of classifying cerebral palsy. The system of classification is as follows:

1. Monoplegia, involvement in one limb.
2. Hemiplegia, involvement on one side of the body.
3. Triplegia, involvement in three limbs.
4. Paraplegia, involvement in the legs.
5. Quadriplegia, involvement in all four limbs.
6. Diplegia, involvement in all four limbs, with more involvement in the legs.
7. Double hemiplegia, involvement in all four limbs, with more involvement on one side of the body.

The third way of classifying cerebral palsy is according to the time of onset of the condition. Cerebral palsy may occur during the prenatal, perinatal, or postnatal periods, although it is difficult to separate prenatal and perinatal factors.

The degree of involvement may be classified on a continuum from mild to moderate to severe as well as in relation to the associated disabilities of speech, hearing, vision, mental ability, and learning. The extent and nature of brain damage is difficult to determine except as the damage is manifested in motor and sensory impairments.

Etiology. Cerebral palsy is caused by damage to the portion of the central nervous system that affects motor coordination. Such damage may occur in the prenatal, perinatal, or postnatal periods. The following conditions may cause cerebral palsy in the prenatal period: (1) blood incompatibility; (2) maternal infections, such as measles and toxemia; (3) anoxia resulting from such conditions as anemia and shock; (4) maternal metabolic disturbances; (5) maternal exposure to radiation; and (6) prematurity.

During the perinatal period, cerebral palsy may result from: (1) anoxia, often due to a twisted umbilical cord; (2) stressful birth, including prolonged labor, or difficult birth such as breech birth; (3) brain hemorrhage; and (4) brain injury, including injury caused by obstetrical procedures, like forceps delivery. Cerebral palsy may also be caused by conditions that occur during postnatal development: (1) childhood diseases and infections like encephalitis, meningitis, and influenza; (2) head injuries; (3) toxic conditions like carbon monoxide and lead poisoning; (4) strangulation; and (5) neurological disorders.

Prevalence. It is somewhat difficult to determine the precise incidence of cerebral palsy because mild cases are often undiagnosed, and because cerebral palsy is often associated with other disabilities of greater severity. Although estimates vary greatly, it would be safe to consider an incidence rate of about 3 per 1,000 school-age children. At the present birth rate, more than 14,000 infants are born each year with cerebral palsy. About 50% of the cases of cerebral palsy are of the spastic type; about 20% are of the athetoid type; and the remaining cases are of the ataxic or mixed type. In most cases, children with cerebral palsy have associated disabilities, of which mental retardation and speech impairment are the most prevalent.

Significance. The prevalence of cerebral palsy has significance for educators in terms of prevention and treatment of the resulting motor problems and associated disabilities. Preventive measures could eliminate or at least reduce the circumstances under which brain damage may occur. Prior to conception, the mother should determine the possibility of blood incompatibility, become immunized against rubella, and follow adequate health and nutritional practices. During the prenatal period, the pregnant woman should continue good health and nutritional habits and avoid exposure to radiation. During the birth process, sound medical practices should be followed. Appropriate health and safety measures should be followed during postnatal development.

For the 3,000 school-age children in whom cerebral palsy occurs, treatment has a two-part focus: one part is centered around the condition of cerebral palsy itself, and the other part is concerned with the associated disabilities. Both treatment components can be served by early childhood–special education. Treatment for cerebral palsy, which may be initiated during infancy, includes using unimpaired areas of the brain to perform vital functions. Training in muscle relaxation and the use of braces and other devices minimize muscle incoordination. Recently, operations have been performed on muscles and on the brain to alleviate some of the symptoms of cerebral palsy. The long-range benefits as well as the applicability and practicality of these surgical procedures remain undetermined at this point.

Treatment for the disabilities associated with cerebral palsy may begin during the postnatal period with infant stimulation and corrective procedures for hearing and visual impairments. Speech therapy may be instituted as soon as language begins to develop. Treatment for these disabilities should continue through the preschool years into the regular school program and should operate in tandem with the treatment for cerebral palsy.

Epilepsy

Definition. Epilepsy may be defined as "a sudden onset and sudden offset of phenomena affecting consciousness and/or sensory-motor or autonomic functions" (Torres, 1969, p. 152). It is also referred to as paroxysmal cerebral dysrhythmia. There are usually measurable disturbances in the electrical discharges of the brain and observable seizures. All seizures, however, are not due to epilepsy.

Characteristics. Epilepsy may be classified according to two categories: generalized seizures (involving the whole body) and focal seizures (affecting just one part of the body). Table 3 summarizes the characteristics of both categories of epilepsy.

Etiology. In those cases of epilepsy that are classified as *idiopathic,* there is no known cause; and in the other cases of epilepsy, classified as *symptomatic,* the cause is due to a specific disease or damage. The seizure activity associated with epilepsy is caused by a sudden massive discharge of electrical energy by

Table 3

A Classification of Convulsive Disorders

Major Category	Types	Clinical Manifestations
Seizures generalized from the onset	Grand Mal	Generalized seizure with tensing of muscles and/or twitching and tremors with loss of consciousness
	Petit Mal	Brief lapse of consciousness (3–10 seconds), sometimes rhythmic 3/sec blinking.
	Akinetic-Myoclonic	Sudden generalized jerk or loss of tone without detectable alteration of consciousness.
Seizures focal at the onset (any of these can progress to a generalized major motor seizure)	Motor	Rhythmic movement of one part of body, stationary or progressing to other parts (Jacksonian). May be generalized from beginning without warning.
	Sensory	Somato sensory, visual, auditory, olfactory, or dizzy manifestations. May rapidly spread to become major motor, masking the aura.
	Psychomotor	Feeling of unreality, visual delusions or hallucinations, with alteration of consciousness.
	Autonomic	Paroxysmal abdominal pain, diarrhea, vasomotor changes.

Note: Adapted from "Convulsive Disorders: A Working Classification and Guidelines for Diagnosis and Treatment" by F. Torres, *Medical Times*, 1969, 97, 155.

Personality and other factors influence the effects of the problem and the treatment program.

the neurons in the brain. Such discharges may be triggered by brain injury caused by genetic factors, prenatal or birth injury, metabolic disorders affecting the brain cells, nutritional deficiencies, accidents, infection, high fever accompanying disease and infection, or a structural defect in the brain. Mental retardation, cerebral palsy, and other neurological disorders may have the secondary disability of epilepsy associated with them.

Prevalence. Some researchers (Torres, 1969; Tower, 1960) suggest that approximately 1% of the population may have epilepsy. The Epilepsy Foundation of America estimates that at least 2% of the United States population have some form of epilepsy. The higher incidence may be accounted for by an increase in epilepsy, by more precise diagnostic procedures, and by a trend to separate epilepsy into its own distinct category rather than to lump it with other disabilities such as neurological disorders.

Significance. Epilepsy may be considered in terms of prevention, management, and treatment. Prevention may be possible with the symptomatic kind of epilepsy. Adequate health, nutritional, and safety practices during the prenatal, perinatal, and postnatal periods can minimize the risk of epilepsy caused by brain damage. After the onset of epilepsy, drug therapy and surgery may be used to eliminate or reduce seizures. It has been estimated that, with drug therapy, as many as 50% of persons with epilepsy may become seizure-free, and an additional 35% of epileptics may experience a significant reduction in seizures. In a small percentage of cases, surgery can correct the damaged portion of the brain. Where a known, accessible, and demonstrable lesion in the brain is present, surgical removal of the lesion may eliminate seizure activity without impairing other functions.

When complete prevention is not possible, the epileptic condition may be managed by drug therapy and counseling for emotional adjustment. The goal of drug therapy is to control seizure activity as completely as possible with the fewest side effects. The most widely used anticonvulsant drugs are Dilantin and Phenobarbital. Mebaral and Mysoline are also frequently used for seizure control. A physician determines the most appropriate drug or combination of drugs.

The beneficial effects of drug therapy may be negated without the counseling for emotional adjustment. Fatigue and tension may increase an individual's anxiety about having seizures and in fact hasten seizure activity. Counseling, as well as some experimental techniques like biofeedback, may help the individual learn to relax and thereby minimize the number of seizures.

For those individuals whose epilepsy is controlled to the extent that a normal existence is possible, special educational services are not necessary. Even with drug therapy, which may cause some drowsiness, inattention, and incoordination, the epileptic should be able to participate in a regular education program. However, educators who work with epileptic children should be aware of the proper techniques for managing a child during a seizure.

The aura, a strange sensation in the form of sights, sounds, smells, or skin stimulation, often warns of an impending *grand mal* seizure. When such a seizure occurs, the teacher should help the child lie down on a cot or on the floor, remove nearby objects and furniture so that the child does not injure himself during the convulsions, and place a *soft* object, like a folded handkerchief, between the child's back teeth. After the seizure, the child may want to sleep. The *petit mal* seizure occurs so quickly, within a matter of seconds, that functioning in the classroom is virtually uninterrupted.

The child whose only disability is epilepsy may take part in a regular school program. But his teachers should monitor his learning closely to prevent gaps that can result from seizures during class time. For children with associated disabilities like mental retardation, treatment may focus on the primary disability more than on the associated disability of epilepsy.

Autism

Definition. The term *autism* refers to a severe communication disorder. The term *autistic children,* as used by the National Society for Autistic Children, includes persons, regardless of age, with severe disorders of communication and behavior whose disability became apparent during early childhood. Autistic children include those afflicted with infantile autism (Kranner's syndrome), profound aphasia, childhood psychosis, or any other condition characterized by severe deficits in language ability and behavior and by lack of ability to relate appropriately to others. The autistic child appears to suffer primarily from impairment of his cognitive or perceptual functioning or both, the consequences of which are limited ability to understand, communicate, learn, and participate in social relationships.

Characteristics. The prevailing characteristic of autism is the inability to understand and to use language appropriately. This disability is often accompanied by impairment in motor development and in auditory and visual perception. This cluster of disabilities results in behavior inappropriate to the physical and social demands of the environment. The specific characteristics of autism are as follows:

1. Onset of condition at birth or at about 2 years of age after apparently normal early development.
2. Impaired or complete lack of appropriate social interactions with parents, other adults, and children.
3. Severely impaired or complete lack of language ability.
4. Lack of intellectual development, or retardation in certain areas accompanied by normal or superior abilities in other areas.
5. Self-stimulating behavior, for example, repetitive and peculiar use of objects and toys or repetitive and peculiar body motions such as rocking or spinning.
6. Little or no eye contact with others.
7. Compulsive behaviors and extremely negative reaction to changes in the environment.
8. Extreme distress for no discernible reason.
9. Hyperactivity (excessively active) or hypoactivity (inactive), often accompanied by erratic sleep patterns.
10. Inability to perform certain gross and fine motor activities, for example, walking with a peculiar gait and having limpness in fingers.
11. Unusual reaction to sights and sounds, for example, seeming not to hear certain sounds and overreacting to others by holding hands over ears.
12. Apparent insensitivity to pain, frequently resulting in self-abusive behaviors.

Etiology. At present, the cause of autism is unknown in spite of considerable research in the fields of psychology, neurophysiology, genetics, and biochemistry. One theory about the etiology of autism was based on the "frigid parent syndrome." Parents of autistic children were considered to be incapable of giving their children love in a positive and supportive manner. This lack of affection and concern was believed to cause autism. A second theory was a variation of the first. It contended that a child may have been born with an unresponsive nature and that the parents' reaction to the child's lack of response may have caused them to behave in a negative way.

Neither of these earlier theories is well supported by research. In fact, researchers now feel that autism may be caused by disturbances in the central nervous system or in the chemical balance of the body. Because of these neurological or chemical defects, a distorted or unusual version of reality reaches the child. His reaction is confusion and avoidance of contact with the world that may be too incomprehensible or too painful for him to handle.

Prevalence. The lack of agreement among researchers about the cause of autism extends to the question of the incidence of autism. Specialists, who define autism according to a very limited and unique set of symptoms, maintain that it is a rare condition. Others, who define autism in a broader sense, report figures that range from 2 to 4.5 cases per 10,000 in the general population. The condition is observed to occur two to four times more often in boys than in girls.

Significance. Because the cause of autism is unknown at this time, preventive techniques cannot be employed. However, treatment strategies have been developed. Early childhood–special educational practices are most appropriate for autistic children since the disability may be diagnosed as early as birth and not later than the end of infancy. Indeed, treatment for the condition may have less impact if it is begun after the preschool years.

A variety of treatment strategies have been used to reach the autistic child:

1. *Traditional psychotherapy.* The child remains in the home and has regular sessions with a psychiatrist. Little success seems to be achieved with this approach.
2. *Residential therapy.* The child lives in a residential setting where specially trained therapists make no demands on him but respond to his needs and wait for him to move into the real world. This kind of treatment lasts many years and is successful with some individuals.
3. *Body stimulation.* The child is helped to become more aware of the world and of himself through intensive, highly structured programs designed to stimulate his senses of touch, taste, and body image.
4. *Behavior modification.* By reinforcing or rewarding appropriate responses, the child is trained to take care of his own needs, to behave in more appropriate ways, and to speak. This approach is generally accepted as the most successful therapy.

Research into drug therapy, mega-vitamin therapy, and diet therapy continues to seek more effective treatment techniques for the autistic child. As yet, there is no known cure.

Multiple Handicaps

Definition. The term *multiple handicaps* is defined as the existence of two or more handicapping conditions of equal severity in one person. Used with reference to developmental disabilities, multiple handicaps may pertain to any combination of mental retardation, cerebral palsy, epilepsy, and autism. Multiple handicaps may also be interpreted with regard to that part of the Developmental Disabilities Assistance and Bill of Rights Act which refers to

> any other condition of a person found to be closely related to mental retardation because such condition results in similar impairment of general intellectual functioning or adaptive behavior to that of mentally retarded persons, or requires treatment and services similar to those required for such persons. (Hammer & Richman, 1975, p. 8)

Characteristics. Multiple handicaps may be described by the characteristics of the various handicaps which are present in the individual. Often, the most severe disability is considered to be the primary problem, compounded by secondary disabilities.

Etiology. The causes of the primary developmental disabilities, mental retardation, cerebral palsy, epilepsy, or autism, may be considered the causes of multiple handicaps. Primary disabilities may produce secondary disabilities, but the probability is even greater that the original problem which caused the primary disability had multiple effects.

Paradoxically, two medical advances may be responsible for increased numbers of multiply handicapped individuals. Improved care of premature infants and the perfected surgical treatment for hydrocephalus meningomyelocel (which often accompanies spina bifida) have significantly reduced the rate of infant mortality. Unfortunately, premature infants tend to have a high incidence of physical defects and neurological and visual disabilities. Approximately one-third of the infants treated for hydrocephalus meningomyelocel require special educational services even after surgical correction (Wolf & Anderson, 1973).

Prevalence. Prevalence figures for multiple handicaps are difficult to determine because individuals may be listed either in a single category of exceptionality, depending on the primary disability, or in several disability categories but not in the category of multiple handicaps. Often individuals with multiple handicaps are classified as mentally retarded since mental retardation is the disability most often associated with other disabilities (Dunn, 1973).

Significance. Prevention of any of the developmental disabilities or any other disabilities would also be prevention of multiple handicaps. With regard to treatment, there is a trend in special education to serve all the needs of multiply handicapped children rather than to focus on a primary disability to the exclusion of any other disabilities. This approach seeks to develop the whole child to his fullest potential. Such a goal has a greater probability of being attained through the combined forces of early childhood education and special education.

Sensory Disabilities

Sensory disabilities are caused by handicapping conditions such as injury or malfunction within the sense organs or injury to the central nervous system. Because hearing and sight are the primary senses for acquiring knowledge, impairments which limit their use seriously affect the young child's development.

Hearing Impairment

Definition. Within the category of hearing impairment, there are two subgroups: *deaf* and *hard-of-hearing.* The Committee on Nomenclature of the

Conference of Executives of American Schools for the Deaf (1938) defines these two classifications as follows: (1) the *deaf* are those persons whose sense of hearing is nonfunctional for the ordinary purposes of life and (2) the *hard-of-hearing* are those persons whose sense of hearing, although defective, is functional with or without a hearing aid. The deaf may be subdivided into the *congenitally deaf* and the *adventitiously deaf,* that is, those who were born with normal hearing but whose hearing became nonfunctional through accident or disease (Telford & Sawrey, 1977).

Characteristics. The characteristics of hearing impairment are described quantitatively and qualitatively. A quantitative description is the degree of hearing loss measured audiometrically in terms of decibels (dB), or units of loudness, within the speech range of frequencies.

Class I. Mild losses (20 to 30 dB). Individuals with this range of hearing loss acquire speech and language in the normal manner.

Class II. Marginal losses (30 to 40 dB). Individuals with such losses acquire speech and language by ear but have difficulty in hearing speech more than a few feet away.

Class III. Moderate losses (40 to 60 dB). Individuals with hearing loss in this range may acquire speech and language by ear if the sound is amplified and if they have visual aids.

Class IV. Severe losses (60 to 75 dB). Individuals with this degree of hearing loss will not acquire speech and language without the use of specialized techniques.

Class V. Profound losses (greater than 75 dB). Individuals with such hearing losses rarely will acquire speech and language by ear alone even with maximum amplification of sound (Telford & Sawrey, 1977).

A qualitative description of hearing impairment is concerned with the ways in which the individual functions in his environment. The characteristics of the child with a hearing deficit include the following:

1. Failure to exhibit the Moro reflex during infancy.
2. Failure to respond when spoken to.
3. Unusually delayed speech and unusually faulty articulation.
4. Apparent chronic inattention.
5. Delayed motor development.

Etiology. Hearing impairment is indicative of a defect in the hearing mechanism, and the defect may be classified as conductive or sensory-neural. *Conductive* hearing loss is caused by interference with the sequence of sound vibrations reaching the auditory nerve. *Sensory-neural* hearing loss is caused by defects in the inner ear or in the auditory nerve itself which transmits the electrical impulses to the brain to complete the process of hearing. Although the kind of hearing loss and the amount of hearing loss may be determined, the exact cause of the hearing loss cannot be established in about one-third of the cases. In those cases where cause may be known, it is often the result of specific problems during the prenatal, perinatal, or postnatal periods.

During prenatal development, genetics may determine malformation of some segment of the ear mechanism or of the auditory nerve. For example, the hereditary disease otosclerosis causes degeneration of the auditory nerve. Infections and diseases, especially rubella, as well as toxic agents may also cause hearing impairment. Anoxia, birth trauma, blood incompatibility, and intracranial hemorrhage may impair the central nervous system in general and the auditory nerve in particular during the perinatal period. Causes of hearing impairment during the postnatal period are most of the childhood diseases—measles, mumps, scarlet fever, diptheria, whooping cough, influenza, pneumonia, and meningitis, all of which are now fairly well controlled through immunization. Another infection, serous otitis media, is a frequent cause of hearing loss. Concussions, cerebral hemorrhage, intracranial tumors, prolonged exposure to high-frequency and high-intensity sounds, and the toxic side effects of certain drugs may cause hearing loss. Emotional and psychological stress may also produce a loss of hearing, usually temporary in nature.

Prevalence. There is a lack of agreement among researchers about the exact incidence of hearing impairment. Silverman (1957) suggested that about 5% of school-age children have a hearing impairment and that of this group 5 out of 1,000 require special educational services. The Illinois Commission on Children

Hearing impairment is caused by injury or malfunction within the sense organ or injury to the central nervous system.

(1968) estimates the incidence of hearing impairment to be somewhat higher, with 1 to 3 out of 100 school-age children having a hearing disability severe enough to justify special educational programs.

Significance. Preventive measures include genetic counseling, appropriate health and safety practices, including immunizations against rubella for the prospective mother and against childhood diseases and infections for the infant, and minimum exposure to high-frequency and high-intensity sounds.

Treatment of hearing impairment may begin during infancy or as soon as a hearing loss is detected. The earlier language development is begun, the more effectively the hearing disabled child will function when he reaches school age. At this point, the hearing impaired child is at a decided disadvantage without speech and language.

In the process of language acquisition, the deaf child depends on vision and his senses other than hearing since he has no functional hearing. The hard-of-hearing child, however, has some residual, or remaining, hearing that must be trained along with his other senses for the purpose of language acquisition. Amplification devices, such as hearing aids, strengthen the residual hearing of the child with a conductive hearing loss.

Both groups of the hearing impaired may benefit from a variety of educational techniques that have developed over several centuries. Until recently, two separate approaches to deaf education were utilized. One system was based on *manual communication* only and the other system advocated *oral communication* only. Now the trend is toward *total communication* in which all available resources and techniques are utilized to help the child acquire language and speech. Total communication employs elements of manual communication such as finger spelling and sign languages, like the American Sign Language (ASL) and the technique of signing exact English (SEE), as well as features of oral communication such as lip- or speech-reading, and auditory training for residual hearing.

In order for total communication strategies to be effective, they must be practiced in the home as well as in early childhood–special education settings. Parents have daily opportunities to broaden their child's language base and to stimulate language development during the critical first years. A joint effort by the home and the school narrows the language gap between the hearing impaired child and the normal child when formal schooling starts.

Visual Impairment

Definition. There are both quantitative and functional definitions of visual impairment. The quantitative definitions, often required for legal and administrative purposes, are as follows: *blindness* is visual acuity of 20/200 or less in the better eye with maximum correction, and *partial blindness* or *partially sighted* is visual acuity of between 20/70 and 20/200 in the better eye after maximum correction.

The functional definitions, more important for educational purposes, are as follows: the *blind* are those who cannot learn to read print and must learn

Braille for reading and writing; and the *visually impaired* are those who can learn to read print (Kirk, 1972).

Characteristics. The characteristics of visual impairment may be noted in a number of behavioral symptoms:

1. Chronic eye irritations as evidenced by watery eyes or by sensitive eyelids.
2. Complaints about visual blurring or the inability to see.
3. Rubbing of eyes, frowning, squinting, excessive blinking.
4. Tilting of head when reading or holding reading matter in an unusual position.
5. Nausea, double vision, or blurring when reading.
6. Avoiding reading-related activities.
7. Inattention to visual tasks.
8. Lack of gross or fine motor coordination.
9. Strabismus (crossed eyes).

Visual impairment may also be considered in terms of the types of visual defect that may occur. Defects may be the results of refractive errors, ocular muscle abnormalities, and a variety of other abnormalities. *Refractive errors,* such as hyperopia (farsightedness), myopia (nearsightedness), and astigmatism (faulty curvature of the lens), constitute approximately one-half of all visual defects (Kirk, 1972). Examples of ocular muscle abnormalities are strabismus (crossed eyes) and heterophoria (inability to coordinate the two eyes). Some of the anomalies which produce visual impairment are albinism (a hereditary condition characterized by refractive errors, reduced visual acuity, jerky eye movements, and extreme sensitivity to light) and cataracts (a condition in which the lens becomes opaque, causing loss of visual acuity).

Etiology. The causes of visual impairment fall into several categories, the largest of which is prenatal influences, including genetic factors. The other categories are infections, accidents and injuries, tumors, and excessive oxygen. Of the infections that may occur during the prenatal period, rubella often causes visual impairment in the child. Accidents and injuries and tumors may also produce visual impairment.

Ironically, human error was responsible for an epidemic of blindness caused by a condition known as retrolental fibroplasia. This disease, induced by the excessive use of oxygen with premature infants, was unknown before the 1940s, peaked rapidly in 1952–53 when it accounted for more than half the blindness in preschool children, and virtually disappeared by 1955 when the oxygen therapy used with premature infants was modified.

Prevalence. The incidence of visual impairment, as estimated by the U.S. Office of Education, is 0.1% of school children. Of this percentage, approximately one-third are blind and two-thirds are visually impaired sufficiently to require special educational services. The fact that visual impairment is the smallest category of exceptionality may be due to two circumstances: (1) with the prevention of retrolental fibroplasia, blindness in preschool children was reduced by one-half and (2) more than two-thirds of all individuals with visual impairment are 65 years of age and older.

Significance. In spite of the relatively low incidence of visual impairment, the disability presents significant limitations to the individual. In this regard, Telford and Sawrey (1977) suggest that "blindness (a) prevents direct access to the printed word, (b) restricts independent mobility in unfamiliar surroundings, (c) limits a person's direct perception of his distant environment . . . , and (d) deprives the individual of important social cues" (p. 369).

The first two limitations cited are perhaps the ones of greatest concern to educators. The development of independent mobility is a primary goal of early childhood-special education programs for the visually impaired. Educational strategies focus on the adaptation of the child's other sensory channels for instruction and learning. Later, when formal schooling begins, other special educational practices are used. Examples of these special materials, methods, and techniques are teaching Braille reading and writing to the blind; teaching the visually impaired to read large type or magnified print; using audio aids; utilizing models, relief maps, graphs, and designs; and teaching how to use everyday items that have been modified for the visually impaired.

Physical Disabilities

Physical disabilities refer to structural variations or conditions of health which limit the child's ability to function normally. They are caused by conditions during fetal development, birth injury, or injury after birth. Such disabilities are classified as orthopedic impairments and other health impairments.

Orthopedic Impairment

Definition. An orthopedic impairment may be defined as a crippling condition which interferes with the normal functions of the bones, joints, or muscles to such an extent that special educational provisions are necessary for the impaired individual (Kirk, 1972). Children with orthopedic impairments may be divided into two groups: those who are born with an orthopedic disability and those who acquire the disability later in life.

Characteristics. The category of orthopedic impairment is so broad that it is difficult to identify many general characteristics. Defects noted in the category of children born with an orthopedic disability include clubbed feet or hands, missing limbs, and spina bifida (defective closure of the spinal cord). In the category of children who acquire an orthopedic disability later in life, impairments characterized by deformities of the limbs, immobility or limited mobility, or muscle weakness may be found.

Etiology. Orthopedic impairments may be caused by hereditary factors, by toxic agents taken by the pregnant woman, like the thalidomide ingredient contained in the tranquilizer Contergan, by birth injuries, and by congenital tendencies and accidents. Infections and diseases, like poliomyelitis (infantile paralysis), hemophilia (bleeder's disease), juvenile arthritis, muscular dystrophy, osteomyelitis, scoliosis, and tuberculosis of the bones, may also cause orthopedic impairment in the young.

Prevalence. The U.S. Office of Education (1970) estimates that 0.5% of school-age children have orthopedic or other health impairments. Several counterproductive trends have influenced the incidence of orthopedic impairment. On the one hand, there has been a significant decrease in orthopedic disabilities caused by infectious disease. Advances in medical science have reduced the incidence of conditions like poliomyelitis, arthritis, osteomyelitis, and tuberculosis of the bones. On the other hand, there has been a significant increase in orthopedic disabilities which result from congenital defects and accidents, including child abuse. The National Safety Council (1975) estimates that each year more than 50,000 children, half of whom are under 5 years of age, are permanently crippled and disabled by accident. In addition, the American Humane Society suggests that each year 10,000 children are the victims of child abuse, which can cause significant physical impairment.

Significance. Orthopedic impairment can be prevented by appropriate health and safety practices. Genetic counseling may minimize the risk of hemophilia. Immunization will reduce significantly the incidence of infectious diseases like poliomyelitis. Orthopedic disabilities caused by accidents may be diminished by adequate safety measures in the child's environment.

Special educational services may be provided to the child who does sustain an orthopedic impairment. The young child needs training in mobility and motor control in order to achieve independence. This instruction may be facilitated by the use of special equipment, materials, and methods as well as by classrooms that are designed with the needs of the orthopedically impaired in mind. Preschool early education is desirable. It can take place in the home, special centers such as crippled children's hospitals, cerebral palsy centers, or special preschool classrooms. With early training, a great number of children with orthopedic disabilities need no changes in the regular educational program when they become school age.

Other Health Impairments

Definition. The term *other health impairments* refers to health problems (other than orthopedic impairment) which are physical conditions that render a child sufficiently limited to require special educational considerations. These health impairments may be temporary or permanent in nature.

Characteristics. The characteristics of other health impairments vary depending on the particular condition with which the child is afflicted. Some health impairments like rheumatic fever, pulmonary tuberculosis, infectious hepatitis, and infectious mononucleosis cause a temporary disruption in the child's educational program. During convalescence from these diseases, some special educational services, in the form of homebound or in-hospital instruction, may be warranted. Other health impairments, such as congenital heart defects, diabetes, nephrosis, cystic fibrosis, and asthma, may have more lasting effects on the child. In these cases, long-term special educational services may be necessary to meet the special needs of the health impaired child.

Etiology. Other health impairments are caused by a variety of conditions. The most common conditions are the following:

1. Congenital heart defect—abnormality of the heart or cardiovascular system.
2. Rheumatic fever—infectious disease affecting blood vessels, heart, and joints.
3. Diabetes—disturbance in the body's metabolism characterized by abnormally high sugar content in the blood and insufficient insulin for metabolizing it.
4. Nephrosis (Bright's disease)—disturbance of kidney functions.
5. Cystic fibrosis—disorder of the pancreas resulting in chronic lung dysfunction.
6. Asthma—disease of the bronchial tubes characterized by difficulty in breathing.
7. Infectious hepatitis—disease of the liver characterized by jaundice (abnormal yellow tone in skin and eyeballs).
8. Infectious mononucleosis—disease of the blood characterized by an excess of white blood cells and extreme fatigue.
9. Pulmonary tuberculosis—infection of the respiratory system.

Although several of these health impairments may be hereditary, as in the case of diabetes and asthma, most are caused by infections or viruses.

Prevalence. The incidence of other health impairments is difficult to determine since the category is seldom considered separately from the category of orthopedic impairment. As previously mentioned, the U.S. Office of Education (1970) estimates that 0.5% of school-age children have orthopedic or other health impairments.

Significance. The low incidence of other health impairments may well be a credit to advances in medical science. As with orthopedic impairment, adequate health practices may reduce the incidence even further. In those cases where some health impairment does exist, on either a temporary or permanent basis, the child's educational program, particularly in the first critical years, should continue with appropriate modifications.

Language Disabilities

Language disabilities are the results of brain injury, malfunction of the speech mechanisms caused by injury or deformities, or emotional problems. The strong relationship between language and cognitive development makes the early diagnosis and treatment of language problems critical to the success of later educational programs.

Speech Impairment

Definition. According to Van Riper (1963), "speech is defective when it deviates so far from the speech of other people that it calls attention to itself, interferes with communication, or causes its possessor to be maladjusted" (p. 16). Two important considerations in identifying speech impairment are age and severity of the deviation. For example, broken speech and mispronounced words would not be a cause for concern in a 3-year-old but they would be in a 12-year-old. Similarly, mispronouncing an isolated sound such as *s* would not be unusual, but mispronouncing a number of sounds would be a severe enough deviation to be labeled a speech impairment.

Characteristics. In discussing speech impairment in relation to young children, it is most important to remember that speech and language development are not fully completed until the seventh or eighth year of a child's life. The various stages of development and the approximate ages at which they occur are presented in detail in Chapter 7, Language Skills. Significant deviations from the behaviors presented in Table 1, Chapter 8, may indicate the presence of a speech impairment.

Speech impairments may be classified into four categories: (1) disorders of articulation; (2) disorders of voice; (3) stuttering; and (4) disorders associated with mental retardation, cerebral palsy, hearing impairment, and cleft palate.

Disorders of articulation may be described as mispronunciations. They are characterized by substitutions, distortions, omissions, and additions of sounds. Not as common as disorders of articulation are disorders of voice. Deviations in this category may be present in any of the five basic characteristics of the voice: pitch, loudness, voice flexibility, quality, and duration.

Stuttering is characterized by a disfluency of speech which involves blocks, hesitations, prolongations, and repetitions (Telford & Sawrey, 1977). For some children, stuttering may begin as early as 2½ years, with periods of fluent as well as disfluent speech. For other children, initial speech may be disfluent speech while for still others, the onset of stuttering may not occur until after several years of fluent speech.

Speech impairment may also be associated with other kinds of disabilities. The incidence of speech disabilities of all types is much greater in the mentally retarded population than in the general population (Dunn, 1973). For children with cerebral palsy, their lack of muscle control tends to limit their linguistic development. Approximately 50% of children with cerebral palsy have speech disabilities (Dunn, 1973). Problems with articulation and voice are the most common among cerebral palsied youngsters. The single most disabling aspect of hearing impairment is the fact that it hinders the learning of language and speech. The child with a hearing disability not only has difficulty with receiving language but also has trouble with developing speech sounds.

Cleft palate presents another barrier to speech development. Cleft palate, the congenital fissure of the roof of the mouth and/or the upper lip, creates an abnormal opening between the mouth and nasal cavities. The resulting speech impairments are a severely nasal or hoarse quality to the voice and misarticulations.

Etiology. The causes of speech impairment are as varied as the types of speech disabilities. Articulation, or the producing of speech sounds, requires (1) a breathing apparatus, (2) two vocal cords, (3) an auditory mechanism, (4) an intact central nervous system, (5) muscles for swallowing, and (6) an oral mechanism consisting of the tongue, lips, teeth, hard and soft palates, and jaws (Kirk, 1972). Speech disabilities may be caused by the malfunctioning of any of these parts. In the absence of any structural defect, misarticulation may still occur. It can be caused by emotional stress, delayed maturation, or environmental factors such as bilingualism and cultural difference.

Disorders of voice may be caused by inflammation of the laryngeal tissue and the vocal cords, by partial or complete paralysis of the soft palate, and by uneven spurts of growth during adolescence. The child's self-concepts may also cause inappropriate levels of voice intensity—speaking too loud, too soft, or unevenly.

There is a plethora of theories about the causes of stuttering. These theories may be categorized into two broad groups: organic theories, which include the theory of cerebral hemispheric dominance and various neurophysiological theories, and psychological theories, which attribute stuttering to emotional factors or to learned behavior.

Speech impairment associated with other disabilities seems to be a result of the primary disability. Whatever may have produced the conditions of mental retardation, cerebral palsy, or hearing impairment may also be considered the cause, at least indirectly, of speech impairment. The condition of cleft palate or lip is caused by the failure of the bone and tissue of the hard and soft palates to fuse during the first months of pregnancy. Such a condition tends to be hereditary.

Prevalence. The incidence of speech impairment is approximately 3 to 5% of the school-age population (Kirk, 1972). This category of exceptionality constitutes the single largest number of children requiring special educational services. Disorders of articulation are the primary defect in more than 80% of speech-impaired individuals. Stuttering is the second most often diagnosed speech disorder, followed in order of frequency by speech impairment associated with hearing disability, disorders of voice, and speech disabilities accompanying cleft palate, cerebral palsy, and mental retardation (Kirk, 1972).

Significance. The category of speech impairment has a two-fold significance for the field of early childhood–special education. In one sense, it represents a challenge: if language and speech development are guided appropriately during the first critical years of a child's life, then the relatively high incidence of speech disabilities may be significantly reduced. In another sense, speech impairment associated with other disabilities such as mental retardation, cerebral palsy, hearing impairment, and cleft palate may benefit from the special educational practices developed to alleviate the effect of these primary disabilities. The impact of both the primary disability and the secondary disability of speech impairment would be minimized with special educational programs during the preschool years.

Learning Disabilities

Definition. The term *learning disabilities* was defined by the National Advisory Committee to the Bureau of Education for the Handicapped, U.S. Office of Education (1968) as follows:

> Children with special learning disabilities exhibit a disorder in one or more of the basic psychological processes involved in understanding or in using spoken or written language. These may be manifested in disorders of listening, thinking, talking, reading, writing, spelling, or arithmetic. They include conditions which have been referred to as perceptual handicaps, brain injury, minimal brain dysfunction, dyslexia, developmental aphasia, etc. They do not include learning problems which are due primarily to visual, hearing, or motor handicaps, to mental retardation, emotional disturbance or to environmental disadvantage. (p. 34)

This definition of learning disabilities, which provided the basis for the Children with Specific Learning Disabilities Act of 1969, makes several key points. One point is that by excluding other disabilities as a primary problem, particularly mental retardation, the definition assumes the presence of *average or better IQ.* A subsequent point is that the definition implies that a *significant educational discrepancy* exists between the child's potential and actual perfor-

Prevention of learning disabilities may rely, in part, on appropriate preschool experiences.

mance. A final key point in the definition is that the disability involves some aspect of *language processing,* particularly learning to read and write.

Characteristics. Cruickshank (1972) notes that as many as 40 terms have been used to describe the category of learning disabilities. There may be more as additional characteristics are identified as symptoms of this condition. Some of the most frequently observed are the following:

1. Hyperactivity.
2. Perceptual-motor deficits.
3. Specific learning deficits, particularly language deficits.
4. Disorders of memory, sequence and conceptual thinking.
5. Disorders of attention—distractibility and short attention span.
6. Incoordination and general disorientation.
7. Impulsivity.
8. Perseveration.
9. Emotional instability.
10. Poor body image and self-concept (McCarthy & McCarthy, 1969).

Not every child identified as learning disabled will exhibit all of these characteristics. A cluster of some of these symptoms may indicate the possibility of the presence of a learning disability.

Etiology. The suggested causes of learning disabilities are as plentiful as the characteristics and definitions of the exceptionality. A number of definitions attribute the presence of a learning disability to an aberration of neurological functioning, the precise cause of which is unknown. It has been theorized that such a dysfunction may be due to any of the prenatal, perinatal, and postnatal influences on the development of the child. (See Chapter 4.) Hereditary factors, anoxia, minimal brain damage (MBD), and chemical imbalance are all examples of possible causes of learning disabilities.

Prevalence. Statistics on the incidence of learning disabilities are as varied as the suggested terminology and etiologies. Kirk (1972) estimates that from 1 to 3% at the least and 7% at the most of the school population may be *diagnosed* as having learning disabilities. The percentage of the general population, from age 3 to 21, that will be *treated* as having learning disabilities is governed by P.L. 94–142, the Education for All Handicapped Children Act. This piece of legislation limits the category of learning disabilities to not more than 2% of the school-age population.

Significance. Because learning disabilities are usually not observed until the child begins school, when he faces the tasks of learning to read and write, this category of exceptionality has not always been of concern to early childhood–special educators. Prevention of learning disabilities may now rely on the appropriate, preschool stimulation fostered by early childhood programs as well as on the informal observation of early childhood educators to identify those children who may be at risk for learning disabilities. Early childhood–special education may serve to eliminate or at least to minimize the discrepancy between the learning disabled child's potential and actual abilities.

Behavioral Disabilities

Definition. The term *behavioral disabilities* refers to "a deviation from age-appropriate behavior which significantly interferes with (1) the child's own growth and development and/or (2) the lives of others" (Kirk, 1972, p. 389). The category of behavioral disabilities has traditionally been known as emotional disturbance and social maladjustment, and has included conditions such as mental illness, psychosis (serious personality disorder), childhood schizophrenia, autism, and juvenile delinquency.

Characteristics. Quay (1969) developed a classification system in which behavioral disabilities are grouped into one of four dimensions, presented here with their characteristics:

1. *Conduct Disorder.* Behavior is characterized by attention-seeking, unrestrained loudness, inappropriate social actions, hyperactivity, and physical and verbal aggression.
2. *Anxious-Withdrawn.* The main behavior traits are hypersensitivity, sense of inferiority, fear, anxiety, and low self-esteem.
3. *Inadequate–Immature.* Characteristics exhibited are disinterest, daydreaming, reticence, and inactivity.
4. *Socialized Delinquent.* Behavior is displayed in group delinquent acts, gang activities, peer group loyalty, truancy, and failure to conform to the expectations of the dominant culture or society. The term *delinquent* has more meaning for legal purposes than for educational concerns.

Dunn (1973) suggests two additional dimensions of behavioral disabilities: (1) autistic, childhood schizophrenic, or otherwise psychotic, and (2) adjudicated juvenile delinquent. Neither of these categories has been the responsibility of the public school system until recently. At the present time, the field of early childhood–special education is attempting to meet the needs of the young special child with severe behavioral disabilities like autism, schizophrenia, or psychosis.

Other characteristics of children with behavioral disorders have been identified by Morse, Cutler, and Fink (1964). They found in a survey of children in programs for the emotionally disturbed that the range of ages was from 5 to 15, more than 80% were boys, the majority of children had IQs over 100 (though they were educationally retarded), and the majority were classified as having conduct disorders.

Etiology. The causes of behavioral disabilities may be grouped into two broad categories: (1) biological factors and (2) psychological and environmental factors (Dunn, 1973). In the first classification, genetic or organic factors may be the cause of behavioral disorders. For example, in a number of cases, schizophrenia seems to have a genetic etiology, since it has been observed to occur almost equally often in both members of a monozygotic (identical) twin pair (Sagor, 1971). In other instances, ingestion of toxic substances, such as lead-based paint, seems to result in permanent behavioral disabilities.

In the second category, psychological and environmental factors seem to influence behavior in a negative manner. In the tradition of Freud, psychodynamic theorists suggest that behavior is based solely on past experiences whether the individual has a conscious awareness of them or not. Learning theorists, like Skinner, propose the notion that all behavior is learned and is determined by reinforcement from the environment. Environmental reinforcers may be parents, teachers, peers, cultural expectations, and society's mores.

Prevalence. The incidence of behavioral disabilities depends on the definition and the degree of severity considered in estimating the prevalence of the exceptionality. The U.S. Office of Education offers a conservative estimate of 2% of school-age children having behavioral disabilities serious enough to require special educational services. One percent is regarded as socially maladjusted or as having a mild behavioral disorder; the other percent is judged to be emotionally disturbed or to have a severe behavior disorder.

Significance. Like children with learning disabilities, children with behavioral disabilities derive more benefit from special education during the years of formal schooling than during the preschool years. However, prevention of behavioral disabilities may well be within the sphere of early childhood–special education if psychological and environmental factors cause the disability. Early education–special education programs can provide a stimulating, supportive environment in which acceptable behavior is reinforced when it is demonstrated by the child as well as by the significant others in the child's life.

Legislation and Litigation

The idea of equal educational opportunities has become a reality for the exceptional children of this country only recently. During the past several decades, great strides have been made under the leadership of the federal government to insure the right of every child, including the exceptional child, to an education which would maximize his potential. At this time, it is appropriate to examine federal involvement in special education in the past in order to achieve an understanding of the present and the future state of education for exceptional children.

Federal Involvement in Special Education

Legislation. Until the last half of the present century, education for exceptional children was primarily a local and a state concern. The federal government made few specific commitments to children with disabilities. Its first commitment to special education was the establishment of Gallaudet College for the Deaf in Washington, D.C., in 1864. But it was not until 1930 that the federal government really addressed itself directly to the issue of special education and established a Section on Exceptional Children and Youths in the

Office of Education. Besides the Office of Education, the Department of Health, Education, and Welfare had under its jurisdiction several other agencies which were concerned with the exceptional child. These included the Office of Vocational Rehabilitation, the Children's Bureau of the Social Security Administration, and the Public Health Service.

Until the 1960s, the federal government's role in special education was limited. It supported programs for exceptional children by (1) supplying matching funds to state and local agencies; (2) granting funds for research in all areas of exceptionality; (3) disseminating information; (4) providing consultative services to state and local groups; and (5) distributing fellowships for the training of professionals in all areas related to special education (Kirk, 1962). It has been observed that "the best index of maturity in a society is the attention it pays to its handicapped, its poor, its abandoned" (Jordan, 1962, p. 9). In that sense, 1965 was the coming of age in America. P.L. 89–10, the Elementary and Secondary Education Act (ESEA) of 1965, made funds available to public schools for programs for children from low-income families. Congress used the term *educationally disadvantaged,* which was defined to include exceptional children. Later in 1965, P.L. 89–313 amended Title I of the ESEA to provide more direct aid for the education of exceptional children in state-operated or state-supported institutions.

The following year, P.L. 89–750, the ESEA Amendments of 1966, authorized significant sums of money for the "initiation, expansion, and improvement of programs and projects for the education of the handicapped" (Meisgeier & King, 1970, p. 294). The provisions of the amendments were directed to children from ages 3 to 21.

P.L. 89–750 also required the Commissioner of Education to establish within the Office of Education two bodies related to the problems of exceptional children. One was the Bureau of Education for the Handicapped which was responsible for administering programs and projects relating to the needs of exceptional persons. The other group to be organized was the National Advisory Committee on Handicapped Children which was to serve in an advisory capacity to the Commissioner.

P.L. 90–247, the ESEA Amendments of 1967, demonstrated the federal government's increased involvement in special education. It made provisions for a variety of services for the handicapped, including regional resource centers and centers and services for deaf-blind children. The establishment of centers for deaf-blind children met a critical need in the field of education since a rubella epidemic in the early 1960s had resulted in the birth of thousands of children with multiple handicaps.

Entitled the Handicapped Children's Early Education Assistance Act of 1968, P.L. 90–538 authorized experimental preschool programs for the handicapped. It was hoped that the 3 years of operation authorized by the Act would demonstrate conclusively that disabilities would be alleviated or corrected in 50% or more of the exceptional children if medical and special educational services were provided during the formative years (Minskoff, 1970).

One piece of federal legislation related to the handicapped was passed in 1970. It was P.L. 91–230, the Elementary and Secondary Education Assistance

Programs Extension. Under Title VI, the Education of the Handicapped Act was created which encompassed all Office of Education programs established to meet special educational needs. Among the authorizations were special programs for children with specific learning disabilities.

The most recent and most significant piece of legislation for the cause of exceptional children in general, and of young, special children in particular, is P.L. 94–142, the Education for All Handicapped Children Act, enacted in November 1975. The scope of this act, by virtue of its comprehensive requirements, reaches far beyond any past legislation to meet the needs of exceptional children. Some of the major mandates of the new law are

1. A free public education for all handicapped children between the ages of 3 and 18 by September 1978, and for all those between the ages of 3 and 21 by September 1980. Exceptions are allowed in states where school attendance laws do not include children in the 3 to 5 and 18 to 21 ranges.
2. An *individualized educational plan* must be written for each handicapped child. Such a program must be developed through the joint efforts of a qualified school official, the child's teacher, the parent or guardian, and whenever possible, the child.
3. The handicapped and nonhandicapped child must be educated together to the maximum extent appropriate. Special classes and separate schools are possible only when the nature or severity of the handicap is such that education in regular classes cannot be achieved satisfactorily.
4. All tests and other evaluation instruments and their implementation must not be racially or culturally discriminatory.
5. All policies, programs, and procedures for educating handicapped children must have prior public notice and prior parent involvement and consultation.
6. All rights and guarantees of this new law apply to handicapped children in private as well as public schools.
7. All state-level agencies currently responsible for special education will have jurisdiction over all educational programs for handicapped children offered within a given state.
8. Each governor will appoint an *advisory panel* to advise and assist in the overall implementation of the law's requirements (Goodman, 1976).

With the first requirement, early childhood–special education becomes a legal mandate. The downward extension of special education services to the preschool years will have a significant impact on the development of young, handicapped children. Early identification, appropriate placement, and special programming will greatly increase the probability of the special child achieving his full potential.

Litigation. The enactment of P.L. 94–142, the Education for All Handicapped Children Act, was the culmination of more than 20 years of court decisions as well as legislation on behalf of exceptional children. The movement to secure equal educational opportunities for all children had its formal beginning in 1954 when the United States Supreme Court rendered its benchmark ruling in *Brown* v. *Board of Education* (1954). The *Brown* decision established the notion of extending equal educational opportunities to *all* children of school age as a basic constitutional right.

More than a decade later, there was a flurry of litigation brought on behalf of exceptional children and their right to public-supported educational services, based on the Equal Protection Clause of the Fourteenth Amendment to the United States Constitution. Three similar cases—*Madera* v. *Board of Education, City of New York* (1967), *Arreola* v. *Board of Education* (1968), and *Covarrubias* v. *San Diego Unified School District* (1970)—ruled that parents, or surrogate parents, must be informed and have a part in the decision concerning special class placement. In the *Madera* decision, provision was also made for legal counsel to be present at placement hearings.

Another decision, *Diana* v. *California State Board of Education* (1970) was just as important for special children. The Court ruled on several key issues: (1) tests for special class placement must be given in both the primary home language and in English and must exclude vocabulary items and culturally unfair verbal questions; (2) retesting must be accomplished within a specified period of time; and (3) resource or supplemental services must be provided for those students who qualify to return to regular classes.

Perhaps one of the two most significant legal decisions affecting exceptional children was made in *Pennsylvania Association for Retarded Children* v. *Commonwealth of Pennsylvania* (1971). In this landmark case, the Court ruled that public school districts

1. May not postpone or in any way deny to any mentally retarded child free access to a program of public education and training.
2. May not deny home instruction to any mentally retarded child.
3. Must allow each child access to a free public program of education and training appropriate to his learning capacities.
4. Shall provide for immediate evaluation, for reevaluation every year, if requested by parents, and for reevaluation of all special children at least every two years.
5. Shall provide for education and training of children less than 6 years old.
6. Shall secure proper education and training outside the public schools of the district where it is not possible to form a special class or to provide such education for any child in the public schools of the district.

The other most significant and precedent-setting case was *Mills* v. *Board of Education of the District of Columbia* (1972). In this decision, the ruling in the Pennsylvania case served as a basis for securing the right to a public education for *all* children, including exceptional children. With support from federal legislation, in the form of P.L. 94–142, and from legal precedents like the *Pennsylvania* and *Mills* decisions, the needs of all special children should be met appropriately.

Summary

Early childhood–special education addresses the needs of children from birth to age 6 who, because of some handicapping conditions, require special educational services. It is felt that the first 5 or 6 years of a child's life are the most important ones for establishing the foundation for later learning. The needs of young exceptional children are unique in that they require special treatment during these formative years in order to maximize their potential.

In the field of special education, a number of terms are used to define specific conditions. The term *disability* is used here to denote an incapacity in one or more aspects of development that may be classified in one of the following categories of exceptionality: developmental disabilities (mental retardation, cerebral palsy, epilepsy, autism, and multiple handicaps), sensory disabilities (hearing impairment and visual impairment), physical disabilities (orthopedic impairment and other health impairments), language disabilities (speech impairment and learning disabilities), and behavioral disabilities. Each of these classifications was discussed in terms of definition, characteristics, etiology, prevalence, and significance. The categories of learning disabilities and behavioral disabilities seem to have the least importance for the field of early childhood–special education since these exceptionalities are most often precipitated by the demands of formal school experiences.

In the past decade or so, the federal government, in the legislative and judicial branches, has fostered efforts to make equal education a reality for all children, including exceptional children. P.L. 94-142, the Education for All Handicapped Children Act, and the precedents set in the *Pennsylvania* and *Mills* court decisions provide a mandate for educational services that meet the needs of all children but particularly the needs of young, special children.

REFERENCES

Brown v. Board of Education, 347 U.S. 483, 493 (1954).

Condon, W. S., & Sander, L. W. Synchrony demonstrated between movements of the neonate and adult speech. *Child Development,* 1974, **45,** 456–462.

Conference of Executives of American Schools for the Deaf. Report of the Conference Committee on Nomenclature. *American Annals of the Deaf,* 1938, **83,** 1–3.

Cruickshank, W. M. Some issues facing the field of learning disabilities. *Journal of Learning Disabilities,* 1972, **5,** 380–388.

Cruickshank, W. M., & Johnson, G. O. (Eds.). *Education of exceptional children and youth.* Englewood Cliffs, N.J.: Prentice-Hall, 1975.

Dunn, L. M. (Ed.). *Exceptional children in the schools.* New York: Holt, Rinehart & Winston, 1973.

Gold, M. W. Research on the vocational rehabilitation of the retarded. In N. R. Ellis (Ed.), *International review of research in mental retardation* (Vol. 6). New York: Academic Press, 1973.

Goodman, L. V. A bill of rights for the handicapped. *American Education,* July, 1976, **12**(6), 4–7.

Grossman, H. J. (Ed.). *Manual on terminology and classification in mental retardation.* Baltimore: American Association on Mental Deficiency Special Publication Series, No. 2, 1973.

Hammer, P., & Richman, G. (Eds.). *A compilation of the developmental disabilities legislation, 1975.* Chapel Hill, N.C.: University of North Carolina, Developmental Disabilities Technical Assistance System, (December) 1975.

Haring, N. G., & Schiefelbusch, R. L. (Eds.). *Teaching special children.* New York: McGraw-Hill Book Co., 1976.

Heber, R. F. A manual on terminology and classification in mental retardation. *American Journal of Mental Deficiency,* 1959, **64,** Monograph Supplement (Rev. Ed.), 1961.

Illinois Commission on Children. *A comprehensive plan for hearing impaired children in Illinois.* Springfield, Ill.: The Commission, 1968.

Jordan, T. E. *The exceptional child.* Columbus, Ohio: Charles E. Merrill Publishing Co., 1962.

Kirk, S. A. *Educating exceptional children.* Boston: Houghton Mifflin Co., 1962.

Kirk, S. A. *Educating exceptional children.* Boston: Houghton Mifflin Co., 1972.

Mayo, L. W. A proposed program for national action to combat mental retardation: A report to President Kennedy's Panel on Mental Retardation. Washington, D.C.: U.S. Government Printing Office, 1962.

McCandless, B. K., & Trotter, R. J. *Children, behavior and development.* New York: Holt, Rinehart & Winston, 1977.

McCarthy, J. S., & McCarthy, J. F. *Learning disabilities.* Boston: Allyn & Bacon, 1969.

Meisgeier, C. H., & King, J. D. (Eds.). *The process of special education administration.* Scranton, Pa.: International Textbook Co., 1970.

Mills v. Board of Education of the District of Columbia, 348. F.Supp., 866 (D.D.C. 1972).

Minskoff, J. G. Washington perspective: Notes on federal activities in learning disabilities. *Academic Therapy,* 1970, **5**(2), 129–131.

Morse, W. C., Cutler, R. L., & Fink, A. H. *Public school classes for the emotionally handicapped: A research analysis.* Arlington, Va.: The Council for Exceptional Children, 1964.

National Advisory Committee on Handicapped Children. *First annual report, Subcommittee on Education of the Committee on Labor and Public Welfare, U.S. Senate.* Washington, D.C.: U.S. Government Printing Office, 1968.

National Safety Council. *Accident facts.* Chicago: National Safety Council, 1975.

Pennsylvania Association for Retarded Children v. Commonwealth of Pennsylvania, 334. F. Supp., 1257 (E.D.Pa. 1971).

Quay, H. C. Dimensions of problem behavior and educational programming. In P.S. Graubard (Ed.), *Children against schools.* Chicago: Follett, 1969.

Resources in Maryland for the developmentally disabled. Baltimore: Developmental Disabilities Council of Maryland, 1975. (Grant #54–P–15381, U.S. Department of Health, Education and Welfare, Div. of Developmental Disabilities.)

Sagor, M. Biological bases of childhood behavioral disorders. In W. E. Rhodes & M. L. Tracy (Eds.), *A study of child variance; conceptual project in emotional disturbance.* Ann Arbor, Mich.: Institute for the Study of Mental Retardation and Related Disabilities, 1971.

Silverman, R. Education of the deaf. In L. E. Travis (Ed.), *Handbook of speech pathology.* New York: Appleton-Century-Crofts, 1957.

Smart, M. S., & Smart, R. C. *Children: Development and relationships.* New York: Macmillan Publishing Co., 1977.

Stephen, E. Cerebral palsy and mental defect. In A. M. Clarke & A. D. Clarke (Eds.), *Mental deficiency: The changing outlook.* New York: Free Press, 1958.

Telford, C. W., & Sawrey, J. M. *The exceptional individual.* Englewood Cliffs, N.J.: Prentice-Hall, 1977.

Torres, F. Convulsive disorders: A working classification and guidelines for diagnosis and treatment. *Medical Times,* 1969, 97(10), 152–156.

Tower, D. B. *Neurochemistry of epilepsy: Seizure mechanisms and their management.* Springfield, Ill.: Charles C Thomas, 1960.

Trotter, R. J. The Milwaukee Project. *APA Monitor,* September, 1976.

United Cerebral Palsy Research and Educational Foundation. *Program for calendar year 1958.* New York: The Foundation, 1958.

United States Office of Education. *Better education for the handicapped: Annual report, fiscal year 1969.* Washington, D.C.: U.S. Government Printing Office, 1970.

Van Riper, C. *Speech correction: Principles and methods.* Englewood Cliffs, N.J.: Prentice-Hall, 1963.

Wolf, J. M., & Anderson, R. M. *The multiply handicapped child.* Springfield, Ill.: Charles C Thomas, 1973.

2

Identification, Assessment, and Intervention

P.L. 94–142, the Education for All Handicapped Children Act, enacted in November 1975, required public school districts to provide appropriate educational services for all exceptional children from 3 to 18 years of age by September 1978, and for all exceptional children from 3 to 21 years of age by September 1980. To satisfy the requirements of P.L. 94–142, school districts must provide a three-pronged battery of special educational services consisting of *identification, assessment,* and *intervention* for exceptional children. This chapter will focus on this three-step process as it relates to young, special children.

Identification

In the past, many exceptional children who needed special educational services were not identified until they reached school age. There were a variety of reasons why large numbers of children did not receive special treatment during their preschool years. The child's condition was often undiagnosed or misdiagnosed and no special services were even sought. If an accurate diagnosis of a handicap was made, many parents did not seek help because they were reluctant to accept the diagnosis and hoped the condition could be outgrown. Other parents were uninformed or misinformed about available services and pro-

In writing this chapter, **Jill E. McGovern** used material about medical identification of disabling conditions from *David A. Draper.*

grams for their child. The result has been few opportunities for handicapped children to reach their potentials. A primary goal of early childhood–special education is to identify exceptional children as early as possible so that the formative years may be spent in ways that make the most of the special child's potential.

Identification of special children may occur at any point from conception through birth, infancy, the preschool years, and the first years of formal schooling. The identification of a disability may be made by any one of the persons who come in contact with the child during the early years of development. These persons include the obstetrician, the pediatrician, the pediatric nurse, the public health nurse, the dentist, the social worker, and the early childhood educator, as well as the parent or primary caregiver. Within their specific spheres of knowledge of the child, each person has the opportunity to pinpoint any deviation from normal development.

The initial identification of a disability is often made by a physician, either the obstetrician or the pediatrician. The obstetrician may become aware of a disability as early as the first few months of pregnancy. Techniques such as amniocentesis and ultra-sound echograms enable obstetricians to determine the presence of a disabling condition. For example, amniocentesis is a process by which a sample of fetal cells is extracted from placental fluids. A genetic analysis of the fetal cells can reveal chromosomal aberrations such as trisomy 13, trisomy 18, or trisomy 21, all of which manifest themselves as Down's Syndrome, or mongolism. In a similar way, ultra-sound echograms can expose orthopedic impairments, physical abnormalities, and multiple fetuses—all conditions which may require special treatment at the moment of birth. While multiple births do not necessarily result in any disability, such births are often premature and do present the risk of some disability associated with prematurity.

The obstetrician is able to recognize the presence or at least the possibility of a disability at the moment of birth. Among the conditions that will alert the obstetrician to the possibility of a disability for the infant are anoxia caused by a twisted umbilical cord or excessive bleeding; a forceps delivery; prolonged, stressful labor; prematurity; and low birth weight.

Other predictors of abnormality may be observed during routine screening of the infant immediately following birth. This process generally involves routine blood and urine tests for metabolic disorders such as PKU and the *Apgar rating* (Apgar, 1965) in which heart rate, breathing effort, muscle tone, reflex irritability, and color are rated. The Apgar instrument predicts survival and indicates newborns who need special care. Other, more detailed examinations of the newborn may be accomplished using such tests as the Brazelton Neonatal Assessment Scale (Brazelton, 1973), Rosenblith's adaptation of the Graham Scale (Rosenblith, 1973), and other newborn neurological examinations (Smart & Smart, 1977). A scale like the Brazelton allows the obstetrician to identify abnormalities in the central nervous system and in the sensory abilities of the newborn. For an even more precise measure of hearing acuity, a new technique using electrodes on the skull of the infant can determine any hearing disability.

If the infant receives medical care from a pediatrician or general practitioner, any deviations from normal development may be identified from the physician's observations and from the child's medical history. The pediatrician would be aware of possible disabilities if she found a record of amaurotic familial idiocy in the child's family, knew that the birth was stressful, or treated the child for a high fever with one of the childhood diseases. Likewise, if the child did not walk and talk at the appropriate age, the pediatrician would see the need for further examination of the child's abilities.

For two major reasons the role of the pediatrician can be a key one in the identification of exceptional children. One reason is that she is the one professional who has the opportunity to observe the child's development frequently and over an extended period of time. The other reason is that the pediatrician is the primary source of help when parents believe their child is having a problem. Early identification of a disability, accurate assessment, and effective intervention may minimize the detrimental effects of the disability.

Another professional in the field of health services who may be able to identify a disability in a young child is the nurse. Both the pediatric nurse and the public health nurse have opportunities similar to those of the pediatrician to note abnormal development. The pediatric nurse may work in a hospital nursery, in a clinic, or in a pediatrician's office, and in any of those environments, she may observe the child over a period of time. The public health nurse serves a similar role in health clinics and home visitations. Seeing the child in her home may reveal factors other than health that would cause the child to be at risk for a disability.

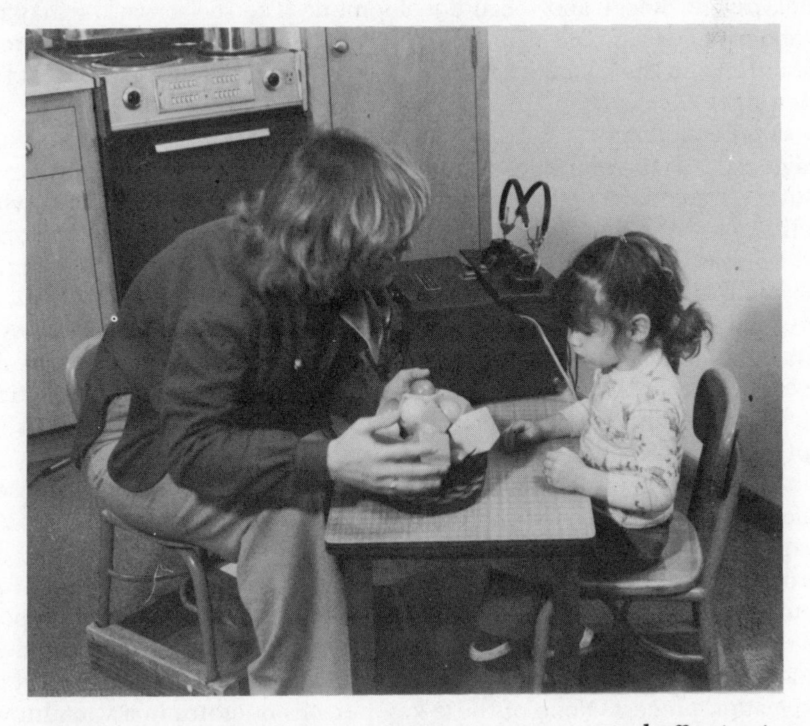

Early identification of a disability, accurate assessment, and effective intervention may minimize the detrimental effects of the disability.

Both the pediatric nurse and the public health nurse have an increasingly critical role in early identification of special children. There is a current trend for nurses to perform some tasks that were formerly performed by the pediatrician. Some of these duties include general screening practices to measure the child's development, discussing appropriate health care with the parent, and referring the child to special health services when needed. The nurse is by no means usurping the role of the doctor, rather she is serving as an adjunct to the pediatrician.

Still another professional who can identify real and potential health problems of the young child is the dentist. Although infants are not usually seen by a dentist, it is important for preschoolers to receive dental care. In caring for the preschooler, the dentist observes the condition of the teeth as well as the structure of the mouth and jaw. The dentist will be able to pinpoint specific dental problems such as decayed teeth and malocclusions which could lead to speech impairment and poor self-concept. The dentist's early identification of such conditions, followed by adequate dental care and nutrition, may prevent any serious disabilities in the child.

In addition to the professionals from the health care fields, the social worker may play an important role in the early identification of handicapped children. As a firsthand observer of the home environment, the social worker is in a position to detect inadequacies in the training and intellectual stimulation provided for the child. Such inadequacies may be harmful to the child's physical, mental, psychological, and social development. The social worker may recognize abnormalities as well as inappropriate environments and be able to refer the children and their families to appropriate sources for assessment and intervention.

Persons involved in day care services and preschool programs have a unique vantage point in the identification of children with disabilities. They have the advantage of regular, and in many cases, daily observation of the child, whereas the other professionals—like the pediatrician, the nurse, the dentist, and the social worker—may see the child on a regular but not necessarily as frequent a basis as the educator. Early childhood educators are also in a position to observe many aspects of the child's development. While the other professionals may take related factors into consideration, they are primarily concerned with a specific facet of the child's development. Physical, mental, linguistic, and social behaviors may all be observed within the early education center, and a comprehensive profile of the child may be obtained.

The expertise of professionals is valuable in the early identification of the handicapped child, but even more critical in this process is the parent. As the primary observer of the child, the parent has firsthand knowledge of the child's total development. If a disability is suspected, the parent may seek further screening of the child by one or several professionals. Parents are in a position to confirm the suspicions of any of the professionals who have noted a risk situation. The cooperation of the parent and the professionals is crucial in the identification process. None of these key persons operates in a vacuum where the child is concerned. An interdisciplinary approach to the problem of identifying young, special children insures accurate assessment and appropriate intervention.

Assessment

Identification of a disabling condition is the first step in the process of meeting the needs of young children. The second step is *assessment*, which is also known as evaluation. The assessment process determines the precise nature and extent of the child's disability so that appropriate prevention and intervention measures may begin.

The interdisciplinary approach, involving professionals from the fields of health care, psychology, and education, seems to provide the most complete assessment of the special child. Each professional contributes information about the child, and all the bits of information merge together to form a complete profile of the child's special needs. The assessment procedures of each of the fields involved in serving the young, special child, are described here.

Medical Assessment. The medical assessment of the child consists of two basic parts: the medical history and the physical examination. The medical history includes specific information about the prenatal, perinatal, and postnatal development of the child. Complications during pregnancy, birth, infancy, and the preschool years are noted, as well as any unusual aspects of the family's medical history. The developmental history of the child is also recorded. Key developmental milestones such as the onset of walking and talking are included in this history. Finally, a social history may be incorporated into the child's medical record. Information about the family and the home environment is important to the medical professional, particularly those involved in family practice. With such a multifaceted medical history of the child, the medical practitioner may begin to make an accurate evaluation of the child.

The physical examination serves two main purposes: it presents a current picture of the child from the medical point of view and it detects abnormalities. Obvious disabilities such as Down's syndrome, severe hearing or visual impairment, and gross neurologic, orthopedic, or other health impairments may be readily discerned by a thorough physical examination. If the doctor suspects disabilities such as mild mental retardation, epilepsy, autism, moderate hearing or visual impairment, inadequate language development, and hyperactivity, he may refer the child for specialized medical examinations. The following specialists may be involved in medical assessments:

1. *Geneticist:* to determine the presence of a disability caused by genetic factors; for example, mental retardation due to recessive genes (galactosemia, phenylketonuria, Tay-Sachs disease) or to chromosomal aberrations (Down's syndrome) or orthopedic impairment also resulting from recessive genes (hemophilia).
2. *Neurologist:* to ascertain the presence of a disability caused by central nervous system dysfunction; for example, cerebral palsy, epilepsy, and hyperactivity.
3. *Biochemist:* to determine the presence of a disability caused by biochemical disorders; for example, mental retardation galactosemia, phenylketonuria, and amaurotic familial idiocy), autism, and hyperactivity accompanying learning disabilities.

4. *Otologist:* to assess hearing impairment caused by defects in the hearing mechanism or in the auditory nerve.
5. *Ophthalmologist:* to assess visual impairment caused by refractive errors, ocular muscle abnormalities, and other visual anomalies such as cataracts.
6. *Orthopedist:* to determine the presence of a disability caused by defects in the bones, joints, or muscles; for example, orthopedic impairment due to diseases such as poliomyelitis, juvenile arthritis, and tuberculosis of the bones.
7. *Psychiatrist:* to ascertain the presence of a disability caused by psychological factors; for example, speech impairment manifested as stuttering, or behavioral disabilities traditionally known as emotional disturbance and social maladjustment.
8. *Dentist:* to determine the presence of a disability caused by decayed teeth or malocclusions; for example, speech impairment.

Occasionally other specialists like the cardiologist, hematologist, internist, and otolaryngologist may also participate in the medical assessment.

Behavioral Assessment. The behavioral assessment encompasses both the psychological evaluation and the education evaluation and presents a picture of the child in terms of her mental, motor, linguistic, and social development. A key component of the psychological assessment is the *measurement of intelligence.* Although there are a number of tests of infant intelligence, their accuracy in assessing or predicting intelligence is questionable. The factor that these infant tests usually measure is sensorimotor development rather than intellectual development, so test results are in terms of DQ (developmental quotient) instead of IQ (intelligence quotient). DQs obtained during the child's first 18 months are accurate predictors of later mental retardation only in cases of severe developmental impairment; however, DQs may have usefulness as indicators of abnormal development in combination with other assessment data (McCandless & Trotter, 1977). Some tests of infant development are the following:

Bayley Scales of Infant Development (Bayley, 1969)—a motor scale and a mental scale covering the age range of 2 to 30 months.

Cattell Infant Intelligence Scale (Cattell, 1940)—a downward extension of the Stanford-Binet Intelligence Scale which yields a mental age score that may be converted to an IQ.

Gesell Development Test (Gesell & Amatruda, 1951)—a measure of developmental age in motor, adaptive, language, and personal-social behavior which is useful in detecting neurological abnormalities (Smart & Smart, 1977).

Ordinal Scales of Psychological Development (Uzgiris & Hunt, 1975)—seven scales to assess psychological development in infancy. By shedding light on development of ability and motivation, this approach to assessment may prevent retardation and apathy in infancy.

After infancy, at about two years of age, *intellectual development* may be assessed more accurately and predictions about later intellectual functioning may be made with more credibility. There are a number of tests of intelligence that are appropriate for use with preschool children. Some of these tests include:

Ammons Full-Range Picture Vocabulary Test (Ammons-Ammons, 1948)—test of receptive language vocabulary for use with preschoolers.

McCarthy Scales of Children's Abilities (McCarthy, 1973)—a general cognitive index with scores for verbal, quantitative, perceptual performance, memory, and motor development, covering an age range of 2½ to 8½ years.

Merrill-Palmer Test (Stutsman, 1930)—a scale of mental tests for preschoolers.

Minnesota Preschool Scale (Goodenough, Maurer, & Van Wageneng, 1940)—assessment of intellectual capacity in children ages 1.5 to 6.0 years.

Peabody Picture Vocabulary Test (Dunn, 1965)—a quick screening measure.

Pictorial Test of Intelligence (French, 1964)—useful measure of motor and speech disabilities, covering an age range of 3 to 8 years.

Slosson Intelligence Test for Children and Adults (Slosson, 1963)—quick screening tool, yielding an IQ, and covering an age range of .5 months to 27 years.

Early childhood educators are in a position to observe many aspects of the child's development.

Stanford-Binet Intelligence Scale (Terman & Merrill, 1960)—measure of mental age (MA) from which an intelligence quotient (IQ) may be derived for an age range of 2 to 18 years.

Wechsler Preschool and Primary Scale of Intelligence (WPPSI) (Wechsler, 1967)—verbal and nonverbal scores for children ages 2 to 6 years.

In addition to assessing intellectual development, the psychological evaluation may include assessment of *motor development.* Table 1, compiled from a variety of sources by Smart and Smart (1977, p. 212), summarizes normal motor develpment from ages 2 to 5. Besides the sources cited which may be used to assess motor development, one of the subtests of the *McCarthy Scales of Children's Abilities* (McCarthy, 1973) may also be used for the same assessment purpose.

Still within the realm of the psychological evaluation is assessment of *perceptual-motor development.* Gross and fine motor behaviors are a function of a child's perceptions, or interpretations of what he receives through his senses. Perceptual-motor growth occurs rapidly between the ages of 3 and 5 years, and provides a basis for building body image (self-concept) as well as for developing the skills involved in reading and writing. Various tests of perceptual-motor development, including visual perceptual ability, are available for assessment purposes. A selection is presented here:

Bender Visual-Motor Gestalt Test for Children (Bender, 1962)—nine designs copied by child and interpreted by trained diagnostician to detect any neurological or psychological defects.

Developmental Test of Visual-Motor Integration (Beery & Buktenica, 1967) —a series of 24 geometric forms to be copied by children from age 2 to 15 years.

Developmental Test of Visual Perception (Frostig, 1963)—measure of five perceptual skills in kindergarten children.

Purdue Perceptual-Motor Survey (Roach & Kephart, 1966)—survey of five general areas of perceptual-motor development.

The psychological and the educational evaluations may be combined into a single assessment instrument which measures *psychoeducational development.* Such an evaluation tool may have the most relevance to the educational program for the special child. Two measures of psychoeducational ability are the:

Psychoeducational Evaluation of the Preschool Child (Jedrysek, Klapper, Pope, & Wortis, 1972)—a five-part assessment of physical, perceptual, memory, language, and cognitive abilities.

Valett Developmental Survey of Basic Learning Abilities (Valett, 1968)—a 230-item survey of a broad range of tasks, applicable at the preschool and kindergarten levels (ages 2 through 7 years).

Language development may be assessed by several evaluation instruments. A number of the previously mentioned tests of intelligence contain subtests of language ability. For instance, the McCarthy Scales of Children's Abilities

Table 1

Some Landmarks in Motor Development During the Years from Two to Five, from Basic Normative Studies. The Item Is Placed at the Age Where 50 Percent or More of Children Perform the Act. (Initials in parentheses refer to sources. See footnotes.)*

	Age Two	Age Three	Age Four	Age Five
Eye-Hand	Builds tower of 6 or 7 blocks (KP) Turns book pages singly (KP) Spoon into mouth without turning (KP) Holds glass in one hand (KP) Imitates vertical and circular strokes (KP) Puts on simple garment (KP)	Builds tower of 9 blocks (KP) Makes bridge of 3 blocks (TM) Catches ball, arms straight (MW) Spills little from spoon (KP) Pours from pitcher (KP) Unbuttons, puts shoes on (KP) Copies circle (TM) Draws straight line (TM)	Cuts on line with scissors (GI) Makes designs and crude letters (GI) Catches small ball, elbows in front of body (MW) Dresses self (GI) Throws ball overhand (KP)	Folds paper into double triangle (TM) Copies square (TM) and triangle (KP) Copies designs, letters, numbers (GI) Catches small ball, elbows at sides (MW) Throws well (G) Fastens buttons he can see (GI)
Locomotion	Wide stance, runs well (KP) Walks up and down stairs alone (KP) Kicks large ball (KP) Descends large ladder, marking time (MW) Jumps 12 inches (MW)	Walks tiptoe (KP, B) Jumps from bottom stair (KP, B) Stands on one foot (KP, B) Hops, both feet (MW) Propels wagon, one foot (J) Rides tricycle (KP) Descends long steps, marking time, unsupported (MW) Jumps 18 inches (MW)	Gallops (G) Descends small ladder, alternating feet easily (MW) Stunts on tricycle (G) Descends short steps, alternating feet, unsupported (G) Skips on one foot (KP)	Narrow stance (GI) Skips (G, MW) Hops on one foot, ten or more steps (MW) Descends large ladder, alternating feet easily (MW) Walks straight line (GI)

Note: From *Children: Development and Relationships*. New York: Macmillan Publishing Co., 1977. Copyright 1977 by Macmillan Publishing Co. Reprinted by permission.

*Sources:

B —N. Bayley. Development of motor abilities during the first three years. *Monographs of the Society for Research in Child Development*, 1935, **1**.

GI —A. Gesell, and F. L. Ilg. *Child development*. New York: Harper & Row, Publishers, Inc., 1949.

G —M. V. Gutteridge. A study of motor achievements of young children. *Archives of Psychology*, 1939, **244**.

J —T. D. Jones. *Development of certain motor skills and play activities in young children*, Child Development Monographs. New York: Teachers College, Columbia University, 1939, No. 26.

KP —H. Knobloch and B. Pasamanick. *Developmental diagnosis*, 3rd ed. New York: Harper & Row, Publishers, Inc., 1974.

MW—C. L. McCuskill and B. L. Wellman. A study of common motor achievements at the preschool ages. *Child Development*, 1939, 9, 141–150.

TM —L. M. Terman and M. A. Merrill. *Stanford-Binet intelligence scale*. Boston: Houghton Mifflin Company, 1960.

(McCarthy, 1973), the Peabody Picture Vocabulary Test (Dunn, 1965), the Stanford-Binet (Terman & Merrill, 1960), and the WPPSI (Wechsler, 1967) all measure aspects of language development.

In addition, several other tests may be used to assess language development in a more comprehensive manner.

Houston Test of Language Development (Crabtree, 1963)—in two parts: one for children between the ages of 18 and 36 months, the other for children between the ages of 3 and 6 years; items in linguistic categories of reception, conceptualization, and expression.

Illinois Test of Psycholinguistic Abilities (Kirk, McCarthy, & Kirk, 1968)—assesses several facets of linguistic behavior in children as young as 2 years, 4 months of age, utilizing a battery of 12 subtests.

Northwestern Syntax Screening Test (Lee, 1969)—a test of receptive and expressive language for children ages 3 to 7.

Preschool Language Scale (Zimmerman, Steiner, & Evatt, 1969)—measure of auditory comprehension, verbal ability, and articulation for an age range covering 2 to 6.

Utah Test of Language Development (Meacham, Jex, & Jones, 1959)—a test of language ability and skills.

Verbal Language Development Scale (Meacham, 1959)—an extension and restandardization of the communications items on the Vineland Social Maturity Scale (Doll, 1965), covering a range of ages from 1 month to 16 years.

There are also three tests which assess a specific aspect of language, that of *auditory perception.*

Auditory Discrimination Test (Wepman, 1960)—a diagnosis of auditory discrimination of initial, medial, and final sounds in minimal word pairs (words such as *slap–slip*).

Goldman-Fristoe-Woodcock Test of Auditory Discrimination (Goldman, Fristoe, & Woodcock, 1970)—measurement of speech–sound discrimination ability; to be used with children as young as 4 years of age.

Test for Auditory Comprehension of Language (Carrow, 1973)—assessment of a child's understanding of language structure, covering an age range of 3 years, 10 months to 6 years, 11 months.

There are a variety of assessment instruments for *educational evaluation.* Some tests focus on general learning aptitude while others measure achievement. Still others may serve as screening as well as assessment tools for diagnosing learning problems experienced by exceptional children.

A Basic Screening and Referral Form for Children with Suspected Learning and Behavioral Difficulties (Valett, 1972)—a survey of a variety of behaviors and academic skills of kindergarten children and older.

CIRCUS: Comprehensive Assessment in Nursery School and Kindergarten (Educational Testing Service, 1974)—a screening tool for preschool-age children with potential learning problems.

Denver Developmental Screening Test (Frankenburg & Dodds, 1969)—a diagnostic instrument for four major areas of development: personal-social; fine motor-adaptive; language; and gross motor, covering an age range of birth to 6 years.

Detroit Tests of Learning Aptitude (Baker & Leland, 1935)—a comprehensive individual test of mental ability that may be used as a diagnostic tool for an age range of 4 years to adult; various batteries of the 19 subtests may be used with all kinds of special children.

Developmental Potential of Preschool Children (Haeussermann, 1958)—an evaluation of intellectual, sensory, and emotional functioning for children between 2 and 6 years of age, or functioning on that level, who have disabilities in expression and other areas.

DIAL (*Developmental Indicators for the Assessment of Learning*) (Mardell & Goldenberg, 1975)—a screening test for identifying preschool children, ages 2½ to 5½, with learning problems.

Hiskey-Nebraska Test of Learning Aptitude (Hiskey, 1966)—originally designed to evaluate the learning ability of hearing impaired children, now includes norms for hearing children as well, covering an age range of 2 years, 6 months to 17 years, 5 months.

The Meeting Street School Screening Test (Hainsworth & Siqueland, 1969)—a screening and diagnostic instrument for early identification of children with learning disabilities, ages 4½ to 6.

Peabody Individual Achievement Test (Dunn & Markwardt, 1970)—a general measure of achievement for children 5 to 12 years of age.

Preschool Attainment Record (Doll, 1967)—a measure of achievement in arithmetic, motor, oral language, and social skills.

Preschool Inventory (Caldwell, 1970)—a general measure of achievement for children ages 3 to 6.

Southern California Test Battery for Assessment of Dysfunction (Ayres, 1972)—a battery of separate tests for children ages 3 to 10: *Ayres Space Test; Southern California Figure-Ground Visual Perception Test; Southern California Kinesthesia and Tactile Perception Tests; Southern California Motor Accuracy Test;* and *Southern California Perceptual-Motor Tests.*

Teacher Rating Scale for the Identification of Handicapped Children (Arizona State Department of Education, 1973)—assessment of a wide range of abilities (academic, emotional, social) for children in kindergarten to eighth grade.

Wide Range Achievement Test (Jastak & Jastak, 1976)—a quick individual test of basic school abilities, covering an age range of 5 years to adult.

Another portion of the behavioral assessment may be considered the *affective and social evaluation.* In some cases, it may be measured in the psychological and educational evaluation. Subtests of some of the previously mentioned instruments assess affective and social behaviors. Other tests which measure these specific abilities are the following:

Adaptive Behavior Scales (Nihira, Foster, Shellhaas, & Leland, 1974)—a measure of independence and ability to cope with the environment for use with children from 3 years to adulthood.

California Test of Personality (Thorpe, Clark, & Tiegs, 1953)—assessment of affective development.

Children's Apperception Test (Bellak, Bellak, Haworth, & Hurvich, 1959)—a projective measure which is a test of personality in children ages 3 to 10.

Vineland Social Maturity Scale (Doll, 1971)—designed to measure social competence as a function of social maturation and independence, utilizing an informant (usually a parent) and interview format, appropriate for an age range of birth to adult.

Information gathered through various assessment techniques enables the educator to plan appropriate instruction.

Informal Assessment. Although the formal assessment procedures just presented garner valuable data about the handicapped child, the profile of the child and her special needs may be enhanced by informal evaluations. Observations made by the medical practitioner, the psychologist, and the educator during the formal testing sessions may contribute significantly to an understanding of the child. For example, the psychologist may see that the child is easily distracted, a fact that would not be revealed in any test scores. Although the child's overall pattern of behavior as indicated by the test results is important, knowledge of the child's distractibility is just as vital in planning a program of intervention to meet her specific needs.

Informal assessment may be accomplished by a variety of observation techniques: *anecdotal records, measurements of behavior, inventories and rating scales,* and *individual observation methods.* The teacher is perhaps the most effective observer in terms of his objectivity and ability to record the child's behavior on a regular and systematic basis in the school setting.

Pasanella and Volkmor (1977) suggest several distinct advantages of the use of observation techniques:

1. Observation measures behavior in natural settings, rather than the artificial settings of a medical examination room or a psychologist's testing center.
2. The observer's attention is focused on the child's actual behavior.
3. Observation increases educational effectiveness by monitoring the intervention strategies and techniques in action.
4. Observation removes the element of isolation inherent in formal assessment; a child's behavior is observed in context and factors compounding the child's disability may be more readily apparent.
5. Observation and subsequent educational planning may rely on the intuition and judgment of the experienced educator.

One observation technique which may be employed by the teacher is that of *anecdotal records.* Anecdotal records are reports of the teacher's informal observations of children and certain aspects of their adaptive behavior. By recording unexpected behaviors or incidents, the educator is able to discern patterns of behavior and thereby make a more precise assessment of the child.

A second technique used in observation of the young child is one that utilizes *measurements of behavior.* Several approaches to measuring behavior are frequency recording, duration recording, time sampling, and Planned Activity Check, or the Placheck Method (Pasanella & Volkmor, 1977).

All of these techniques are used for the purpose of gathering baseline data about a special child's behavior. Baseline data—measures of a behavior under a set of stable conditions (Pasanella & Volkmor, 1977)—provide a constant against which intervention plans may be assessed.

The use of *inventories and rating scales* constitutes a third observation technique. A number of checklists, inventories, and rating scales are available to the early childhood–special educator to assess a child's behavior in an informal but efficient fashion. The resulting information indicates the child's functioning in a broad range of critical areas of behavior and enables the educator to plan appropriate instruction. Some of the inventories that may be useful are the following:

Developmental Checklists for 3-, 4-, and 5-year olds (Frost & Kissinger, 1976).

Preliminary Evaluation Information (Frost & Kissinger, 1976).

Pupil Behavior Rating Scale (Gearheart, 1973).

A Teacher's Estimate of Kindergarten Pupils' Abilities (Kirk, 1966).

The Pupil Rating Scale (Myklebust, 1971).

Preschool Evaluation Form (Pasanella & Volkmor, 1977).

A Program for Early Identification of Learning Disabilities (Peterson, 1970).

A Psychoeducational Inventory of Basic Learning Abilities (Valett, 1968).

A final observation technique is that of *individual observation methods.* These methods may include any observation tools and tricks the teacher has found to be particularly useful in diagnosing the young, special child. Among such tools may be a homemade checklist of behaviors the teacher expects to occur in the classroom; interviews with persons involved with the special child such as the parent, the social worker, and the medical practitioner; and a situational evaluation of the home and the school environments in which the child's behaviors occur. An example of the situational evaluation is the *Evaluation Checklist* developed by Harms (1972) for assessing the strengths and weaknesses of the classroom environment. Pasanella and Volkmor (1977) stress the value of a situational evaluation in attempting to "maximize the handicapped child's effective interaction with the regular curriculum, subject matter, peers, and adults" (p. 93).

Task Analysis. So far, assessment of the young, exceptional child has been based on formal and informal evaluation techniques. A third approach to assessment is task analysis. "Task analysis is the process of isolating, describing, and sequencing all the essential subtasks which, when the child has mastered them, will enable him to perform the objective" (Pasanella & Volkmor, 1977, p. 161). A task or skill is broken down into its simplest parts, and the parts are then arranged in sequence of steps by which the child may achieve the *stated behavioral objective.*

By examining the skills involved in a specific behavior, the teacher is able to compile a list of skills which becomes a tool both for assessing the child's progress and for planning appropriate intervention. The length of the list of skills or subtasks depends on the nature of the task and the abilities of the child. Each subtask in the sequence needs to be simplified enough to allow the child to experience success at each step. The instructional sequence leads to mastery of the desired behavior.

The principles of task analysis are incorporated into the more formalized assessment technique of criterion-referenced measurement or testing. *Criterion-referenced measurement* is "any test which is purposely designed to provide measures which can be interpreted in terms of specific performance standards" (Pasanella & Volkmor, 1977, p. 115).

Criterion-referenced tests are designed to discriminate between mastery and nonmastery of specific behaviorally stated objectives. The student's score is a listing of behaviors or skills she has acquired and those which she has not yet mastered. The test items are selected to reflect the standing of a student with respect to the curriculum (and thus sensitive to instruction) and not from the relation of her scores to the scores of others. From the results of a criterion-referenced test the teacher can plan intervention strategies and techniques that take into consideration the child's present level of functioning, rate and style of learning, and potential for mastering specific behaviors. Specific skill deficiencies may be clearly identified, and in this way, the needs of the handicapped child may be met more appropriately.

Intervention

The third component of the process of meeting the special needs of young, handicapped children is *intervention,* which may be considered as any modification or addition of services, strategies, techniques, or materials to maximize the child's potential. While the other two phases of the diagnostic process, *identification* and *assessment,* are critical prerequisites for planning a program of intervention, they are static operations. *Intervention* is dynamic and flexible as well as essential for effecting positive changes in the development of exceptional children. Decisions about intervention are based on the information acquired during the identification and assessment procedures, and they take into consideration appropriate *placement* and interdisciplinary *treatment.*

Placement is governed by the child's special needs and the kinds of special services that are available. Generally, the more severe the child's disability, the more restrictive the environment. The Education for All Handicapped Children Act (P.L. 94–142) recognizes the need for institutional programs for severely and profoundly disabled youngsters, and at the same time encourages *mainstreaming,* that is, placing the special child in the least restrictive environment. This philosophy is supported by at least two arguments: (1) there should be a single educational system that effectively serves all children rather than one for the disabled and another for everyone else (Abeson, Burgdorf, Casey, Kunz, & McNeil, 1975) and (2) there is less need for labeling and categorizing when the majority of special children are served within the regular educational program, and the problem of stigmatization is thereby minimized.

Until recently, the options for placing a handicapped child were limited, with few alternatives between home care and institutionalization. With the current trend toward early childhood–special education, more choices are available to parents of special children. Some of the kinds of instructional settings, in order of most restrictive to least restrictive, include:

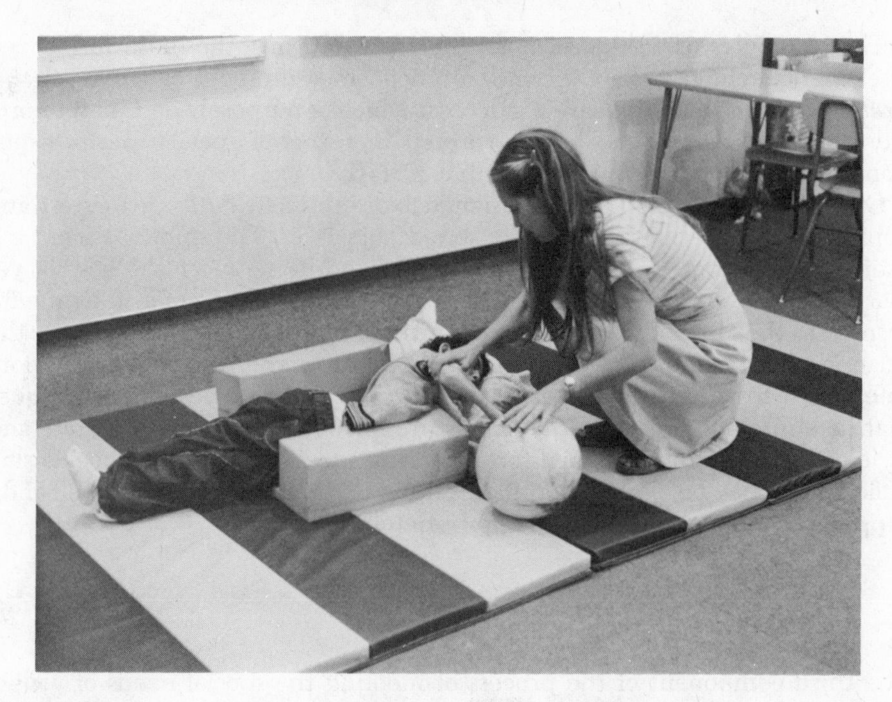

Each subtask of a skill needs to be simplified enough to allow the child to experience success at each step.

1. *Hospital* or *Residential Setting.* These environments are appropriate for the most profoundly and severely disabled children. In some cases, the *hospital setting* may be a temporary placement. For example, the Down's syndrome child often experiences serious cardiac and respiratory problems which require hospital care. In other cases, the institution or residential setting meets the rigorous needs of young children disabled by conditions such as severe mental retardation, multiple handicaps, hearing and visual impairments, or serious behavior disorders. To be effective for these children, care must be the comprehensive and constant kind that institutionalization provides.
2. *Home Setting.* For some special children whose disability is severe enough to limit mobility but sufficiently treated so as to be managed by the parents, the home is appropriate during the child's early years. An example is a young child with physical impairment. Her mobility may be decidedly limited but her impairment can be managed within the home where she profits from the relationships with her family members.
3. *Special School Setting.* This environment is appropriate for children whose disability requires intensive treatment and who can function adequately in the home environment. Children with moderate mental retardation, cerebral palsy, autism, hearing or visual impairment, moderate physical impairment, or moderate behavior disorders may benefit from a special school setting in which the program of intervention is concentrated on their special needs.

4. *Regular School Setting with Special Support Services.* Handicapped children placed in regular early childhood programs may be appropriately served with special *support services.* Examples of special support services are physical therapists, speech therapists, language therapists, and play therapists. Children with mild disabling conditions can have their special needs met while they benefit from interaction with their nondisabled peers.

In addition to placement considerations, effective intervention for young, handicapped children requires *interdisciplinary treatment.* Each discipline—medical, social, psychological, and educational—has an obligation to provide the most appropriate treatment for the handicapped child. But, because the field of education has perhaps the greatest responsibility for meeting the needs of young special children, early childhood–special education has the greatest impact on these children.

Medical Intervention. The physician is frequently the first professional whom parents of disabled, or suspected disabled, children contact. In some cases, the disability may be controlled or eliminated by medical treatment. Epilepsy is an example of a disability that may be controlled by medication such as Dilantin and Phenobarbitol. Another example is hyperactivity associated with learning disabilities that may be effectively treated for some children with the use of stimulants like Ritalin. Health impairments such as hepatitis or infectious mononucleosis may be eliminated by medical treatment. With these disabilities which can be effectively controlled or eliminated, special educational services may still be warranted, either on a short-term basis for the child with temporary health impairments, or on a long-term basis for the child with more lasting disabilities.

In other cases, medical intervention may be effective in arresting a disabling condition but only after irreversible damage has occurred. Several kinds of mental retardation, specifically galactosemia, phenylketonuria, and cretinism, may be prevented by modification of the child's diet. But, if treatment does not begin immediately after the child is born, the damage is irreparable. While medical intervention may inhibit further damage, it needs to be supplemented by educational intervention. Hearing impairment caused by the infection serous otitis media is another example of medical treatment ending the harmful condition, but not in time to prevent lasting detrimental effects. Still another example is any of a number of physical impairments like tuberculosis of the bones which may cause orthopedic impairment even though the disease is arrested. In these cases, special educational services will be essential to minimize the effects of the disabling condition.

Medical intervention may be effective in reducing the detrimental aspects of a young child's disability. For example, mental retardation caused by environmental factors such as malnutrition and inadequate health care may be moderated by medical treatment. Some cases of cerebral palsy, epilepsy, hearing impairment, visual impairment caused by muscle defects and cataracts, and speech impairment caused by cleft palate may be alleviated by surgery. Recent medical advances have also proved to be effective in treating certain disabilities. One such technique is biofeedback, which seems to be of some usefulness with individuals who have cerebral palsy, epilepsy, speech impairment caused by stuttering, hyperactivity associated with learning disabilities, and some behavior disorders. In these instances where the effects of the disability may be minimized, the need for special educational services may be reduced correspondingly.

Social Intervention. Treatment recommended by social workers is usually implemented in conjunction with treatment by other disciplines, such as medicine or education. For example, the diet prescribed by the physician or the nurse may require new skills on the part of the parent in shopping and food preparation. The social worker is in a position to assist and monitor the new nutritional practices.

The social worker may function in several roles on behalf of the exceptional child and her family. One role is *advocate* for the child, so that all special services to which the child is entitled, such as health care, legal assistance, and educational programs, are made available to her. In the role of liaison, the social worker attempts to maintain the channels of communication between the home and the school. As counselor, the social worker acts as a resource for parents who desire guidance in handling themselves in relation to their handicapped children as well as in working with the children in the home. Such counseling may occur on an informal basis or in a more formal, structured format, such as a course in Parent Effectiveness Training (Gordon, 1970). This training program is designed to improve communication between parents and children, employing techniques such as active listening and responding.

Psychological Intervention. The field of psychology has made a number of significant contributions to the treatment of exceptional children. Psychological intervention has proved effective with children with behavioral disabilities as well as with children with other kinds of disabilities. Several of the approaches found to be effective are the psychodynamic approach, the behavioral-deficit approach, and the behavior modification approach (Dunn, 1973). In the psychodynamic approach, therapy, like play therapy, serves to reveal the underlying causes of the maladaptive behavior. The behavioral-deficit approach suggests that a child's inappropriate behavior is the result of frustration and failure in the educational setting. Once the deficits are determined, they may be treated.

The two kinds of psychological intervention just described have more relevance with children with behavioral disabilities than with children with other exceptionalities. The behavior modification approach has more universal application. Behavior modification is a technique for shaping a person's behavior in a manner desired by the behavior modifier, who may be a psychologist, an educator, or a parent. The technique uses the principles of reinforcement for desirable behavior and follows a basic pattern:

1. Acceptable behavior is clearly defined.
2. Appropriate behavior is reinforced immediately with an effective reinforcer, like a smile, a compliment, a treat, a token, or a privilege.
3. Inappropriate behavior is ignored, or punished when absolutely necessary.

The effectiveness of behavior modification has been well documented (Charles, 1976) and has been proven in a great number of studies with exceptional children (Birnbauer, 1971; McKenzie, 1968; Patterson, 1965). The approach seems to be an effective form of psychological intervention with children with mental retardation, autism, speech impairment, learning disabilities, and behavioral disabilities.

Educational Intervention. Medical, social, and psychological intervention strategies are essential in the treatment of young, special children. Yet, they function as adjuncts to educational intervention. The field of education seems to bear the greatest responsibility in treating exceptional children. It is toward the fulfillment of that responsibility that this book has been prepared. The remaining chapters present specific strategies, techniques, and materials for implementing an effective program of educational intervention. It is appropriate at this point, however, to discuss two general strategies that are utilized in the educational treatment of young, special children.

The first strategy is that of *diagnostic-prescriptive teaching.* Charles (1976) says that diagnostic-prescriptive teaching consists of four parts:

1. *Determination of behavioral objectives* which are statements describing educational goals and intentions.
2. *Diagnosis* to determine which objectives have been reached by the child.
3. *Prescription,* which is the process of planning educational activities that will help the child achieve the objectives.
4. *Criterion measurement* or *evaluation* to determine if the child has achieved the behavioral objectives.

In addition to determining behavioral objectives, diagnosing, prescribing, and measuring a child's progress, the teacher is responsible for implementing the prescriptions and keeping records of the behavioral objectives achieved by the child.

The diagnostic-prescriptive teaching strategy is presented as a part of the intervention procedure because it seems to dovetail so naturally into the process of assessment. All of the data obtained by the assessment procedures previously discussed are only useful to the educator when they are considered in terms of intervention. The results of assessment should provide the teacher with a complete picture of the child's abilities and disabilities and enable him to plan an appropriate educational program for the child.

Another form of educational intervention is required by the Education for All Handicapped Children Act (P.L. 94–142). One of the mandates of the federal legislation is that each child diagnosed as exceptional and placed in a special educational setting must be given an *individual educational plan.* Such a plan must include the following information:

1. Suggested educational placement.
2. Individual child's capabilities.
3. Barriers to normal learning.
4. Additional services required.

5. Recommendations for instructional activities, techniques, and materials.
6. Time frame in which educational intervention should be accomplished.

The individual educational plan is the outcome of the process of identification and assessment and requires specific statements about all important aspects of educational intervention. It is intended to insure that the special needs of exceptional children are met in the most effective manner possible.

Summary

This chapter has presented a discussion of *identification, assessment,* and *intervention* with young, special children. Identification may be made by those professionals who are involved with exceptional children as well as by the parents. Assessment of the special needs of these children includes formal assessment (medical evaluation and behavioral evaluation), informal assessment based on observation techniques, and task analysis.

Intervention may be implemented by professionals in the medical, social, and psychological fields, but it is predominantly implemented by educators. Diagnostic-prescriptive teaching and an individual educational plan are two forms of educational intervention that may be used to meet the special needs of young, exceptional children.

REFERENCES

Abeson, A., Burgdorf, R. L., Casey, P. J., Kunz, J. W., & McNeil, W. Access to opportunity. In N. Hobbs (Ed.), *Issues in the classification of children* (Vol. II). San Francisco: Jossey-Bass, 1975.

Ammons, R. B., & Ammons, H. S. *Full-Range Picture Vocabulary Test.* Missoula, Mont.: Psychological Test Specialists, 1948.

Apgar, V. *Perinatal problems and the central nervous system.* In U.S. Dept. of Health, Education and Welfare, Children's Bureau, *The child with central nervous system deficit.* Washington, D.C.: U.S. Government Printing Office, 1965.

Arizona State Dept. of Education. *Children.* Phoenix: Author, 1973.

Ayres, A. J. *Southern California Test Battery for Assessment of Dysfunction.* Los Angeles: Western Psychological Services, 1972.

Baker, H. J., & Leland, B. *Detroit Tests of Learning Aptitude.* Indianapolis: Bobbs–Merrill Co., 1935.

Bayley, N. *Bayley's Scales of Infant Development.* New York: Psychological Corp., 1969.

Beery, K. E., & Buktenica, N. A. *Developmental Test of Visual-Motor Integration.* Chicago: Follett Publishing Co., 1967.

Bellak, L., Bellak, S. S., Haworth, M. R., & Hurvich, M. S. *Children's Apperception Test.* Larchmont, N.Y.: C.P.S., 1959.

Bender, L. *The Bender Visual-Motor Gestalt Test for Children.* Los Angeles: Western Psychological Services, 1962.

Birnbauer, J. Preparing "uncontrollable" retarded children for group instruction. In W. Becker (Ed.), *An empirical basis for change in education.* Chicago: Science Research Associates Inc., 1971.

Brazelton, T. B. *Neonatal Assessment Scale.* Philadelphia: J. B. Lippincott Co., 1973.

Bush, W. J., & Waugh, K. W. *Diagnosing learning disabilities.* Columbus, Ohio: Charles E. Merrill Publishing Co., 1976.

Caldwell, B. M. *Preschool Inventory.* Princeton, N.J.: Cooperative Tests & Services, 1970.

Carrow, E. *Tests for Auditory Comprehension of Language.* Austin, Tex.: Learning Concepts, 1973.

Cattell, P. *The measurement of intelligence of infants.* New York: Psychological Corp., 1940.

Charles, C. M. *Individualizing instruction.* St. Louis: C. V. Mosby Co., 1976.

Circus. Princeton, N.J.: Educational Testing Service, 1974.

Crabtree, M. *Houston Test of Language Development.* Houston, Tex.: Houston Press, 1963.

Doll, E. A. *The measurement of social competence (A manual for the Vineland Social Maturity Scale).* Washington, D.C.: Educational Testing Bureau, 1953.

Doll, E. A. *Preschool Attainment Record.* Minneapolis: American Guidance Service, 1967.

Doll, E. A. *Vineland Scale of Social Maturity.* Circle Pines, Minn.: American Guidance Service, 1965.

Dunn, L. M. (Ed.). *Exceptional children in the schools.* New York: Holt, Rinehart & Winston, 1973.

Dunn, L. M. *Peabody Picture Vocabulary Test.* Minneapolis: American Guidance Service, 1965.

Dunn, L. M., & Markwardt, F. C., Jr. *Peabody Individual Achievement Test* (PIAT). Circle Pines, Minn.: American Guidance Service, 1970.

Frankenburg, W., & Dodds, J. B. *Denver Developmental Screening Test.* Denver: Ladoca Project & Publishing Foundation, 1969.

French, J. L. *Pictorial Test of Intelligence.* Boston: Houghton Mifflin Co., 1964.

Frost, J. L., & Kissinger, J. B. *The young child and the educative process.* New York: Holt, Rinehart & Winston, 1976.

Frostig, M. *Frostig Developmental Test of Visual Perception.* Palo Alto, Calif.: Consulting Psychologists Press, 1963.

Gearheart, B. R. *Learning disabilities: Educational strategies.* St. Louis: C. V. Mosby Co., 1973.

Gesell, A., & Amatruda, C. *Developmental diagnosis.* New York: Hoeber, 1951.

Goldman, R., Fristoe, M., & Woodcock, R. W. *Goldman-Fristoe-Woodcock Test of Auditory Discrimination.* Minneapolis: American Guidance Service, 1970.

Goodenough, F. L., Maurer, K. M., & Van Wagenen, M. J. *Minnesota Preschool Scale.* Minneapolis: American Guidance Service, 1940.

Gordon, T. *Parent effectiveness training.* New York: Peter H. Wyden/Publisher, 1970.

Haeussermann, E. *The developmental potential of preschool children.* New York: Grune & Stratton, 1958.

Hainsworth, P. K., & Siqueland, M. L. *The Meeting Street School Screening Test.* Providence, R.I.: Crippled Children and Adults of Rhode Island, 1969.

Harms, T. Evaluating settings for learning. In B. C. Mills and R. A. Mills (Eds.), *Designing instructional settings for young children.* Dubuque, Iowa: William C. Brown, 1972.

Harris, D. B. *Goodenough-Harris Drawing Tests.* New York: Harcourt Brace Jovanovich, 1963.

Hiskey, M. S. *Test of Learning Aptitude.* Lincoln, Nebr.: Union College Press, 1966.

Jastak, J. F., & Jastak, S. R. *Wide Range Achievement Test.* Wilmington, Del.: Guidance Associates of Delaware, 1976.

Jedrysek, E., Klapper, Z., Pope, L., & Wortis, J. *Psycho-educational evaluation of the preschool child: A manual utilizing the Haeussermann approach.* New York: Grune & Stratton, 1972.

Kirk, S. A., McCarthy, J. J., & Kirk, W. O. *Illinois Test of Psycholinguistic Abilities,* (Rev. ed.). Urbana, Ill.: University of Illinois Press, 1968.

Kirk, W. O. A tentative screening procedure for selecting bright and slow children in kindergarten. *Exceptional Children,* 1966, **33,** 235–241.

Lee, L. *Northwestern Syntax Screening Test.* Evanston, Ill.: Northwestern University Press, 1969.

Mardel, C. D., & Goldenberg, D. S. *Developmental Indicators for the Assessment of Learning.* Highland Park, Ill.: DIAL, Inc. 1975.

McCandless, B. R., & Trotter, R. J. *Children: Behavior and development.* New York: Holt, Rinehart & Winston, 1977.

McCarthy, D. *The McCarthy Scales of Children's Abilities.* New York: Psychological Corp., 1973.

McKenzie, H. Behavior modification of children with learning disabilities using grades as tokens and allowances as back-up reinforcers. *Exceptional Children,* 1968, **34,** 745–752.

Meacham, M. J. *Verbal Language Development Scale.* Circle Pines, Minn.: American Guidance Service, 1971.

Meacham, M. J., Jex, J. L., & Jones, J. D. *Utah Test of Language Development.* Salt Lake City: Communication Research Associates, 1959.

Myklebust, H. R. *The Pupil Rating Scale.* New York: Grune & Stratton, 1971.

Nihira, K., Foster, R., Shellhaas, M., & Leland, H. *Adaptive Behavior Scale.* Baltimore: American Association on Mental Deficiency, 1974.

Pasanella, A. L., & Volkmor, C. B. *Coming back . . . or never leaving.* Columbus, Ohio: Charles E. Merrill Publishing Co., 1977.

Patterson, G. An application of conditioning techniques to the control of a hyperactive child. In L. Ullmann and L. Krasner (Eds.), *Case studies in behavior modification.* New York: Holt, Rinehart, & Winston, 1965.

Peterson, W. *A program for early identification of learning disabilities.* Seattle: Special Child Publications, 1970.

Roach, E., & Kephart, N. *The Purdue Perceptual-Motor Survey.* Columbus, Ohio: Charles E. Merrill Publishing Co., 1966.

Rosenblith, J. K. Manual for behavioral examination of the neonate. Workshop conducted at meetings of American Psychological Association, Montreal, 1973.

Slosson, R. L. *Slosson Intelligence Test* (SIT). New York: Slosson Educational Publications, 1963.

Smart, M. S., & Smart, R. C. *Children: Development and relationships.* New York: Macmillan Publishing Co., 1977.

Stutsman, R. *Scale of Mental Tests for Preschool Children.* New York: World Publishing Co., 1930.

Terman, L. M., & Merrill, M. A. *Stanford-Binet Intelligence Scale.* Boston: Houghton Mifflin Co., 1960.

Thorpe, L. P., Clark, W. W., & Tiegs, E. W. *California Test of Personality.* Monterey, Calif.: CTB/McGraw-Hill, 1953.

Uzgiris, I., & Hunt, J. *Assessment in Infancy: Ordinal Scales of Psychological Development.* Urbana, Ill.: University of Illinois Press, 1975.

Valett, R. E. *A Basic Screening and Referral Form for Children with Suspected Learning and Behavioral Difficulties.* Palo Alto, Calif.: Fearon Publishers, 1972.

Valett, R. *The Valett Developmental Survey of Basic Learning Abilities.* Palo Alto, Calif.: Fearon Publishers, 1968.

Wechsler, D. *Wechsler Preschool and Primary Scale of Intelligence.* New York: Psychological Corp., 1967.

Wepman, J. M. *Auditory Discrimination Test* (Rev.). Chicago: Language Research Assoc., 1973.

Zimmerman, I. L., Steiner, V. G., & Evatt, R. L. *Preschool Language Scale.* Columbus, Ohio: Charles E. Merrill Publishing Co., 1969.

3

Principles of Learning and Instruction

Although educational programs for young children with disabilities were found throughout the nation before the 1970s, they were scattered, leaving large areas and thus many handicapped children and their families with few if any services. With the passage of federal and state legislation in the 1960s and 1970s, early childhood education for the handicapped is becoming widespread. The new services and programs deal with skill development in areas which once were not considered education and were rarely taught in a formal manner. The federal legislation also requires local officials to conduct "child-find programs" to search out children who are not being served by any program. These searches will undoubtedly reveal rare combinations of handicapping conditions that present instructional challenges never before encountered.

To meet these new challenges and to insure equal opportunity for handicapped children, it is essential that special education programs be based on sound educational theories. Those who work with exceptional children must understand the principles of learning and instruction that apply to all children. These principles should be the basis for decisions concerning curriculum content and choice of teaching techniques.

William A. Horn and *Sue Ellen Horn* contributed to the section on learning theory. The material on task analysis and related procedures was developed by *Paul Wehman*. *David A. Herr* provided the ideas on reinforcement. Remaining portions, including the results of her research on program components, were supplied by the senior author.

The purpose of this chapter is to review different learning theories and conditions believed to contribute to learning, consider instructional procedures which are proving effective with disabled children from birth to 5 years of age, and survey program components for the delivery of services.

Principles of Learning

Gagné defines learning as a change in human disposition or capability which can be retained, and which is not simply the natural result of growth (Bigge, 1976). If the individual is placed in a learning situation, the occurrence of learning is inferred when the individual's previous behavior is compared with the behavior exhibited following the placement. Hurlock (1972) describes learning as development that comes from exercise and practice. Through learning, the child becomes competent in using his innate abilities, those traits which are inherited rather than acquired. She stresses, however, the need for the opportunity to learn. Similar definitions have been made by Lawther (1968) and by Breckenridge and Murphy (1969).

The young child acquires many skills during the preschool years. Whether they are "learned" may depend upon how learning is defined. The normal child develops skills during this period without formal, planned learning sessions. There is much evidence that handicapped children need formalized pro-

To insure equal opportunity for exceptional children, it is essential that special education programs be based on sound educational theory.

cedures over a period of time in order to learn the same skills (Hayden & Dmitriev, 1975). For example, the nonhandicapped child will turn over, sit up, pull himself to standing, handle his bottle, pull off his shoes, and perform many other tasks without training. For many handicapped children these same skills are learned only after carefully planned, precise instruction. The efficiency with which the handicapped child acquires skills will depend on the type of learning necessary, the theories employed, and the conditions that are provided.

Learning Theories

Two learning theories are predominant at the present time: the S-R (stimulus-response) conditioning theories of the behavioristic group and the cognitive theories of the Gestalt-field group (Bigge, 1976). Detailed accounts of each theory with all the existing variations cannot be presented within the scope of this textbook. The basic tenets of each theory and other viewpoints which are influencing the movement in preschool education for the handicapped will be discussed. For more detailed discussions of the theories, the reader is encouraged to study the references for this chapter.

S-R (Stimulus-Response) Conditioning Theory. Proponents of this theory believe that learning is a change in behavior. They believe learning occurs when stimuli and responses become related according to certain principles. Stimuli, or the causes of learning, are environmental factors which act upon the organism, causing it to respond or at least to increase the probability of a response. Responses are physical reactions of the organism to either external or internal stimulation (Bigge, 1976). Examples of external stimuli are sounds, sights, tastes, and motion. Hunger and fear are examples of internal stimuli.

Thorndike's association theory is based on the principle of reinforcing the association between the stimulus and the desired response. When a desired response occurs, it is rewarded, thereby strengthening the child's association of the stimuli and the response. Repeated failure to reward a response is the procedure for eliminating that response. According to this theory, learning occurs faster when the child experiences early successes and more successes than failure. This implies that there must be a teacher who provides guidance, organization of the learning environment, and encouragement (Lawther, 1968). Behavior modification in early childhood educational programs is an example of the S-R Conditioning Theory.

Gestalt-field Theory. Gestalt-field theorists believe that learning is a process of gaining insights, viewpoints, expectations, or thought patterns. These theorists use the word *person* instead of *organism* and view the environment as psychological instead of physical. Followers of this theory believe that the child (person), his environment, and his interactions with the environment influence and change each other during the learning process (Bigge, 1976).

The Gestalt theory of learning emphasizes the mind's reorganization of the stimulus situation into a meaningful pattern, or Gestalt. The Gestalt psychologist assumes that stimuli arriving through "the senses is being constantly organized and interpreted into units of meaning" (p. 39). This process of organizing and interpreting is the development of insights which, for the Gestalt theorists, is learning (Lawther, 1968).

The Gestalt theorists believe the whole stimulus situation, including the figure and the background, is organized; and the perception and meaning (insight) comes as a whole unified pattern. "The organization provides more than an aggregation of parts" (Lawther, 1968, p. 40).

Preschool programs based on the Gestalt theory do not teach basic concepts but instead provide an environment in which the child may explore and thus gain an understanding of his world.

The differences between the two theories may be summarized thusly: The S-R Conditioning theorist interprets learning in terms of changes in the strength of two variables—associations and behavior. Gestalt-field theorists define learning in terms of organization of what one experiences into meaningful patterns (Bigge, 1976).

Educators rarely embrace one theory exclusively. They may espouse one of the many variations which have developed from each theory, or they may assume an eclectic position, "selecting and modifying knowledge from incompatible positions, adding new thinking" (p. 13) and developing new ideas. Gagné's view of learning is considered a behavioristic-oriented eclectic approach, while Bruner's views on learning and teaching are considered cognitive-oriented eclectic psychology (Bigge, 1976). Both of these men have greatly influenced modern-day educational thought. Bigge (1976) has provided an overview of both Gagné and Bruner's beliefs.

Gagné distinguishes between external conditions (arrangement and timing of stimulus events) and internal conditions (attention, motivation, and recall) of learning. In order to identify the classes or varieties of a child's learning, one must look first at the capabilities (internal) of the learner and then at the stimuli present in the child's environment (external).

He emphasizes the role of instrumental conditioning, or information processing, in learning. This is seen as a complex of processes that take place in a learner's central nervous system. "Learning as a total process begins with a phase of apprehending the stimulus situation, proceeds to the stage of acquisition, then to storage and finally to retrieval" (Gagné, 1965, p. 78).

Gagné's pivotal idea is that learning a new capability, or skill, requires prior learning of subordinate capabilities, or prerequisite skills, of the new capability (Bigge, 1976, p. 172). Any significant learning can be analyzed into progressions of subordinate learnings. Gagné calls such progression a *learning hierarchy.*

According to Gagné, five categories of human capabilities are outcomes of learning. They are (1) verbal information, (2) intellectual skills, (3) cognitive strategies, (4) attitudes, and (5) motor skills. *Verbal information* refers to mere statements of information, while *intellectual skills* involve knowing how to perform an act as contrasted with knowing that certain conditions exist. *Cognitive strategies* are capabilities that a learner employs in attending, learning, remembering, and thinking. *Attitudes* are internal states which influence the learner's actions toward classes of things, persons, and events. *Motor skills* are used in such activities as pouring sand in a bucket or riding a tricycle.

For Gagné, learning is a change in observable behavior that happens under observable conditions; however, it takes place in the brain. Learning is a process comparable to respiration or digestion. Gagné psychology underpins the mechanistic instruction (designed to produce a certain result) that is associated with behavior modification and competency-based education.

Although Bruner has not developed a systematic learning theory, a generalized theory and a viewpoint are implicit in his writings. His principal concern has been how people select, retain, and transform information. To him this is the essence of learning. He has directed his attention to what people do with information they receive "to achieve generalized insights and understandings that give them competence" (Bigge, 1976, p. 247).

Bruner believes that learning involves three "almost simultaneous processes": (1) acquisition of new information, (2) transformation of knowledge, and (3) checking the pertinence and adequacy of knowledge. New information may be a refinement of prior learning or of a nature that runs counter to previous information. Transformation of knowledge is the manipulation of learning to make it fit new tasks. The pertinence and adequacy of knowledge or information is evaluated as to its adequacy to the task at hand. Such evaluation judges the plausibility of knowledge (Bigge, 1976, p. 250).

He is critical of those who have not given enough attention to matters such as which versions of subject matter are appropriate for various childhood periods. He believes they have overlooked the pedagogical problem of how to represent knowledge, how to sequence it, and how to put it in forms that are appropriate to the age of the learner.

He feels that psychologists and teachers tend "to disregard the puzzling problem of the relationship of knowledge as detached information and knowledge as a guide to purposeful action or performance" (Bigge, 1976, p. 249). They should be concerned with what keeps learners interested in learning and achievement beyond necessity.

Bruner acknowledges the need for praise and reward for each successful act of learning but warns of the danger of creating too much dependence upon reward and the rewarder. The rewarding function must be gradually given back to the learner so that his sense of accomplishment is rewarding (Bigge, 1976).

Bruner sees the learner not as a passive, reactive organism, but as a person who actively selects information. He believes that mental growth is not a gradual accumulation but "more like a staircase with rather sharp risers, more a matter of spurts and rests." Spurts seem to be touched off when certain skills begin to develop. Unlike Piaget, Bruner does not see the steps or spurts in human development linked with age; some environments can slow the sequence while others move it faster. He describes the steps as a series of prerequisites (Bigge, 1976, p. 252).

While Piaget is seen more as a developmental psychologist than a learning theorist (Bigge, 1976), his studies of the nature of children at different ages have influenced a growing cadre of leaders in the field of early childhood education for the handicapped (Anastasiow & Mansergh, 1975). Piaget's stages of development include sensorimotor (0–2 years), pre-operational (2–5 years), concrete operational (5–12 years), and abstract reasoning (12 to maturity). Each stage "extends the preceding period, reconstructs it on a new level, and later surpasses it to an even greater degree" (Bigge, 1976 p. 19). The key processes in development are *assimilation,* by which the child filters or modifies the information from his environment, and *accommodation,* by which the child modifies his thinking and beliefs to fit reality. The quality of the child's involvement with his environment provides the materials which influence his cognitive development. The richness of the environment influences what the child can learn but does not determine what he will learn. "In a less rich or less structured environment the child will be delayed in his cognitive development, not because of a lack of training but because of a lack of opportunities to experience" (Anastasiow & Mansergh, 1975, p. 315). Development is viewed by Piaget as an inherent, unalterable, evolutionary process of which the phases listed above are a part. Maier (1965) summarizes Piaget's concept of development with six generalizations:

1. There is an absolute continuity of all developmental processes.
2. Development proceeds through a continuous process of generalizations and differentiation.
3. This continuity is achieved by a continuous unfolding. Each level of development finds its roots in a previous phase and continues into the following one.
4. Each phase entails a repetition of the processes of the previous level in a different form of organization . . .Previous behavior patterns are sensed as inferior and become a part of the new superior level.
5. The differences in organizational pattern create a hierarchy of experience and actions.
6. Individuals achieve different levels within the hierarchy. (p. 102)

Tangential to learning theory has been the influence of Arnold Gesell and other developmental theorists. Largely through observations of various stages of child development, Gesell proposed that all areas of human development result from maturation of the organism. He believed that environmental factors "merely support, inflect and modify but do not generate the progressions of development" (Ausubel & Sullivan, 1970, p. 26).

From his observations of children Gesell developed detailed lists (scales) of skills and the expected ages at which children would accomplish them. Educators who have developed programs around the scales believe that teachers should introduce an activity as near as possible to the time most children can accomplish the skill involved (Anastasiow and Mansergh, 1975).

Learning theories applied to preschool programs for handicapped children have been studied by Anastasiow and Mansergh (1975). Three operational models were found to be in agreement on instructional content and materials to be used, but sharp differences were discovered in the instructional techniques. A hypothetical continuum was used to describe how the models viewed the child as a learner. The views ranged from one extreme of those who perceive the child as a passive receptor to the other extreme of those who perceive the child as an active transactor. Methods on the continuum ranged from a behavioristic program which uses drill and small-step procedures to a program which uses discovery or guided discovery. The two extremes match the methods expected of proponents of the behavioristic theory of Gagné and the cognitive development theory exemplified by Piaget. Between these two extremes is a third approach, which the authors termed the normal development approach. It reflects the work of Gesell and Hilgard, who established age expectancies for skill acquisition.

In the opinion of Hill (1963), the value of studying learning theory is twofold. It provides a vocabulary and conceptual framework for observing and interpreting actual learning situations. Also, the teacher who is familiar with different theories will know where to look for solutions to practical problems. While the theories do not give solutions, they do direct the teacher's attention to variables that are critical in finding solutions. Table 1 summarizes the behavioristic and the cognitive-field viewpoints on many different aspects of the learning process which should be considered in educational planning for young children with special needs.

Table 1

Comparative Schema of Contemporary Learning Theories

Issues	Behavioristic Theories	Cognitive-Field Theories
Learning	Observable	Not necessarily observable
Behavior	Measurable	Not necessarily measurable
Humans	Reactive organism (product of stimulus-response history in determining environment)	Purposive person interacting with his psychological environment
Motivation	Organic drives and basic emotions or conditioned ones accumulative from past conditioning and current drives	Goal, expectancy, intention, and purpose; immediate; outgrowth of one's life space
Experience	Basic principle of universe is cause and effect; conditioning	One's experience grows out of one's pursuing one's purpose. Rooted in insightful behavior
Approach to education	Environmentalist and determinist	Interaction of child with environment alters both child and environment
Environment	Physical and social surroundings	What person believes to be his surroundings (life space)
Truth	Ultimate reality	Anticipatory accuracy
Reality	Physical objects and processes	Person's interpretation of meaningful patterns
Perception	Analogous with taking photographs	Relevance of object to purpose constitutes its meaning
Interaction (with environment)	Serial alternating reaction, first of organism, then of environment	Simultaneous and mutual

Note: Compiled from M. L. Bigge, *Learning Theories for Teachers*. 3rd ed., pp. 60–77. New York: Harper & Row, 1976. Copyright 1976 by Harper & Row.

Conditions for Learning

In the writings of learning theorists, one finds repeated references to learning conditions, that is, the stimuli and environments which contribute to the process of learning. Without any attempt to rank these conditions by their importance to learning, they are presented here in summary form.

Orientation and Attention. Orientation refers to the act of becoming aware of information and getting ready to respond to it. Attention refers to the child's focusing on a particular bit of information (Blake, 1974). Attention involves looking, listening, or feeling. Also, it may be searching movements that end when the desired information is found. Past experience and the present situation interact through the process of paying attention. How the presented information affects the individual depends on what aspects of it he pays attention to (Hill, 1963). The figure-ground difficulties evidenced by many young handicapped children result from their inability to focus attention. For such children, the teacher must develop techniques that help them give their attention to relevant items. Examples of techniques used to draw attention to objects or other stimuli include color coding, loud sounds, and textured surfaces (Blake, 1974).

Attention span is the length of time the child's attention can be focused on the learning task. Baroff (1974) has stated that teaching any task clearly depends on getting and holding the attention of the learner. Generally the attention span in children increases and becomes more complex with age. Older children not only can attend for longer periods of time but they also have less difficulty focusing on the relevant instead of irrelevant features (Ausubel & Sullivan, 1970).

Maturation. Differing views of maturation and its role in the learning process seem not to be related to the concept but to its explanation. Ausubel and Sullivan (1970) acknowledge two schools of thought: one regards the term as descriptive of a process whereby all development is essentially regulated by internal factors; and the other equates maturation with becoming "ready" in certain capacities or with changes in the anatomical and physiological foundations of behavior.

For Lawther (1968), the term *maturation* refers to the extent to which changes in the human body are predetermined by the person's genetic constitution. In the infant, it is difficult to make a real distinction between maturation and learning because the child's hereditary potential, that is, ability to talk, walk, and so forth, develops according to the environment provided by others. In all maturation there is learning; in all childhood learning there is hereditary maturation. Hurlock (1972) points out that maturation provides the raw material for learning and determines to a large extent the more general patterns and sequences of the child's behavior.

A somewhat different view has been expressed by Breckenridge and Murphy (1969), who define maturation as those changes which make it possible for a child to begin functioning or to function at progressively higher levels. As the physical structure (bones, sensory equipment, and particularly the nervous system) become more complex, the child becomes more capable of acquiring skills. Maturation patterns tend to be similar from one human being to another. Maturation is characterized by a fixed order of progression, by a tendency of inevitability, by irreversibility, and by universality in that it is found among all races in all environments. It is the rate of maturity that tends to vary from one individual to another.

Both Ausubel and Sullivan (1970) and Hurlock (1972) explain the effects of maturation on the acquisition of skills. Skills related to phylogenetic functions develop as the child matures while skills related to ontogenetic functions require some training. *Phylogenetic functions* are common to the human race and include crawling, creeping, sitting, and walking. Training offers little advantage for these functions; however, a depriving environment can reduce opportunities for practice and thus retard development. *Ontogenetic functions* are specific to the individual and include skills, such as tricycle riding, skating, or skipping rope, for which some training is essential.

Closely related to maturity is the concept of critical periods for learning. Hurlock (1972) has said that effective learning is dependent upon proper timing. If the child is not ready to learn, teaching will be a waste of effort and may lead to resistant behavior. On the other hand, if a child is mature enough but is not permitted to learn, he may become disinterested in all learning activity.

McGraw (1969) believes that if the child is denied the proper experience at the critical time and is offered instead other subsequent development experiences, there will be a greater number of interferences when the child finally attempts the delayed activity.

Two hypotheses concerning critical periods for learning have been presented by Banus (1971). The first hypothesis concerns a critical period for learning beyond which the child's receptiveness will not appear. There is a point in time which marks the onset of total indifference or resistance to certain patterns of stimulation. The second hypothesis is that a critical period exists during which the child is especially sensitive to various developmental modifiers (e.g., nutrition, experience) which, if identified at a different time in the life of the child, would have little or no effect. In other words, there is a critical period of maximum susceptibility to learning. Banus believes that the longer development is delayed, the more difficult it is to stimulate.

McGraw (1969) concluded that educational hints can be gained from studies of the maturing nervous system of the infant and offered the following suggestions:

1. Training in any particular activity before the neural mechanisms have reached a certain state of readiness is futile.
2. Exercise of a newly developing function is inherent in the process of growth, and if ample opportunity is afforded at the proper time, specific achievements can be advanced beyond the stage normally expected.
3. Periods of transition from one type of neuromuscular organization to another are an inherent part of development and are often characterized by disorganization and confusion.

4. Spurts, regressions, frustrations, and inhibitions are an integral part of growth, and there is reason to believe that they also influence the development of behaviors.
5. Maturation and learning are not different processes, merely different facets of the fundamental process of growth.
6. Evidence that a child is ready for a particular educational subject is to be found in certain behavior signals which reflect the maturity of the nervous system.

Readiness. While some writers view readiness as the result of maturation, others use the term to signify that skills needed before new learning is introduced have been acquired. Gagné advanced the notion that the prerequisite capabilities must be already acquired before new learning can take place (Bigge, 1976). The absence of any prerequisite, or subordinate, capability indicates a state of unreadiness. Accordingly, Gagné has identified eight types of learning, each a prerequisite or building block for the one which follows. Each type of learning establishes a condition from which more complicated types of learning can emerge.

Gagné's eight types of learning are as follows:

1. *Signal learning*—child learns to make general, diffuse responses to a signal (signal learning is better known as *classical conditioning*).
2. *Stimulus-response learning*—learner acquires a precise response to a stimulus that he is able to discriminate from others.
3. *Chaining*—learner combines two or more stimulus-response connections.
4. *Verbal association*—learner uses verbal chains.
5. *Discrimination learning*—individual learns to make a number of different responses to as many different stimuli.
6. *Concept learning*—learner makes a common response to a class of stimuli that may differ from each other in physical appearance.
7. *Rule learning*—learner uses a chain of two or more concepts.
8. *Problem solving*—the kind of learning that requires thinking.

Piaget's hierarchy of learning stages implies the concept of prerequisite skills. For example, learning which takes place during the sensorimotor stage (0–2 years) provides the child with skills he will use during the pre-operational stage (2–5 years). The process extends throughout the four stages (see pp. 67–68).

A concept related to readiness and prerequisite skills has been presented by Banus (1971). She explained that there are not only critical times for learning but also critical events, each of which is "the most important factor in determining the development of a behavior" (p. 9). For example, the child's first word is the critical event in language development. If a critical event is inhibited, the omission will be detrimental to the child's development. The critical events hypothesis gives support to the need for early identification and treatment of young handicapped children and demonstrates at least one danger of the wait-and-see policy.

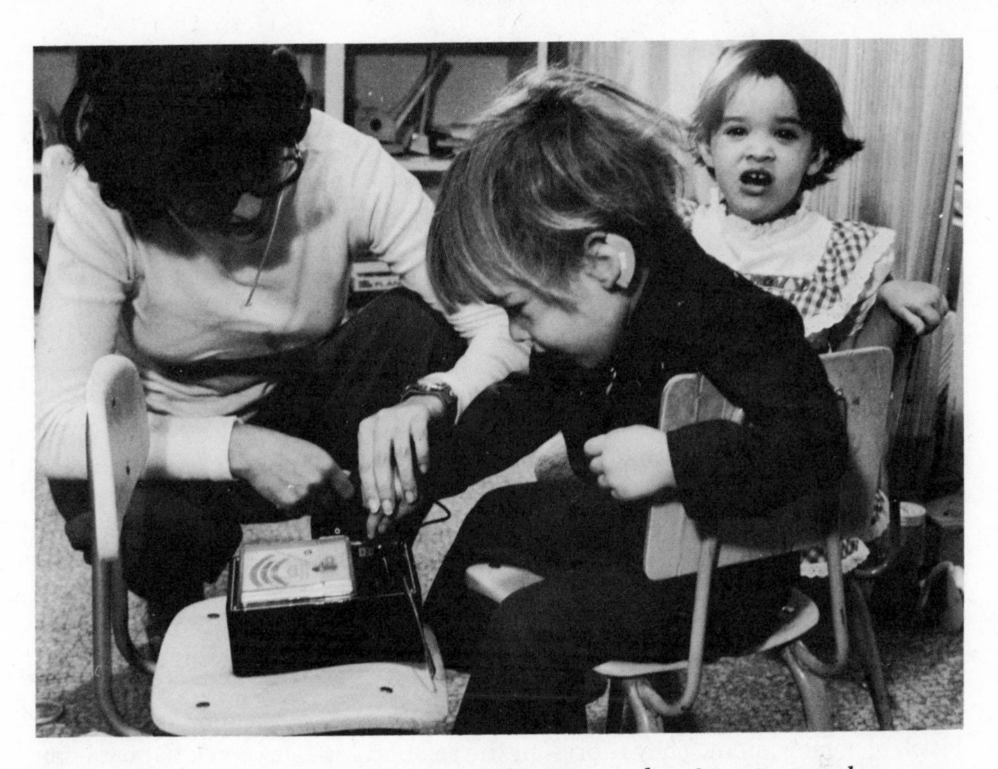

The child's interest in a task significantly affects other functions such as memory and attention span.

Lawther (1968) warned against attempts to force learning on the very young child before prerequisite skills were developed. However, he believed that most errors in teaching tend to be ones of postponing learning rather than of starting too soon.

Somewhat different ideas concerning readiness have been expressed by Ausubel and Sullivan (1970). They believe that a child's readiness to learn a new task may be determined by the instructional methods and materials used in his educational program. Also, the child's present state of readiness is partly determined by the appropriateness and efficiency of his previous instruction. The quality of his educational program determines developmental readiness as well as skill readiness for further learning.

Motivation. Little has been written concerning motivation in the young child and even less concerning motivation in the young child with special needs. However, from the writings about motivation in general, certain facts seem pertinent to preschool education for handicapped children.

Robinson and Robinson (1965) used the term *effectance,* a general kind of motivation in contrast to physiological motivation such as hunger and thirst. Effectance, the child's motivation to interact with his environment, is not a characteristic that the human being acquires rapidly at first. On the other hand, Ausubel and Sullivan (1970) hypothesize that motivation becomes progressively a less important factor as children grow older. As the child's cognitive abilities, attention span, and ability to concentrate increase, learning becomes easier and there is less need for others to stimulate the learning process. One can assume that if learning does not become easier, as it may not for the young handicapped child, motivation then remains a highly significant factor.

Baroff (1974) said that the child's motivation or interest in a task significantly affects other functions such as memory and attention span. Mouly (1968) said that interests are acquired as a result of satisfying experiences. Once established, such interests tend to last as long as they are satisfying. Among young children, interests are based on limited experience and tend to be narrow and directed toward the trivial. In spite of these characteristics, the interests of young children may be used as a wedge for further learning.

Hill (1963) believes motivation is a component of the individual's drives. She distinguishes between the physiological drives such as hunger, thirst, and pain and nonphysiological drives such as pride and affection. Other possible drives include curiosity, exploration, manipulation, and novelty seeking as well as drives satisfied by new experience, by activity, and by certain kinds of physical contact. It is this last drive which is important in the attachment of infants to mothers and also in other aspects of love and social relationships. Lawther (1968) said that the person who is completely satisfied and contented makes no progress, makes no attempt to adjust, adapt, and learn.

Bigge (1976) viewed success and failure as intrinsic motivation, not merely levels of achievement. They represent the relationship between what has been attempted and what has been achieved. When a child attains success at one task he is more likely to perform successfully on another task. For many children, success is the only reinforcement necessary to stimulate positive attitudes toward the task and increased performance. Many researchers (Gardner, 1959; Heber, 1951; Levy, 1974) have found slowly developing children do not expect to be successful and, consequently, avoid trying new tasks. As a further consequence, when they do try, their performances do not begin to reach what they are capable of achieving. Teachers can overcome low expectations by designing activities so that the child will have successful experiences.

Although some studies have shown that anxiety is a motivational factor, Ausubel and Sullivan (1970) reported that highly anxious children have poor visual discrimination, show less curiosity, exhibit more rigidity, and show less interest in novel toys than less anxious children do. In young children it appears that anxiety depresses achievement. Robinson and Robinson (1965) reported similar findings, adding that anxious children are less open to new experiences, more preoccupied with internal stimuli (e.g., motivation, fear, hunger) and less responsive to possible incentives offered by their surroundings. Ausubel and Sullivan found these facts to be consistent with the findings that anxious school-age children do much better in highly structured learning situations where they encounter little novelty or need to improvise.

Rate. Rate may refer to the percentage of lifetime learning accomplished during various periods of life or to the length of time required for a child to master a task.

In his summary of growth based on the percentage of development completed by age 18, Bloom (1964) concluded that about one-third of the general achievement pattern at age 18 has been developed by the age of 6. He has compared this with other learning periods as follows:

	Percentage of Age 18 Development	
	Each Period	Cumulative
Ages Birth–6	33	33
Ages 6–13	42	75
Ages 13–18	25	100

When Bloom reported these figures, he also expressed his belief that further investigations would reveal even larger values for the preschool period.

Bloom stated that the most rapid period of growth for the child's general intelligence is during the first 5 years of life. Again, he anticipated that further study would indicate a greater rate of growth during the preschool period. Bloom warned that those influences which affect the growth of intelligence and other characteristics will have even greater impact during the periods of most rapid development. Reporting his findings from a study of the early years, White (1975) acknowledged that the most rapid development occurs in the early years but warned that the first three years are the critical ones.

The rate of development is one of the individual differences found among children. Ausubel and Sullivan (1970) have delineated three primary methods of expressing rate of growth:

1. An individual may serve as his own basis of comparison.
2. His status may be compared to that of the *mean* child of like age.
3. His status may be assessed in terms of progress achieved by a particular subgroup of his age mates who match him in level or rate of growth in a given function.

Each method of expressing growth rate provides valuable information. Used together they supplement each other in the task of evaluating growth processes. In young handicapped children, the crucial decision concerns whether the rate of development is predetermined genetically or if the handicapping condition poses a barrier to development.

McGraw (1969) emphasized the need for recognizing periods of regression or loss of achievement as part of the process of growth. The emergence of a new skill may for a time act as a deterrent of some skill that was previously well developed. She indicated that rate of growth is characterized by periods of rapid development, periods of apparent rest, and in some cases, periods of decline.

Environment. The Gestalt-field theorists have had much to say about the learning environment. For instance, Wertheimer and Köhler pointed out the importance of arranging learning situations so as to foster real creative understanding rather than mere memorization. Lewin believes teachers should try to reconstruct the learner's life space in order to determine what the child perceives as barriers to learning (Hill, 1963). The more one knows about an individual, the more one is able to identify possibilities that are open to him.

The environment as a condition for learning has been a topic for discussion and research. Blank (1973) suggested that educational environments viewed by adults as helpful can be confusing and threatening to a child. She advocated game-like environments as a means of reducing anxiety and goals that are relevant and attractive to children. To support learning, Blank encouraged one-to-one and small-group instruction environments.

Research (Cairns & Butterfield, 1975) concerned with how normal infants use their environment concluded that the human infant cannot be characterized as a passive recipient of sensory stimulation. It was found that the infant actively seeks out stimulation and selects what he will pay attention to, exercising, to some degree, control of his stimuli. On the other hand, Caldwell (1973) believes the environment of the young handicapped child is depriving. If there are sensory impairments, he cannot take in what is there for him to learn about; if there are motor impairments, he has difficulty moving his body to explore beyond his immediate surroundings; other impairments limit meaningful interaction with the environment. The child with the least abilities gets less from his environment.

Practice. Practice is viewed differently by various writers concerned with child development. Hurlock (1972) views practice from the standpoint of the learner as the mere repetition of an act and from the standpoint of a teacher as selected, directed, and purposive activity. To Blake (1976), practice is the amount of time spent on learning. Cratty (1973) has said that although basic performance seems to depend on motivation, skill development is attributable to practice. Guthrie indicated that practice responses should be learned under the particular conditions in which they will be used. Practice under varied conditions helps to establish learning (Hill, 1963).

The terms used to describe practice methods give clues to current thought concerning practice as a condition of learning. Distribution of practice refers to the way practice sessions are spaced over time. In *massed practice,* practice sessions are few in number and last a substantial period of time, while in *distributed practice,* there are more sessions of comparatively shorter time. If 15 hours could be devoted to teaching a child to throw a ball, under massed practice, one 15-hour session or three 5-hour sessions would be scheduled. With distributed practice, 15 one-hour sessions or even 60 15-minute sessions could be scheduled.

The ideal way to distribute practice sessions has been the subject of many studies. While it is not known exactly what spacing is ideal, it is generally considered better to spread short sessions over a period of time rather than to practice all at once. Blake (1976), however, suggests that the characteristics of individual children and the tasks be considered. Children with short attention spans who need variety in programming will not do well with massed practices. Children who get confused by trying to deal with too many things at one time will have difficulty handling distributed practice.

Reminiscence refers to an almost paradoxical improvement in learning which often occurs after a long delay between practice sessions. Reminiscence is common in skill training and may be attributable to rest. It is also possible that such improvement may, in part, be due to self-initiated practice sessions on the part of the child or to thinking about the skill.

Reinforcement and Punishment. The key learning principle underlying reinforcement and punishment is that behavior is controlled by its consequences. Generally, the consequence of a given behavior, or response, may be classified as reinforcement, punishment, or extinction. *Reinforcement* refers to those consequences which increase the likelihood of the behavior being repeated or becoming stronger (Bugelski, 1971). Reinforcers may be further classified as positive or negative.

Positive reinforcers are rewards or incentives. They may be social, tangible, or activity reinforcers. *Social reinforcers* include praise, attention, approval, and physical affection. Sulzer and Mayer (1972) have prepared an extensive list of possible social reinforcers. *Tangible reinforcers* are prizes, food, and money. *Activity reinforcers* are opportunities to do things that bring pleasure such as playing, staying up beyond bedtime, or going to the zoo.

Negative reinforcement is the second major type of reinforcement. It is the removing of something unpleasant as opposed to the giving of a reward for the desired behavior. Punishment can have the effect of a negative reinforcer when its intended effect, to decrease behavior, has the opposite effect, that is, makes the response more fascinating to the child and increases the likelihood that the response will be repeated (Robinson & Robinson, 1965).

Punishment, the second classification of consequences, consists of either the *presentation* of something undesired or the *removal* of a positive reinforcer. Punishment such as isolation or depriving the child of a privilege may be immediately effective in decreasing undesired behavior; however, the use of such techniques often results in avoidance and escape behaviors and other negative feelings on the part of the punished child.

Extinction consists of permitting an undesired response to occur without reinforcement and, like punishment, results in a decrease in the rate, persistency, or intensity of the response. For example, deviant behaviors decrease when the teacher stops giving the children the attention she previously gave them. It must be noted, however, that extinction is not a very efficient technique since its use is most often characterized by an immediate increase in the undesired response as well as subsequent recurrence of the response after the extinction procedures appear to have been effective.

Eight Phases in the Act of Learning

The conditions for learning are part of or implied in the eight phases in the act of learning identified by Gagné (1974). Listed in the order of their occurrence, they are as follows:

1. Motivation—incentive.
2. Apprehending—attending and perceiving a stimulus.
3. Acquisition —the essential incident of learning.
4. Retention—storage.
5. Recall—retrieval.
6. Generalization—transfer.
7. Performance—observable behavior.
8. Feedback—knowledge concerning degree of success; reinforcement (Bigge, 1976).

It is essential that the teacher be aware of the phases as they are accomplished by the child. Weakness in any phase will be reflected throughout the remaining phases.

Learning is a complex process. Each behavioral change is dependent upon learning that preceded it. A definite relationship exists between a given stage of development and the stages which precede or follow it.

Mental development, the product of learning, is not a uniform process. It is characterized by different rates for different abilities; however, it is more rapid for all abilities during the early years than at any other time during life (Bloom, 1964).

Most children learn with little difficulty during the early years. However, without effective instruction, the handicapped child is in jeopardy. The handicapping condition (blindness, deafness, retardation, autism, and so forth) may deprive the young child of opportunities to learn. The purposes of instruction for this child are (1) to reverse the effects of deprivation, (2) to help the child use the critical periods for learning developmental tasks which contribute to later learning, and (3) to establish patterns of learning for the child. The ultimate goal of instruction for the young child with special needs is to help him enter the mainstream of education when he reaches school age. Early childhood education programs throughout the nation have demonstrated that this goal is attainable (DeWeerd, 1977).

Principles of Instruction

The remainder of this chapter focuses on principles and procedures which can be effectively and efficiently used in the instruction of young handicapped children. The intention is to outline general practices based on learning principles which can be applied to individual problems.

Individualization

No two learners learn at the same pace or in the same manner. Each child should be considered a school within himself: the instructional objectives and procedures and the program components must be individualized to the child's unique abilities and limitations. No one program or approach will be successful for every child; in fact, techniques successful with one child may deter the progress of another child even though both are the same age and have similar abilities and deficiencies. While applying the general learning conditions which are used with all children, teachers of the handicapped child must continually search for, implement, and evaluate methods with the principle of individualization in mind. Such an approach is time-consuming, somewhat "trial-and-error," sometimes exhausting, and yet rewarding from the knowledge that each child has had appropriately designed instruction and thus an opportunity to learn.

Basic Components of an Instructional Program

Williams, Brown, and Certo (1975) expanded a four-step model used in special education programs into the eight-step model presented here.

> I. *What* skill does a teacher intend for the student to perform? (What does a teacher intend to teach the student?)
> II. *Why* does a teacher want the student to perform a specific skill?
> III. *How* does a teacher intend to teach the student to perform a skill?
> IV. How can a teacher *empirically verify* that the skill of concern is being or has been taught?
> V. Can the student perform the skill at a situationally acceptable *rate?*
> VI. What does a teacher intend to use as *vehicles* (instructional materials) for the skill to be acquired and performed?
> VII. Can the student perform the skill across
>   a. *Persons*
>   b. *Places*
>   c. *Instructional materials*
>   d. *Language cues*
> VIII. Can the student perform a skill without directions to do so from persons in authority? (p. 124)

Although this model was developed for use with severely handicapped students, its design and rationale reflect similar, less detailed models used in the education of young handicapped children. Each component is explained below with practical suggestions for use in instruction.

I. *What skill does a teacher intend for the student to perform?* A number of researchers have delineated the skills which develop during the preschool years (*see* Chapter 2). From such work, criterion-referenced assessment tools have been developed. The Learning Accomplishment Profile (LAP) (Sanford, 1973) is one example.

The LAP translates the skill categories identified by Gagné to those of the developmentalists. The skill categories are (1) gross motor skills, (2) fine motor skills, (3) language skills, (4) cognitive skills, (5) social skills, and (6) self-help skills. These are the broad areas of development from which the teacher can decide *what* to teach.

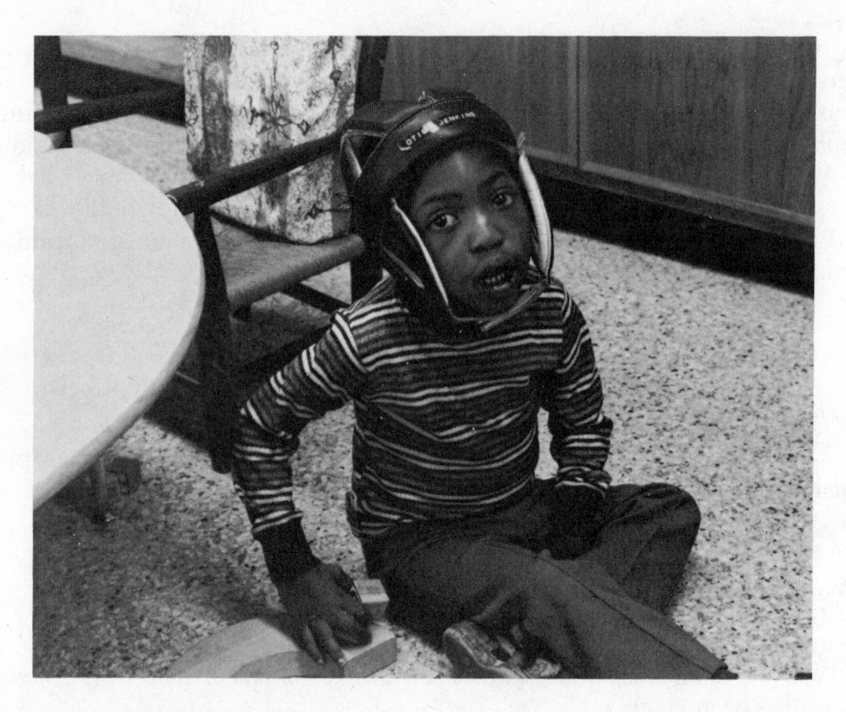

Successful learning experiences help to improve his sense of himself.

Criterion-referenced assessment instruments provide a detailed, sequential order of skills in each of the areas of development. Table 2 shows the parallel development of selected skills expected of normal children across the preschool years.

From observing the child in various activities, the teacher evaluates or identifies what the child can do (entry skills) in each development area. If the teacher is aware of the sequential steps which are prerequisite to later skills and has analyzed the child's entry skills, she is able to select appropriate learning objectives for the child (Sanford, 1974).

Task Analysis. Task analysis requires the precise identification of skills within a developmental task. Each skill is separated into its component parts (subskills) and these subskills are sequenced in logical order from simple to complex. Task analysis is a means for determining the child's functioning level and for indentifying the subskills required to develop new skills (Williams, Brown, & Certo, 1975).

According to Hallahan and Kauffman (1976), the extent to which a task must be analyzed depends on the functioning level of the child. Tasks must be more finely analyzed for the very young and for more severely handicapped children than for those without handicaps. Task analysis of a behavior can range from a few subskills for mildly handicapped children to an indefinite number for more deficient children. The task analysis is thorough enough if the child's

Table 2

Parallel Development of Selected Skills

Areas of Development	First Year 0–12 Months	Second Year 12–24 Months	Third Year 24–36 Months	Fourth Year 36–48 Months	Fifth Year 48–60 Months
Gross Motor	Rolls over Sits without support Walks with assistance Walks alone	Throws ball Creeps backward down stairs Kicks large ball Jumps in place	Pedals tricycle Walks on tip-toe Balances on one foot for 5 seconds	Skips on one foot Jumps from bottom step Walks on a line Catches bounced ball	Climbs ladder and trees Walks full length of board (6 cm) without stepping off
Fine Motor	Holds hands together Lifts cup with handle Grasps string Neat pincher grasp of raisin	Builds tower of 2–6 cubes Can pick up and hold 2 small objects in one hand	Enjoys finger pointing Cuts with scissors Manipulates eggbeater Makes mud and sand pies	Drives nails and pegs Holds crayon with fingers Strings 4 beads	Draws with pencil and crayon Draws simple house Prints simple words
Language	Responds to voice Vocalizes – not crying Imitates speech sounds Indicates wants	Points to 1–3 named body parts Names one object Refers to self by name Imitates 2–4 words	Names common objects Gives full name upon request Follows a 2-stage command	Can whisper Can increase volume of voice Uses plurals Listens eagerly to stories	Gives home address Gives age and birthday Asks meaning of abstract words
Cognitive	Responds to name Rings bell purposely Responds to No-No Looks at pictures in a book	Fetches and carries familiar objects Uses names of familiar objects Matches familiar objects	Associates use with objects Repeats 2 digits Points to teeth and chin upon request	Names all colors Tells actions in pictures Can count two blocks	Names 14 of 18 pictures of common objects Can define 6 words Knows day and night
Social	Smiles and laughs Plays peek-a-boo Discriminates strangers	Demands personal attention Reaches for familiar persons Imitates housework	Parallel play predominates Domestic make-believe play Helps put things away	Shows affection for younger siblings Understands taking turns and sharing Performs for others	Goes on errands outside house Shows concern and sympathy Bosses and criticizes
Self-Help	Picks-up spoon Feeds self cracker Fusses to be changed after bowel movement	Drinks from cup Can unzip zipper Unwraps candy Pulls off socks	Removes coat or dress Dries own hands Gets drink unassisted	Unbuttons accessible buttons Is usually dry all night Dresses with supervision	Laces shoes Can cut with knife Washes face and hands unassisted

Note: Selected from *Learning Accomplishment Profile* by A. R. Sanford. Chapel Hill, N. C.: Training Outreach Project, 1973. Used by permission.

errors in performance can be precisely identified and needed subskills are obvious (p. 140).

The best point to begin instruction can be determined by assessing the skills which the child demonstrates independently (Knapczyk, 1975). Selection of the appropriate skill for training minimizes the likelihood of teaching skills which are too simple or too advanced. Skill selection is directly related to the teacher's knowledge of the task (Siegel, 1972).

II. *Why does a teacher want the student to perform a specific skill?* The purposes for educating young handicapped children are (1) to minimize the effects of handicapping conditions on the child's ability to learn, (2) to establish success patterns for subsequent learning, and (3) to help the child enter the mainstream of education at school age, even if this is only remotely possible. These goals which imply optimal development for the child, independence appropriate to his level of maturity, and a positive self-concept should be the justifications for decisions concerning *why* a skill should be performed.

The *why* of skill selection in instructional programming is answered by the long-range and short-range objectives established for each child.

Long-range Objectives. Task selection for young children centers around the areas of development (language, gross motor, and so forth). To discover the child's position in the developmental sequence, the teacher will look at all available information from other professionals working with the child, from the child's parents, and from the analysis of the child's functioning level. The tasks which are determined to be next in the developmental sequence are chosen as long-range objectives. These are instructional objectives which state the desired terminal behavior. For example, a long-range objective in the gross motor area for the child who has learned to sit without support could be to pull himself to a standing position. This objective implies complete mastery of the task. A long-range objective for the same child in the area of self-help skill development could be (now that he can sit without support) to drink from a cup independently. Because skill development in all areas is possible at the same time, long-range objectives may be developed in more than one area. The number of different long-range objectives for a child will depend on many variables, including the child's age, vitality, interest, and so forth. Teachers should be careful not to require too much or to overstimulate the child. Generally two or three long-range objectives, carefully selected, can be handled.

Short-range Objectives. Short-range objectives are the skills the child must learn in order to accomplish the long-range objective. A task analysis might show that between the two long-range objectives (sits without support and pulls himself to a standing position) and what the child is able to do now, there are four intermediate skills. For example, the child must be able to (1) stand while holding on, (2) reach for a supporting ledge, (3) grasp a supporting ledge, and (4) support his body weight with hands. A normal child may accomplish each of the subskills in a relatively short period or even accomplish two subskills simultaneously. It is likely that the slowly developing child will require more time and explicit instruction for each subskill. Furthermore, it may be necessary to further analyze the subskill into very small steps (approximations).

To assure that each step is mastered before the next step is taught, short-range objectives should be precisely stated to indicate the behavior expected and degree of mastery. Mager (1962) suggests three components of a behavior or performance objective:

1. Specifying conditions under which behavior is to occur.
2. Defining the behavior to be changed in precise and observable terms.
3. Establishing a criterion which signals completion of the task.

Requiring a criterion to be met before beginning the next skill introduces accountability and objective evaluation in programming. Furthermore, through carefully defining behaviors and specifying exact teaching conditions, it is more probable that the results of the instructional program can be replicated by other teachers and the child's parents.

Platt (1977) developed the following plan for development of short-term objectives:

Subject	Active Verb	Condition	Standard
Who	What	When, Where	How Well
	(Observable)	How, with What	(Measurable)
Child	Will Grasp	Nearby Supporting Ledge	10 out of 12 Trials

Even more precisely expressed short-range objectives result when they state first the provisions under which the child's actions will be expected. For example, the same short-range objective would read: When placed near object of appropriate height, the child will grasp a supporting ledge 10 out of 12 trials.

Carefully defined short-range objectives arranged in logical order identify *what* to teach. Mastery of each short-range objective in order leads to the accomplishment of the long range-objective, the *why* of instruction.

III. *How does a teacher intend to teach the student to perform a skill?* The *how* of instruction includes the procedures, strategies, and tactics teachers use to help the child develop new skills (Williams, Brown, & Certo, 1975). While no one approach will be appropriate for all ages, for all handicapping conditions, and for all degrees of impairment, the following techniques of instruction provide a basis which may be modified for the individual.

The Learning Environment. The likelihood that the child will benefit from preschool instruction is dependent upon a number of factors other than his own abilities. Baroff (1974) indicated that the skills of the teacher, appropriateness of the curriculum, physical environment, and attitudes toward the child's ability to learn contribute heavily to the learning environment and largely determine the child's success.

The attitudes of teachers, parents, and staff concerning the child's ability to learn are critical to the child's success. If little achievement is expected and demanded because he is handicapped, the child will accomplish little. On the other hand, if the child is viewed as a learner and expected to master appropriately selected tasks taught with skill, the child will learn.

McKee (1976) warned that assessment of the child's characteristics is an insufficient basis upon which to build a program. Success must be engineered through a child-by-task-by-setting analysis. Such analysis not only considers the child's strengths and weaknesses and prerequisite skills but also assesses the quality of the environment. Learning is promoted when the task is taught in a natural setting, one in which the skill is used. For example, dressing skills are more likely to be learned where dressing takes place than in some contrived situation. To facilitate learning, the environment must fit the child, not the reverse.

Task Analysis and Skill Sequencing. The method by which material is presented to the developmentally delayed child plays a critical role in the acquisition of skills and, equally important, the rate at which behavior is acquired. In recent years, the move to present learning content through easy-to-hard sequencing and task analysis has gained in popularity and acceptance (Brown, Bellamy, & Sontag, 1971; Williams, 1975).

The values of a task analysis method of presentation include

1. It makes the learning task or behavior easier for the student, thus increasing the probability of success; that is, part learning is easier than whole learning (Blake, 1974).
2. It allows the teacher to assess a student's level and place him at a certain program level to begin instruction.
3. It gives the teacher explicit direction in determining skill content through structure and order.
4. It facilitates replicability of the child's instructional program.

Task analysis allows for the breaking down of behaviors and skills into smaller components. In this way, the child is faced with less amounts of material at one time, and the opportunities for reinforcement are more frequent. A general strategy for employing task analysis was suggested by Brown and his colleagues (1971):

1. After studying available information and observing the child, the teacher determines the long-range objective and identifies the observable responses for criterion performance.
2. The teacher analyzes the responses and divides them into a series of less complex responses (subskills).
3. The teacher arranges the responses necessary to complete the long-range objective in a logical series.
4. The teacher verifies the child's ability to perform each response (subskill) in the series.
5. The teacher teaches the child to perform each response in the series.

6. The teacher records the child's performance during each training phase in order to make adjustments as they are needed.

Shaping and Chaining. Behavior shaping by reinforcers is used to implement the task analysis approach. With shaping, the behavioral objective is gained through reinforcing small steps or approximations. When developing new behavior, reinforcement may have to be given for each small step of the desired skill. As the response becomes more accurate, reinforcement is given only for the correct response, and previously reinforced approximations are ignored.

A sequence of responses is referred to as *chaining.* As Kazdin (1975) noted, "The component parts of a chain usually represent individual responses already in the repertoire of the individual. Yet the chain represents a combination of the individual responses ordered in a particular sequence" (p. 38).

One sequence commonly used with young handicapped children is backward chaining. With backward chaining, the last step in a response sequence is trained first. Table 10 (Chapter 6) provides an illustration of how backward chaining may be employed when teaching developmentally delayed children how to eat with a spoon. In this sequence, the trainer places his hand over the child's hand with the spoon in place and guides him through the entire chain. The initial training takes place at the final step in the chain, that is, placing the spoon filled with food into the mouth. The trainer gradually reduces the guidance and supervision and allows the child greater independence.

Prompting, Fading, and Modeling. Three tactics of building new behavior which have enjoyed much success with the developmentally young are *prompting, fading,* and *modeling.* Frequently, handicapped children either do not comprehend verbal instructions or do not comply with instructions. This is particularly characteristic of children with severe behavior or language handicaps. When this occurs in a learning situation, the teacher must find other ways to get a desired behavior to occur. If the child does not demonstrate the behavior, there is little opportunity for reinforcement.

Physical guidance is frequently required to develop new skills in the severely developmentally delayed child. For example, to encourage a delayed child to put on a shirt, the teacher may have to manually guide the child through the skill, providing praise and affection for each successful step in the task (Martin, Kehoe, Bird, Jensen, & Darbyshire, 1971).

Fading is the gradual withdrawing of the physical guidance which is initially given in the development of the behavior (Berkowitz, Sherry, & Davis, 1971). Correct timing for the withdrawal of physical guidance is an art which a teacher gains only with experience. When to fade is critically important. Removal of physical prompting too early or before the behavior is well established will result in loss of the response. Failure to fade a prompt, on the other hand, often leads to dependence on the teacher. It then becomes increasingly difficult to encourage independent, self-initiated behavior.

The use of modeling and demonstration is also a valuable means of instruction (Nelson, Cone, & Hanson, 1975; Wehman, 1976; York, Williams, & Brown,

1976). In order for instruction to be effective, the teacher must have the attention of the child. Frequently, children with severe developmental delays do not imitate nor do they make eye contact. Until these prerequisite skills are taught, modeling and demonstration will not be effective teaching methods.

Imitation. Young children learn from copying behaviors which they observe in their family members. Emphasis on this form of learning may help young handicapped children acquire new skills. If a child does not develop an interest in imitating others or the ability to learn from observation, the child's learning in all areas of development may be adversely affected.

In teaching imitation, the teacher actually performs the activity she wishes the child to reproduce, at the same time encouraging the child to copy the activity. Johnson and Werner (1975) have defined the steps in developing the skills of imitation:

1. Teach the child to attend (to look at, to listen to).
2. Teach simple nonverbal behaviors first, then more complex ones.
3. When the child is old enough, teach imitation of verbal cues.

Because imitation of verbal cues is directly related to speech, the development of speech in the young handicapped child can be greatly facilitated if the child has been taught to imitate.

The skills of the teacher contribute heavily to the learning environment and largely determine the child's success.

Cueing. Cueing, the use of verbal instruction, gestures, or other physical means of prodding or supporting performance, may teach the child to remember a response. The child receives the cue immediately prior to the expected action. For example, saying "Get your truck" may signal the child to pull himself to a standing position in order to reach his toy. Other examples of cueing are lip reading and the use of sounds to prompt responses. In order to respond to individual needs, the teacher must use on-the-spot analysis of the child and his environment to identify existing elements which can function as cues (Hayden, McGinness, & Dmitriev, 1976).

The basic sequence which teachers should follow in teaching a given skill involves the following:

1. Get the child's attention.
2. Give the instruction to perform the response. Instruction may include demonstration and encouragement to imitate.
3. Help the child make the correct response by prompting, cueing, and modeling, and give the instruction again.
4. If the child still does not perform the skill, the teacher must *manually guide* the child through the response.
5. Reward appropriate responses immediately.
6. Correct inappropriate responses immediately. Retest (Badger, 1971).

With this sequence the teacher may manipulate any of a number of other possible variables which might positively influence the acquisition of the skill. For example, the use of oversized buttons (Karen & Maxwell, 1967) which are gradually reduced in size will minimize errors in dressing training. Color-coded shoe eyelets will help the child attend more closely to the relevant dimensions of lacing his shoes (Gold & Scott, 1971). The amount of practice or trials provided on a given skill may lead to rapid acquisition of dressing skills (Azrin, Schaeffer, & Wesolowski, 1976).

Positive Reinforcement. Positive reinforcement of correct responses is a critical component of any instructional program. It should result in an increase in that response. Positive reinforcers may be praise, attention, food, tokens, money, or affection.

Reinforcer Sampling. A reinforcer has little value unless it is something the child wants. To discover what motivates the child, and to introduce him to possible reinforcers, a reinforcer sampling technique has been developed (Ayllon & Azrin, 1968). It consists of presenting new types of stimuli and events to the child and allowing him to become familiar with these reinforcers, thus increasing the probability that they will become reinforcing to the child.

Reinforcement Menu. The reinforcement menu is another method of introducing reinforcer options to children. The menu shows a number of high preference activities represented by stick figures or other symbols. It should be mounted on a large board. As Gardner (1974) notes, color photographs or illustrations may be used to make the board more attractive and meaningful to younger children. The menu also has an added value because it can be observed and is not totally abstract. Before beginning each training session, the child can choose an item or activity from the menu to work for.

Observation. Many times simple observation and trial-and-error will reveal how effective certain reinforcers are. For several days the teacher may use a certain reinforcer for a desired behavior to see if any behavior change occurs. Significant alterations in behavior would indicate that the reinforcer is instrumental in increasing desired behavior.

Direct observation can also reveal reinforcer preferences. Children who enjoy certain activities or show great enthusiasm for special privileges may demonstrate changed behavior if these events are made contingent on the desired behavior.

Usually, trial-and-error is used in combination with direct observation. Though it may appear that a child shows interest in certain activities or events, this does not necessarily mean that these events will effect a significant change in behavior. The teacher must systematically evaluate reinforcing events and order them into a reinforcement hierarchy. In a reinforcement hierarchy, "events should be arranged in terms of their relative importance to each child" (Gardner, 1974, p. 253).

The Need for Specificity. In determining reinforcing events for developmentally disabled children, it is important to be specific. Each child may respond differently under varied types of reinforcement. Praise, physical affection, peer attention, or attention from teachers are possible combinations in which reinforcement may be delivered. Certain children may perform best when a male delivers the reinforcement rather than when a female is giving praise. These reinforcement variables also give clues for the best motivation conditions to be used in an instructional program.

Maximizing Reinforcer Effectiveness. The *immediacy* of reinforcement is one variable which influences the effectiveness of a reinforcer. Reinforcers need to be delivered when the desired behavior occurs, particularly when a new skill is initially being developed. A child who goes to the toilet for the first time without a verbal reminder needs to be reinforced at once. Only in this way can the child gradually associate positive results with the behavior.

A second factor which influences the effectiveness of a reinforcer is *labeling,* or telling the child why he is being rewarded. When a child acts in an appropriate manner or begins to acquire a desired skill, the teacher must reinforce this behavior. However, it is also important to tell the child why he is being reinforced. A common drawback of many instructional programs with the developmentally delayed is the failure of the teacher to label the reinforcement contingency placed on the behavior. For example, if a teacher is providing gum drops for each correct response in hand washing, the child must be told, "Good, you turned on the water, Johnny," or "Good, you dried your hands, Johnny." Severely delayed children may not connect the reinforcing consequence with the desired behavior unless the contingency is labeled.

The *amount* of reinforcement given will also influence rate of learning. A general rule is—the greater the amount of reinforcement given for a response, the more frequent or stronger the response. This is true only to a certain point, however. If the amount of reinforcement is progressively increased, or is not varied with other reinforcers, the reinforcer will lose its effect. Satiation may occur with any reinforcing stimulus or event, but it is more likely to develop when primary reinforcers (food or liquid) are given excessively. Secondary reinforcers such as praise or attention are much more resistant to satiation effects.

Generally, it is best to use only social reinforcers unless the desired responses will not develop without using food or liquid reinforcers. If secondary reinforcers are used, the child does not become dependent on primary reinforcers and learns to respond to the more natural reinforcement of praise and attention.

Reinforcement may be given for each correct response or on a varied *schedule.* A reinforcer for each correct response is the best approach in developing a new behavior, but after the behavior is learned, an intermittent schedule promotes the maintenance or durability of the new behavior. As a behavior becomes increasingly durable, the amount of reinforcement should be diminished, the delivery of reinforcers should be gradually delayed, and the schedule of reinforcement more intermittent.

IV. *How can a teacher empirically verify that the skill of concern is being or has been taught?* If the instructional program for young children with special needs has been based on a task analysis approach, then evaluation has been an integral part of the entire instructional program. Evaluation in a task analysis approach to teaching has three components: observation, task decisions, and records.

Observation. In the task analysis approach, the teacher uses observation to determine entry skills and the child's approach to the task. Later, observations help to determine the appropriateness of the short-term objectives and if, in fact, the short-term objective has been stated in observable and measurable terms. If observation shows that these conditions exist, evaluation is relatively easy.

Observations provide the basis for making decisions about the tasks, determining the effects of minor modifications in the instructional plans, and determining the effectiveness of the reinforcement program.

Task Decisions. Evaluation takes place when determinations are made concerning not only whether the child has performed the task but also the quality of the performance. Decisions to further analyze a subskill, to provide more trials or practice time, or to move on to a new task are the direct results of an ongoing evaluation.

Records. Records of the child's entry-level skills, the number of trials per session, the length of sessions, and skills accomplished contribute to evaluation and thus to verification and decision making. Records should be maintained for the following purposes:

1. Determine further learning possibilities.
2. Assess individual growth.
3. Determine personal characteristics of the child.
4. Involve parents in the learning process.
5. Plan for materials and resources needed to enrich the instructional program (Kaplan, Kaplan, Masden, & Gould, 1975).

V. *Can the student perform the skill at a situationally acceptable rate?* Rate may refer to the number of times a particular response occurs in a given time period or to the length of time required to complete a response. In the development of basic skills in young handicapped children, the length of time required to complete a task is an important concern.

The rate of performance is directly related to the quality of the performance. Both quick, impulsive performance and overly slow, deliberate performance provide opportunities for mistakes which, if not corrected, will persist and affect subsequent learning. Performance rates that are different enough to call attention to the child will be a liability in his interactions with other children.

A slow rate of responding increases the probability that some responses in the chain will not be recalled. Because skill acquisition in young children is cumulative, it is desirable that teachers and parents use rate of response as one criterion for determining that the skill has been learned.

Teaching materials must be matched to the characteristics of the individual child and to the method of instruction.

VI. *What does the teacher intend to use as vehicles for the skill to be acquired and performed?* Teaching materials must be matched to the characteristics of the individual child and to the method of instruction. Persons working with young handicapped children must have an extensive knowledge of the materials available. Parts of Chapter 5, Chapter 6, and Appendix B describe some of the many materials available. Each of the cited sources provide activities and materials for skill development.

VII. *Can the student perform the skill across persons, places, instructional materials, and language cues?* Learning to perform newly acquired skills in a variety of settings and situations is a critical part of the child's instructional program. This section identifies several methods which can be used to ensure that the child will retain and transfer newly acquired skills to other environments.

Use of Naturally Occurring Reinforcers. Naturally occurring reinforcers are those events which are normal consequences of a behavior. Illustrations of naturally occurring reinforcers are finding a toy by one's own efforts and eating. Feelings of accomplishment are naturally occurring reinforcers for learning a new skill.

Alterations in Reinforcement Variables. Altering the schedule for reinforcement is another way of improving the likelihood that the child will maintain the new behavior. Ways of altering reinforcement include:

1. Gradually fading the reinforcement contingencies.
2. Delaying the delivery of the reinforcers after a desired behavior occurs.
3. Providing reinforcement on an intermittent schedule of reinforcement.
4. Gradually reducing the amount of reinforcement given.

These methods correspond closely with everyday reinforcement conditions common to most people. Initially, the reinforcers for the developmentally young must be structured and artificial if results are to be significant, but reinforcement variables must also be modified as the child acquires the behavior.

Use of Parents and Peers. Parents, relatives, siblings, and peers can help the child transfer his newly learned skill to new settings. Family knowledge and understanding of training procedures being utilized in the preschool or other training programs can be instrumental in generalizing the behavior to the home.

Parents are also able to give the teacher information about the child's behavior at home. For instance, in developing a toilet training program, the parent can give the teacher some indication of how often the child goes to the bathroom, if the bed is wet at night, and so forth. This information may be used in classroom training.

Varying Stimulus Conditions. One of the more frequently used methods of promoting generalization is to vary the learning conditions. This may include:

1. Introducing irrelevant or distracting stimuli.
2. Utilizing a variety of teachers or trainers.
3. Conducting the training in different settings.

The aim of these procedures "is to increase the number and type of stimuli which will set the occasion for the target behavior(s)" (Wehman, Abramson, & Norman, 1977, p. 218). It should be observed that the basic purpose of generalization training is to help the child pick out the salient or critical components required to make the learning transfer.

Implications drawn from a review of the literature can be summarized as follows:

1. Tasks should be selected with consideration for the child's functioning level and with consideration for the quality of his prerequisite skills.
2. Teachers must gradually reduce the amount of reinforcement once the child has demonstrated proficiency in the skill.
3. Children must be helped to practice newly acquired self-help skills in a number of different settings.
4. Teachers and parents must be sensitive to the kinds and effectiveness of various reinforcers.
5. Teachers must weigh the influence which peers and siblings have on the durability of a newly acquired skill.

VIII. *Can a student perform a skill without directions to do so from persons in authority?* If the answer to this question is no, then the child is externally controlled. The young handicapped child may easily become externally controlled. When it is appropriate for a particular skill to be performed without specific cues, the child's training should provide for such performance. Toilet training implies the complete act of toileting; the same is true of dressing, feeding, talking, and the other skills appropriate to young children.

Williams, Brown, and Certo (1975) suggested that self-regulation may be incorporated into a curriculum. When a skill is taught, the child should be required to initiate all components to complete the task without verbal cueing. Self-regulation strategies should not be taught as segmented or isolated curriculum entities but as integral parts of the learning activity.

With young handicapped children, it would be unreasonable to expect self-regulation in tasks for which the same would not be expected of nonhandicapped children. However, skill training which ends short of self-regulation is insufficient and unfair to the child and to his parents. If early intervention programs for young handicapped children are to achieve the goals for which they were established, independence in skill performance must begin at an early age.

Individualized Educational Programs

A written individualized educational program (IEP) for each handicapped child ages 3–21 is required by P.L. 94–142. The IEP is developed for each child by a group which includes a representative of the local education agency (LEA), the parents or guardians, and the teacher. The plan includes the specifically designed instruction to meet the needs of the handicapped child. Also included is documentation of decisions reached about the objectives, implementation, and evaluation of the child's IEP. The components of an individualized education program are as follows:

1. A statement of the child's present level of educational performance. It must include the level of performance with regard to the following needs: educational, social and emotional, language, perceptual, motor, physical education, and medical.
2. A statement of annual goals for the child's education program. The annual goals should include affective–social skills, physical skills, and mental–cognitive skills.
3. A list of short-term objectives. These should be child-oriented, positive, measurable, and observable subtasks which lead to the annual goals. The short-term objectives should state what the child will do, under what conditions, and with what degree of success (number of successful performances in a given number of trials).
4. A statement of educational services needed by the child (determined without regard for the availability of those services) and related services needed, including the type of physical education program in which the child will participate.
5. A description of the extent to which the child will participate in a regular education program, showing how he will work toward the least restrictive alternative placement. Justification must be given for the type of educational placement the child will have.
6. Date for the initiation and alteration of services.
7. Evaluation criteria.
8. Schedules for determining if objectives have been met.

The school is responsible for calling meetings of specific people, including one or both of the child's parents for the purposes of developing, reviewing, and revising (not less often than annually) the child's education program. Table 3 shows procedures that have been suggested to facilitate the writing of the IEP.

Program Components for the Delivery of Services

Those who develop programs for young children with special needs must select from many options and consider the developmental needs of each child (Caldwell, 1973). To develop a statewide program for the education of young handicapped children, Fallen (Division of Special Education, 1974) conducted a nationwide survey of service delivery systems and found that programs had

Table 3

Sample Format for Data Gathering and Writing the IEP

1. Examine initial referral information.
2. Examine all available information about the child.
3. Consider what other sources of data need to be investigated. (If outside agencies need to be contacted, obtain parental permission.)
4. Decide which evaluations or additional information would be necessary, submit request for type of data desired.
5. Gather all past and present material and develop summary paragraph(s) attempting to synthesize what the information sources indicate.
6. List child's present level of performance:
   - A. major needs or areas of concern
   - B. strengths and weaknesses of the child
   - C. priority of concerns
   - D. styles of learning
   - E. other major trends or themes regarding the child
   - F. specific questions that need to be answered
7. Decide on the procedure for writing the IEP.
8. Determine and prioritize goals for the child.
9. Establish specific performance objectives.
10. Select educational and related services needed.
11. Note the percent of time to be spent in the regular classroom.
12. Determine initiation and completion dates for each service or action recommended.
13. Decide on evaluation criteria.
14. Make placement decision.
15. Note the personnel responsible for implementing the IEP.

Note: From J. Platt, *IEP In-service Training Materials*. Washington, D.C.: Mid-East Regional Resource Center, George Washington University, 1977.

developed around patterns which include one, several, or all of the following features:

Parent Involvement. Almost all of the programs capitalized on the widely held belief that there is no better teacher than the parents who have been taught to recognize and to meet the developmental needs of their child. Parent education may include knowledge of the child's program, instruction directed toward improving the quality of family life, and the opportunity to work with other parents. Parent counseling, closely related to parent education, provides services for those families who find it difficult to accept the presence of a handicapped child. Foster parents and other parent substitutes receive the same training and services as parents. Foster grandparents are helped to understand young handicapped children and encouraged to provide grandparent-like favors for children whose parents are absent. This service has been effective in pediatric wards, clinics, and treatment centers.

Home Program. The professionally trained child development specialist visits the home regularly to help the parent or parent substitute acquire skills and knowledge concerning the child's development and the school program. The professional works with the parent and the child in activities designed to minimize problems caused by the handicapping condition and to promote improvement in the child's functional abilities. The parent and professional agree on the child's home learning program, and written instructions are prepared as reminders and for records.

Home Visitor. The difference between the home visitor program and the home program is the training level of the person who works with the parent. The home visitor is a paraprofessional trained by the educational child development specialist (a professional) to provide parent instruction.

Small-group Programs. Programs similar to the home visitor or home program have been developed to train parents in groups of two, three, or four rather than individually. As the children acquire skills, the size of the group can be increased.

Day Care Centers. Existing day care centers for nonhandicapped children have become able to provide effective educational programs for young handicapped children by adding appropriately trained staff members. The educator works with four or five children. Interpretation of the children's problems to other staff members and to the parents is one of the educator's responsibilities.

The neighborhood day care home is a center which is established in close proximity to the homes of children served. A day care mother is specially trained to provide for the physical, social, emotional, and educational needs of each child enrolled. Play equipment, books, and other instructional materials are provided, and the program is supervised by a professional who provides assistance in the planning for each child.

Neighborhood Group Centers. Centers similar to neighborhood day care centers have been developed to care for all of the children in a family. Thus the age range for the group center could include infants to school-age children.

Nursery Schools. Nursery schools for the young child with special needs may be special schools or regular schools also serving nonhandicapped children. In either case, the program is designed to meet the educational, emotional, social, and physical needs of the child.

Classroom Programs. Classroom programs are designed for 8 to 10 young handicapped children who can travel from home to school without serious problems and who can benefit from association with other children. Classroom models are similar to nursery schools, and programs are individualized for each child. Teachers working in this type of setting usually have the help of aides, parents, or volunteers.

Child Development Hostels. Hostels have been developed to care for severely and profoundly handicapped children in a homelike environment.

Transportation. A means of getting from their homes to existing services is the greatest need of some handicapped children. For those in home programs, transporting the instruction to the child is essential. Many programs for young exceptional children provide transportation or assume its cost.

Child Information Library. Libraries of educational information for parents of young handicapped children have been established. Additionally, some of these facilities provide a loan service of games, records, films, and other learning materials.

The Toy Lending Library. Similar to the child information library, the toy lending library provides equipment, toys, and other educational materials on loan. If a toy is broken, its parts are returned to the library for repair.

Educational Facilitator. Some persons have received special training to increase the effectiveness of babysitters or caretakers for young handicapped children. Through such training these persons know how to change daily routines into learning experiences.

Hospital–Clinic-Based Classrooms. Instructional programs have been established for young children waiting for treatment or recovering from illness.

Learning Centers. The learning center provides special instruction requiring equipment which is too expensive to be housed and used in individual classrooms or day care centers. These are usually centrally located to serve a large geographic area and are equipped to accommodate children with a variety of handicapping conditions.

Out-patient Institutional Care. Services of some institutions have been extended to provide residential care on a short-term basis for children whose parents need a vacation or need to attend to family emergencies. Special programs are provided to make the children's stay a happy vacation from their parents. *Respite care* provides the same service on a community basis.

Television Programs. Several types of televised instruction have been developed to meet the needs of young developmentally delayed children and their parents. One type is designed to assist the child in skill development. Parents are notified concerning program dates, and the children are prepared for lesson periods. The content of the televised lesson is coordinated with other phases of the child's program. Another use of television has been the closed-circuit instructional program shown on a prescriptive basis. This type of instruction is coordinated with a home program. Public television has provided educational programs designed not only for parents but also for public awareness. Similar programs have been developed for radio.

Parent's Guide. The parent's guide used in connection with television and radio programs provides background information and suggests activities to make the programs more meaningful to young children. Guide books and newsletters are publications which inform parents of existing resources in the community and activities to use with their children for skill development.

Mobile Classrooms. These are vans which travel to designated locations where children meet in groups for social and educational experiences. The vans are equipped with instructional materials and equipment appropriate for the children they serve. In one preschool program each unit made two stops daily. During the first hour of the morning, 20 three-year-olds and their parents came aboard for instruction. After their departure, 20 four-year-olds and their parents arrived for the class session. After lunch, the staff drove the van to another location in the community where two similar groups received instruction. The schedule operated four days a week. The fifth day was reserved for staff inservice training. Mobile libraries, laboratories, day care units, and clinics have made use of vans to provide a variety of services for sparsely populated areas and where transportation is a problem.

Adaptations and elaborations of these basic ideas have been used to develop needed services for children from birth through age five, their parents, and other members of their families. First Chance programs described by Karnes and Zehrbach (1977) have included, in addition to those features mentioned, (1) technical assistance and consultative services, (2) prenatal instruction of high risk potential parents, and (3) intervention into higher level systems models.

Summary

This chapter has presented a summary of learning theories which have provided the theoretical framework for instructional procedures used with young handicapped children. Various conditions which contribute to learning have been considered. Procedures relative to designing the child's instructional program have been identified. The intention has been to contribute to the understanding of those who plan to work with young handicapped children. Chapters 5 through 10 are concerned to some extent with the application of these principles and procedures to various areas of skill development. In order to understand the development of young handicapped children, it is necessary to have a background of knowledge about the development of normal children, a topic that is discussed in the next chapter.

REFERENCES

Anastasiow, N. J., & Mansergh, G. P. Teaching skills in early childhood programs. *Exceptional Children,* 1975, **41**(5), 309–317.

Ausubel, D., & Sullivan, E. *Theory and problems of child development* (2nd ed.). New York: Grune & Stratton, 1970.

Ayllon, T., & Azrin, N. H. Reinforcer sampling: A technique for increasing the behavior of mental patients. *Journal of Applied Behavior Analysis,* 1968, **1**, 13–20.

Azrin, N. N., Schaeffer, R., & Wesolowski, M. A rapid method of teaching profoundly retarded persons to dress. *Mental Retardation,* 1976, **14**(6), 29–33.

Badger, E. *Infant learning program.* Washington, D.C.: Edufax, 1971.

Banus, B. *The developmental therapist: A prototype of the pediatric occupational therapist.* Thorofare, N.J.: Charles B. Slack, 1971.

Baroff, G. *Mental retardation: Nature, cause and management.* New York: John Wiley & Sons, 1974.

Berkowitz, S., Sherry, P., & Davis, B. Teaching self-feeding skills to profound retardates using reinforcement and fading procedures. *Behavior Therapy,* 1971, **2**, 62–67.

Bigge, M. L. *Learning theories for teachers* (3rd ed.). New York: Harper & Row, 1976.

Blake, K. *Teaching the retarded.* Englewood Cliffs, N.J.: Prentice-Hall, 1974.

Blank, M. *Teaching learning in the preschool.* Columbus, Ohio: Charles E. Merrill Publishing Co., 1973.

Bloom, B. *Stability and change in human characteristics.* New York: John Wiley & Sons, 1964.

Breckenridge, M., & Murphy, M. *Growth and development of the young child.* Philadelphia: W. B. Saunders Co., 1969.

Brown, L., Bellamy, T., & Sontag, E. *The development and implementation of a public school prevocational training program for trainable retarded and severely emotionally disturbed children.* Madison, Wis.: Madison Public Schools, 1971.

Bugelski, B. *The psychology of learning applied to teaching* (2nd ed.). New York: Bobbs-Merrill, 1971.

Cairns, G., & Butterfield, E. *Assessing infant's auditory functioning.* In B. Friedlander, et. al. (Eds.), *Exceptional infant: Assessment and intervention.* New York: Brunner/Mazel, 1975.

Caldwell, B. The importance of beginning early. In J. Jordan, *Not all little wagons are red.* Reston, Va.: The Council for Exceptional Children, 1973.

Cratty, B. *Intelligence in action: Physical activities for enhancing intellectual abilities.* Englewood Cliffs, N.J.: Prentice-Hall, 1973.

DeWeerd, J. Introduction. In J. Jordan, A. Hayden, M. Karnes, & M. Wood (Eds.), *Early childhood education for exceptional children: A handbook of ideas and exemplary practices.* Reston, Va.: The Council for Exceptional Children, 1977.

Division of Special Education, State Department of Education. *A comprehensive state plan for the education of young handicapped children below age 5 in Virginia.* Richmond, Va.: author, 1974.

Gagné, R. *The conditions of learning.* New York: Holt, Rinehart & Winston, 1965.

Gagné, R. *Essentials of learning for instruction.* Hinsdale, Ill.: Dryden Press, 1974.

Gardner, W. *Reactions of intellectually normal and retarded boys after experimentally induced failure: A social learning theory.* Unpublished doctoral dissertation, George Peabody College for Teachers, 1959.

Gardner, W. I. *Children with learning and behavior problems.* Boston: Allyn & Bacon, 1974.

Gold, M. W., & Scott, K. C. Discrimination learning. In W. B. Stephens (Ed.), *Training the developmentally young.* New York: John Day, 1971.

Hallahan, D., & Kauffman, J. *Introduction to learning disabilities: A psycho-behavioral approach.* Englewood Cliffs, N.J.: Prentice-Hall, 1976.

Hayden, A., & Dmitriev, V. The multidisciplinary preschool program for Down's syndrome children at the University of Washington Model Preschool Center. In B. Friedlander, G. Sterritt, & E. Kirk (Eds.), *Exceptional infant: Assessment and intervention.* New York: Brunner/Mazel, 1975.

Hayden, A., & McGinness, G. Bases for early intervention. In E. Sontag, J. Smith, & N. Certo (Eds.), *Educational Programming for the Severely and Profoundly Handicapped.* Reston, Va.: The Council for Exceptional Children, 1977.

Hayden, A., McGinness, G., & Dmitriev, V. Early and continuous intervention strategies for several handicapped infants and very young children. In N. Haring & L. Brown, *Teaching the severely handicapped* (Vol. I). New York: Grune & Stratton, 1976.
Heber, R. *Expectancy and expectancy changes in normal and mentally retarded boys.* Unpublished doctoral dissertation, George Peabody College for Teachers, 1951.
Hill, W. *Learning: A survey of psychological interpretations.* San Francisco: The Chandler Publishing Co., 1963.
Hurlock, E. *Child development* (5th ed.). New York: McGraw Hill Book Co., 1972.
Johnson, V., & Werner, R. *A step-by-step learning guide for retarded infants and children.* Syracuse, N.Y.: Syracuse University Press, 1975.
Kaplan, S., Kaplan, J., Masden, S., & Gould, B. *A young child experiences.* Pacific Palisades, Calif.: Goodyear Publishing Co., 1975.
Karen, R., & Maxwell, S. Strengthening self-help behavior in the retardate. *American Journal of Mental Deficiency,* 1967, **71**, 516–550.
Karnes, M., & Zehrbach, R. Alternative models for delivering services to young handicapped children. In J. Jordan, A. Hayden, M. Karnes, & M. Wood, *Early childhood education for exceptional children: A handbook of ideas and exemplary practices.* Reston, Va.: The Council for Exceptional Children, 1977.
Kazdin, A. *Behavior modification in applied settings.* Homewood, Ill.: Dorsey Press, 1975.
Knapczyk, K. D. Task analytic assessment of severe learning problems. *Education and Training of the Mentally Retarded,* 1975, **10**(2), 74–77.
Lawther, J. *The learning of physical skills.* Englewood Cliffs, N.J.: Prentice-Hall, 1968.
Levy, T. Social reinforcement and knowledge of results as determinants of motor performance among educable mentally retarded children. *American Journal of Mental Deficiency,* 1974, **78**, 752–758.
Mager, R. *Preparing instructional objectives.* Palo Alto, Calif.: Fearon, 1962.
Maier, H. W. *Three theories of child development* (Rev. ed.). New York: Harper & Row, Publishers, 1965.
Martin, G., Kehoe, G., Bird, E., Jensen, V., & Darbyshire, M. Operant conditioning of dressing behavior in severely retarded girls. *Mental Retardation,* 1971, 9, 27–30.
McGraw, M. *The neuromuscular maturation of the human infant.* New York: Hofner Publishing Co., 1969.
McKee, B. An interaction approach to learning disabilities. *Journal of Learning Disabilities,* 1976, 9(7), 423–426.
Mouly, G. *Psychology for effective teaching.* New York: Holt, Rinehart & Winston, 1968.
Nelson, G., Cone, J., & Hanson, C. Training correct utensil use in retarded children: Modeling versus physical guidance. *American Journal of Mental Deficiency,* 1975, **80**, 114–122.
Platt, J. IEP *In-service training materials.* Washington, D.C.: Mid-East Regional Resource Center, George Washington University, July 1977.
Robinson, H., & Robinson, N. *The mentally retarded child: A psychological approach.* New York: McGraw Hill Book Co., 1965.
Sanford, A. R. *Learning accomplishment profile.* Chapel Hill, N.C.: Training Outreach Project, 1973.
Sanford, A. R., with Bailey, D., Johnson, W. C., Leonard, J., & O'Connor, P. D. *A manual for use of the learning accomplishment profile.* Winston-Salem, N.C.: Kaplan School Supply Corp., 1974.
Siegel, E. Task analysis and effective teaching. *Journal of Learning Disabilities,* 1972, 5(9), 5–19.

Sulzer, B., & Mayer, G. *Behavior modification procedures for school personnel.* Hinsdale, Ill.: Dryden Press, 1972.

Wehman, P. Imitation as a facilitator of treatment for the mentally retarded. *Rehabilitation Literature,* 1976, **37**(2), 41–48.

Wehman, P. *Helping the mentally retarded acquire play skills.* Springfield, Ill.: Charles C Thomas, 1977.

Wehman, P., Abramson, M., & Norman, C. Transfer of training in behavior modification programs: An evaluative review. *Journal of Special Education,* 1977, **11**(2), 217–231.

White, B. *The first three years of life.* Englewood Cliffs, N.J.: Prentice-Hall, 1975.

Williams, W. Procedures of task analysis as related to developing instructional programs for the severely handicapped. In L. Brown, T. Crowner, W. Williams, & R. York (Eds.), *Madison's alternative to zero exclusion: A book of readings.* Madison, Wisc.: Madison Public Schools, 1975.

Williams, W., Brown, L., & Certo, N. Basic components of instructional programs. *TIP theory into practice,* 1975, **14**(2), 123–136.

York, R., Williams, W., & Brown, P. Teacher modeling and student imitation: An instructional procedure and teacher competency. *American Association for Education of Severely/Profoundly Handicapped Review,* 1976, **1**(8), 11–15.

4

The Development of the Young Child

A basic understanding of the development of the young child from conception through birth, infancy, and the preschool years is necessary in order to have a continuum of normal development against which to compare the development of the young, special child. This chapter presents a discussion of the child's development during the prenatal, perinatal, and postnatal periods, infancy, and the preschool years. Influences on the child in each of these phases are also discussed. Such a review is intended to serve as a background against which the development of the young child with special needs may be viewed more meaningfully. Subsequent chapters of the text present discussions of the specific skills (motor, cognitive, language, play, emotional and social, and self-help) acquired by the young child during her early years, and of the ways in which the young, exceptional child may deviate from the normal child in learning these specific skills.

Conception and Prenatal Development

The child's development is influenced by factors occurring as early as the moment of conception. Conception takes place when the ovum, or egg, of the female is fertilized by the sperm of the male. The ovum is produced by the

---

The author of this chapter was **Jill E. McGovern.**

ovaries, and when it is released by one of the two ovaries, it moves through the Fallopian tube. The sperm, deposited in the female's vagina, travel through the uterus, or womb, to the Fallopian tube where they surround the ovum. Several of the sperm cells penetrate the ovum, and finally one sperm moves to the nucleus of the ovum and thereby completes the fertilization process. Each of the sex cells, the ovum and the sperm, contributes 23 chromosomes and together they form one cell of 46 chromosomes, the normal number for a human cell.

The prenatal period may be divided into three distinct phases. The first prenatal stage, known as the *period of the ovum,* or the *germinal period,* begins when the ovum is fertilized and continues for one or two weeks. During this time, the fertilized ovum, also known as the zygote, undergoes cell division or mitosis. As the zygote divides and grows, it leaves the Fallopian tube and moves into the uterus where it implants itself in the lining of the uterus. During the first 10 to 14 days of existence, the zygote receives its nourishment from its own yolk. After implantation, all nourishment is received from the mother's body.

The second prenatal stage, the *embryonic period,* occurs when implantation takes place and continues until the end of the second month. It is at this time that the various organs and tissues are being differentiated and formed. The embryo's development proceeds in a cephalocaudal manner, that is, from head to tail, and in a proximodistal manner, that is, from the inside outward. The head develops first, and by the end of 8 weeks, the features of the face—eyes, ears, nose and mouth—are clearly differentiated. Fingers and toes are recognizable by this time as are the sex organs which are beginning to form. The embryo's height and weight increase greatly as a result of the rapid growth that occurs during the second prenatal period.

During the embryonic stage, the developing child's nourishment is obtained from the mother through a system that consists of the placenta, the umbilical cord, and the amniotic sac. The organ that lines the wall of the uterus and partially surrounds the embryo is the placenta. The embryo is connected to the placenta by the umbilical cord. The bloodstream of the mother feeds into the placenta, from which the embryo draws nourishment and oxygen and into which it releases carbon dioxide and other waste materials by way of the umbilical cord.

The embryo itself is surrounded by fluids known as amniotic fluids, which are contained within the amniotic sac. The fluid serves two important purposes: it protects the embryo from bumps and shocks, and it allows the embryo freedom of movement. Recent medical science has found another important purpose for the amniotic fluid; it provides the cells that are extracted during amniocentesis, a process which is used to detect chromosomal aberrations or other deficiencies such as sickle-cell anemia in the embryo.

The third prenatal period, the *fetal period,* begins at the end of the eighth week and continues until birth. This final stage of development is one of differentiation and integration of the internal organs and of growth of the fetus in length and weight. Some of the notable features of this phase are the sex of the fetus becomes distinguishable by the 12th week; the head makes up one-third of the length of the fetus by the 16th week; the body axis begins to straighten and the head, arms, and legs begin to move independently by the 20th week; the eyes of the fetus open by the 28th week; and after the 28th week, the fetus is sufficiently developed to be born and survive. In the majority of cases, however, fetal development continues until approximately the 40th week of gestation.

Prenatal Influences

The development of the unborn child is influenced by a number of factors such as nutrition, drugs, radiation, infections, blood incompatibility, stress, and other environmental factors. The negative effect of any of these factors may prove detrimental to the fetus.

Fetal malnutrition is one of the most common causes of death of a fetus and of lasting postnatal damage to the brain development of an infant. Inadequate maternal diet and placental insufficiency are the two primary sources of fetal malnutrition. A number of studies (Vore, 1973) support the contention that poor maternal diet results in fewer brain cells in both the fetus and in the child in later life, low birth weight, and, in general, poor development. Low birth weight is associated with infant deaths as well as with underdevelopment. Such a child may be stunted in growth, have insufficient brain cell growth, and have more illnesses and behavior problems than a normal child. Supplementing the pregnant woman's diet with vitamins, proteins, and calories has been shown to reduce or eliminate the detrimental effects of inadequate maternal nutrition (Coursin, 1973).

Placental insufficiency may result from maternal malnutrition as well as from frequent or closely spaced pregnancies. The pregnant woman requires greater amounts of many nutrients, such as calcium, iron, iodine and zinc, than the nonpregnant woman. If the mother has an inadequate supply of these substances in her blood and the fetus is unable to obtain these nutrients from the placenta, the newborn may exhibit mental and motor deficiency, hearing and visual loss, cerebral palsy, and other impairments.

In addition to fetal malnutrition, chemical and physical agents may have a harmful effect during the prenatal development of the child. Although the placenta filters out many substances from the mother's blood, some pass through the placenta and damage the fetus. Many chemical agents, or drugs, may adversely affect the fetus. It has been documented that pregnant women addicted to heroin give birth to infants also addicted to the drug (Katchadourian & Lunde, 1975). Other drugs may have harmful effects on the infant: quinine may result in deafness; tranquilizers like chlordizepoxide (Librium), meprobamate (Miltown), and thalidomide may produce infants with deformed or missing limbs if the drug is taken during the embryonic period. Oral contraceptives may increase the levels of vitamin A in the blood to such degree as to cause deformities in the embryo. Still another drug, alcohol, is associated with abnormal fetal development. Several studies have suggested that one out of five alcoholic mothers may produce children with facial, limb, and heart defects (Jones & Smith, 1973). Even more recently, The National Institute on Alcohol Abuse and Alcoholism maintained that the consumption of as little as one ounce of pure alcohol a day by pregnant women would increase their risk of producing a deformed or retarded child ("Alcohol and the Fetus," 1977). There also may be a threat to the fetus if its father engages in heavy drinking since there is a possibility that such drinking may damage the genes in the male's sperm cells ("A Man's Drinking May Harm His Offspring," 1975).

Not only are chemical agents injurious to the fetus but so are physical agents such as cigarette smoking and marijuana. Recent investigations support the premise that women who smoke cigarettes during pregnancy are more likely to produce physically and mentally retarded children (Pasamanick & Knobloch, 1972). Like oral contraceptives, cigarette smoking induces abnormally high levels of vitamin A in the mother's blood, which may cause deformities in the developing embryo. Other by-products of cigarette smoking, nicotine, carbon dioxide, and cyanide, may reduce the amounts of blood, oxygen, and nutrients, respectively, reaching the fetus. Likewise, marijuana smoking has been associated with birth defects (Sharma, 1972).

Radiation is a source of serious harm to the developing fetus. Although the small amounts of radiation given off by X-rays may not injure the fetus, larger doses may result in mental and physical deficiencies. Similarly, another kind of radiation, ionizing radiation, may cause abnormal development of the child's head and brain if it is received by the pregnant woman in sufficiently heavy amounts at specific times during pregnancy (Kappelman, 1971). Still a third type of radiation, atomic radiation, seriously affects fetal development as evi-

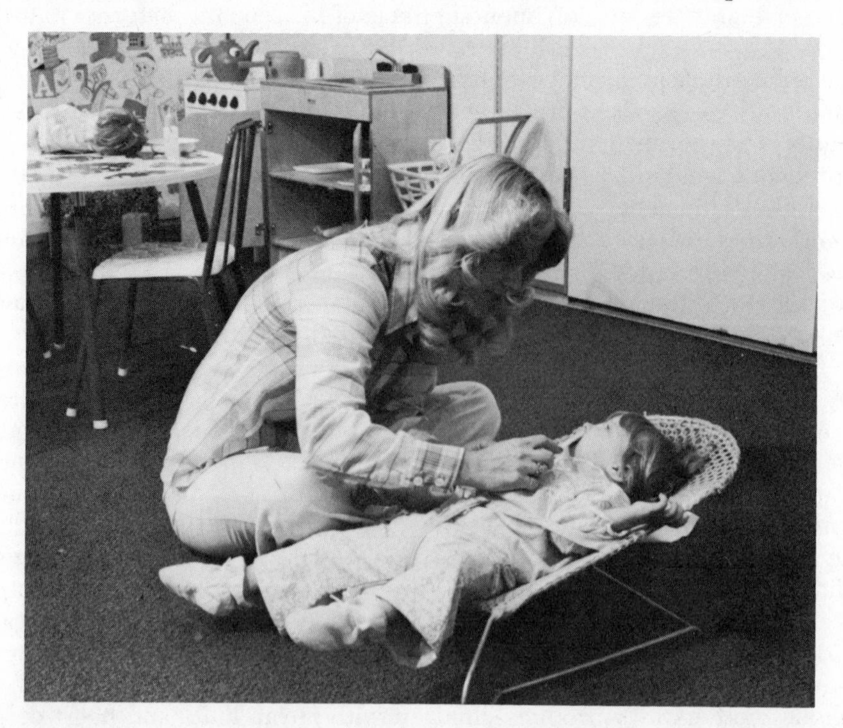

Children born to women who contracted rubella during the early months of pregnancy are at risk for cardiac, neurological, hearing, and visual defects.

denced by the great number of deformed children born to women who, during their pregnancy, were exposed to the atomic bomb dropped on Hiroshima, Japan, in 1945. It may also be possible that one or more of the different types of radiation cause the chromosomal abnormalities that result in Down's syndrome, or mongolism (Kochupillai, Verna, Grewal, & Ramalingaswami, 1976).

Normal fetal development may also be impaired if the pregnant woman contracts infections. Infections or viral diseases such as rubella, chicken pox, smallpox, hepatitis, scarlet fever, syphilis, and toxoplasmosis may be pernicious to the fetus and, even more so, to the embryo.

A dramatic example of the effect of infection on the unborn child occurred with the worldwide epidemic of rubella in 1964. Only 20% of the children born to women who had contracted rubella during their pregnancy were free of apparent defect. Eleven percent of children born to this same group of women had cardiac, neurological, hearing, and visual defects; 40% were premature; and more than 50% exhibited various combinations and degrees of mental retardation and emotional disturbance. The devastating effects of this one disease have since been minimized by the use of a vaccine that immunizes women against rubella.

Blood incompatibility may also adversely affect the fetus. This condition occurs when the mother's blood is Rh negative and the fetus's blood is Rh positive. In this case, the fetus produces antigens which are passed through the placenta into the mother's blood, which in turn makes antibodies that are returned through the placenta to the blood of the fetus. The resulting problems include brain damage and anemia. Since the danger from blood incompatibility increases significantly after the first birth, damage to subsequent children may be alleviated by the administration of the medication Rhogam to the Rh negative mother immediately after the birth of the first child.

Still another factor affecting the development of the fetus is maternal stress. The mother's physical and emotional stresses may result in physical abnormalities, birth complications, and later increased frequency of illness for the child. Physical stresses, such as standing for long periods of time or carrying heavy loads, and situational stresses, such as unwanted pregnancy, marital problems, and personal tensions, may cause harm to the fetus.

A final, important influence on the development of the fetus is the environment in general. Environmental factors that may affect the fetus include maternal socioeconomic status, maternal age and physical stature, and birth order and family size.

The socioeconomic status of the pregnant woman is a determinant of her health, nutrition, and use of health and social services. The emotional and physical stresses of frequent or closely spaced pregnancies may impair the mother's health in general and result in placental insufficiency in particular. Such pregnancies often occur among women of a low socioeconomic level, although the growing awareness and availability of birth control methods and family planning counseling may minimize this health risk.

Socioeconomic status also affects the mother's nutrition. One study revealed that women from low-income groups received fewer calories and proteins than women from high-income groups (Abraham, Lowenstein, & Johnson, 1974). In addition, low-income white women were lacking in vitamin A, and black women at all income levels were deficient in calcium. The appropriate use of health and social services during pregnancy can insure adequate prenatal care in such areas as health and nutrition, but socioeconomic status again plays a role in the pregnant woman's use of these services. Low socioeconomic status frequently reflects low educational level, which often means inadequate information about proper prenatal care.

The mother's age has a decided influence at both extremes of the childbearing period. More than any other age group, mothers under the age of 15 are likely to have premature births as well as have their infants die in the first year of life. The exception is over-35, primiparous mothers (bearing a child for the first or second time) who have a higher prematurity rate than any other age group (Illsley, 1967). Mothers over the age of 45 are the second most likely group to experience the death of their children in the first year of infancy. Older mothers are also more likely to produce children with Down's syndrome, the probability of which increases significantly with age. The risk of having a Down's syndrome child before age 30 is 1 in 1,000; at age 40, it is 1 in 100; and by age 45, the chance is 1 in 45. In general, it may be noted that very young mothers, age 15 and under, and older mothers, age 35 and over, are more likely to give birth to infants with impairments than are mothers from the ages of 16 to 34.

Just as maternal age has an impact on fetal development, so does maternal physical stature. Studies have suggested a relationship between the mother's stature and her ability to reproduce normal offspring. Short mothers seem to have more complications during pregnancy and delivery and to produce premature infants as well as infants with low birth weight (Illsley, 1967). A mother's short stature may be the result of environmental factors, particularly low socioeconomic status.

Birth order and family size also influence fetal development. One study indicated that IQ decreases with birth order and that the more children per family, the lower the average IQ (Belmont & Marolla, 1973). Another study found that babies born within one year of a previous pregnancy had lower birth weights and lower scores on both the Bayley tests at 8 months and on the Stanford-Binet IQ tests at 4 years when compared with babies born 2 to 5 years after the previous gestation (Holley, Rosenbaum, & Churchill, 1969).

In summary, some of the factors that may have a harmful influence on the development of the fetus are maternal nutrition, chemical and physical agents, radiation, infections, blood incompatibility, maternal stress, low socioeconomic status, maternal age and physical stature, and birth order and family size.

Perinatal Development

The birth process is a critical physical experience for both the mother and the child. In giving birth, the mother goes through labor, which can be divided into three distinct stages. The first stage, lasting approximately 12½ hours out of an average total labor of 14 hours, is the opening of the cervix, or neck of the uterus. Rhythmic contractions set in motion the muscular processes which cause the cervix to dilate to a point where the diameter of the opening is about 4 inches. The second stage, lasting about an hour and a half for a first child, and less for subsequent births, continues from the time that the cervix is completely dilated until the baby emerges from the mother. The third and final stage of labor, lasting only a few minutes, occurs when the placenta and membranes are expelled.

Occasionally, a normal birth may not be possible. In that case, a Caesarian section is performed: the mother's abdomen and uterus are cut open, and the baby and placenta are then removed. Formerly a risky procedure, a Caesarian section is now relatively safe and eliminates the danger to both mother and child of a breech birth or a possibly damaging forceps delivery.

Perinatal Influences

Anoxia, prematurity, and low birth weight are factors that can complicate the birth process. One of these problems, *anoxia,* occurs quite commonly at birth. Defined as oxygen deprivation, anoxia may be tolerated by the infant for brief moments during the birth process. Prolonged anoxia, however, will result in brain damage. The severity of the damage is directly related to the length of time the infant is without oxygen. Such brain damage may manifest itself in a variety of disabilities: mental retardation, cerebral palsy, epilepsy, and disorders of behavior, language, and speech.

There are several causes of anoxia. One is interference with the blood flow through the umbilical cord from the mother to the infant. This situation may occur when the umbilical cord becomes so twisted during the birth process that blood flow is impeded, or when the umbilical cord is cut before the infant begins breathing on its own. A French obstetrician, Frederic Leboyer, has introduced a practice that may prevent the latter cause of anoxia. He advocates allowing the newborn infant to lie quietly on the mother's abdomen, with the umbilical cord intact until the child's respiratory system begins to operate independently. Then, the umbilical cord will cease to function and, after five minutes or so, may be cut without endangering the flow of blood and oxygen to the neonate, or newborn.

Another cause of anoxia is hemorrhaging or severe bleeding by the mother during the birth process. The flow of blood to the infant is thus diminished and so is the crucial supply of oxygen.

A second birth complication is prematurity, which is determined by the length of the gestation period or the birth weight of the infant. In the former case, gestation is less than 37 weeks, and in the latter, the birth weight is less than 2,500 grams. The physical and behavioral development of premature infants, while typical of their gestational age, is not advanced enough to insure survival without special assistance. The premature baby will be placed in an incubator or isolette to control the temperature since the baby does not yet have a stabilized body temperature. Mechanical devices are also used to feed premature infants because they often are not able to suck and swallow. Although the isolation of the incubator is beneficial to the infant's physical devel-

The sense of touch plays a critical role in the development of the child for gaining concrete knowledge and establishing a feeling of security.

opment, it may be detrimental to her psychological development. Physical separation from the parents, particularly the mother, prevents adequate interaction and stimulation.

The problems just described decrease the chance of survival for approximately 7% of premature infants. If they do survive, they tend to be at risk for many development problems: lower than average IQ, learning and motor difficulties, hearing and visual impairments, and certain types of cerebral palsy (Feinbloom, 1972). Several studies of prematurity, however, have found that delayed mental ability noted in infancy often disappeared by age 4 (Berges, Lezine, Harrison, & Boisselier, 1973).

A third birth complication, low birth weight, occurs in conjunction with prematurity but may also be noted in full-term infants who are small for their gestational age. About one-third to one-half of low birth-weight babies are growth-retarded rather than premature. Growth-retarded babies are more likely to survive than premature infants, but they are also more likely to have genetic defects as well as mental and neurological impairment. The severity of a child's later handicap seems to be strongly related to her birth weight: the lower the birth weight, the greater the handicap. The recent advances in intensive care practices in the nursery may minimize the harmful effects of low birth weight and prematurity.

Postnatal Development

The first few months of the newborn infant's life are spent in making basic adjustments to the environment outside the womb. During this time, motor, perceptual, mental, psychological, and social abilities are also beginning to develop.

Certain inborn reflexes or instinctive responses to a stimulus are exhibited by the newborn. Some appear to be vestiges of mechanisms used for protection by primitive man and even earlier in the development of the species, and some appear to be important survival responses. In the first group are several reflexes less related to survival. The startle or Moro reflex occurs in response to a loud noise or sudden change in position and results in movement of the legs and arms and the opening and closing of the hands into a clenched fist. The grasp or Darwinian reflex happens when pressure is put on the infant's palm. A fist is made so tight that the infant can be lifted and supported by his own grasp. The Babinski reflex occurs when the sole of the infant's foot is stroked lightly. The infant's toes turn upward. The tonic neck reflex reflects the typical newborn posture. When an infant is lying on its back, its head turns to one side, the arm and leg on that side are extended, and the arm and leg on the opposite side are flexed.

In the second group of reflexes are the ones necessary for survival. The rooting reflex is a response to tactile stimulation on the cheek or lip and is the infant's attempt to locate food. The sucking reflex serves two purposes: obtaining sustenance and soothing and inducing sleep. Sucking is also closely related to looking. Initially the infant is not able to coordinate these two actions; if she looks, she stops sucking. The antismothering reflex enables the infant to keep air passages clear. Several other physiological reflexes related to the newborn's respiration serve the same function. Coughing and sneezing also clear the air passages and lungs, and yawning provides quick intake of air when needed.

In addition to the reflexive actions just described, the motor or muscular development of the infant manifests itself in crying, maintaining posture, and grasping. Crying is a motor response which involves the entire body as well as the vocal apparatus of the infant. The ability to maintain posture and hold the head upright is observed when an infant who is held in a sitting position pulls her head forward to a balanced state. When the infant is held on a caregiver's back without support to the head, she quickly gains control of her head movement. Newborn reaching and grasping begins at 2 weeks of age and ends at 4 weeks of age, to recur at 20 weeks of age. During the first occurrence, the motion is a single reach-grasp pattern; during the later occurrence, two distinct patterns, reaching and grasping, are demonstrated.

As important as an infant's motor abilities are her perceptual abilities. *Perception* may be defined as the ability to identify, discriminate, and interpret sensation (Myklebust, 1964). For the infant, perception begins when she begins to receive information about her environment through the sense organs.

The tactile senses include the skin and body senses, which will be considered separately. The skin senses provide the infant with information about her external environment. Receptors, or nerve cells, in the skin respond to pressure, pain, and temperature as well as to touch, or tactile, sensation. The infant's early reactions to tactile stimulation may be observed in the rooting, grasping, and Babinski reflexes previously described. The sense of touch plays a critical role in the development of the child, not only in her gaining concrete knowledge of the environment but also in establishing a feeling of security and trust between the child and the parent or other caregiver (Erikson, 1956).

Closely related to the skin senses are the body senses: the vestibular sense and the kinesthetic sense. The *vestibular system* supplies feedback to the infant about the balance, movement, and orientation of her body as a whole. The receptors for this system are located in the inner ear. The *kinesthetic system* also provides information about movement through receptors in the muscles, tendons, and joints. These two closely related systems enable the infant to develop basic motor abilities, such as balance and coordination.

Just as the tactile senses are highly developed in the fetus, so are the chemical senses of taste and smell. The newborn has more taste receptors, or taste buds, on the tongue than does an adult. But like adults, infants prefer sweet tastes; sour and salty tastes are next preferred, in that order, and bitter tastes are avoided.

The sense of smell is strong in the newborn, and she is able to locate and discriminate between odors during the first few days of life. While the sense of smell is important to the newborn for identifying odors from her mother and other caregivers, it is probably more important later in life and in combination with other senses for establishing food preferences.

Information acquired through the senses of taste and smell is not utilized by the infant as much as that from the senses of hearing and vision. The human ear is thought to be completely developed at birth so that newborn infants have the ability to distinguish between pitches and the ability to locate the source of the sound. With regard to pitches, infants prefer low-frequency or low-pitched sounds like a whisper. For most infants, the sound of human speech is the most meaningful one in their environment. Although they are able to respond to most sounds from the moment of birth, infants tend to pay more attention to human speech than to any other sounds. Infants as young as 12 hours old have been observed to follow the rhythm of any human language but not of meaningless sounds (Condon & Sander, 1974). In this manner, they seem to be absorbing the form and structure of the language of their particular culture.

Unlike the ear, which is fully developed at birth, the eye and the visual system of the newborn are the least mature of all the senses at birth. For example, the pupil, which controls the amount of light that enters the eye, reacts slowly during the infant's first few days. As a result, the infant is startled by a sudden increase in brightness and closes her eyes. Although newborns do not respond favorably to brightly lighted surroundings, they do fixate, or focus, on the source of light with at least one eye within the first hours after birth. The ability to *fixate* on a light with both eyes as well as to *track* a moving object within the field of vision develops within 3 and 4 days after birth.

Two other aspects of visual perception that may be observed in newborns are *preference for complexity* and *perception of depth.* Newborn infants seem to prefer looking at complex patterns, a preference that appears to be inborn. The ability to recognize the human face, as complex as it is, does not appear to be inborn, but rather has to be learned through experience. Besides a preference for complexity, newborns also seem to possess depth perception, which enables then to reach and grasp objects and thereby learn about the world around them. During the first 6 months of life, the visual-perceptual skills of infants become increasingly well developed and great amounts of learning take place through the visual sense.

The senses and perceptual abilities do not operate in isolation. At least one researcher (Bower, 1974) maintains that the perceptual system is a well-integrated one, even from birth. Using the combination of touch and vision, infants will reach out and grasp objects they see before them. Coordinating hearing and vision, infants will look in the direction of a sound as early as 10 minutes after birth.

In addition to motor and perceptual abilities, mental abilities are developing in the infant. Any learning would be impossible without the ability to focus on selected sections of the environment. Even premature infants seem to have the ability to make an *orienting response* to sensory stimulation. Such a response is considered the beginning of *attention.* The orienting response is present but undeveloped in the newborn and becomes more refined during the first few months of life. Another mental ability that improves with age is that of *habituation* which may be defined as the process whereby humans disregard meaningless stimulation.

Infants' language ability begins its development from the moment of birth. Early language is mostly *reflexive crying* which is replaced by *cooing, gurgling,* and *babbling* as well as alarm crying at about 6 weeks of age. This stage is supplemented by the *lalling* stage in which sounds are echoed by the infant, beginning around 5 or 6 months of age. Several months later the infant imitates the sounds made by others. Finally, speech begins between 12 and 18 months.

As important as the infant's motor, perceptual, and mental development is her psychological and social development. The mother-child attachment serves as a basis for the child's emotional and social growth. Initially, this attachment is nonspecific as long as the infant's needs are met; between 6 and 9 months, however, the infant demonstrates a specific attachment. The food, comfort, protection, and attention provided by the mother are necessary for normal physical, psychological, and social growth.

Postnatal Influences

There are a number of factors that may interfere with the infant's normal postnatal development. Diseases, such as those related to gastrointestinal and respiratory infections, those accompanied by high fever, and those related to malnutrition, may have a lasting effect on the child. Infants whose parents smoke have a high incidence of bronchitis and pneumonia during their first

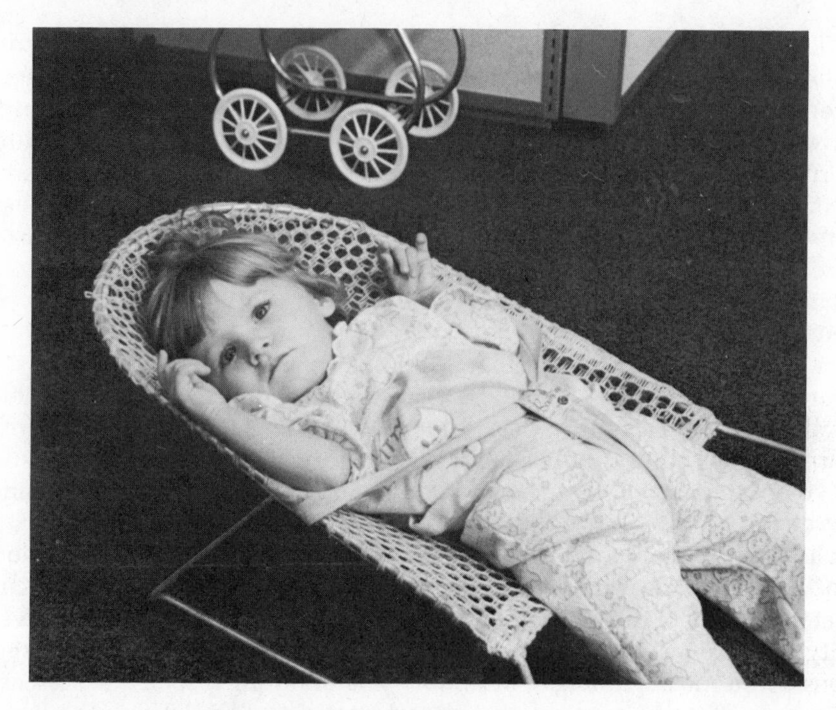

The ability to focus both eyes on a light and track a moving object within the field of vision develops early in life.

year. After respiratory infections, gastrointestinal illnesses are the most common in North American infants.

Diseases such as encephalitis, meningitis or rubella that are accompanied by a high fever may cause permanent brain damage and subsequent mental retardation. Accidents involving physical injury to the head may produce the same result.

Some immunity to disease and illness is transferred from the mother to the child while nursing continues. When the child is weaned, however, her resistance to infection may be lowered until her system builds up its own immunity. At this time, the infant is more susceptible to infections. One such infection, serous otitis media (SOM), may linger as a low-grade infection of the middle ear after the other symptoms of infection have disappeared. Untreated, SOM can cause hearing loss and subsequent speech deficiencies ("Hearing: A Link to IQ," 1976).

Protein-calorie malnutrition often causes death, but for those malnourished children who survive, the result is permanent impairment. Two severe diseases caused by malnutrition are maramus and kwashiorkor. The former is caused by undernutrition due to early weaning from breast milk to inadequate food, and it results in lasting physical abnormalities. The latter disease occurs in infants and children whose diets are low in protein but not so low in calories. Kwashiorkor also results in physical deficiencies.

Perhaps most devastating to the developing infant is the combination of malnutrition and inadequate stimulation in the home. The detrimental effects of malnutrition are compounded by intellectual and emotional deprivation which may permanently harm the child's physical, mental, psychological, and social development.

Even when the factor of malnutrition is not a consideration, stimulation in the child's environment is critical for normal development. A number of studies have found that infants deprived of mental, emotional and social stimulation often exhibit delayed or retarded behavior in many facets of their development (Goldbarb, 1947; Goldenson, 1970).

Even though the influence of genetic factors is predominant at birth, it is gradually balanced by the impact of the environment on the infant's development. The child's physical, perceptual, mental, psychological, and social growth is determined to a large extent by the environment in which she is born and nurtured. The amount and kind of stimulation the child receives from her environment, especially during the first few years of life, may affect her functioning throughout the rest of her life. Infants can achieve their maximum potential with the support of a nurturing, stimulating environment.

Development During Infancy

While the periods leading up to infancy and the preschool years are critical in the child's development, they account for only a portion of the child's growth during the formative years. The description of the child's development during infancy and the preschool years will be less detailed than the foregoing discussion concerning the prenatal, perinatal, and postnatal periods because later chapters are devoted to specific areas of development.

The period of infancy lasts for the first 2 years of the child's life. During this period the child undergoes a gradual transformation from horizontal to vertical posture, from passive to active mobility, and from vocal to verbal expression. The changes in the infant's ability to move appear to be a result of the spurt of brain growth that occurs in the cerebellum during the first year and a half of life. This portion of the brain controls balance and coordination. Creeping, which is the mode of locomotion during the infant's first year, is basically a horizontal posture. In the second year, vertical posture emerges, and the child begins to hold her head and shoulders erect, sit, step, stand, and finally walk at about 15 months of age. After walking is mastered, running and climbing are added to the child's repertoire of locomotion skills. As the environment becomes more accessible, the child's opportunities for stimulation expand tremendously.

The acquisition of language is a passive or receptive process during the infant's first year. As previously mentioned, the newborn infant is able to perceive meaningful human speech patterns. By the end of the first year the child is able to understand specific words such as "no" and the names of family members when spoken to her and to say a few words herself. During the second year, the process of language acquisition changes from passive to active. The child's understanding now extends to whole sentences, and her ability to speak increases to putting two words together. The normal vocabulary of an 18-month-old ranges from 3 to 50 words (Lenneberg, 1967).

Influences on Development During Infancy

The role of the environment is a critical one in the development of the child's locomotion and language competencies. Infants need a chance to practice each of the skills required for walking: raising the chin and chest, sitting with support, sitting alone, standing with support, standing while holding on to furniture, walking with support, standing alone, and finally walking alone. Confinement to a crib or playpen limits a child's opportunity to experience each of these stages. In an extreme example of the harmful effects of environmental deprivation, Spitz (1945) found infants who spent all of their time in cribs in a foundling home still lying on their backs at 10 and 12 months of age and unable even to sit alone.

Such environmental deprivation may also retard language acquisition. A child's competence in language is related to the amount and variety of the mother's or other caregiver's speech to the child. In one study, it was found that 10-month-old infants received more maternal vocalization and had more verbal interaction in middle-class families than in lower-class families (Tulkin & Kagan, 1972). Language delays and deficiencies may have their roots in inadequate and deprived physical, social, and verbal environments.

Development During the Preschool Years

If infancy may be considered as ending at 2 years of age, the preschool years may be regarded as those years from 2 until 5 or 6. Most states in the United States require school attendance no later than age 6. The term *preschool*, nevertheless, may not be entirely appropriate since these 3 or 4 years in a child's life are judged to be an important time for providing the child with basic educational experiences. Many preschoolers are, in fact, enrolled in early childhood development programs, and more children in these preschool years will benefit from early stimulation as the trend toward early childhood–special education continues and expands.

The business of the preschool child is play, through which she is able to develop many facets of her total being like her body, language, emotions, and personality. During the preschool years, physical growth is slower than in infancy; the rate of growth in height and weight decelerates during this period. In contrast, the motor skills mastered by the child during these years increase in complexity. The repertoire of walking, running, and climbing of the 2-year-old is enlarged to include walking tiptoe, jumping, hopping, skipping, skillful climbing, and riding a tricycle. As a result of changes in the distribution of the

Recreational programs provide unique opportunities for learning.

fat tissues and the growth of the muscle and skeletal tissues, the child appears less like a baby and more like a child.

Language development, like motor development, proceeds in an orderly sequence. In the preschool years, the language of the child advances from two-word utterances and a vocabulary of 40 to 50 words at age 2, to complete mastery of the rules of the language (grammar and syntax) and a vocabulary of more than 1,500 words by age 4. After this age, the child simply embellishes this foundation through the addition of more complex and varied linguistic structures and an ever-increasing vocabulary.

The emotional and social development of the child also undergoes some significant changes during the preschool years. In infancy, bonds of attachment were established between the child and her parents, siblings, and other family members. As the preschool child's world expands, she adds other children to her sphere of attachments. The child's interaction with these friends and peers, particularly through play, fosters continued intellectual as well as emotional development.

Personality development in the preschool child is influenced by two closely related factors: the achievement of a sense of autonomy during the first years of the period and the achievement of a sense of initiative from 3 to 6 years of age. The sense of autonomy or independence is based on the sense of trust established during infancy. The roots of initiative may also be observed in infancy in the different activity levels of the infant. Later, at about 4 years of age, the child more fully develops the sense of initiative by demonstrating active, curious, exploratory behavior.

With the development of the sense of autonomy and the sense of initiative, the preschool child is able to become aware of herself as an individual. A clear, positive self-concept is the product of movement experiences and exploration as well as the reactions of the family, significant others, and peers to the individual child.

Influences on Development During the Preschool Years

The normal development of the preschool child may be impeded by factors affecting her physical, linguistic, or emotional and social growth. The rate of physical growth slows down during this period. Slower than average growth in height and weight due to malnutrition may result in retarded physical development. Such growth retardation has been noted in children from low-income families.

The harmful effects of malnutrition as well as of disease and lack of dental care can be minimized by preventive health care. Without proper home cleanliness and safety and immunization against diseases, children may suffer the permanently damaging effects of infection, disease, and accidents. For example, infections accompanied by high fever may result in lasting brain damage; a disease such as polio may cause a child to have a lifelong physical disability; and accidental ingestion of lead-based paints during the preschool years may lead to permanent brain damage and irreversible mental retardation.

The physical development of the preschool child's ear accounts for her susceptibility to middle ear infections. At this point in the child's growth, the Eustachian tube is shorter, wider and more horizontal than in an older child or an adult. Pathogenic organisms from the throat have easy access to the middle ear. As described on page 112, middle ear infection, serous otitis media (SOM), may cause hearing loss as well as language and speech impairments and possible mental retardation.

Language development may also be impeded by an impoverished environment. In comparing children from a middle-class, enriched environment to children from a lower-class, deprived environment, it has been noted that the former group tends to be more advanced in grammar, syntax, vocabulary, and pronunciation than the latter group (Templin, 1957). Whether the lower-class language is actually deficient or merely different from the middle-class language remains in question. What is significant for young children is that the language patterns and styles that are acquired during the formative first 5 or 6 years may affect their later functioning in the school setting. Because language and mental abilities are so closely related, delayed or deficient language skills may retard a child's intellectual and psychological development.

The emotional and social development of the preschool child may suffer lasting damage if the child is not supported by an accepting, loving, nurturing environment. Several conditions may lead to emotional and social disabilities.

One, that of child abuse and neglect, often is the result of the child being unwanted. Aggressive behavior, fear, withdrawal, and low self-concept are often characteristics of the abused and neglected child. Just as likely to occur are brain damage and other physical impairments.

Another condition resulting in severe intellectual as well as emotional and social deficiencies is institutionalization of young children. Children observed in institutions devoid of affection and stimulation suffered devastating harm. Many 1-year-olds could not sit alone or creep, many 2-year-olds could not walk, and most of them had IQs around 50 (100 is average) (Dennis, 1973). The same kind of lack of stimulation can occur in the home as well. Several studies have shown that there is a direct relationship between the child's intellectual and social competence and the mother's competence and the environment she provides for the child (Ainsworth, 1973).

Whether the source of deprivation is abuse, neglect, institutionalization, or an impoverished home, one of the most apparent consequences is a negative self-concept on the part of the child. Low self-esteem has a negative, pervasive effect on all aspects of the child's development. The resulting lack of competency may be permanently disabling to the individual.

Summary

This chapter has presented a discussion of the development of the young child from conception, through the prenatal, perinatal, and postnatal periods, infancy, and the preschool years. Influences on the child during each of these stages of development were also discussed. Factors that may affect the child's growth include nutrition, toxic agents, radiation, infections, blood incompatibilities, stress, and other influences during the prenatal period; anoxia, prematurity, and low birth weight during the perinatal period; and diseases, infections, malnutrition, accidents, child abuse, and the environment during the postnatal period and early childhood. The focus of the chapter has been on normal growth and development as well as on the various ways in which this typical progression may be impeded to the extent that young children would require special educational services to maximize their potential to the fullest.

REFERENCES

Abraham, S., Lowenstein, F. W., & Johnson, C. L. *Preliminary findings of the first health and nutrition examination survey, United States, 1971–1972: Dietary intake and biochemical findings* (DHEW Publication No. (HRA) 74-1219-1). Washington, D.C.: U.S. Government Printing Office, 1974.

Ainsworth, M. D. S. The development of infant-mother attachment. In B. M. Caldwell & H. N. Ricciuti (Eds.), *Review of child development research* (Vol. 3). Chicago: University of Chicago Press, 1973.

Alcohol and the fetus. *Time,* June 13, 1977, p. 56.

Belmont, L., & Marolla, F. A. Birth order, family size and intelligence. *Science,* 1973, **104,** 1096–1101.

Berges, M., Lezine, E., Harrison, A., & Boisselier, F. The "syndrome of the post-premature child": A study of its significance (Part II). *Early Child Development and Care,* 1973, **2,** 61–94.

Bower, T. G. R. *Development in infancy.* San Francisco: W. H. Freeman & Co., Publishers, 1974.

Condon, W. S., & Sander, L. W. Neonate movement is synchronized with adult speech: interactional participation and language acquisition. *Science,* 1974, **183,** 99–101.

Coursin, D. B. Maternal nutrition and the offspring's development. *Nutrition Today,* 1973, **8**(2), 12–18.

Dennis, W. *Children of the crèche.* New York: Meredith Corp., 1973.

Erikson, E. H. The problem of ego identity. *Journal of the American Psychoanalytic Association,* 1956, **4,** 56–121.

Feinbloom, P. I. Prematurity. In J. H. Durston (Ed.), *Pregnancy, birth and the newborn baby.* Boston: Delacorte Press/Seymore Lawrence, 1972.

Goldbarb, W. Effects of psychological deprivation in infancy and subsequent stimulation. *American Journal of Psychiatry,* 1947, **102,** 18–33.

Goldenson, R. M. Prenatal development. *The encyclopedia of human development.* New York: Doubleday, 1970.

Hearing: A link to IQ? *Newsweek,* June 14, 1976, p. 97.

Holley, W. L., Rosenbaum, A. L., & Churchill, J. A. Effects of rapid succession of pregnancy. In *Perinatal factors affecting human development.* Pan Am Health Organization, Pan Am Sanitary Bureau, Regional Office of World Health Organization, 1969, p. 41–45.

Illsley, R. The sociological study of reproduction and its outcome. In S. A. Richardson & A. F. Guttmacher (Eds.), *Childbearing—its social and psychological aspects.* Baltimore: Williams & Wilkins Co., 1967.

Jones, K. L., & Smith, D. W. Recognition of the fetal alcohol syndrome in early infancy. *The Lancet,* 1973, **2**(2), 999–1001.

Kappelman, M. M. Prenatal and perinatal factors which influence learning. In J. Hellmuth (Ed.), *Exceptional infant: Studies in abnormalities* (Vol. 2). New York: Brunner/Mazel, 1971.

Katchadourian, H. A., & Lunde, D. T. *Fundamentals of human sexuality.* New York: Holt, Rinehart & Winston, 1975.

Kochupillai, N., Verna, I. C., Grewal, M. S., & Ramalingaswami, V. Down's syndrome and related abnormalities in an area of high background radiation in coastal Kerala. *Nature,* 1976, **262,** 60–61.

Lenneberg, E. H. *Biological foundations of language.* New York: John Wiley & Sons, 1967.

A man's drinking may harm his offspring. *Science News,* 1975, **107**(8), 116.

Myklebust, H. R. Learning disorders: Psychoneurological disturbances in childhood. *Rehabilitation Literature,* 1964, **25,** 354–359.

Pasamanick, B., & Knobloch, H. Epidemiologic studies on the complication of pregnancy and the birth process. In S. Harrison (Ed.), *Childhood psychopathology.* New York: International Universities Press, 1972.

Sharma, T. Marijuana: Recent research and findings, 1972. *Texas Medicine,* 1972, **68**(10), 109–110.

Spitz, R. A. Hospitalism: An inquiry into the genesis of psychiatric conditions in early childhood. *Psychoanalytic Study of the Child,* 1945, **1,** 53–74.

Templin, M. C. *Certain language skills in children.* Minneapolis: University of Minnesota Press, 1957.

Tulkin, S. R., & Kagan, J. Mother-child interaction in the first year of life. *Child Development,* 1972, **43**, 31–41.

Vore, D. A. Prenatal nutrition and postnatal intellectual development. *Merrill-Palmer Quarterly,* 1973, **19**, 253–260.

5

Motor Skills

Evidence that the very young child is learning often appears in his movements. The baby's ability to raise his head, to turn over, to sit up, to stand, to walk are all noted accomplishments, visible signs of progress from helplessness toward independence. On the other hand, the absence of such skills, at the time they are expected, causes alarm.

This chapter reviews some of the basic knowledge about normal motor skill development and its relationship to the young child with special needs; procedures for assessing and evaluating motor skills of young children; and instructional techniques and adaptive equipment designed to facilitate motor skills development.

The intention is not to supply detailed coverage of motor development, but instead to emphasize information directly related to the young handicapped child's acquisition of motor skills. The purpose of this chapter is to guide professionals in decision making and to help them choose wisely among procedures and equipment designed to facilitate the development of motor skills.

Motor, in the context of development, means muscular movement. Motor skills are learned in a process called motor learning. Contrasted with other types of behavior, the primary characteristic of motor learning is movement. Motor *skills* refer to levels of competence in carrying out certain motor behaviors or tasks (Whiting, 1975). *Motor development* is a global term which refers to the sequence and rate at which the child acquires motor skills and thereby

---

Major contributions of two professionals were combined with additional information to form this chapter. *David E. Herr* provided the information on the many facets of motor development. *Roberta L. Goodwyn* provided the portion on adapted equipment.

learns to use and control his body. The terms *psychomotor, perceptual motor,* and *sensorimotor* are used by scholars in various disciplines, but all refer to motor behavior (Singer, 1975).

The Importance of Motor Skill Development

Motor learning, as with learning in all other skill areas, is part of the person's total development. While it is true that the skill areas are synergetically related, do not develop in isolation, and are indeed inseparable, a separate study of each area can promote sound educational planning and practices.

Few forms of human behavior do not involve some type of movement, a fact noted by Malpass (1963) who emphasized the importance of motor skills development. Mobility is one biological criterion of life itself. The person who is unable to perform motor skills has great difficulty participating in educational programs and becoming independent (p. 602).

The contributions of motor development to the child's life include: (1) good health, (2) emotional catharsis (stability), (3) independence, (4) self-entertainment, (5) socialization, and (6) self-concept (Hurlock, 1972, p. 133). It is known that certain movements help to make bones, muscles, and joints stronger. Training can develop agility, balance, and strength (Baumgartner, 1971).

Correlation studies of intellect and movement have indicated that there is a motor base to intellect and have concluded that participation in physical training programs will improve not only perceptual and motor skills but other abilities as well, most notably, academic performance (Ismail & Gruber, 1968). However, Cratty believes that evidence does not support the hypothesis that motor ability change is inevitably accompanied by change in other traits. There are indications, however, that if "started early enough and contained in a highly individualized program, appropriate movement activities offer promise in the general remediation of developmental lag" (1972, p. 243).

Hammill and Bartel (1975), in presenting the perceptual-motor approaches of Barsch, Frostig, Getman, and Kephart, warned their readers that even though these teaching systems are widely used in schools, they are still experimental, nonvalidated techniques (p. 216). On the other hand, Hallahan and Cruickshank (1973), after reviewing the literature pertaining to perceptual-motor training in depth, concluded it is not yet known if perceptual-motor training deserves or does not deserve approval. They felt that systematic, empirical investigation of the theories and procedures had not been accomplished (p. 216).

From any point of view, it seems that improvements in motor skills resulting from perceptual-motor skill training would be considered sufficient rewards. As long as the development of motor skill proficiency is the overriding aim of motor training programs, evaluation of the programs and children's achievement should be based on the extent to which the aim has been accomplished. Moreover, since most forms of human behavior can be positively or negatively affected by numerous variables, it is equivocal whether improvement in motor skills is exclusively responsible for improvement in other behaviors. Although it is very likely that improvement in self-concept, peer relationships, academic achievement, and other behaviors accompany improvement in motor skill training (or perceptual-motor training), it is difficult, if not impossible, to isolate the specific cause and effect.

For the child with learning problems, achievement in motor areas may be his only avenue to feelings of success. It has been said that a genius can afford to be a "motor moron," but a person whose functional IQ measures 50 cannot (Stevens & Heber, 1964). In addition to attaining a reasonable degree of social competence, improved fitness and motor ability may lift one's level of aspiration (p. 37).

Motor Skill Development

Most attempts to classify motor skills result in either two or three classifications: gross motor skills, fine motor skills and, often, visual motor skills. *Gross motor skills* refer to tasks which involve contractions and use of the large muscles of the neck, trunk of the body, arms, and legs. The abilities to lift the head, creep, crawl, roll, walk, run, jump, and skip are all gross motor skills. In gross motor activity, the whole body may be in movement.

Fine motor skills are more precise movements of the small muscles in the lips, tongue, eyes, hands, and feet. Fine motor skills include grasping, releasing, pinching, sucking, and blinking.

Visual motor skills refer to those tasks which are said to require eye-hand coordination such as placing pegs in holes, stringing beads, and using scissors. In light of the fact that visually handicapped children learn many such tasks, it is felt that a more accurate term would be *perceptual motor activities* or simply *motor coordination,* teams of muscles working together and monitored by sensory perceptions.

It is questionable, in fact, that this two- or three-dimensional classification system is realistic. According to Hallahan and Kauffman (1976), "most attempts to place a movement into a specific category based on the muscles involved will prove unsatisfactory" (p. 124) since many tasks, particularly those of a somewhat complex nature (e.g., running, picking up toys, drinking liquid from a cup), involve large and small muscles and must be monitored by sensory information as well.

From a number of studies involving thousands of subjects asked to perform up to 200 different motor tasks, Fleishman (1964) defined 20 basic skill areas which appear to constitute the motor skill domain or field. He separated them into psychomotor abilities and physical proficiencies.

Psychomotor Abilities

1. Control Precision: Fine, highly controlled muscular adjustments, primarily where larger muscles are involved (p. 17).
2. Multilimb Coordination: Simultaneous coordination of either both hands, both feet, or hand and foot.

3. Response Orientation: Ability to make appropriate movement in response to a stimulus, especially under conditions which demand speed (p. 19).
4. Reaction Time: Speed with which the individual is able to respond to a stimulus when it appears (p. 19).
5. Speed of Arm Movement: Speed with which an individual can make a gross, discrete arm movement where accuracy is not a requirement (p. 21).
6. Rate Control: Continuous anticipatory motor adjustments relative to changes in speed and direction of a continuously moving target or object (p. 21).
7. Manual Dexterity: Manipulation of fairly large objects under speed conditions (p. 23).
8. Arm-Hand Steadiness: Ability to make precise arm-hand positioning movements where strength and speed are minimized; the steadiness with which such movements are made (p. 24).
9. Finger Dexterity: Ability to make skillful, controlled manipulations of tiny objects involving, primarily, the fingers (p. 24).
10. Arm-Hand Steadiness: Ability to make precise arm-hand positioning movements where strength and speed are minimized (p. 24).
11. Wrist-Finger Speed: Speed with which the wrist and finger dexterity are coordinated.
12. Aiming: Similar to eye-hand coordination.

Physical Proficiencies

1. Explosive Strength: Ability to mobilize one's energy effectively in making single or repeated movements requiring a maximum expenditure of force (p. 99). Skills such as the broad jump, softball throw, and shuttle run require this type of strength.
2. Extend Flexibility: Ability to flex or stretch the trunk and back muscles as far as possible in either a forward, sideways, or backward direction (p. 99). Toe touching, abdominal stretch, and twist and touch exercises require this ability.
3. Dynamic Flexibility: Ability to make repeated, rapid, flexing movements (p. 99). Activities that require resiliency of the muscles such as repeated bending or twisting depend upon this ability.
4. Gross Body Equilibrium: Ability of an individual to maintain total body equilibrium, despite forces pulling him off balance, where he has to depend mainly on nonvisual (e.g., vestibular and kinesthetic) cues (p. 99).
5. Balance with Visual Cues: Ability to maintain body balance, when visual cues are available (p. 99).
6. Speed of Limb Movement: Speed with which an individual can make rapid movements (throwing, adjusting) of arms or legs, when accuracy and force requirements are not involved (p. 99).
7. Dynamic Strength: Continuous and repeated use of muscular force, particularly in the arms, as required in pull-ups and push-ups.

8. Static Strength: Capacity to apply force against an immovable object (dynamometers); the capacity to lift or push weights with the arm or feet (p. 65).

While the norms developed on these abilities and proficiencies have been derived from adults and children over 12, a knowledge of them should be useful for persons working with young, motor-handicapped children. The skill and proficiency areas described by Fleishman provide a realistic picture of the expansiveness of the motor skill domain. They also narrow the focal point of programs aimed at developing motor skills in children.

Motor skill development involves extremely complex interaction between a number of attributes or processes which are unique to each individual. While no two individuals are endowed with the same potential, and no two individuals acquire motor skills in exactly the same manner, each person's motor skill development is strongly influenced by three variables: biological and anatomical attributes, growth and maturation processes, and environmental factors. These variables are presented briefly with reference to handicapping conditions found in young children.

Biological and Anatomical Attributes

The inherited biological and anatomical attributes possessed by the child at birth constitute the support system for motor skill development. These attributes are unique to each child and are dependent on genetic transmission and prenatal development. Ausubel (1958) states, "Contrary to popular belief, individual differences in the emergence of locomotor abilities are not determined by weight or body build but by genetic factors concerned with their development" (p. 508). The particular combination of genes transmitted to the child from his parents plays a dominant role in determining the child's abilities. Thus, genetic endowment is important because it establishes the basic parameters within which subsequent motor development can take place. Genetic errors, for example, such as those resulting in PKU, mongolism and cystic fibrosis, place drastic limitations on the motor potential of afflicted children. On the other hand, the skill development of the world's greatest athletes had its beginning in genetic transmission.

Factors other than genetic transmission and inheritance may have a severe impact on the child's biological and anatomical potentialities before, during, or after birth. The nutrition and general health and physical condition of the mother during pregnancy, for example, are directly related to the condition of the child at birth. Other conditions, including anoxia, prematurity, birth injury, and traumas after birth (neurological, physiological, and biological) also can have a limiting effect on motor skill development.

Growth and Maturation

During the first six years of life, the body structure of the child grows and develops with amazing rapidity. The average boy, for example, grows in length

Motor development refers to the sequence and rate at which a child acquires motor skills and thereby learns to use and control his body.

from 19½ inches to 33¾ inches in the first two years of life and from 7½ pounds to 27¾ pounds in the same period of time. By 5½ years of age, the same child will grow almost a foot and weigh over 17 pounds (Watson & Lowrey, 1967).

The motor skills the child is capable of performing increase at a similar pace. In the first 6 years of life, the motor activities of the infant expand from a limited number of primitive reflexive movements to the development, but not refinement, of most of the skills which characterize adults. By the age of 16, most children have developed motor skills as well as they will in their lifetime.

Attempts to teach the child motor skills before his muscles and nervous system have matured to a state of readiness will be wasted effort. "The development of body control parallels the development of the motor area of the brain. Skilled movements cannot be mastered until the muscular mechanism of the child matures" (Hurlock, 1972, p. 134).

Certain principles of human growth and development characterize the growth and maturation of motor skills. It must be noted, however, that the following principles are generalizations which apply to most developing children; exceptions exist within a substantial number of children.

Developmental Direction. Two major principles relate to developmental direction. The first, cephalocaudal, refers to the fact that motor development proceeds from head to foot. At birth the head of the newborn is substantially larger and approximates the head of an adult more closely than the other bodily

Table 1

Sequence of Motor Development

Head Region	*Arms and Hands*
▪ Ocular pursuit movements: 4 weeks	▪ Defensive movements: 2 weeks
▪ "Social" smiles (in response to another's smile): 3 months	▪ Thumb-sucking: 1 month
▪ Eye coordination: 4 months	▪ Reach and grasp: 4 months
▪ Holding the head up: In a prone position: 1 month In a sitting position: 4 months	▪ Grasp and hold: 5 months
	▪ Picking up object with opposed thumb: 8 months
Trunk Region	*Legs and Feet*
▪ Turning: From side to back: 2 months From back to side: 4 months Complete: 6 months	▪ Hitching (backward movement in sitting position): 6 months
▪ Sitting: Pulls to sitting position: 4 months With support: 5 months Without support: 9 months	▪ Crawling (prone body pulled by arms and leg kicks): 7 months
▪ Organs of elimination: Bowel control: 6 months Bladder control: 15 months	▪ Creeping: On hands and knees: 9 months On all fours: 10 months
	▪ Standing: With support: 8 months Without support: 11 months
	▪ Walking: With support: 11 months Without support: 13 months

Note: From *Child Development* by E. Hurlock. Copyright 1972 by McGraw-Hill Book Company. Used with permission of McGraw-Hill Book Company.

structures. Both body and motor skill development proceed downward in the following order: neck, arms, chest, back, legs. As McCandless (1961) points out, this sequence is not immutable, and notable exceptions do exist. He provides two examples: the growth of a tail during the fifth and sixth week of fetal life and the manipulations of the feet during the first six months of life.

The proximodistal principle indicates that growth and development tend to proceed from the midline or axis of the body to the outer extremities. The first movements of the arm, for example, consist of relatively gross movements involving mostly the shoulder muscles. Next, movements involving the elbow, then the wrist, and finally the finger muscles are used, developed, and refined by the child.

Developmental Sequence. In the main, motor skill development occurs in a fairly rigidly defined developmental sequence. Due to the work of many researchers in the early 1930s, including Gesell and his associates, relatively definitive sequences have been outlined and norms established with which the development of individual children can be compared. Such normative standards are useful for ascertaining the current development of a child in comparison to others his age since most children tend to reach the same motor skill milestones at approximately the same age.

When using normative data to make such comparisons, however, it is important to consider the range of variability around the average or mean. Among children who are developing normally, some will develop faster than others; some will be slower. However, all will be within the normal range.

Rate Variations. Closely related to developmental sequence is the rate at which milestones are being accomplished. Rates of development vary considerably not only between individuals but also within an individual. No two human beings develop at exactly the same pace or reach the various developmental stages at precisely the same time. According to Gesell and Ilg (1943) even identical twins do not grow up in just the same way. They are individuals from the moment of birth. Developmental rates within individuals are also variable. That is, children often have spurts of growth which are followed by plateaus in maturation. Thus, variability is the rule rather than the exception and should be considered as a characteristic of normal maturation, except in the cases where significant variability exists.

Sequence and rate of motor development follow predictable patterns for most children. Among some handicapped children significant divergence in both sequence and rate can be found. While mentally retarded youngsters tend to follow the same sequence in acquiring motor skills as their normal peers, the rate of development is significantly slower for some. It is the significantly slower rate of acquiring skills that characterizes the motor development of the developmentally delayed. Many children with learning disabilities never achieve motor skills in the usual sequence. The sequence of skill acquisition and the rate of development are markedly different for some children with cerebral palsy. The rate of acquiring motor skills among the blind may be slower, not because of motor impairments but because their visual impairment denies them a concept of space. Other handicapping conditions may affect the sequence and rate of skill development, but the problems are individual; no pattern seems to characterize the hearing impaired, the multiply handicapped, or the emotionally disturbed.

Skill Refinement. Generally two principles of maturation govern the manner in which skills become refined. Most motor skills tend to mature or develop from general to specific or from gross movement to skill refinement. That is, generally smaller and more specific movements (picking up objects) develop out of gross movement patterns (waving arms). However, McCandless (1961) has indicated that motor development from the specific to the general does occur and that the processes complement each other (p. 280).

Similarly, the second principle indicates that motor skill development involves the sequential building of skills; that is, new skills develop from previously developed skills. For example, the gross motor skill of walking is built from, and is a refinement of, creeping, crawling, and standing.

FIGURE 1. The development of posture and locomotion in infants.

Note: From "The First Two Years: A Study of Twenty-five Babies" by Mary M. Shirley. *Institute of Child Welfare Monograph No. 7.* Minneapolis: University of Minnesota Press. © Copyright 1933, renewed 1961 by the University of Minnesota. By permission.

Environmental Variables

While maturation establishes the sequence of motor skill development, the quality and rate of development can be enhanced or impeded by environmental factors. Genetic and maturational processes provide the potential for motor skill development while environmental variables, such as experience and learning, determine how well the child uses that potential. Once the body has matured to the extent necessary for the development of particular motor skills, a number of environmental variables greatly influence the rate and extent of their development. Most notable among these variables appear to be the child's opportunities for practice; his motive or incentive, which is greatly influenced by the culture; his attitudes toward motor tasks; and the attitudes of others toward the child as well as their methods of interactions with him. While these factors are discussed separately below, it is important to note that they are not mutually exclusive; in fact, they are complexly interwoven and interrelated.

Culture. The culture in which a child is reared plays an important role in shaping his motor skill behavior. According to Fleishman (1964), cultural forces often prescribe what shall be learned and at what age. Children reared in different cultures tend to develop different patterns of basic abilities. Different cultures tend to differentially value, extoll, and reinforce virtues within their populace; thus, persons striving to be valued, extolled, and reinforced focus on the development of skills and abilities valued by the culture. Similarly different subcultures, including families, differentially reinforce, extoll, and value less ostentatious forms of human behavior. Child-rearing practices which vary among cultures also tend to account for differing motor skill development and proficiency among cultures.

Child's Attitudes Toward Motor Skills. Ausubel (1958) has avouched that, in addition to genetic factors, other "such temperamental characteristics as eagerness, persistence, and curiosity" account for "individual differences in the emergence of locomotor abilities" (p. 508). That is, our attitudes, feelings, likes, and dislikes can greatly influence our performance, since we tend to do well, or at least, strive to do well, in those tasks from which we derive pleasure, "good feelings," self-satisfaction, and reinforcement.

The development of attitudes, feelings, likes, and dislikes is extremely complicated, yet it appears that reinforcement or lack of reinforcement plays a substantial role in their development. Most children develop a somewhat positive attitude toward motor skill activities. They sense a feeling of accomplishment or other forms of pleasure in motor tasks, and thus, continue to engage in such activities. However, for others, motor skill activities are the source of frustration and anxiety resulting in the failure cycle, that is, failure begets failure. As a result, they develop negative attitudes toward the activities. Soon the child refuses to work on motor skill development and avoids motor activity. Consequently, few new skills develop, and the child becomes less proficient in performing previously acquired ones.

Attitudes of Others and Their Interactions with the Child. Persons associated with the motor skill activity in which the child engages influence his level of interest and the extent of participation. Reactions to the child's performance serve as reinforcement or punishment for the child and thus help to shape his attitudes toward his own abilities and toward motor skills in general. As with other forms of human behavior, praise, approval, or other positive reactions to his motor skills from persons near the child tend to create positive feelings and encourage him to participate in future activities. Negative reactions usually have the opposite effect. Moreover, the willingness and eagerness of the child's parents and other persons to play with the child or otherwise involve themselves with the child in motor activities can have a reinforcing effect.

Similarly, biases of persons toward children who have been labeled mentally retarded, epileptic, learning disabled, and so forth, will affect the performance of these children and bring on what is called the self-fulfilling prophecy effect. This "involves the transmission of expectancy of the subject (children) in such a way that alters the normal functioning of the subject" (Gephart & Antonoplus, 1969, p. 580). For example, the expectation that a child's motor achievement will be low because he is mentally retarded is reflected in actions toward the child. If little is expected, the child obligingly achieves at a low level. His performance is judged acceptable because not much was expected. In this way a mentally retarded child with normally developing motor skills can be shaped into a "motor moron" by the action of teachers, parents, and others who hold low expectations.

Unreasonably high expectations can be so defeating to the child that he learns to avoid the cause of his failure. If motor activity is the source of trouble, the young child with learning problems may be denied his only avenue to feelings of success.

Another effect of persons on the motor skill development of children is that of modeling. Children tend to copy (model) the behaviors and actions of persons who are especially significant to them. It is possible that a wide range of motor behaviors (e.g., eating habits, walking techniques) develop from modeling. Children tend to model both the idiosyncratic and refined behaviors of persons important to them. Thus, some motor skill deficiencies may be traced back to the imitation of an inappropriate model.

Motor Skill Characteristics of Young Children with Special Needs

The range and variability of motor skill deficiencies found among young handicapped children are great. Likewise, within each subgroup of this population, extremes in range and variability are evident. Generally, a 5-year-old child with epilepsy is more capable of performing most motor skills than the 5-year-old mentally retarded child; yet some 5-year-old retarded children can outperform some 5-year-old children with epilepsy. Just because motor skill deficiencies are not unusual characteristics among the subpopulations of handicapped children, there is no reason to assume that all handicapped youngsters lack motor skills potential or, in fact, have any motor disability.

This section describes the general characteristics of different handicapping conditions found in young children. While it is recognized that each child's motor skill deficiencies may be caused by any one or more of the variables previously discussed, the predominant etiology of each condition is discussed with only minor mention of other sources of disabilities. Many of the motor skill deficiencies characteristic of individual children may have their roots in a vast number of complex variables.

Cerebral Palsy. Motor disorders are the most predominant characteristics of cerebral palsy. The nature of these disorders vary considerably from child to child and between the various types of cerebral palsy. Some children afflicted by cerebral palsy have only minimal muscular incoordination; others have almost total loss of muscular control. As outlined by Smith and Neisworth (1975), the major motor disorders found in each of the types of cerebral palsy are the following:

1. *Spasticity:* "Loss of control of the voluntary muscles . . . flexor and extensor muscles contract simultaneously . . . movements are jerky and poorly coordinated . . . hypertonicity" (pp. 378–379).
2. *Athetosis:* "Jerky, involuntary, slow, irregular and twisting movements . . . involuntary movements occur when deliberate, voluntary exertion is made . . . major problems occur most frequently in the hands, then in lips and tongue, and least often in the feet" (p. 378).
3. *Ataxia:* "Characterized by disturbance of balance . . . movements are awkward . . . (in walking) individual appears to be dizzy . . . falls easily" (p. 378).
4. *Tremor:* "Characterized by involuntary movement (small and rhythmic) of flexor and extensor muscles" (p. 378).
5. *Rigidity:* "The limbs are rigid and hard to bend . . . rigidity is constant in some instances, intermittent in others . . . able to perform only slow movements" (p. 378).

Moreover, children with cerebral palsy are characterized by the number of extremities involved: monoplegia (one limb), paraplegia (both legs), diplegia (primary involvement in both legs, and slight affliction in the arms), hemiplegia (arm and leg on same side are afflicted), triplegia (three limbs affected), and quadraplegia (involvement of all four limbs).

A secondary problem common to many cerebral palsied youngsters is the effect of not using some muscles on other muscles that were not originally afflicted by the disorder. Such muscles are likely to atrophy or become weakened through disuse; the result is more serious motor skill deficiency.

Mental Retardation. Studies of retarded children's motor skill development indicate that they are inferior in motor proficiency when compared to their normal peers (Kirk, 1972, p. 205). Following a review of the literature pertaining to motor skills development among the mentally retarded, Malpass (1963) concluded that, as a group, they demonstrated less motor competence in tasks requiring precise movements and reactions as well as those requiring complex skills and motor coordination. Blake's conclusions were expressed along similar lines (1976). Singer (1972) indicated that the mentally retarded have difficulty learning manual skills and that generally their motor attributes are both qualitatively and quantitatively different from the same trait patterns in normal children.

Several other related and important conclusions can be made from research pertaining to the motor skill development and proficiency of the mentally retarded. First, there is a definite relationship between the age and perfor-

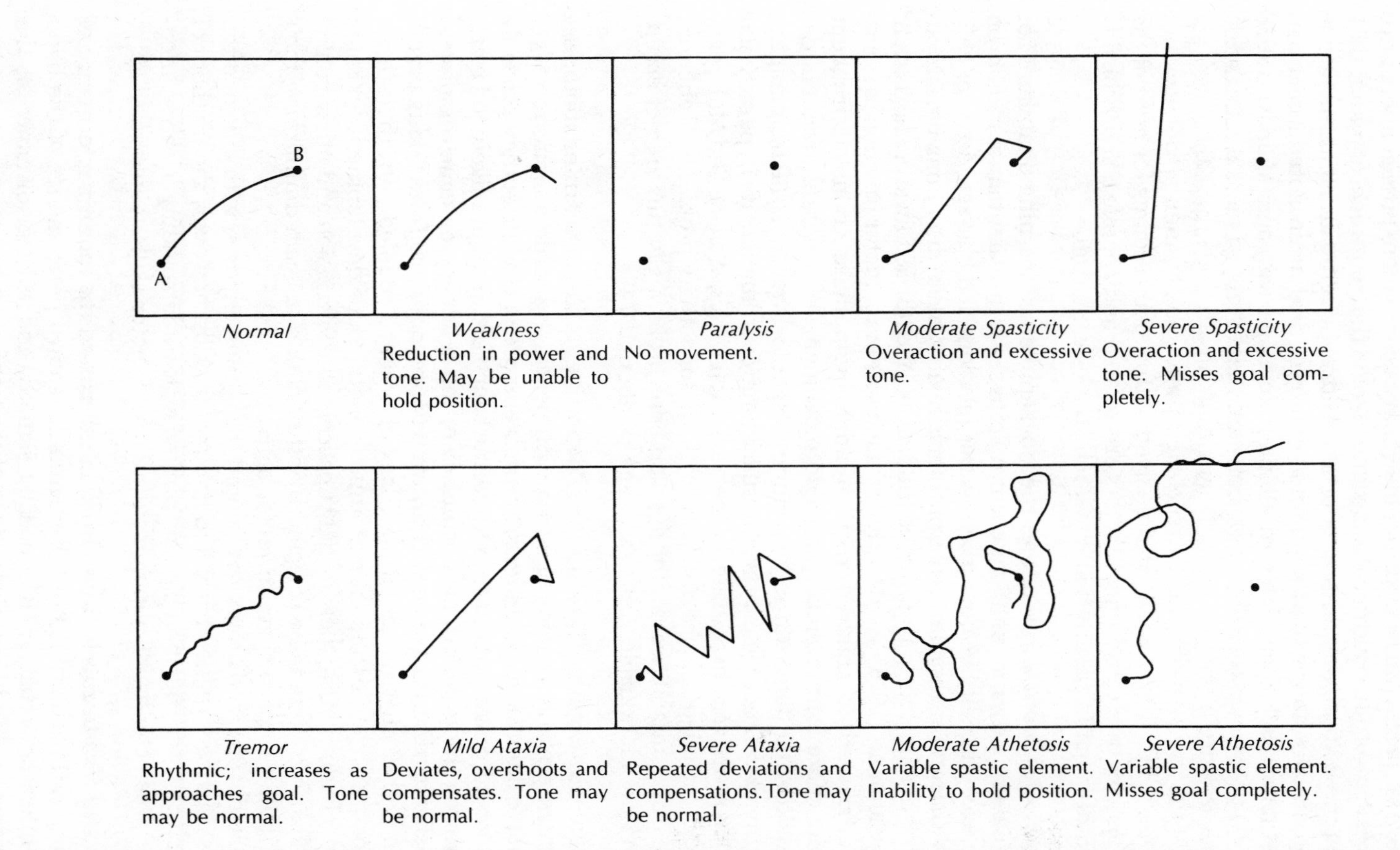

FIGURE 2. Diagrammatic representation of a single movement from position A (point of origin) to position B (goal) under various conditions of neuromotor control.

Note: From *Developmental Diagnosis* by H. Knobloch and B. Pasamanick. Hagerstown, Md.: Harper & Row, 1972. © Copyright 1972 by Harper & Row. Reprinted by permission.

mance. As retarded children grow older, they become more proficient in motor skills, just as other children do. Second, while the sequence of motor skill development approximates that of other children, discrepancies in the rate of growth, usually slower than for normal children, have been noted as early as infancy (Share & French, 1974) and tend to increase with age (Malpass, 1963). Finally, a definite relationship exists between the severity of mental retardation and the severity of motor skill deficiencies (Malpass, 1963, p. 626).

The etiology of motor skills deficiencies and developmental delay is not clear-cut. While it is probable that delayed maturation accounts for most of the discrepancies, the cause–effect factors are related and complex, and probably more individual in nature than research studies can assume.

Learning Disabilities. Whether the label applied is "learning disabilities" or "minimal brain dysfunction," motor problems seem prevalent among children in this exceptionality. Among the most often identified characteristics of children with learning disabilities are problems related to: (1) directionality, laterality, and dominance; (2) motor coordination; and (3) self-awareness (Fallen, 1970). Clements (1971) listed the following disorders of motor function as symptoms attributed to children with minimal brain dysfunction: (1) frequent athetoid, choreiform, tremulus, or rigid movements of hands; (2) frequent delayed motor milestones; (3) general clumsiness or awkwardness; (4) frequent tics and grimaces; (5) poor fine or gross visual-motor coordination; (6) hyperactivity; and (7) hypoactivity. In addition to these characteristics, Wallace and McLoughlin (1975) included balance and rhythm as motor activity problems of children with learning disabilities. Motor development problems in this area of exceptionality are identifiable at an early age (Weber, 1974).

Behavior Disorders. The absence of definitive studies concerning motor development problems among children with behavior disorders seems to reflect several pertinent facts. One, if motor problems are in evidence, they probably do not have the same etiology as the disturbance but are more likely to be one of many resulting behaviors. For instance, the tendency of some youngsters with behavior disorders to be withdrawn will prevent them from taking part in play and other physical activities. A lack of practice coupled with their disregard for social reinforcement can impede motor skills development for some of these children. Also, their socially unacceptable aggression and other behaviors may cause them to be rejected by other children, again diminishing their opportunities to participate in motor activities.

Rimland (1964) and others have noted that young children with autism often possess relatively refined gross and fine motor skills; however, the plethora of research on this population has contributed little understanding of the relationship between the handicapping condition and motor skills acquisition.

Visually Handicapped. Kirk (1972) has discussed the motor performance of the blind and partially sighted. Research has shown performance of the blind to be inferior to that of the partially sighted, and the performance of the partially sighted to be inferior to that of the normal child. One may speculate that if the blind and partially sighted enjoyed equal opportunities as their sighted peers to imitate the motor skills of others, to ride vehicles and play games, motor problems among this group would be related to deficits other than visual impairment.

Generalizations concerning the motor development of the blind are unwarranted. Conflicting evidence concerning motor skills development among young blind children has been presented. Other reports have reported differences in the motor skills of those blind from birth and those who acquire blindness at a later time. If the blind child also has a hearing impairment, the absence of auditory clues negatively affects his motor performance (p. 307).

Other Handicapping Conditions. Motor development among young children with speech handicaps and hearing impairments has received little attention in the professional literature. Moores (1976) indicated that the communication problems of the deaf set extreme limits on opportunities to fully interact and manipulate the environment in meaningful ways. If compensatory means of communication are not provided, "the impairment leads to impoverished communication skills that set limits on all aspects of his development" (p. 92). The same implications exist for the young child with a severe speech handicap.

Assessment and Evaluation of Motor Skills

Assessment and evaluation of motor development problems are the shared responsibilities of the medical and allied health professions. While the parents and professionals working with the child can supply information which may not be available from other sources, theirs is a facilitating role in the assessment and evaluation of motor skills deficiencies in young children.

Assessment of motor development is the process of determining the level of the child's performance through the administration of one or a group of instruments and the observations of the examiner. *Evaluation* applies to the interpretation of the test results with consideration for the quality of the child's performance, the limitations of the instrument, the child's ability to understand what is expected, and other testing conditions. Evaluation of the child's motor development must also take into account his developmental and medical history and other personal information (Pyfer, 1976).

When the medical professionals have completed the neurological and neuromuscular evaluations of the child, psychologists, psychiatrists, and educators specially trained to administer motor development instruments aid in the assessment and evaluation process. The most commonly used instruments for the assessment of motor development include:

1. *The Bayley Scales of Infant Development* (Bayley, 1969). This is an individually administered test for children between the ages of 2 months and 30 months. The motor development portion of the test assesses the degree of body control, coordination of the large muscles, and the finer manipulatory skills of the hands and fingers. As with other motor tests,

the child's current level of functioning is established so that the extent of any deviation from normal expectancy can be determined.

2. *The Bruininks-Oseretsky Test of Motor Proficiency* (Bruininks, 1977). This test is designed for use with children ages 4 through 18. It assesses eight areas of motor performance through an individually administered procedure. The subtests include: running speed and agility, balance, bilateral coordination, strength, upper limb coordination, response speed, visual-motor control, and upper limb speed and dexterity. A short form is available for a brief survey of motor proficiency and a long form provides for comprehensive assessment of motor development.
3. *The Denver Developmental Screening Test* (Frankenburg & Dodds, 1969). This individual test was designed for use in depicting slow development in children from birth to 6 years of age. Of the four sections, two assess motor skills. The fine motor section, which consists of 30 items, assesses "the child's ability to see and use his hands, to pick up objects and draw" (p. 3) while the gross motor section, containing 31 items, is used to determine "the child's abilities to sit, walk, and jump" (p. 3). Most items are scored by directing the child to do a particular activity, yet some items allow the report of a parent or other person familiar with the child. No single test score is calculated to estimate the degree of development; rather, the extent of developmental delay is calculated by counting how many "delays" (i.e., items failed below chronological age) appear on the child's test.
4. *The Developmental Schedules* (Banus, 1971). The schedules of Gesell and his associates charted the characteristic behaviors of infancy and early childhood under four categories, one of which is motor development. The schedules are standardized and are the foundation upon which the Bayley Scales of Infant Development and A Developmental Screening Inventory have been developed (White, 1975). These developmental scales require either performance by the child or information concerning the child's performance at home. The Gesell schedules create a structure within which the child's performance can be compared with that of other children. The purpose of the instrument is to find the child whose development is significantly slow. It also has been used in research to describe particular groups of children for the purpose of comparing sample behaviors (p. 24).
5. *A Developmental Screening Inventory* (Buros, 1972). This instrument consists of selected items from the Gesell Developmental Schedules for use with children between 1 month and 18 months of age. It is individually administered to assess abnormal development. Two of its five skill areas apply to adaptive gross motor and fine motor skills.
6. *A Developmental Test of Visual Motor Integration* (Buros, 1972). The short form of this test includes an age range from 2 to 8; the long form includes ages 2 to 15. The test items are geometric drawings, arranged in order of increasing difficulty, to be copied in a test booklet. The child's

score is calculated as the number of forms that have been copied successfully prior to three consecutive failures. Educational assessment is the stated purpose of the test. Standardization is adequate only for ages 5 through 13.

7. *Marianne Frostig Developmental Test of Visual Perception* (Buros, 1972). This test is designed to measure the development of perception in children ages 3 to 8. One of the five subtests is a measure of eye–hand coordination.
8. *The Learning Accomplishment Profile* (Sanford, 1974). The Learning Accomplishment Profile (LAP) is one of many developmental scales emerging from Head Start and First Chance, federally funded programs for normal and handicapped children. It is designed to provide the teacher of the young handicapped child with a criterion-referenced record of the child's existing skills. The LAP consists of a hierarchy of both gross motor and fine motor skills compiled and assimilated from many sources including the Bayley Infant Scales, Denver Developmental Scale, Cattell Intelligence Test, Gesell schedules, and the Vineland Social Maturity Scale. The scale allows the examiner to assess the child on 64 gross motor and 59 fine motor skills. In using the LAP, the teacher assesses the individual child in terms of whether or not he possesses each skill. The evaluative items are then used to designate the teaching sequence in both gross or fine motor areas. An individual record sheet is provided for each child.
9. *The Primary Visual Motor Test* (Buros, 1972). This test is designed for use with children ages 4 through 8. The child is given 16 geometric designs to copy. The test purports to evaluate the ability to translate from the visual (receptive) to the motor (expressive) mode and certain integrative processes which are involved in successful performance.
10. *Southern California Motor Accuracy Test* (Buros, 1972). This test is used with children ages 4 through 7 who have nervous system dysfunction. The test consists of tracing a line design. The scores show degrees of accuracy and speed.
11. *Southern California Perceptual Motor Test* (Buros, 1972). This test is designed to evaluate dimensions of perceptual-motor function in children ranging in age from 4 through 8 years. Six subtests, including imitation of postures, crossing the midline of body, bilateral motor coordination, right-left discrimination, standing balance—eyes open, and standing balance—eyes closed, are presented. No reading is required and no verbal response is necessary except for two responses on one subtest. Administration requires no special equipment (only a stopwatch) and minimal practice.
12. *Vane Kindergarten Test* (Buros, 1972). The perceptual-motor part of this test requires children between the ages of 4 and 11 to make three copies each of a box, a cross, and a hexagon. The whole test yields a total IQ which is a fair approximation of a Stanford-Binet IQ. The test is intended for use by psychologists.

While these instruments can be useful in assessing motor performance among young children, it should be noted that they are not comprehensive and therefore should be used in conjunction with keen observations and other information. It is important to note also that motor ability tests have limited value and should be used not as specific measures but as general ones (Singer, 1975).

Several variables may influence the child's performance on motor tests: (1) the presence of an observer and test materials may be distracting; (2) the child may not be accustomed to shifting his attention from one task to another on command; and (3) the child's level of excitement may be a problem (Cratty, 1969). Informal observations and testing followed by retesting will probably yield a more nearly true-to-life picture of the young child's motor achievement.

The purpose of the assessment and evaluation program is to determine the level of motor achievement in terms of quality of performance as well as numbers of skills mastered. This determination, compared with normal motor development, aids in the identification of skills that need additional practice and new ones to be learned. In this way, the assessment and evaluation process leads to an individualized motor development program.

Principles of Instruction for Motor Skill Development

The fundamental purpose of motor skill training is to help the child acquire skills which will enable him to continue learning and to lead a life that is as independent as his age and his ability allow. Although it is questionable whether maturational processes can be enhanced by training programs, it is definite that all children, regardless of degree of impairment or developmental delay, can benefit from a carefully designed motor skills training program. Moreover, since motor skill learning is governed by the same general principles of learning which affect all types of learning (Blake, 1976), the training program should be centered around these principles. This section briefly describes how the principles and conditions of learning and instruction discussed in Chapter 3 apply to motor skill development in the young child with special needs.

Curriculum Selection. Several tangential facts have a bearing on curriculum selection. It should be emphasized that motor skill instruction for the handicapped child follows medical examination and communication between the doctor and the instructor. If the child has not been examined medically, it is the responsibility of the professional working with the child to help the parents secure appropriate services. If the child is receiving therapy, communication between the therapist and instructor is essential. Professionals working together will determine which motor skills the child is ready to learn and who is responsible for each phase of instruction.

Motor skill instruction is based on knowledge of motor development and the usual sequence in which specific skills occur. Such information is found in existing developmental scales of motor ability. While there are many versions of these scales, they are similar and should be useful as guides to curriculum

Table 2

Learning Accomplishment Profile (LAP) in part

Gross Motor Skills				
Behavior	Age (Dev.)	Date of Achievement		Comments
Held sitting—head . . . erect	2 mos.	1/10/77	+	
Rolls over	3 mos.	3/1/77	+	
Held standing, lifts foot	3 mos.	3/10/77	+	
Pulls to sit—no head lag	4 mos.	5/1/77	+	
Turn from back to side	4 mos.	5/1/77	+	
Sit without support	5 mos.	6/30/77	+	
Stands, holding on	6 mos.	7/28/77	∓	
Pull self to stand	8 mos.	9/1/77	+	
Walk with assistance	11 mos.	11/28/77		
Stands alone well	11 mos.			

Note: Adapted from *Learning Accomplishment Profile* by A. R. Sanford. Chapel Hill, N.C.: Training Outreach Project, 1973. Used by permission.

selection. Table 2 shows a small adapted portion of the Learning Accomplishment Profile presented here for reference purposes.

Regardless of the child's chronological age, if he has achieved all of the skills up to and including "pull self to stand" his motor developmental age is 8 months. Although he may master skills out of sequence through his own efforts, expecting him to skip developmental tasks can have serious consequences. He should not be expected to stand alone well until the preceding skills are mastered. With reference to his present level of achievement, the next skill to be learned is, "walk with assistance." Activities designed to help the child acquire this skill constitute, for the time being, his motor curriculum.

Instructional Procedures. Principles of instruction discussed in Chapter 3 apply to all areas of learning including motor skills development. A lesson from the video series, *Next Steps Together,* (Project FEATT), an instructional program for parents of young handicapped children, illustrates the practical application of these principles to the teaching of motor skills. The program "Walking with Support" is directed to the gross motor skills implied in the task "walking with assistance" on the LAP scale. The subskills required to master the larger task are the *selected motor curriculum* at this time.

As the program begins, the host makes the audience aware of the fact that if the child can: (1) pull himself up with help, (2) stay up for a short while, and (3) balance himself reasonably well, he is ready to learn the new task. The host

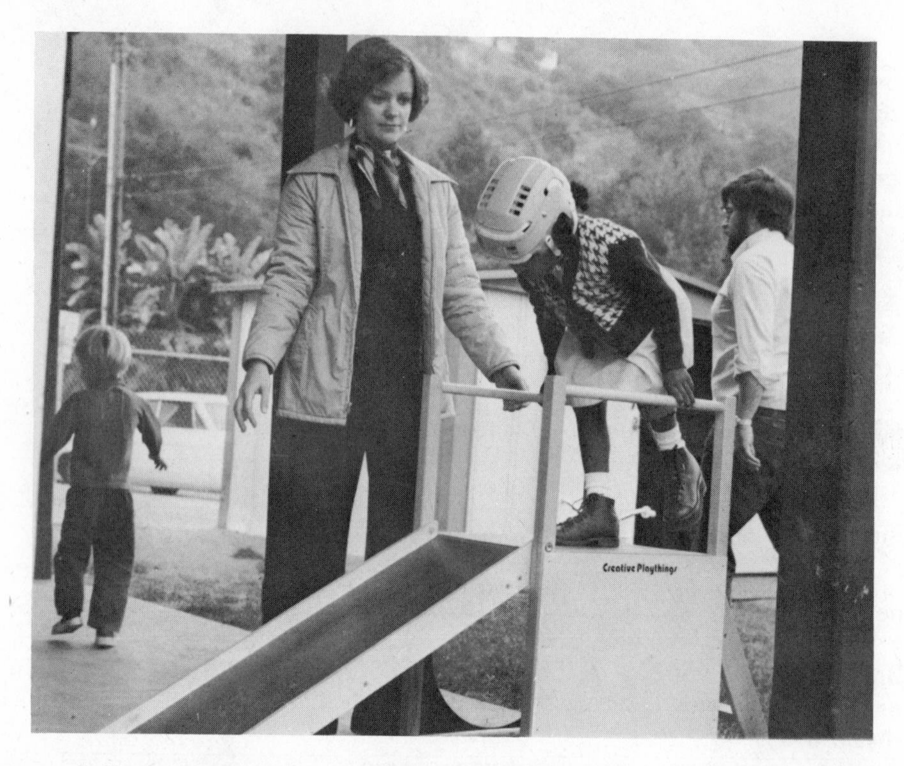

Motor skill instruction of a handicapped child follows medical examination and communication between the doctor and the instructor.

was stating the prerequisite skills, what the child must know before he is ready for new learning.

The purpose of teaching the task is made clear by examples of learning experiences which are available only if you can move around. The child who moves in an upright position has many more opportunities to learn than the one who is crawling or creeping on the floor. The objective is to have the child master the task of walking with support.

The audience is told that an object for support is needed, preferably a chair or a stool of a size that allows the seat to be as high as the child's waist and no higher than his chest. A toy which the child likes is also needed. It will be placed in the seat of the chair. Thus the learning environment has been arranged and the instructional materials selected. In other words, the *conditions for learning* have been considered and provided.

The child uses his previously learned tasks to pull himself up and to reach for his toy. His instructor determines that he is supported by the chair and that his legs are straight. Two more conditions for learning have been met: the child's interest and his security. These factors shape the child's attention.

The instructor has turned the chair in order to see the child. Then she places herself on the side of the chair opposite to the one supporting the child. By kneeling or stooping, she puts herself on the child's level. In other words, every effort has been made to meet the particular needs of the learner.

The instructor gently moves the chair away from the child. She is careful not to remove his support but to encourage the child to step forward in order to reach his toy. As the child lifts one foot (subtask 1) and puts it down (subtask 2), the instructor says, "Step." The child must shift his weight (subtask 3), lift the other foot (subtask 4) and put it down (subtask 5). *Task analysis* has identified the subtasks; *verbal cues* (promptings) have been provided. Excitement in the instructor's voice provides some reinforcement, but having the toy seems to be reinforcement enough for the child.

If the child does not step as the support is carefully moved away, a third person picks up the child's limbs in stepping fashion until the pattern has been established. *Modeling* and *fading* have been used.

Two additional uses of this skill are demonstrated, one of which the child can initiate. In this way the lesson has provided for *practice* and *use* of the newly acquired task.

Johnson and Werner (1975) have presented instructional procedures for 17 gross motor tasks and 6 fine motor tasks.

Therapy Techniques. For young children with severe deficits in motor skill development, programs of physical therapy will be required. Among the physical therapy programs which are widely used are those advocated by Phelps, Bobath, Rood, and Doman-Delacato (Banus, 1971). The Phelps program is based upon the development of muscle tone and strength through activities that provide resistance. The Bobath approach involves positioning the child in postures which inhibit the unwanted movements followed by controlled inhibition and voluntary movement by the child. The approach advocated by Rood provides for muscle stimulation by brushing action. The Doman-Delacato approach has been popular in the past with the lay population, but highly criticized by professionals. For children with less severe physical involvement, Chaney and Kephart (1968) have advocated many procedures that have been popular with both parents and professionals. Programs advocated by Kephart and his followers are detailed, but usually are not broken down to the more minute segments as are the previously mentioned physical therapy programs.

Instructional Approaches. Bits of information scattered in the literature on motor development provide answers to frequent questions concerning instructional approaches in programs for young children with special needs. Although the points of view are limited in number, they are based on experience and study and may be helpful to those designing programs and for those researching various methods and techniques.

1. Is motor achievement potentiality increased by early training? Available information indicates that children seem to reach higher levels of achievement if they start developmental training and practice quite young (Lawther, 1968). With handicapped children early training may prevent secondary handicapping conditions. DeWeerd has pointed to the children in First Chance programs who disproved the prognosis that they would never walk and others who, after early training, have entered regular kindergarten programs (Jordan, Hayden, Karnes, & Wood, 1977).

2. *If handicapped children enter regular programs at the kindergarten level, what skills should they have?* From one study (Mullen, 1975) it is assumed that basic gross motor and fine motor skills would be needed in addition to achievement in the following visual motor tasks: tie shoelaces, dress independently for outdoor play and home, color and trace between lines, catch and throw ball, and hop on one foot. It would seem, however, that each program would have its own entrance requirements and each child's abilities assessed accordingly.

3. *Which is more effective, structured or unstructured physical activity on motor skill development?* Best (1967) found structured physical activity significantly more effective for young children with learning disabilities. Kirk (1972) has said motor development for the trainable mentally retarded is best stimulated through games and recreational activities. The two points of view are not contradictory because activities may be selected for the skills they develop, and games provide structure to the program. Simplified yoga has been used to promote body awareness, balance, laterality, and crossing the midline (Hopkins & Hopkins, 1976). The authors found this approach highly effective as well as relaxing and calming to handicapped youngsters.

4. *Which is more effective, individual instruction or group instruction in motor development activities?* Rarick and Broadhead (1968) studied this point and concluded that individual instruction was more effective.

5. *If the only available instruction in motor development is group instruction, how often is it needed for effective training?* In an early childhood education program for institutionalized retarded children emphasizing gross motor, balance, arm-hand coordination, and manual activities, group instruction was provided twice each day. The session lasted one-half hour. The results of the program were dramatic, especially in the areas of balance and arm-hand coordination (Smeets & Manfredini, 1973).

6. *What are the deterrents to motor development?* According to Ayers (1966), whose point of view has been expressed by many teachers, overprotection of the young handicapped child, too much help, exasperation with too slow a rate of skill development, and harsh attitudes are inhibiting in motor skill development. Donlon (1976) saw the child's inability to imitate as the absence of a valuable learning tool.

7. *What equipment is needed for motor skill development in young handicapped children?* Werner (1974) used bean bags, yarn balls, playground balls, hoops, bowling pins, scooter boards, balance beams, trampolines, ropes, parachutes, tricycles, swings, slides, and jungle gyms. The reader is referred to the next part of this chapter and to Appendix B.

Adapted Equipment for Motor Development

The unique requirements of some young children with developmental problems are such that special equipment is needed. In spite of the increasing supply of instructional materials for special education, what is available is not always suitable, and the expense involved may be prohibitive.

Parents and teachers are accustomed to devising materials and equipment to help children learn. Much of the equipment needed for motor skills development can be created from household articles and items that are usually thrown away.

Parents often complain that they are not creative enough to design adapted equipment that might help their child; nevertheless, some of the most creative ideas have come from parents. It might seem that teachers and medical professionals would be best equipped to evaluate a child's needs and devise adaptations. However, having been taught a few possible solutions to a few specific problems may make it more difficult for professionals to think of new ones. More often parents are the ones who devise the most effective solutions.

Apparently, neither innate creativity nor technical knowledge is the key to implementing adaptive equipment to meet the needs of special children. The most important key is observation. If you observe that a child has difficulty bringing a spoonful of food to his mouth with coordination, then you will begin to ask, "How can I make it easier for him to hold the spoon and bring it to his mouth?" Once the problem is identified, various ideas can be used. Neighbors, teachers, and grandparents can be asked to help find a good solution. This should provide numerous suggestions.

Observing the child, the task he is attempting, and the problems he encounters will lead to many practical solutions. The emphasis of this chapter will be on general ideas to encourage observation and understanding of the child's problems. It is impossible to predict what will work with each child, and adapted equipment which aids one child may not aid another.

For children with special needs, therapy follows normal development by trying to normalize the child's experiences. Adapted equipment should be used the same way; that is, the equipment should enable a child to participate in the daily life experiences he might otherwise miss.

The information which follows presents different kinds of adapted equipment and the particular use of each for motor skill development.

Positioning

Children with delayed motor skills can benefit from equipment which helps develop or compensate for poor physical development. Whether the child has a general lag in development or a definite mental or physical handicap, if his problem interferes with movement or hand activities, special positioning may be helpful.

The one position used most often during the day is sitting. Whether the child is involved with academics, eating, playing, toileting, socialization, or just observing his environment, if he can sit, he will be more successful. The sitting position allows the hands to be free and the eyes to see straight ahead, and therefore becomes an important stage in his progress.

If a child cannot sit well, even with adaptations, the advantages of eye-hand positioning can be achieved lying down. For a child with poor muscular control throughout his body, a foam roll can be placed under his chest while he lies on

The sitting position.

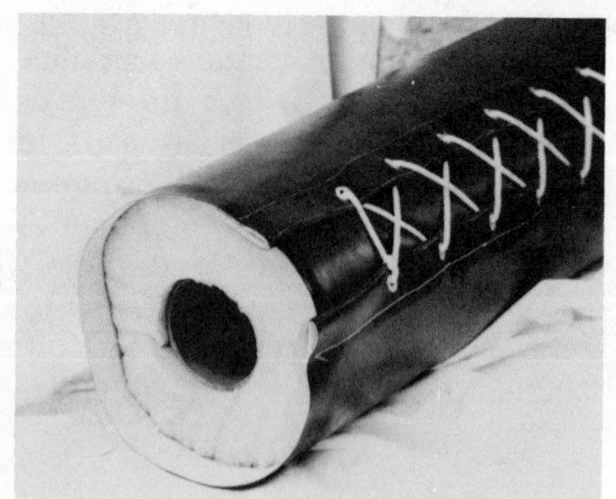

Two types of foam rolls.

his stomach. This lifts his body weight off the floor, allows him to get his hands out in front of him, and positions his head so he can focus on his hands or on objects placed in front of him. He is also in a good position for head and shoulder control.

The foam roll can be made firmer by rolling corrugated cardboard into a cylinder and taping it before covering with foam. For larger rolls, use several layers of cardboard taped or tied into a cylinder or use hollow plastic pipe. The cylinder should be firm and strong enough to support the child's weight, but can be more comfortable if covered with foam. Use canvas to make a drawstring bag to fit over the roll. This can be removed and easily washed when soiled.

It is advisable to encourage a child to be on his stomach, with face and arms lifted off the floor, if normal sitting isn't possible. This position leads to higher developmental levels such as creeping, kneeling, and standing. It also allows for eye-hand development, assuming his head and body are held off the floor so the child can move his arms and reach objects. A child whose development has prevented his learning to roll, sit, and crawl may prefer to lie on his back or sit in a reclined chair. In general, this is not advisable because there are no other motor milestones reached from this position and all he can see while lying on his back are lights, ceilings, and adult's faces.

The scooter board (belly board or crawler) is another piece of equipment that has multiple uses including positioning the child for a specific function such as eating or working at a table. A child can lie on his stomach on the scooter board while he learns to hold his head up, to prop on his elbows, and to reach out. The scooter board is a rectangular board (¾-inch plywood) with heavy-duty casters attached to each corner. The board can be padded with a layer of foam and covered with vinyl.

In addition to positioning, the scooter board allows movement. If the child has poor balance, weak arms, flaccid or weak muscle tone (as in learning disabilities or retardation), temporary leg casts, or is unable to crawl, he may gain both strength and mobility from pushing himself around on the scooter board. Activities to encourage hand skills, pencil and paper work, or conceptual develop-

The scooter board.

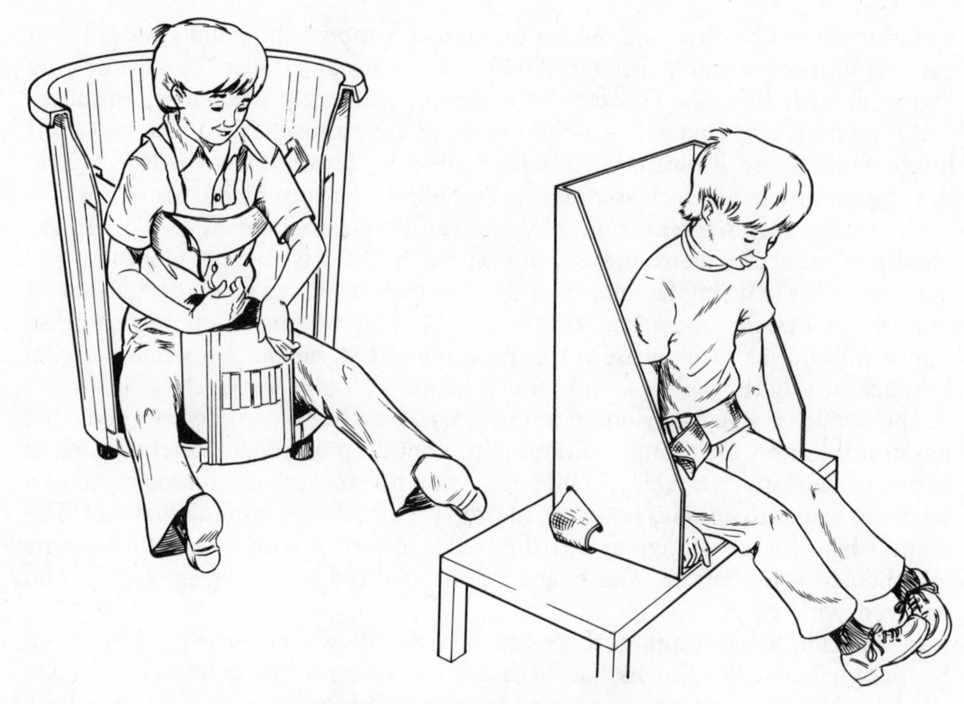

Trash can seat and box seat.

ment may be done in this position. The scooter board may be used to send a child on errands or to provide him an opportunity of carrying out verbal instructions which require motor responses. Even if the child has difficulty moving the board, he can experience "forward," "backwards," and "around" by being pulled when a rope is attached to the board. If there is any chance of the child falling off, a strap or belt should be fastened around the scooter board and the hips of the child.

If the child can partially maintain a sitting position, an adaptation can be made from containers to help him sit on the floor or participate in group play. A cardboard box, plastic trash can, or laundry basket can be cut away on one side to allow the child to sit with minimal support.

Quite often difficulty in sitting stems from problems with the hips, when the legs tend to straighten out and pull together. This makes the child slide forward in his chair, possibly falling sideways and losing head control at the same time. The simplest addition to a chair to prevent this is a box or large block placed under the child's feet to allow him to push himself back when his legs begin to straighten. With a box or footrest under his feet, he is more likely to keep his knees bent and this in itself may prevent abnormal positioning. If the footrest is not sufficient, a cloth harness can be used to keep his hips back in the chair to help maintain an upright position. This cloth tie-in is better than a single strap around his hips because the single strap will allow him to continue sliding forward into the strap causing pressure on the stomach.

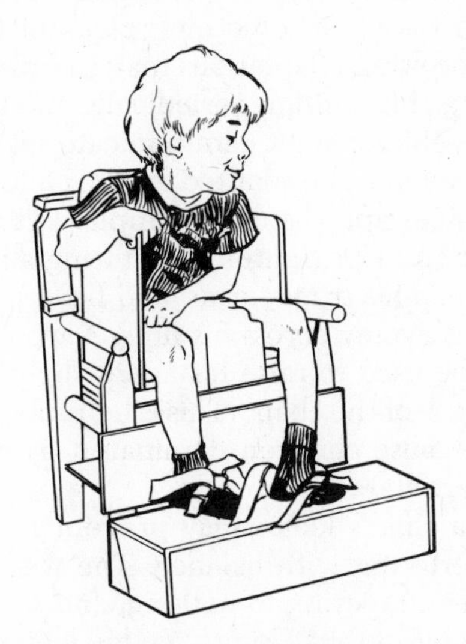

Chair with footrest.

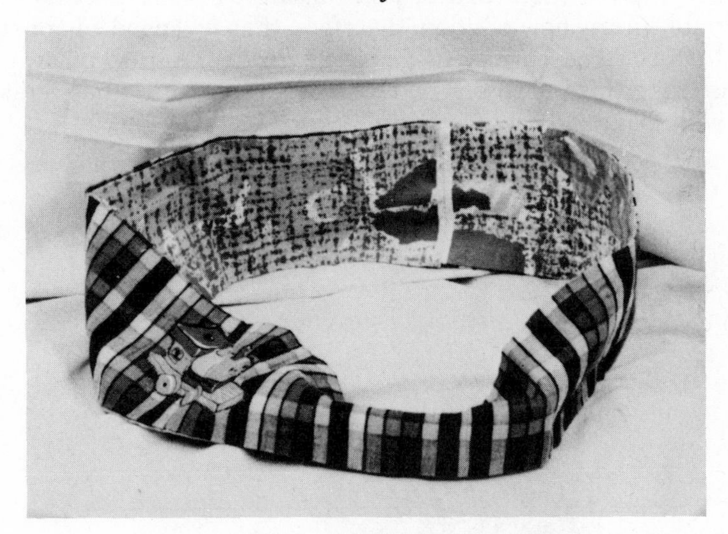

Cloth tie-in.

The cloth tie-in is a rectangle of fabric with two holes for the legs to slip through and straps for tying. After the child's feet are put through the holes, the harness is then pulled up under the child's bottom and tied on both sides of the chair. The harness should be made of sturdy, washable material. It should be sewn securely because there will be much stress on the straps. The leg holes should be bound with seam binding to prevent raveling.

It should be emphasized that one must be constantly aware of the child's tolerance to a new position. Changing his usual position may be so uncomfortable that it makes him inattentive, restless, or fussy. Tolerance to a new position can be built by giving the child something pleasant to do. Since bending his body a different way or using adaptations may interfere with circulation, care must be taken to change his position periodically and to check for red pressure spots, especially if the child cannot communicate his discomfort.

At times the chair itself must be adapted for the child; adding a wedge to keep his hips bent or his knees apart is one example. Often, sitting balance is impaired because the leg muscles tighten up, putting all of the child's weight on one hip. In order to keep his trunk, arms, and head in a balanced position, his weight must be spread evenly across his hips. A wooden wedge covering the seat of the chair can be used to raise his knees slightly, thus keeping his hips bent and against the back of the chair. (This is helpful to some children but must be used judiciously because children dominated by flexion patterns may fall forward if their hips are flexed.)

A wedge between a child's knees may prevent him from pressing his legs together, thereby interfering with balance. The wedge may be a few inches wide between the knees, tapering to nothing, and short enough to enable the child to sit behind it comfortably. Using a wedge which is too wide may stretch the muscles, making them tighter and causing discomfort. Children will be uncomfortable in any new position; therefore, they will need an opportunity to get used to it. Hard or sharp areas should be padded. A small pillow or a towel can be used for this purpose. For more permanent use, the wedge can be covered with foam and then with vinyl.

A chair with tray and footrest.

Construction of this wedge and other chair adaptations requires some skill in carpentry. This wedge is made of three rectangles of plywood beveled and glued together to form a triangle. A fourth triangular piece is glued to the bottom of the wedge so it can be bolted to the chair. The chair and the bottom of the wedge are drilled in two places and bolted.

A tray or table can be incorporated with the wedge seat or used separately. The tray chair can be a complete unit—a wooden chair with small wheels for mobility, a footrest, a wedge or straps as needed, chair arms, back support, and tray. This allows a child to be well positioned for play, work or eating at his own table. Too often special chairs do not fit the height of his table so the child loses the opportunity to use his hands while he sits.

Construction of a tray securely attached to a chair is complicated. Basically, the tray can be made for any chair with arms by cutting a rectangular form from ½-inch plywood. A small curved section should be cut to fit around the child's body. Toys and food are lost into the lap when a generous hole is cut. A screen-door hook or a dog-leash snap should be added to each side to lock the tray to the chair. Beneath the tray, wide straps or a wooden trough to fit around the arms of the chair can be added to keep the tray from tipping. Gluing a 2-inch by ½-inch strip of wood around the edge of the tray prevents the child from pushing objects over the edge. Holes may be drilled into the strip so that pencils and toys can be tied to the tray. By tying objects with heavy cord, the child who knocks them away can attempt to retrieve them independently.

Another type of seat which emphasizes leg position to maintain the hip and trunk in alignment employs a curved base which the child straddles. The straddle seat keeps the knees apart and keeps even weight on the hips. It can be incorporated with other equipment by adding foot and back supports and a tray. Heavy-duty casters can be added for mobility. In its simplest form, the straddle seat is similar to sitting over the foam roll. For more permanent seating, two end-pieces are cut from plywood and connected with wooden slats or a flexible sheet of masonite or plywood. The larger the chair, the more supports need to be added. The chair can be covered with carpeting for comfort and tactile experience. Footrests can be added, or the floor can be used as a footrest. The straddle seat stimulates balance and postural muscle tone.

Children who need to practice kneeling for balance and hip strength can do their schoolwork at a bench or low table. A simple kneeling table can be made by inverting a sturdy cardboard box. The child may need to keep his feet against a wall if his knees tend to slide out from under him.

Before encouraging a child to walk, one should remember that there are neurological and medical factors which must be evaluated by a physician before standing or walking should be attempted. If the medical opinion is that no harm will come from standing or walking, and if the child has the readiness to walk but lacks motivation, push toys may be used to encourage him. A long-handled toy that rattles or plays music when pushed can make walking more interesting. A doll carriage or sturdy-wheeled toys with a handle can be used for walking. If the child has poor balance and tends to push the toy too far ahead, a wooden chair or a large box of toys added for extra weight may be pushed instead.

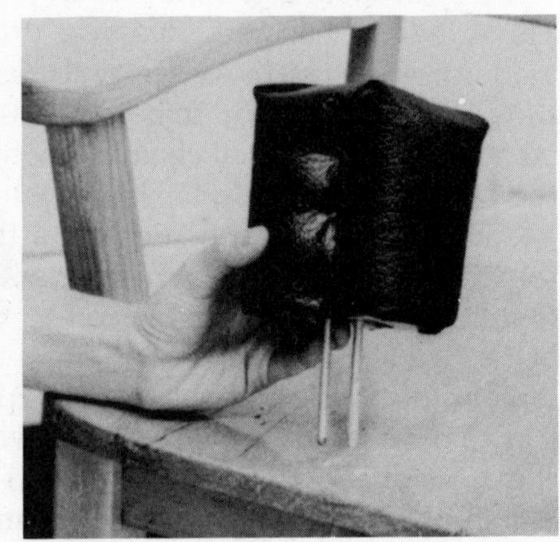

Another chair adaptation.

A chair with wedge and footrest.

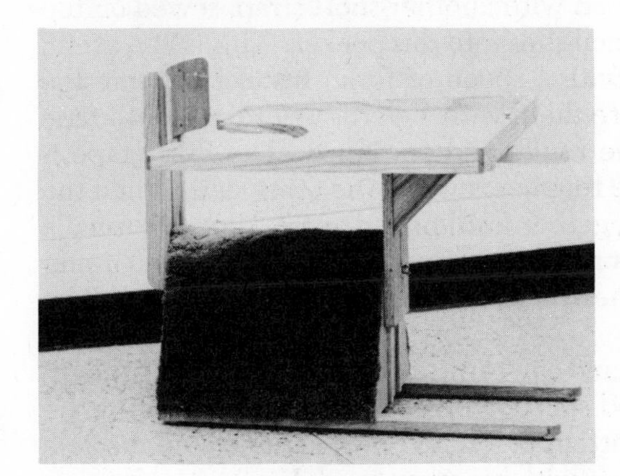

Straddle seats.

If a child can walk, additional skill in balance can be encouraged with a balance board. A straight 2-inch by 4-inch by 10-foot board can be placed flat on the floor as a balance beam. (A warped board must not be used.) To facilitate more balance and create more challenge, the board can be lifted a few inches off the floor by using wooden brackets.

Hand Skills

Play is a child's work and toys are his tools. Play is a natural way of practicing acquired skills and learning new ones (see Chapter 10). Toys and equipment that stimulate hand skills and eye-hand coordination can facilitate physical development and incorporate it with conceptual learning. Only a few of many possible examples are presented here.

Several solutions are available to the child for whom holding a pencil is a problem. He could simply use large, primary size crayons and pencils, or a regular pencil can be wrapped with foam or sponge and secured with plastic tape. The nonslip surface as well as the spongy texture help the child grasp. Putting a pencil through the middle of a small foam ball (3-inch) or through a chunk of foam sponge may make maintaining a grip easier for the child. If a child cannot grip the pencil or releases it intermittently, a pencil holder may be helpful. A pencil holder can be any device which helps to keep the pencil in the child's palm.

One type of holder consists of a strap which fastens around the hand while securely holding the pencil (crayon, paintbrush, eating utensil). A strip of fabric is folded double or triple and stitched across both ends and down both sides to form a strap about ¾-inch wide. It needs to be long enough to fit across the palm of the hand, going between the thumb and index finger, and long enough to be tied. Two buttonholes are then put in the palm part of the strap. The pencil is slipped into the first hole and out of the other. Both ends of the pencil are free, but the center is held against the palm.

A variation of the holder is made by using a pocket for the pencil instead of two holes. The same strap may be used with another short strap, sewed on top of the first, in the palm area. The pencil slips into this pocket. (This is also useful as a utensil holder for self-feeding with a spoon or fork.) Instead of tying the ends of the strap, it is easier to secure them with Velcro. Velcro is a cloth tape closure that comes in two parts, one rough and one fuzzy. The fuzzy tape is sewn to one end of the strap and the rough is sewn to the other end. When the two are overlapped they will stick together until pulled apart. Velcro is usually available in fabric stores as well as from medical supply dealers. (It is also useful in replacing buttons, snaps, and other difficult fasteners to help a child dress himself.)

Paper tends to slide on a table top and can cause a child to become frustrated. If he has difficulty with the eye-hand skills involved in coloring or writing, he is probably going to put his cortical attention on his crayon and will not be able to concentrate on stabilizing the paper with his other hand. His frustration may be reduced by securing the paper to the table using masking tape or by making a paper-holding frame. A simple one is made from two sheets of corrugated cardboard stapled or taped together on three sides. The top sheet is cut out in the center to form a frame nearly the size of the paper. The paper is slipped in between the two sheets of cardboard on the untaped edge.

To increase dexterity, bean bags are easy for children to use. Their plasticity allows a child to grip them in numerous positions, even if his grasp is limited. They can be thrown like a ball either overhand or underhand to encourage eye-hand coordination, upper extremity strengthening, or joint range of motion. Unlike a ball, they do not bounce and therefore stay put when they land. While bean bags are generally small, and therefore difficult for a child to catch, a coordinated adult can toss them so they will land on the child's lap if he misses them with his hands. Even if the child cannot catch the bean bag, he has it in his lap ready to throw again.

A circular hoop or a shallow box placed on the floor can be a target. The target can be varied by putting the box on the floor or by putting it above eye level on a table. Since the bean bag will drape, if it hits the rim of the target it may stay there. Add interest to the target by using a favorite toy (the bed of a dump truck) as the target or by suspending jingle bells (from a rhythm band) to provide the child with auditory reinforcement when he hits the target.

Bean bags can be made in various colors, sizes, and shapes for use in conceptual development activities. They can be used to match colors when the colored bean bag is thrown to the same color target, such as a piece of construction paper. Counting can be practiced. Concepts such as "up" and "down" can be taught by throwing to targets up on the table or down on the floor. The concept of little and big can be reinforced by having bean bags of different sizes and matching them to little and big targets. Likewise, bean bags can be made in several shapes (circle, square, triangle). Auditory memory and understanding of verbal instructions can be enhanced by telling the child which shape to throw. Corresponding targets can be made in the same shapes from cardboard or construction paper. Unlike a ball, a bean bag will stay where it is thrown; therefore, the target can be flat on the floor.

Color, shape, or size of bean bags should be varied in order for the child to exert autonomy in choosing the ones he likes best. Long thin ones (the size of a corncob) are especially easy for a child with small hands or limited grasp. Round ones are more fun when a few tiny ones are added (3-inch diameter; 5-inch for larger ones) or a smiling face is made with magic marker or felt appliqué. Because bean bags will receive vigorous use, they must be made of sturdy material and the seams should be stitched twice. Loosely woven knit fabric may allow the filling to fall out. The selection of filling is important. Navy beans seem to make the best filling. It has been noticed that when mice find bean bags, they devour the ones filled with birdseed but rarely eat the ones with beans.

For rolling, catching, and developing bilateral skills, a round ball has advantages over a bean bag. A small inflated beach ball is a good size for catching with both hands. A foam rubber ball is soft and harmless. Small plastic infant balls are available with irregular surfaces so the ball can be gripped easily. A cloth clutch ball is extremely easy to grasp, is soft and harmless, and does not bounce away. It is made by sewing together individual sections of stuffed fabric. Each section becomes a handle for the child to grasp or clutch. These can be made in various sizes.

Clutch ball.

Puzzles are helpful in developing hand skills. Simple puzzles (especially wooden ones) are good for fine-motor planning, but often the child cannot manipulate the flat pieces. A wooden knob (dresser drawer pull) glued to each piece may make him more successful.

If two-handed activity is indicated, an interesting game can be made from a coat hanger. The center of the opened wire must be bent into several loops, curves, or right angles. Place a metal washer or plastic ring on the wire and make the two ends into handles. Do this by bending the ends of the wire into shallow loops and covering with foam or slipping them into cardboard tubes cut from empty paper towel rolls. The child holds the handles in both hands and by moving them in different directions he tries to slide the ring over the obstacle course from one side to the other. These can be made in a series of simple curves or can be complicated to require more visual-motor coordination and motor planning.

Additional motor planning skill can be acquired by placing blocks correctly into holes of the same shape. A plastic gallon milk bottle can have the basic shapes cut out of the front and a large hole cut from the back so the blocks can be retrieved. Ready-made blocks in various shapes may be used if a hole is cut to match each shape. Also various shapes may be sawed from wood.

Wooden clip clothespins may be used for finger strengthening and color matching. The child will improve both skills by clipping printed clothespins to poster board of the same color. They may be used for clipping together pictures that are alike or pictures of items that go together (i.e., foot and sock, cup and saucer, moon and stars). Also clothespins can be used as items for counting.

A matching game can be made by marking a 9-square grid on each of two pieces of cardboard. Colored squares of construction paper are cut to fit grid sections. A design is made on one grid to be copied by the child. Covering the game pieces with clear plastic will make them last longer.

Other ideas include: (1) covering cubes of foam with fabric of different textures, colors, or designs, to teach tactile awareness, colors, words, numbers, or letters; (2) using squares of perforated masonite for lacing boards (although the extra holes may be distracting); (3) making people-puzzles out of cardboard and having the parts overlap and fastened with small pieces of Velcro or other adhesive material that can be reused; and (4) making cut-out dolls and appropriate clothing, using Velcro to make the clothing stick to the doll.

Adapted equipment need not be elaborate nor expensive. If it improves the child's performance, enables him to function more efficiently, and contributes to his further development, its purpose has been well served.

Summary

In this chapter, various aspects of motor skills development have been presented with reference to the special needs of the young handicapped child. Assessment, evaluation, teaching procedures, and the use of adapted equipment as each applies to motor skills development have been included.

REFERENCES

Abravanel, E., Levin-Goldsmidt, E., & Stevenson, B. Actions imitations: The early phase of infancy. *Child Development,* 1976, **47,** 1032–1044.

Ausubel, D. *Theory and problems of child development.* New York: Grune & Stratton, 1958.

Ayers, J. Interrelationship of perception, function and treatment. *Physical Therapy,* July 1966, **46**(7), 741–744.

Banus, B. *The developmental therapist.* Thorofare, N.J.: Charles B. Slack, 1971.

Baumgartner, B. Goals for self-help and independence. In W. B. Stephens (Ed.), *Training the developmentally young.* New York: John Day, 1971.

Bayley, N. *Bayley Scales of Infant Development: Manual.* New York: Psychological Corp., 1969.

Best, H. *The effects of structured physical activity on the motor skills development of children with learning disabilities.* Memphis: Memphis State University, 1967.

Blake, K. *The mentally retarded: An educational psychology.* Englewood Cliffs, N.J.: Prentice-Hall, 1976.

Bricker, W., & Bricker, D. A program of language training for the severely language handicapped child. *Exceptional Children,* 1970, **37,** 101–111.

Bruininks, R. *The Bruininks-Oseretsky Test of Motor Proficiency.* Circle Pines, Minn.: American Guidance Service, 1977.

Buros, O. *The seventh mental measurement yearbook.* Highland Park, N.J.: The Gryphon Press, 1972.

Chaney, C., & Kephart, N. *Motoric aids to perceptual training.* Columbus, Ohio: Charles E. Merrill Publishing Co., 1968.

Clements, S. Symptomatology—identification of the child. In R. Jones (Ed.), *Problems and issues in the education of exceptional children.* Boston: Houghton Mifflin, 1971.

Clinton, L., & Boyce, K. Acquisition of simple motor imitative behavior in mentally retarded and nonretarded children. *American Journal of Mental Deficiency,* 1975, **79,** 695–700.

Cratty, B. *Motor activity and the education of retardates.* Philadelphia: Lea & Febiger, 1969.

Cratty, B. *Perceptual and motor development in infants and children.* New York: Macmillan, 1970.

Cratty, B. Special education. In R. J. Singer (Ed.), *The psycho-motor domain: Movement behavior.* Philadelphia: Lea & Febiger, 1972.

Donlon, E. *The severely and profoundly handicapped.* New York: Grune & Stratton, 1976.

Fallen, N. *A review of literature concerning learning disabilities.* Unpublished manuscript, The University of Maryland, Department of Special Education, 1970.

Fleishman, E. *The structure and measurement of physical fitness.* Englewood Cliffs, N.J.: Prentice-Hall, 1964.

Frankenburg, W., & Dodds, J. B. *Denver Developmental Screening Test.* Denver: University of Colorado Medical Center, 1969.

Gephart, W. J., & Antonoplus, D. P. The effects of expectancy and other research-biasing factors. *Phi Delta Kappan,* 1969, **51,** 579–583.

Gesell, A., & Ilg, F. *Infant and child in the culture of today: The guidance of development in home and nursery school.* New York: Harper, 1943.

Hallahan, D., & Cruickshank, W. *Psychoeducational foundations of learning disabilities.* Englewood Cliffs, N.J.: Prentice-Hall, 1973.

Hallahan, D. P., & Kauffman, J. M. *Introduction to learning disabilities: A psychobehavioral approach.* Englewood Cliffs, N.J.: Prentice-Hall, 1976.

Hammill, D., & Bartel, N. *Teaching children with learning and behavior problems.* Boston: Allyn & Bacon, 1975.

Hewett, F., & Forness, S. *Education of exceptional learners.* Boston: Allyn & Bacon, 1974.

Hopkins, L., & Hopkins, J. Yoga in psychomotor training. *Academic Therapy,* 1976, **11** (4), 461–465.

Hurlock, E. *Child development.* New York: McGraw-Hill, 1972.

Ismail, A., & Gruber, J. *Motor aptitude and intellectual performance.* Columbus, Ohio: Charles E. Merrill Publishing Co., 1968.

Johnson, V., & Werner, R. *A step-by-step learning guide for retarded infants and children.* Syracuse, N.Y.: Syracuse University Press, 1975.

Jones, R. (Ed.). *Problems and issues in the education of exceptional children.* Boston: Houghton Mifflin Co., 1971.

Jordan, J., Hayden, A., Karnes, M., & Wood, M. *Early childhood education for exceptional children: A handbook of ideas and exemplary practices.* Reston, Va.: The Council for Exceptional Children, 1977.

Kirk, S. *Educating exceptional children.* Boston: Houghton Mifflin Co., 1972.

Lawther, J. *The learning of physical skills.* Englewood Cliffs, N.J.: Prentice-Hall, 1968.

Levy, T. Social reinforcement and knowledge of results as determinants of motor performance among educable mentally retarded children. *American Journal of Mental Deficiency,* 1974, **78**, 752–758.

Malpass, L. Motor skills in mental deficiency. In N. R. Ellis (Ed.), *Handbook of mental deficiency: Psychological theory and research.* New York: McGraw-Hill, 1963.

McCandless, B. *Children and adolescents: Behavior and development.* New York: Holt, Rinehart & Winston, 1961.

Moores, D. Early childhood special education for hearing handicapped children. In H. Spicker, N. Anastasiow, & W. Hodges (Eds.), *Children with special needs: Early development and education.* Minneapolis: University of Minnesota Leadership Training Institute, 1976.

Mullen, J. Identifying LD kindergarten children. *Academic Therapy* 1975, **11**(1), 117–118.

Project FEATT. *Next steps together* (video series). Lafayette, Ind.: Purdue University, 1976.

Pyfer, J. *Assessment and evaluation of the handicapped child.* Paper presented at the American Alliance of Health, Physical Education and Recreation Convention (Milwaukee, Wis., April 6, 1976).

Rarick, L., & Broadhead, G. *The effects of individualized versus group oriented physical education on selected parameters of development of educable mentally retarded and minimally brain injured children.* Final Report. Madison, Wis.: Wisconsin University, Department of Physical Education, 1968.

Rimland, B. *Infantile autism: The syndrome and its implications for a neural theory of behavior.* New York: Appleton-Century-Crofts, 1964.

Robinson, H., & Robinson, N. *The mentally retarded child: A psychological approach.* New York: McGraw-Hill, 1976.

Rosehan, D. Effects of social class and race on responsiveness to approval and disapproval. *Journal of Personality and Social Psychology,* 1966, **4**, 253–259.

Sanford, A. R. *Learning accomplishment profile.* Chapel Hill, N.C.: Training Outreach Project, 1973.

Share, J., & French, R. Early motor development in Down's syndrome children. *Mental Retardation,* 1974, **12**(6), 23.
Singer, R. N. *Motor learning and human performance.* New York: Macmillan Publishing Co., 1975.
Singer, R. N. (Ed.). *The psychomotor domain: Movement behavior.* Philadelphia: Lea & Febiger, 1972.
Smeets, P., & Manfredini, D. Scope and perspective in special education. *Education and Training of the Mentally Retarded,* 1973, **8**(3), 124–126.
Smith, R., & Neisworth, J. *The exceptional child: A functional approach.* New York: McGraw-Hill, 1975.
Stephens, W. (Ed.). *Training the developmentally young.* New York: John Day, 1971.
Stevens, H., & Heber, R. *Mental retardation: A review of research.* Chicago: University of Chicago Press, 1964.
Wallace, G., & McLoughlin, J. *Learning disabilities: Concepts and characteristics.* Columbus, Ohio: Charles E. Merrill Publishing Co., 1975.
Watson, E., & Lowrey, G. *Growth and development of children.* Chicago: Year Book Medical Publishers, 1967.
Weber, R. (Ed.). *Handbook on learning disabilities: A prognosis for the child, the adolescent, the adult.* Englewood Cliffs, N.J.: Prentice-Hall, 1974.
Werner, P. Education of selected movement patterns of preschool children. *Perceptual and Motor Skills,* 1974, **39**, 795–798.
White, B. *The first three years of life.* Englewood Cliffs, N.J.: Prentice-Hall, 1975.
Whiting, H. *Concepts in skill learning.* London: Lepus Books, 1975.

6

Self-help Skill Development

This chapter is concerned with teaching self-help skills such as grooming, eating, toileting, and dressing. The ability to take care of one's self-care needs is fundamental in achieving self-sufficiency and independence. It should be considered a critical part of the educational curriculum for any young handicapped child. However, the success of training in grooming, eating, toileting, and dressing skills will depend on the effectiveness with which parents can follow through, as well as implement, self-help programs. With the current proliferation of home-based early education programs (Erickson, 1975), parents are increasingly becoming involved as partners in the self-help training process.

This chapter suggests ways professionals can help apply instructional techniques and guidelines to the development of self-care skills in young handicapped children. It includes consideration of normal self-help skill development, and its relevance to assessment, program development and evaluation, assessment techniques, and specific instructional guidelines and techniques. Guidelines are presented for young children at different levels of development and with various handicapping conditions.

Normal Self-help Skill Development

Knowing how self-help skills develop in children who have no learning problems will aid the teacher and others in understanding the nature and scope of

---

The major part of this chapter was written by *Paul Wehman.* The section on adapted equipment was provided by *Roberta L. Goodwyn.*

the learning problems among handicapped children. Such knowledge can provide a basis for assessing the child's current functioning level and give direction for educational planning.

The Learning Accomplishment Profile (LAP) (see pp. 161, 163–64) lists the skills of toileting, eating, dressing, and grooming in sequential order of development among nonhandicapped children. A developmental age or age range provided for each skill listed is an approximation of when the skill is mastered. Included among the behaviors of grooming, eating, toileting, and dressing are other skills which indicate signs of emerging independence in the young child. A small portion of the scale is shown in Table 1.

Table 1 shows that different types of behavior are expected to develop during the same period of time. In many instances the age range during which children may be expected to master some skills is as much as one year. A 4-year-old handicapped child who masters the skill of pouring liquid from a pitcher with little spilling is performing that skill at a level commensurate with her chronological age. The handicapped 5-year-old who has not mastered the same skill would be considered developmentally delayed in that one skill. Further analysis of the child's achievement level would be required before this skill becomes a part of her instructional program.

The hierarchy of self-help skill behaviors is used in assessment to determine what the child can and cannot do. A manual for use with LAP provides further description of acceptable performance (Sanford, 1974). In educational planning, the unaccomplished tasks below the child's chronological age become a part of her instructional program.

Table 1

Self-help Skills

Behavior	Age (Dev.)	Assessment Date	Date of Achievement
Is usually dry at night	36–48 mos.		
Pours well from pitcher	36–48		
Undresses self	36–48		
Washes hands and face unaided	36–48		
Pulls on shoes	36–48		
Buttons coat or dress	40		
Dresses without supervision	42		
Brushes teeth	42		
Separates easily from mother	42		

Note: From *Learning Accomplishment Profile* by A. R. Sanford. Chapel Hill, N.C.: Training Outreach Project, 1973. Reprinted by permission.

The value of developmental scales as indicators of what can be reasonably expected of the young child cannot be overemphasized. For example, if it is normal development for a child of 3 or 4 to stay dry all night, it is unreasonable to expect a 2-year-old to do as well. If a 2-year-old is consistently dry all night, her development is considered advanced for that one behavior. Expecting all 2-year-olds to master the skill is a matter of ignorance. The child whose rate of development is slower than normal will accomplish self-help tasks in approximately the same order as other children but will require more time.

According to the LAP list of self-help skills, 20 behaviors or tasks are related to eating, 8 to toileting, 16 to dressing, 6 to grooming and 8 to other emerging skills of independence. These skills have been grouped according to categories and are presented in Tables 2–6.

The earliest emerging behaviors are eating skills. Dressing and grooming skills become prominent after 2 years of age. The first toileting skills, based on maturation and conditioning, emerge at one year of age. Other self-help skills of emerging independence appear as early as 18 months.

The lists of skills by categories clearly show the relationship of early accomplishment to the development of later skills. For example, the child lifts the cup by its handle at approximately 6 months; drinks from the cup with some spilling at 11 months; drinks from the cup independently at 17 months; and gets a drink unassisted between ages 2 and 3.

The lists help to delineate skills that may be emerging simultaneously. Behaviors such as finger feeding, fussing to be changed after a bowel movement, and taking off shoes and pants are all expected in normal development at one year of age.

The lists fail to show the relationship between emerging self-help skills and emerging motor skills. For instance, the ability to pick up a spoon (an eating skill) is expected at approximately the same time as the child is expected to sit without support (a motor skill). Although the young child seems to become

Table 2

Grooming Skills (LAP)

Behaviors	Age (Dev.)
Dries own hands	24–36 mos.
Washes hands and face unaided	36–48 mos.
Brushes teeth	42 mos.
Dries face and hands	42 mos.
Washes face and hands unassisted	54 mos.
Can brush and comb hair unassisted	60–72 mos.

Note: Tables 2–6 from *Learning Accomplishment Profile* by A. R. Sanford. Chapel Hill, N.C.: Training Outreach Project, 1973. Reprinted by permission.

Table 3

Other Self-help Skills (LAP)

Behavior	Age (Dev.)
Remembers where objects belong	18–23 mos.
Indicates desires by gesturing & utterance	18–23 mos.
Picks up toys and puts them away	18–23 mos.
Separates easily from mother	42 mos.
Can carry, breakable objects	36–48 mos.
Goes about neighborhood unattended	48–60 mos.
Puts toys away neatly in box	60–72 mos.
Crosses street safely	60–72 mos.

aware of herself at one year of age, grooming skills emerge much later because the complex motor skills required have not developed.

Each of these relationships between development and chronological age are important considerations in assessment, program development, and instruction.

Program Development: General Considerations in Developing Self-help Programs

Information about a child's proficiency in a given skill is obtained from an assessment. There are a number of assessment methods. Eaves and McLaughlin (1977) have outlined seven types. These include:

1. Inspection of previously collected data about child.
2. Informal consultation with others who know child.
3. Structured interviews.
4. Screening devices (i.e., questionnaires, rating scales).
5. Standardized tests.
6. Nonstandardized tests.
7. Direct observation.

Although each of the above methods may provide useful information about the self-help skills of the child, the most valuable form of assessment may be completed through achievement identification and task analysis (see Chapter 3).

Table 4

Eating Skills (LAP)

Behaviors	Age (Dev.)
Picks up spoon	5 mos.
Lifts cup with handle	6 mos.
Feeds self cracker	6 mos.
Holds, bites and chews biscuit	9 mos.
Drinks from cup when held (some spilling)	11 mos.
Finger feeds self for part of meal	12 mos.
Holds spoon, brings to mouth, licks it	14 mos.
Uses spoon, spilling little	16 mos.
Drinks from cup	17 mos.
Lifts and holds cup between hands	18–23 mos.
Unwraps candy	22 mos.
Inhibits turning of spoon	24 mos.
Masticates food	12–24 mos.
Discriminates edible substance	12–24 mos.
Gets drink unassisted	24–36 mos.
Feeds self with little spilling	36–48 mos.
Spreads butter on bread with knife	36–48 mos.
Pours well from pitcher	36–48 mos.
Eats with fork and spoon	36–48 mos.
Can cut with knife	48–60 mos.

Achievement Identification. Entry skills are determined by observation and consultation with the child's parents and other professionals working with the child. An analysis of the self-help, motor and language skills which the child has achieved gives direction for program planning and instruction.

Task Analysis. Each item in the hierarchy of self-help skill development represents a skill to be learned, an objective. However, each behavior is com-

Table 5

Toileting Skills (LAP)

Behavior	Age (Dev.)
Fusses to be changed after B-M	12 mos.
Usually dry after nap	12 mos.
Indicates wet pants	15 mos.
Has bowel control	15 mos.
Dry at night if taken up	24 mos.
Is usually dry all night	36–48 mos.
Cares for self at toilet	45 mos.
Uses bathroom unassisted	60–72 mos.

Table 6

Dressing Skills

Behavior	Age (Dev.)
Enjoys taking off hat, shoes & pants	12 mos.
Can unzip zipper	18–23 mos.
Pulls off socks	12–24 mos.
Removes coat or dress	24–36 mos.
Unbuttons accessible buttons	36–48 mos.
Undresses self	36–48 mos.
Pulls on shoes	36–48 mos.
Buttons coat or dress	40 mos.
Dresses without supervision	42 mos.
Undresses except for back buttons, laces and ties	48–60 mos.
Laces shoes	48–60 mos.
Distinguishes front from back of clothing	48–60 mos.
Dresses self except tying	48–60 mos.
Buttons 4 buttons	50 mos.
Dresses and undresses alone	60–72 mos.
Ties shoe lace	72 mos.

posed of smaller components which must be identified. For example, the subskills for one eating skill—drinks from cup—are the following:

1. Child picks up cup.
2. Child moves cup to mouth.
3. Child wets lips with liquid.
4. Child tilts head back slightly.
5. Child pours liquid into mouth.
6. Child replaces cup on table.

Each subskill may be broken into smaller components. For example, before the child can pick up the cup, she must have the following skills:

1. Child can sit (is upright).
2. Child has awareness of cup.
3. Child can reach.
4. Child can grasp.

Further analysis of the above skills is possible. If any one subskill is missing, the skill cannot be learned. In a task analytic assessment (Knapczyk, 1975), the teacher can determine what motor skills are required to complete the self-help task and the level of language development required for the child to understand verbal cues. An analysis of the child's entry skills is the key to determining the best point at which to begin instruction. Knowing the child's present skills reduces the likelihood of teaching skills which are already known or those that are too advanced.

As an illustration, a task analysis for putting on pants is presented in Table 7. If the child repeatedly responded to the request, "Pull up your pants" by performing only the first 5 steps, it could be assumed that steps 6 through 25 were unlearned tasks. From incorrect, poor, or no performance on steps 6 through 25, the teacher would determine that instruction should begin at step 6, raising the first knee.

Objectives

Once it has been decided which self-help skills need to be taught, and the specific functioning level of the child has been assessed, realistic program objectives may then be formulated. It will be recalled from Chapter 3, that the three components of behavioral objectives are:

1. Specifying conditions under which behavior is to occur.
2. Defining the behavior to be changed.
3. Establishing a criterion which shows that the objective has been reached.

The following examples demonstrate a poorly developed objective and a well-developed objective.

Bad Example: Jerry will display more independence and self-confidence in brushing teeth by the end of the year.

Table 7

Task Analysis for Putting on Long Pants

Steps:

1. Pick out pants.
2. Pants in position on lap.
3. Grasp at waistline.
4. Maintain hold.
5. Open waistband.
6. Raise first knee.
7. Insert foot.
8. Push foot through leg.
9. Pull first leg.
10. Raise second knee.
11. Insert foot.
12. Push foot through leg.
13. Pull second leg.
14. Bend over.
15. Grasp lower pants leg.
16. Pull pants completely over feet.
17. Stand up.
18. Grasp at waistline.
19. Maintain hold.
20. Pull up to hips.
21. Position hands.
22. Grasp waistband.
23. Maintain hold.
24. Pull to waistline.
25. Adjust waistband.

Good Example: Given a toothbrush, Jerry will demonstrate proficiency in at least 90% of the steps in the brushing task analysis for 4 out of 5 days.

A performance objective which calls for complete mastery of a self-help skill is illustrated as follows:

Objective: To drink from an uncovered child's cup.
Task: Put a small amount of milk or juice into an uncovered child's cup. Assist the child in raising the cup and drinking from it, and returning the cup to the table. When the child can drink from the cup without assistance and without spilling, gradually increase the amount of liquid placed in a cup. (Johnson & Werner, 1976, p. 90)

Selecting a Teaching Procedure

In selecting appropriate teaching procedures, the most important consideration is the uniqueness of each child's needs. The needs of a bright visually handicapped child will be very different from those of a multihandicapped infant. Although the self-help tasks to be learned may be similar, the learning abilities of the children will determine which teaching procedures should be used. In addition to learning abilities, the teacher should also consider the previous strategies used with the child and their effect on self-help development.

The techniques of instruction described in Chapter 3 can be applied to the teaching of self-help skills to young handicapped children. Some of these techniques are applied to teaching specific self-help skills in Tables 8, 9, and 10.

Tables 8 and 9 show task analysis as it applies to brushing teeth and washing one's face. The task analyses provided in these tables illustrate examples of behavioral chains. Table 10 provides an illustration of backward chaining which is especially effective with children whose handicapping conditions are severe.

Table 8

Brushing Teeth

Steps:

1. Remove toothbrush and toothpaste from cup.
2. Unscrew toothpaste cap.
3. Squeeze appropriate amount of toothpaste onto brush.
4. Lay toothbrush down.
5. Screw cap back on tube.
6. Pick up brush in preferred hand.
7. Lean over sink.
8. Brush in down motion over top teeth from one side of mouth to the other.
9. Spit out excess at least once.
10. Brush in up motion over bottom teeth from one side of mouth to the other.
11. Spit out excess at least once.
12. Brush in down motion over back of top teeth from one side of mouth to the other.
13. Spit out excess at least once.
14. Brush in up motion over back of bottom teeth from one side of mouth to the other.
15. Spit out excess at least once.
16. Brush back and forth over crowns of top teeth from one side of mouth to the other.
17. Spit out excess at least once.
18. Brush back and forth over crowns of bottom teeth from one side of mouth to the other.
19. Spit out excess at least once.
20. Pick up cup.
21. Turn on cold water faucet.
22. Fill cup with water.
23. Rinse mouth with water.
24. Spit out excess at least once.
25. Pour excess water out of cup into sink.
26. Replace cup next to sink.
27. Rinse toothbrush in water.
28. Turn off cold water faucet.
29. Replace brush and paste in cup.

Table 9

Washing the Face

Steps:

1. Walk over to sink.
2. Pull up sleeve.
3. Close drain.
4. Turn on warm water spigot.
5. Turn off spigot when basin is halfway full.
6. Pick up face cloth.
7. Place in water.
8. Squeeze cloth.
9. Pick up soap.
10. Rub soap on wet cloth.
11. Replace soap on sink.
12. Bend over basin.
13. Close eyes.
14. Rub cloth all over face with slight pressure.
15. Rinse cloth in water; squeeze excess water out.
16. Rub wet cloth again over face to remove all soapy film.
17. Rinse cloth again.
18. Squeeze dry.
19. Dry eye areas.
20. Open eyes.
21. Dry face with towel.
22. Open drain.
23. Rinse basin and replace all materials in correct places.

Table 10

A Backward-Chaining Method for Teaching Spoon Feeding

Steps:

1. Carry spoon to one inch from mouth.
2. Carry spoon to midpoint between bowl and mouth.
3. Carry spoon to two inches above bowl.
4. Lifts spoon out of bowl.
5. Fills spoon with food.
6. Dips food into bowl.
7. Pick up spoon.

Note: From *Helping the Mentally Retarded Acquire Play Skills: A Behavioral Approach* by P. Wehman. Springfield, Ill.: Charles C Thomas, 1976. Copyright 1976 by Charles C Thomas. Reprinted by permission.

Specific Guidelines in Teaching Self-help Skills

The attainment of self-help skills is important to the child for several reasons. Primarily, they are skills which are used daily requiring repetitive activities which facilitate learning and retention. Because they are daily activities, learning them emphasizes normal experiences and gives the child some equality with peers and siblings. Dressing and eating, especially, are concrete activities in which the child can assess her own progress. Learning to do something for herself will boost her self-concept and motivate her to attempt other tasks. Also, when she becomes independent in tasks family members once had to do for her, she will gain their respect.

Many young children with special needs cannot acquire self-help skills unless they are taught with extraordinary skill. To assist their teachers and other professionals who work with them, the following teaching guidelines are presented.

Toilet Training

Using the toilet independently is an important self-help skill which nonhandicapped children typically begin to learn between 24 and 30 months of age. That handicapped children have been trained through operant conditioning to void properly in the commode is well documented in the literature (Baumeister & Klosowski, 1965; Kimbrell, Luckey, Barbuto, & Love, 1967; Levine & Elliot, 1970; Mahoney, Van Wagenen, & Meyerson, 1971).

Essentially, toilet training is the sequencing of skills which are required for appropriate toileting. This includes finding the toilet, pulling down pants, sitting on the toilet, defecation or urination, use of toilet tissue, pulling up pants, flushing the toilet, and washing and drying hands. Usually, the supervisor provides reinforcement for each step of the training. Careful data and records are kept to indicate progress being made.

While operant conditioning has been successful, recent advances in behavior modification have led to even more dramatic improvement in the speed and effectiveness with which toileting skills can be acquired (Foxx & Azrin, 1973). As Azrin and Foxx (1971) note, many of the previous studies performed in the 1960s failed to provide conclusive follow-up data on the maintenance of newly acquired toileting skills.

The Azrin and Foxx rapid method of toilet training decreased training times to an average of four to five days. The 9 steps below, which have been adapted from Foxx and Azrin (1973), represent the instructional sequence involved in the bladder training procedure:

1. Give as much fluid to the child as he will drink while seated in his chair.
2. Direct the child to sit on toilet seat using the least possible prompting.
3. Direct the child to pull his pants down using the least possible prompting.
4. a. When child voids, give him a food reinforcer and praise while seated, then direct him to stand.
   b. If the child does not void within 20 minutes after drinking the fluids, direct him to stand.
5. Direct the child to pull up his pants using the least possible prompting.
6. Direct the child to his chair using the least possible prompting.
7. After the child has been sitting for 5 minutes, inspect him for dry pants.
   a. If his pants are dry, give him edible and praise.
   b. If pants are wet, only show him the edible and admonish him.
8. Check child for dry pants every 5 minutes.
9. At the end of 30 minutes, begin the sequence of steps again. (p. 45)

Each task must be taught in small steps in the right order.

The emphasis on self-initiated or independent toileting is an important milestone in toilet training of the developmentally young. This training eliminates the need for prompting or control from others, and develops independent behavior in the child. Foxx and Azrin (1973) describe how to program for self-initiated toileting in the child once bladder control has been learned. These steps are the following:

1. Give fluids immediately following an elimination.
2. Do not give further prompting.
3. Continue to provide guidance for dressing and undressing and for flushing the toilet, if necessary, but never at a greater level than that needed on previous toiletings.
4. Move child's chair farther from the toilet after each successful self-initiation.
5. Gradually lengthen the time between dry-pants inspections.
6. Intermittently reward correct toileting.
7. Have the child demonstrate that he can find the toilet from various areas on the ward. (p. 54)

Eating Training

There are a number of eating skills which the young delayed child may be unable to perform independently.[1] These may range from the inability to

---

1. Paul Wehman acknowledges his indebtedness to Katy Pierce, OTR, Cedar Rapids, Iowa, for her help in assembling these guidelines.

swallow to using a spoon or eating family style with a number of utensils, plates, and bowls. For example, the severely physically handicapped child may be unable to eat properly unless the correct type of positioning or prosthetic devices are employed (Schmidt, 1976). Because the number of skills involved is so great, only the critical points in each of the basic eating functions are outlined here. Parents and professionals should be able to develop an effective eating program from this outline.

When to Feed the Child

1. At the beginning of the feeding training, work with the child alone. Give her undivided attention and as much time as she needs.
2. As she advances, graduate her to feeding prior to the family meal. Then let her sit with family members while they eat. During the meal, the child should have an easy-to-eat food such as a cracker.
3. Feeding training always should be a pleasant experience. It should be done when the child is ready for food and the child's preference for different foods should be respected to a certain extent. Introduce new food slowly and always accompany it with a familiar one.

Positioning. Feeding in the correct position should start as soon as possible. With parents of very young children, it is important to give clear and detailed instructions and, if at all possible, they should be given to both parents.

1. The child's head should be in a slightly downward position (the normal position during eating).
2. The spoon should be placed into the mouth from either side rather than directly from the front, with a slight downward pressure to counteract the often present tongue thrust. Use a spoon with a small shallow bowl for early eating experiences.
3. Encourage the child to take the food off with her lips and not with the teeth.
4. To assist swallowing, if needed, stroke the child's throat slightly. If the child gags or chokes, put the head forward and down; the child will probably throw his head back and put a stretch on the esophagus, preventing the food from getting dislodged.
5. The child should sit in a correct position, with the feet supported and the elbows resting on the table. It may be necessary to use special supports such as straps and sandbags to secure proper position. However, try to keep this to a minimum, because it may be hard to wean the child away from these later.

Swallowing. In order to teach voluntary swallowing the following points should be considered:

1. The head should be in a slightly downward position.
2. Use only a small amount of liquid in the cup; it is easier and keeps the child from being discouraged.
3. Stroke the throat to facilitate swallowing.
4. Discourage child from biting the cup.

5. If there is no lip closure (due to overbite or involuntary motion), hold the lips shut, applying very slight pressure to upper and lower lips with your fingers.
6. Teach the child to take one sip and swallow.
7. If the child stiffens on approach of the cup, wait until she relaxes again. She will soon learn that she will get food only when relaxed.

Drinking from a Straw. Even if the child is not able to handle a cup, she can be taught to drink from a straw. This type of drinking has several advantages:

1. It is a step towards independent feeding for the child who has difficulty lifting a cup.
2. It is also a speech development activity, providing breath control and lip mobility.
3. It is a help in controlling drooling.
4. It is an excellent means of getting liquids into a severely handicapped child.

Some of the important points to remember are:

1. Use a short plastic straw with a small circumference.
2. Only a small amount of liquid should be placed in the cup.
3. Let the child take only one sip at a time, gradually increasing speed until it becomes a continuous procedure.
4. Encourage child to close only her lips and not her teeth. If lip closure is not present or insufficient, again apply slight pressure to lips around straw with your fingers.
5. A good way to start is to use a small cup with a lid and a straw running through it. It is possible to push milk into the child's mouth by pressing on the lid, after which the child will swallow and gradually get the idea of sucking up. A sweet syrup applied to the tip of the straw also encourages sucking. Later several small holes may be punched in the lid to allow easier flow.
6. Increase the length of the straw and change to liquid with a heavier flow (milkshakes) as the child progresses.
7. Use a paper straw and see how many the child needs to empty a cup.

Using a Cup. First, see if the child will grasp the handle of the empty cup. If so, guide the cup to his mouth as if to drink. If not, assist the child in holding the cup. Put a small amount of liquid in the cup. Help him to get the cup to his mouth for drinking. At a later time, allow the child to try by himself, even if he spills the contents.

Chewing. Start with semisolid foods, such as lima beans and cooked carrots, which the child likes. Bread or vanilla crackers are also appropriate because they are soft and unlikely to cause choking. Encourage the child to chew each bite before swallowing until chewing becomes a habit. By putting food between the teeth from the side of the mouth (alternate) you hope to set off chewing reflexes by stimulating the inside of the cheek; the same method seems to counteract the tongue thrust. Give more and more solid foods as chewing strength increases.

Self-feeding. Devices which can be used to facilitate self-feeding include:

1. Built-up handle on spoon, or handcuff to hold spoon (see p. 179). Use the fork as much as possible; it is easier to spear than to push food onto a spoon.
2. Plate with sides, so food will fall back onto plate (see p. 179).
3. A cut-out board to hold plate if necessary.
4. A cup which is not too large. (Cups with spouts should not be used for children with drinking difficulties to avoid relapse to primitive sucking.)
5. Cup holder if child cannot hold cup.
6. Sticky foods like mashed potatoes that will not fall off the spoon easily. (Use these initially to help child learn to use a spoon.)

Points that are important to remember in feeding training include:

1. Be sure of good body position.
2. Stabilize feet and other hand, if necessary.
3. Support hands on the table.
4. Let child decide which hand she wants to use.
5. Make a "dry run" until child is familiar with activity and understands exactly what she is supposed to do.
6. Give her some assistance at first, gradually reducing it.
7. Let her try by herself and see what she does when she thinks she is unobserved. (This might give you some helpful clues.)

The development of appropriate eating behavior has received increased attention in recent years. A number of reports describe spoon-feeding training with severely delayed children (Berkowitz, Sherry, & Davis, 1971; Christian, Holloman, & Lanier, 1973; Eaton & Brown, 1974; Groves & Carroccio, 1971; O'Brien, Bugle, & Azrin, 1972). Through a backward chaining teaching procedure, the child is physically guided through most of the spoon-feeding behavior and initially required only to empty the spoon into her mouth. As the child becomes more proficient, the teacher gradually fades hand support until total independence is achieved.

Dressing and Undressing

Dressing skills are best taught in realistic situations such as toileting sessions, preparing for daytime activities, or removing garments before bedtime. It is also necessary to schedule daily sessions at home and at school to work on skills which need special attention. The following instructional guidelines may be implemented during such sessions:

1. Each child should be assessed to determine which steps of a skill she is able to perform unassisted. A task analysis of each activity will help the teacher assess the child. Each person working with the child should be aware of what level of assistance she needs in order that no more physical assistance is given than the child actually requires.

2. Undressing is usually easier for a child than dressing so training should begin with this. Backward chaining is usually the best instructional technique for dressing since the child receives early satisfaction.
3. Even if the child cannot do the task, she can be an active participant by bending an arm or stooping slightly when garments go over her head. Involvement of the child is a beginning first step and may be fostered by talking to her about the garment and the part of her body that is being clothed. Dressing time can be used to emphasize colors and movement concepts such as push, pull, up and down.
4. Several concrete suggestions for dressing-undressing instruction include:
   a. Use clothing one or two sizes too large so the child can remove it with ease.
   b. Use socks without heels (tube socks) for first sessions. Backward chaining helps child learn to manipulate the heel area effectively. When child can pull this type sock on, introduce stretchy type cotton-blend sock with heel. Follow this with regular nylon sock.
   c. For training putting on or removing crew-neck shirts, first teach the child to raise and lower a hula hoop or similar aid over her head. When child has learned these hand motions, introduce a dressing shirt which has only a hole for the head. Have child learn to raise and lower this over her head by modeling and physically assisting her. From this, move on to an over-sized T-shirt, followed by a regular shirt. Some children will take long periods of training to learn removing the shirt over their head and then from the arms, so it is better to have them learn to pull their arms out before raising the shirt over their heads. It is easier to put the arms in the T-shirt before the head. The shirt should be positioned in front of the child with the bottom opening close to her stomach. She must put one arm into the shirt all the way through the correct sleeve. (If one arm is more difficult to use, it should be the first to be placed into a garment, but the better arm should be removed first when taking off a garment.) The same procedure is used for the other arm. Then the child pushes the shirt up each arm at least to her elbows. This is necessary in order to get it over her head. When both arms are ready, the child simply tilts her head forward, grasps the center of the shirt with either hand, and pulls it over her head. For many children this sequence is simpler than putting their head in first and then attempting to get their arms into the sleeves.

An instructional program designed to help a physically handicapped child begin to acquire buttoning skills is presented in Table 11. In this program an effort has been made to describe the specific child and teacher behaviors required to meet the objective.

Grooming Skills

The development of grooming skills such as bathing, brushing teeth, washing hands, and blowing nose can also be achieved through task analysis, behavior shaping methods, and positive reinforcement. Once the teacher has acquired these basic behavior modification techniques, implementing instructional pro-

Table 11

Predressing Skill: Inserting a Wooden Disc Through Vertical and Horizontal Slots

Prerequisite Skills: Student must be able to grasp with thumb and index finger; also, the student must have gross motor skills of her arms.

Materials: An elevated board with a vertical and horizontal slot, and a wooden disc. At first, the board should be placed parallel to the working surface, later the board should be moved to a perpendicular position.

Objective: Given a wooden block with one vertical and horizontal slot, the student will drop the disc through the slots 8 out of 10 times. The board will be placed on the table in front of the student, the disc will be on the left side of the board. The teacher will be sitting beside the student.

Child Behaviors	*Teacher Behaviors*
1. Child raises dominant arm straight up to her waist level. 2. Child extends dominant arm forward until it is directly over the wooden disc. 3. Child lowers dominant arm straight down until it is 1/2-inch from the wooden disc. 4. Child curls dominant hand fingers downward. 5. Child places dominant thumb on the edge of the disc that is closest to her body. 6. Child places index finger of her dominant hand on the edge of the disc farthest from her body. 7. Child raises hand straight up, thus holding the wooden disc. 8. Child moves dominant hand holding the disc (to right or left) until her hand is directly above the vertical slot. 9. Child lowers dominant hand holding disc until disc is 1/2-inch from the vertical slot. 10. Child releases disc, thus dropping the disc through the slot. 11. Child repeats steps 1–10 ten times in the vertical slot. 12. Child repeats steps 1–10 ten times using the horizontal slot.	Teacher will give the verbal cue "Do this" and model the desired behavior; if there is no response then physical prompting will be used for each step. Reinforcement will be on a continuous basis initially, in the form of clapping, and the statement "Very good," after each correct response and then faded in the form of the statement "Very good" after the student has completed the entire task analysis. Correction Procedure: The student will be told her response was incorrect. The teacher will either model the correct response or physically prompt it depending on the level of assistance required by the child.

grams for grooming should not be difficult. As an illustration of how these techniques can be applied to teaching a child to take a bath, an instructional program is provided in Table 12.

Table 12

Taking a Bath

Prerequisite Skills: Taking off clothes, opening and closing eyes at appropriate times, washing face.

Materials: Soap, cloth, towel, bath mat.

Objective: Given the materials necessary to take a bath, student will wash herself clean with 95% accuracy.

Steps:

1. Walk over to tub.
2. Close drain.
3. Turn on hot and cold water.
4. Fill tub half-full with warm water.
5. Turn off hot and cold water spigots.
6. Take off clothes.
7. Sit in tub of water.
8. Pick up face cloth and soap.
9. Place in tub.
10. Rub small amount of soap on cloth.
11. Wash face and behind ears.
12. Rinse both face and ear areas and dry with towel.
13. Replace towel.
14. Rub wet soapy cloth over neck area (front and back).
15. Rinse soap from neck.
16. Rub wet soapy cloth over shoulder and arms.
17. Rinse soap away.
18. Wash chest and stomach area with soapy cloth.
19. Rinse both areas.
20. Pick up back brush.
21. Wet and lather it.
22. Scrub back all over.
23. Rinse brush and place aside.
24. Rinse back with wet cloth.
25. Wash around pelvic area and buttocks.
26. Wash thighs and knees.
27. Wash legs and feet.
28. Wash between toes.
29. Rinse all body parts.
30. Stand up carefully.
31. Get out of tub and stand on mat.
32. Pick up towel.
33. Dry all body parts from top to bottom.
34. Wrap towel around body.
35. Open drain.
36. Rinse tub.
37. Put on clean clothes.

Teaching Procedures for Taking a Bath: Take baseline information to determine where to start teaching. When teaching, go through the steps one at a time. Tell the child what you want her to do. On the step that she cannot do, repeat the same instructions. If the child does not respond, model correct response. If child still does not respond, physically move

Table 12

Taking a Bath *(cont.)*

the child through the correct response. Reinforce after physical prompting to increase the correct responses made by the child. Social reinforcers should be used if possible; however, if edible reinforcers are more effective, they should be utilized. Reinforcement should be given immediately after the child responds independently. When responses do not occur after physical prompting, the child's readiness to learn the new skill should be reconsidered. Also, the effectiveness of reinforcers and clearness of instruction should be checked.

Additionally, the skill of bathing may be taught through the process of backward chaining. This involves physically guiding the child through all the steps and drilling the last step repetitively until the child has learned it. After the child has learned the last step, the parent or professional then physically guides her up to the next to the last step, drills the next to the last step, and allows the child to carry through the last step alone. This procedure continues until all the steps are learned. Data are recorded after each session.

Adapted Equipment and Approaches for Self-help Skill Development

The reasons for encouraging parents and teachers to create equipment for working with young handicapped children were discussed in Chapter 5. The same reasons and principles apply in the development of self-help skills. Some ideas that have been used to help young children acquire self-help skills are presented here.

Eating

For young children with developmental problems, there are many problems associated with eating. The child may be unable to feed herself; she may want to eat only certain foods; she may need special equipment which may isolate her from others; or her eating habits may be repulsive to others. Teachers and parents must find ways of making mealtime as normal as possible to assist the child in gaining acceptance and independence.

Proper positioning could be the most important aspect of successful eating. The child may need a special seat to keep her legs apart, weight even on both hips, trunk supported and upright, head up and arms in front of her. The more normal the sitting posture, the more normal feeding will be.

Swallowing food is very difficult for the child who is lying down. Even in infancy, the child's body should be slightly inclined with the head a little higher than the feet. For the toddler, a reclined position discourages self-feeding. Proper positioning fosters normal posture which in turn promotes success in eye-hand coordination. Finnie (1975) has illustrated appropriate eating positions for different ages (pp. 116–118).

Many children need specific feeding techniques. These should be devised by a qualified therapist who evaluates the child's strengths as well as weaknesses and then works with the child, her parents and her teacher. If this service is not available, Finnie's book is a helpful resource for general ideas on feeding techniques.

It is not unusual for children to avoid textured foods, preferring instead pureed or baby foods. If they are allowed to continue eating soft foods, it is unlikely that they will learn to chew or to tolerate textured foods. Generally, it is recommended that the child's ability to eat textured foods be increased gradually even if she objects.

Commercially produced items which will help the young child acquire eating skills may be purchased from equipment companies (see Appendix B) or in grocery stores, dime stores, or drug stores. Items often found in local stores include rubber suction cups for stabilizing plates, plastic tumblers, plastic utensils with bent handles, and cups with built-in straws. Narrow plastic tumblers which are easy to grasp are available. Cups are available with two handles for children who can control the cup better when both hands are used. A hole can be punched in the lid to accommodate a straw. Long plastic straws and curly straws are helpful in strengthening a child's sucking ability (but are difficult to clean). Hospital supply dealers carry rolls of clear tubing that can be cut to length for long straws.

Many types of cups, plates, and utensils are available in special equipment catalogs. Cups with suction bases, wide bases, spouts, straws, lids, double handles, or single handles meet the child's specific needs.

Plates are available with suction cup bottoms, divided sections, and high rims. If a regular plate is used, a metal or plastic guard can be attached to the side, which gives the child an edge to push the food against. Utensils come with built-up handles for easier grasp, swivel handles for limited arm motion, and bent handles to substitute for wrist movement. Stabbing chunks of food may be easier for the young child than scooping with a spoon. A combination spoon and fork (spork) has the advantage of both. For the child who tends to bite the spoon,

Plates and cups with special features.

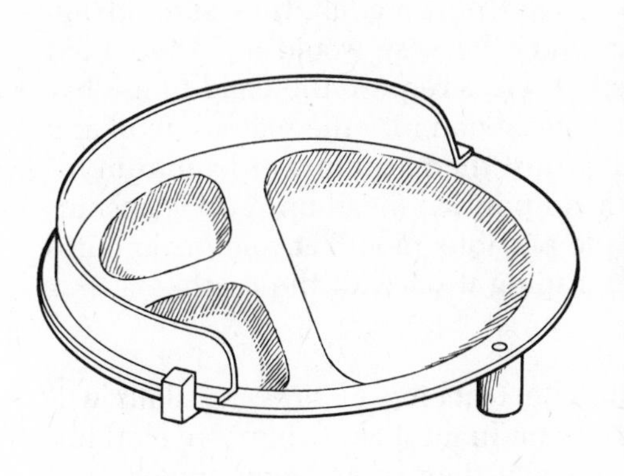

Left, plate with guard; right, plate with feet.

plastic-coated metal spoons are safer than rigid plastic spoons. Soft rubber spoons are sometimes available.

Often a child is better able to feed herself if her spoon has a large round handle. Such a spoon is easily devised from a regular spoon. A hair roller or scrap of plastic pipe may be placed over the handle, or the handle may be wrapped with foam rubber or sponge and secured with plastic electrician's tape.

If the child cannot hold the spoon well, a utensil cuff which will keep the spoon in her palm can be bought or made. The cuff consists of a strap which fits around the hand, fastens with Velcro (trade name for a cloth fastening tape, available from fabric stores), and has a pocket to hold the utensil. If the child can lift her arm toward her face but cannot aim the spoon sideways into her mouth, the handle of the spoon can be bent toward her mouth. The angle needed is opposite for left- and right-handed use. Most metal spoons can be bent slightly.

Cycem is the trade name for a nonslip surface which is available for purchase by the roll and in other forms. It is a flat rubberlike sheet that can be cut in placemat size for use under plates, schoolwork, or toys to keep them in place. It can be wiped clean.

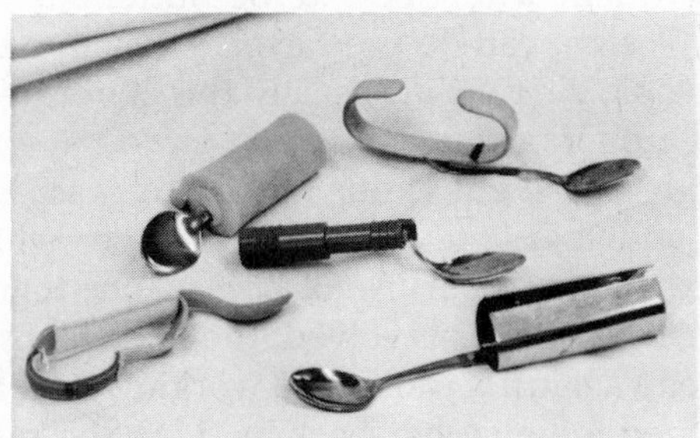

Adaptations of utensils that make eating easier.

Various types of mechanical feeding machines are now available. Although they usually require much adjustment or help from an adult, they offer advantages to severely handicapped children who otherwise would need to be fed every bite at each meal. In general, these devices require the child to use her arm or head to press a lever. This pushes the spoon into the plate of food and raises the spoon to mouth level. The child must then lean forward and remove the food from the spoon. Thus, normal head position (head upright) is encouraged, and other desirable factors are made possible (mouth at midline and lips coming forward to the food instead of scraping it off with the teeth).

Dressing

Careful observation of the child during the teaching of dressing skills will contribute to an understanding of her problem. In most cases, her own clothing and positioning can be used more beneficially than special equipment. It is possible to buy clothing in styles which facilitate self-dressing.

Clothing at least one size larger should be bought for a child with dressing difficulties. The loose fit contributes to the child's ability to master dressing skills. Garments that are tight or difficult to fasten should not be used. Clothing should be simple with a minimum of fasteners. Pants with elastic waists instead of snaps and zippers should be selected. Pants which fasten with a wide hook are easier to use than those with snaps. A wide belt with a single-prong buckle is easier than others.

Pullover shirts will avoid the need for tiny buttons, but pullover shirts must be loose and made with flexible material at the neckline. Otherwise they will be difficult to remove. Short pants are easier than long ones to put on or take off. Sometimes a long-sleeved shirt is easier to manage than a short-sleeved one because a child can pull on the cuff of the shirt to help remove it. The cuff buttons can be sewn with elastic thread to allow the child to put the shirt on without unbuttoning the cuffs.

Iron-on appliqués can be used to distinguish the front of a garment from the back. The child's shoes can be color-coded on the inside sole to remind her on which foot each belongs.

Velcro can replace buttons and zippers. Buttons can be sewn on top of the button hole and a patch of Velcro sewn underneath the hole and on the other surface where the button should be. When a child overlaps the two patches of Velcro, the garment will be fastened until she pulls them apart. In this way the garment will appear to be buttoned.

Velcro can be used over the snap on a pair of pants. It can also replace the whole zipper, but usually this is not necessary. If a child cannot open or close a zipper, a round ring or a large paper clip can be placed through the zipper tab to make it easier for her to grasp. Zippers open and close best when one hand adjusts tension on the zipper while the other pulls the zipper tab. Poor balance or poor use of both hands together may make the task difficult.

If balance is involved, the child's positioning should be considered. Can she lean against a wall while working with her zipper? Can she sit down? Does she need to lie on her back or side? She may be able to accomplish the task if she

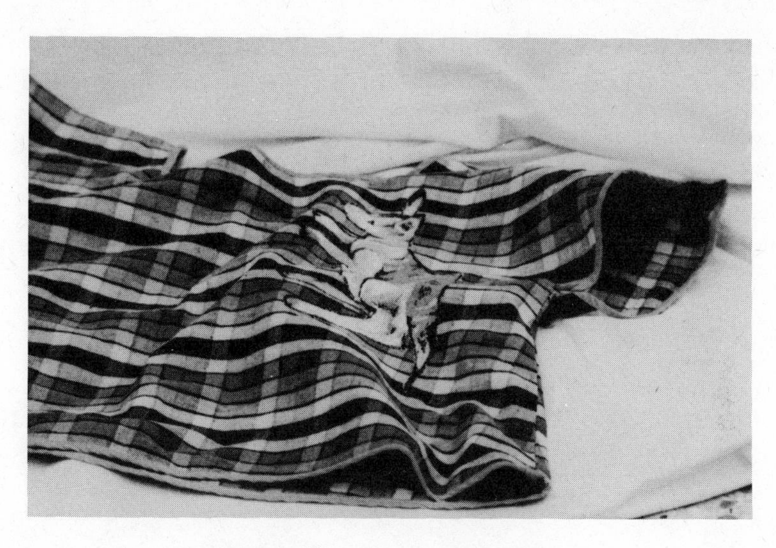

Appliqué on front of garment.

sits in a corner, on a low bench, or perhaps straddling a foam roll. The child's position in all dressing tasks is critical; each position determines the muscles she will use. Young children who are severely handicapped need help in finding the proper position to make the task easier.

Also the positioning of the clothing must be considered. Each piece must be placed the same way each time. Clothing must be flat, right-side out, and corresponding to the child's left and right, front or up. This assistance will give her the visual constancy she is otherwise unable to attain. Once she can put on the clothing, she can then be taught to position it and to change incorrect positioning.

Learning dressing skills on herself is harder than learning the separate skills first; therefore, the child may need to practice with dressing sets in order to understand each step. Horowitz (1967) developed a 6-step set for putting a garment over the head. Initially the child practices the concept and motor skill of putting something over her head by using a small plastic hoop. When she can do this, she advances to a 2-inch wide loop of vinyl. The flexibility of the vinyl adds more skill to the task. The next step is a similar loop of fabric, adding more flexibility and making it more difficult for the child to manipulate it over her head. Each garment in the series has an appliqué on the front so the child can learn to adjust the clothing correctly. The next step is a rectangle of material with an opening for the head but no side seams. The child completes the over-the-head practice without worrying about armholes. The last steps make use of complete shirts, one sleeveless and one with short sleeves. Each complete set can be made in various sizes to accommodate different children.

A similar series can be used for putting on pants, first using a hoop, then a band of fabric, then a loose "sleeve" of material, then loose short bloomers with elastic waist and legs. The child first learns how to lift one leg and put it through the hoop and gradually builds up to putting both legs through the garment.

1. Plastic Hoop

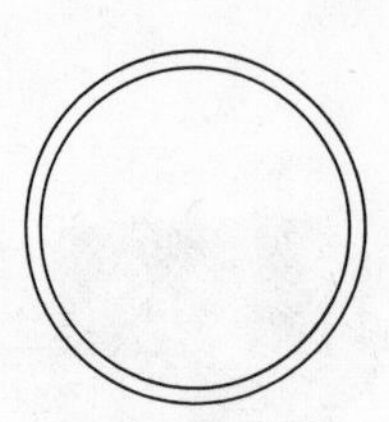

2. Vinyl Loop or Leatherette Loop

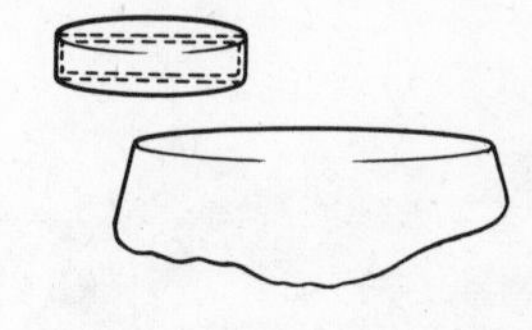

3. Fabric Loop

4. No Side Seams

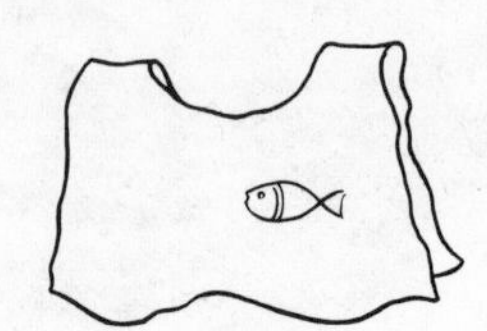

5. Sleeveless

6. Short Sleeves

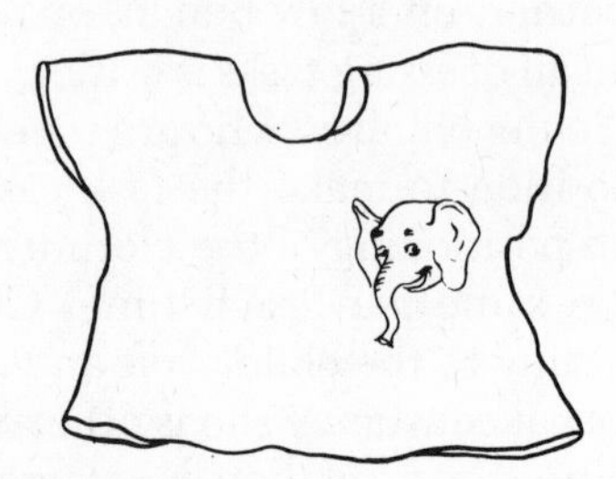

Dressing set.

Fastenings are often the most difficult part of dressing. Because they are next to the body, the child has trouble seeing them. Using dressing dolls or dressing boards gives the child practice with the fastener before she has to incorporate it with her own clothes. Commercial dressing dolls are often too small, and their fastenings tend to be fragile. Using a large stuffed cloth doll (2-feet tall) and making outfits which include snaps, buttons, zipper, buckle, hooks, and lacing may be more beneficial to the child. Large, heavy-duty fasteners should be used. Hooks and snaps should be the large ones used on pants; buttons should be large (1-inch) and flat rather than domed. Zippers should be heavy and could have a zipper-pull ring. Individual fasteners do not have to be used on a doll. They can be sewn to a piece of material and attached to flat boards or incorporated in pillows and other articles.

Lacing and knot-tying boards take the child through each step. In lacing, the child learns to put the string through the hole, cross the midline, keep the strings in proper sequence, and lace alternate strings. In knot tying the child learns to cross the midline, form an X with the strings, and manipulate them into the knot. In both sets, various visual clues are used and then phased out as the child learns.

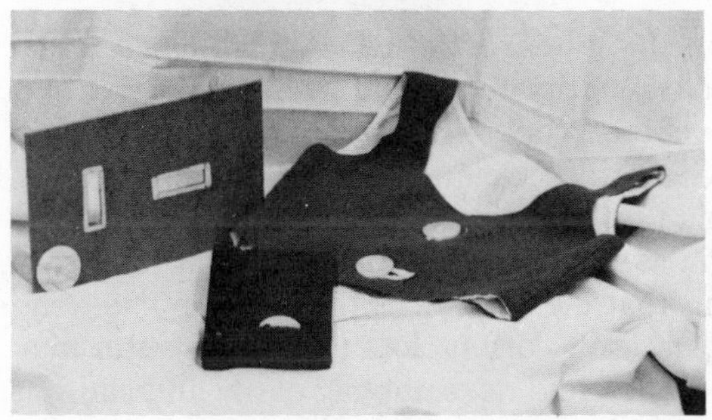

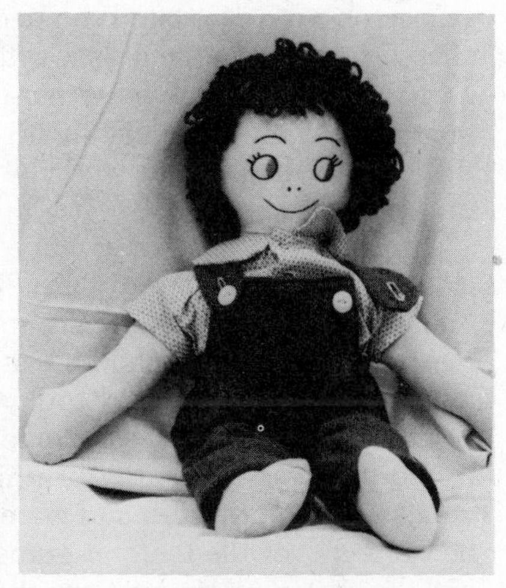

Upper left, fasteners; lower left, buttoning; right, dressing doll.

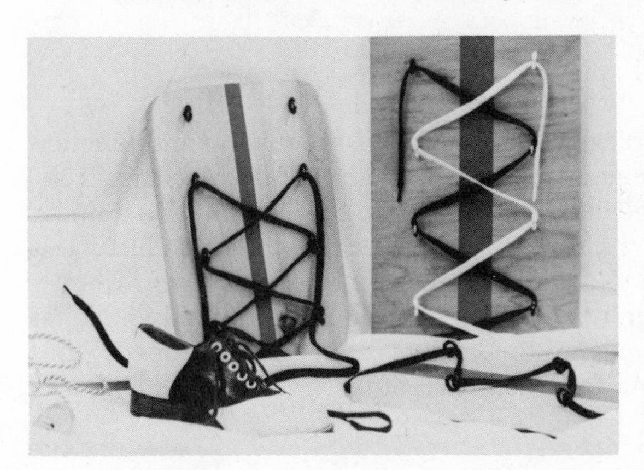

Lacing and knot tying.

Grooming

A young handicapped child may have little concern for grooming skills. However, she should receive training in good habits and become able to participate in her own care. She can assist with combing, hand washing, and bathing.

If she cannot reach her head, a long-handled comb may be used. Liquid soap in a dispenser or squeeze bottle is easier to handle than a loose cake of soap. The cake of soap can be secured to the sink with a suction cup. Supply dealers sell hand brushes and sponges which attach to the sink with suction cups enabling the child to wash each hand independently. For bathing, nonslip treads or rubber mats should be used in the tub. Commercial and homemade tub seats prevent a child from slipping while being bathed (see equipment and material sources in Appendix B.)

Soap on a string around the neck or a bath mitt will simplify bathing for the child. The mitt can be a sock with a cake of soap inside or a washcloth folded in half and sewn. One edge can be left open for the child to put her hand in, or all edges may be stitched with a cake of soap inside. This is easier to handle than either the soap or washcloth by itself. Long-handled bath sponges and brushes are useful.

A young child can also practice brushing her teeth (see p. 167) but the actual cleaning must be done by an adult. Healthy teeth and gums are much too important to entrust their care to a child. Proper cleaning of the teeth is even more important if the child has any feeding problems, tongue thrust, drooling, high palate, or gum hypertrophy due to seizure medication.

The cleaning of teeth should begin as soon as they appear. It is not necessary to use toothpaste; it is the brushing that cleans the teeth and stimulates the gums. A soft toothbrush and water, or a soft cotton cloth dipped in water may be rubbed over the teeth or gums. If the child does not gag easily and can spit out the water in her mouth, then toothpaste may be added for flavor and interest.

Summary

There is little doubt that if handicapped children are to grow up and function independently in society, proficiency in self-help skills will play a critical role. Furthermore, the earlier delayed children are able to receive self-care training through early childhood programs and parent instruction, the more likely it is that such children will be able to avoid placement in special classes. The delayed child who begins to exhibit independent functioning in self-help skills has taken one large step toward removing the label of being "handicapped," thus allowing more instructional time for training in other areas such as language and socialization.

REFERENCES

Azrin, N. H., & Foxx, R. A rapid method of toilet training the institutionalized retarded. *Journal of Applied Behavior Analysis,* 1971, **4,** 89–99.

Baumeister, A., & Klosowski, R. An attempt to group toilet train severely retarded patients. *Mental Retardation,* 1965, 3, 24–26.

Berkowitz, S., Sherry, P., & Davis, B. Teaching self-feeding skills to profound retardates using reinforcement and fading procedures. *Behavior Therapy,* 1971, **2,** 62–67.

Christian, W., Holloman, S., & Lanier, C. L. An attendant operated feeding program for severely and profoundly retarded females. *Mental Retardation,* 1973, **11,** 35–37.

Eaton, P., & Brown, R. The training of mealtime behaviors in the subnormal. *British Journal of Mental Subnormality,* 1974, **20,** 78–85.

Eaves, R., & McLaughlin, P. A systems approach for the assessment of the child and his environment: Getting back to basics. *Journal of Special Education,* 1977, **11**(1), 99–111.

Erickson, A. *Essential early education: A mandate for early intervention.* Unpublished paper, University of Vermont, 1975.

Finnie, N. *Handling the young cerebral palsied child at home.* New York: E. P. Dutton & Co., 1975.

Foxx, R., & Azrin, N. H. *Toilet training the retarded.* Champaign, Ill.: Research Press, 1973.

Gardner, W. I. *Behavior modification in mental retardation.* Chicago: Aldine-Atherton, 1971.

Groves, I., & Carroccio, D. A self-feeding program for the severely and profoundly retarded. *Mental Retardation,* 1971, **9,** 10–11.

Horowitz, I. ADL training of the child with perceptual-motor dysfunction: The basic percepts approach. *American Journal of Occupational Therapy,* 1967, **21,** 10–17.

Johnson, V., & Werner, R. *A step-by-step learning guide for retarded infants and children.* Syracuse, N.Y.: Syracuse University Press, 1975.

Kimbrell, D., Luckey, R., Barbuto, K., & Love, R. Institutional environment developed for training severely and profoundly retarded. *Mental Retardation,* 1967, **5,** 34–37.

Knapczyk, D. Task analytic assessment of severe learning problems. *Education and Training of the Mentally Retarded,* 1975, **10**(1), 74–77.

Levine, M., & Elliot, C. B. Toilet training for profoundly retarded with limited staff. *Mental Retardation,* 1970, **8,** 48–50.

Mahoney, K., Van Wagenen, R., & Meyerson, L. Toilet training of normal and retarded children. *Journal of Applied Behavior Analysis,* 1971, **4,** 173–182.

Moore, B., & Bailey, J. Social punishment in the modification of a preschool child's "autistic like" behavior with a mother as therapist. *Journal of Applied Behavior Analysis,* 1973, **6,** 497–508.

O'Brien, F., Bugle, C., & Azrin, N. H. Training and maintaining a retarded child's proper eating. *Journal of Applied Behavior Analysis,* 1972, **5,** 67–72.

Quick, A., & Campbell, A. *Lesson plans for enhancing pre-school developmental progress: Project Memphis.* Dubuque, Iowa: Kendall/Hunt Publishing Co., 1976.

Sanford, A. R. *Learning Accomplishment Profile (LAP).* Chapel Hill, N.C.: Training Outreach Project, 1973.

Sanford, A. R. (Ed.), with D. Bailey, W. C. Johnson, J. Leonard, & P. D. O'Connor. *A manual for use of the Learning Accomplishment Profile.* Winston-Salem, N.C.: Kaplan School Supply Corp., 1974.

Schmidt, P. Feeding assessment and therapy for the neurologically impaired. *American Association for Education of Severely/Profoundly Handicapped Review,* 1976, **1**(8), 19–27.

7

Cognitive Development

In this chapter, cognitive development in the young child will be viewed as the process of gaining abilities related to knowing, perceiving, and recognizing. Development of awareness and understanding and the ability to experience are implied in this definition. In other words, the chapter will be addressed to how the child adapts to, relates to, and interprets his environment. Its focus will be on instructional considerations which foster cognitive development. Its basic premise is that what one knows influences what environmental information can be perceived and processed, but what is perceived and processed alters previous information, thereby creating new knowledge.

Exactly what happens to change sight or touch (or any of the senses) to perceptions, knowledge, and recognition has been discussed at great length by many people. If there are points of agreement concerning the nature of cognition, they center around the facts of its complexity, the difficulty of separating it from other areas of development (motor, social, language, and so forth), and acknowledgment that its products are more easily identified than its process is understood.

In spite of increasing research on cognitive development in young handicapped children, little fully substantiated knowledge in this field of special education exists. Concern, interest, and funding for early intervention programs have been well in advance of documented knowledge concerning teach-

---

The major portion of this chapter, the section on concept development, was written by *Phillip J. McLaughlin* and *Ronald C. Eaves.* Other sections were supplied by the senior author.

ing strategies and curriculum materials. The situation is further complicated by such factors as the nature and degree of handicapping conditions and the age of the child. For instance, the differences that exist between a mongoloid infant and a normal infant may be small compared to the differences between the two children at age 5. It is expected that the blind 3-year-old who has had the benefits of infant stimulation, parent training, small group instruction, and other supportive services will be further advanced in cognitive development than the 5-year-old blind child for whom no stimulation has been provided. It is well-known that the child who is deaf from birth is greatly disadvantaged compared to the child who loses his ability to hear after he has acquired language.

Because of the sparsity of validated information, the tendency has been to draw conclusions from the many studies of cognitive development of school-age handicapped children. Such information seems of little use because of population differences. There is little reason to assume that a similarity in cognitive styles exists between school-age handicapped children and the younger ones.

On the other hand, there are good reasons for drawing on information concerning young nonhandicapped children. Regardless of the severity of the handicapping condition, there are more similarities than differences between handicapped and nonhandicapped young children.

Cognitive development is the process of gaining abilities related to knowing, perceiving, and recognizing.

Parent education programs and increasing public awareness have increased the opportunities for cognitive development for handicapped youngsters. Some have been in stimulating programs longer than their school-age counterparts. Therefore it appears reasonable to direct the content of this chapter to theories and known facts concerning cognitive development as they apply to young children. In some instances, it will be possible to concentrate on information relative to those with handicapping conditions.

Theories Related to Early Cognitive Development

Cognitive development in young children is rarely discussed without reference to the stages of development in the theories formulated by Jean Piaget. Piaget distinguishes between two major stages of intellectual development: sensorimotor (birth to 2 years) and conceptual intelligence (age 2 to maturity). Considerations here will be limited to those areas which concern children age 5 and younger (Meier, 1976).

Sensorimotor Stages I and II. During the first stage, between birth and 4 months, the child engages in elementary sensorimotor adaptations and progresses from automatic or reflexive behavior to differentiation of responses. In the second stage the child repeats simple acts for their own sake (opening and closing the fist).

Sensorimotor Stage III (4–8 months). The infant begins to make intentional moves toward pleasurable or stimulating goals (repeatedly swinging arms to activate a mobile).

Sensorimotor Stage IV (8–12 months). The infant actively anticipates the goals; activity becomes less generalized, more intentional and goal-directed (kicking over a pillow to obtain a toy hidden behind it).

Sensorimotor Stage V (12–18 months). Active exploration and experimentation become evident. Experimentation is goal oriented, and child varies activities to obtain same goal (pushes down on pillow now as well as kicks it).

Sensorimotor Stage VI (18–24 months). This final stage of the sensorimotor period is characterized by inventiveness and creativity. Most significantly, a primitive form of representation, or imagery used in problem solving, appears. (The child invents a means, not through trial and error, to obtain a goal.)

Within the second major Piagetian stage of intellectual development, only the first developmental stage applies to young children.

Preoperational Thought (2–7 years). During this period the child learns to use his multisensory experiences from previous periods and begins to internalize cognitive and symbolic manipulations of reality. About age 4, the child begins to conceptualize more elaborately and construct more complex thoughts and images. He can group objects into classes according to his perception of their similarities.

It should be emphasized that while Piaget and his followers have documented the occurrence of these cognitive milestones, when and how they are achieved largely depends on the quality of learning opportunities in the child's life. When a child has ample opportunities for cognitive development and fails to develop as rapidly as other children his age, or "even to completely master some of the more advanced milestones, he is considered to have some cognitive deficiency or disability which may result in mental retardation and/or developmental disabilities" (Meier, 1976, p. 98).

Another accepted theory of cognitive development is one found in many writings but not attributed to any one person. Known as the *information-processing* view, it envisions man (child) as a complex machine or device, somewhat like a computer, "that processes elaborate programs for dealing with information in intelligent and adaptive ways" (Flavell, 1977, p. 5). The programs are intricately interrelated and sequenced cognitive operations which manipulate units of information to attain personal goals (Flavell, 1977).

A much earlier theory of cognitive development, one encompassing personality development as well, was formulated by Lewin in 1935. To Lewin, cognition referred to how individuals perceived reality. The significance of reality was relative to each individual's perceptions of it. Meier (1976) has offered this example: A hot school lunch does not mean as much to the well-nourished child who had a good breakfast as it does to the child who has not eaten since yesterday's lunch (p. 93).

Lewin used the term *life space* to mean a distinct collection of experiences through which an individual views his environment. Each person's life space conditions the way he perceives events and experiences of the present. Differences in perception determine different cognitive styles; some persons tend to bring facts and their applications together (convergent), others are analytical, and others are more synthetic (creative and divergent).

Unlike the behaviorists (see Chapter 3), the cognitive-field theorists like Lewin are much concerned with intrinsic drives which motivate individuals to behave as they do. To these theorists, the danger of behavior modification techniques is that they will cause dependency on extrinsic rewards or stop short of proving to the child that learning is a reward in itself (Meier, 1976).

Components of Cognitive Development

Perceptual and Discrimination Learning. Perception has to do with the ways in which we read the information that comes to us from our senses (Elkind, 1974). Its proficiency, like most areas of cognitive development, increases with age and experience. Its complexity increases with the interaction of information that comes from different senses at the same time. As the child develops, his ability to organize, to explore, to integrate, and to rearrange information increases. That perceptual learning can begin soon after birth is no longer questioned. The results of recent studies, according to Flavell (1977), have shown that the infant is able to perceive his world a lot better than he can act upon it.

Rohwer (1976), reporting on research concerning conceptual learning in young children, has provided the following information. Early experiences affect later perceptual efficiency. Enrichment of an infant's visual field increases perceptual activity while deprivation affects the child's ability to perceive and to discriminate. Discriminating between left and right is difficult for children up to age 6 while children as young as 3-1/2 can tell up from down. Young children tend to focus narrowly on stimuli while those from 3 to 7 show increasing ability to scan the stimuli comprehensively.

In discrimination tasks, young children characteristically show preference for color rather than form. Their preferences from most to least tend to be color, size, number, and form. With older children, form is the most preferred dimension with color, size, and number ranging from most to least preferred. When a child's preference is used in the teaching task, his performance efficiency increases.

Another factor that affects discrimination learning is whether the stimuli are presented successively or simultaneously. "Simultaneous presentation of stimuli substantially improves performance presumably because the child can more readily compare two stimuli and thus become sensitive to their distinctive features" (Rohwer, 1976, p. 34). The most critical factor in discrimination learning, however, is the child's need for instructional assistance. Without it, the child finds discrimination tasks very difficult. Rohwer concludes his review of studies with the observation that children in the preschool need substantial instructional assistance in order to learn what it is that they are supposed to learn.

Memory. Memory, viewed simply, is the retention of what has been learned or experienced. It is a process through which information is constructed and transformed in order to be remembered. Memory refers to that part of learning which has to do with recognition, recall, or the facilitation of relearning, not to the results of conditioning (Ausubel & Sullivan, 1970).

The literature on memory distinguishes between short-term memory and long-term memory. Short-term memory refers to the retention of information over periods of seconds or minutes after which time it quickly fades. An example of short-term memory is the retention of the digits in a phone number long enough to dial. Once they have been used to accomplish the task for which they were remembered, they are so quickly forgotten that one is hard pressed to respond if an operator intervenes with, "What number did you call?" Long-term memory refers to the retention and retrieval of information over an extended period of time including hours and days as well as months and years (Robinson & Robinson, 1965).

According to Baroff (1974):

> Things which are experienced are first registered by the short-term mechanism and then (1) either forgotten, (2) actively retained by being recirculated through short-term memory (rehearsal), or (3) passively retained in long-term memory thereby becoming accessible to recall over periods of time. (p. 254)

Evidence of developing memory is apparent when the infant shows recognition of his mother and when the young child persistently reaches for a toy hidden from view. Although some early use of sound may result from conditioning, the correct use of labels for familiar objects is evidence of the memory process.

Early in life memory is involuntary, gradually becoming intentional as the child grows older. Studies of memory in the preschool child have shown that young children retain information more efficiently from games than from laboratory conditions.

Three factors account for the apparent instability of memory in early childhood: the absence of organized and differentiated cognitive structure, the lack of meaningfulness of information, and the absence of adequate vocabulary (Ausubel & Sullivan, 1970). Meaningful experiences and verbal coding appear to facilitate the child's ability to recall.

Verbal Learning. Verbal learning is mentioned here for the purpose of emphasizing the process as a component of cognitive development in early childhood and its relationship to the memory process. It appears that verbal learning facilitates the child's ability to recall, but it is certain that the use of language facilitates his ability to demonstrate recognition and recall. In his research review, Rohwer (1976) indicated that children learn more efficiently when they are helped in verbalizing information presented in pictures and in other forms of verbal elaboration. This subject is covered more comprehensively in Chapter 8.

Concept Learning. A concept is a set of stimuli which are related in some way. Synonyms for concept include set, class, group, and category. Concept learning is frequently described as the type of learning which makes it possible for an individual to put objects, events, or persons into a class and respond to the class as a whole (Gagné, 1970). The acquisition of concepts transforms the child's surroundings into an understandable and organized environment (DeCecco & Crawford, 1974). Concept learning undergirds much of what children learn. In light of its importance to a child's preschool learning and its responsiveness to direct teaching, the emphasis of this chapter is directed to this component of cognitive development.

There are two basic types of concepts: concrete and abstract. Concrete concepts can be observed (Gagné, 1966). Vegetables, automobiles, birds, books, cats, numbers, and vowels are examples of concrete concepts. The child can learn concrete concepts by direct observation. For example, he might learn the concept *cat* by observing several small four-legged animals identified for him as *cats* or *not cats* by his parents.

The second type of concept is called a defined, or abstract, concept. Defined concepts must be learned by definition; they do not refer to observables. Instead, they refer to rules relating simpler concepts (Blake, 1974). For example, counting blocks, telling the actions in pictures, and comparing textures are defined concepts. Learning defined concepts requires the child to learn a rule. For example, when a young child says "where dolly" or "that truck" he is illustrating the first step toward proper grammar. This step toward sentence formation is a forming rule that allows the generation of new sentences, like "where truck" and "that dolly," when "where" had previously been used only with "dolly" and "that" only with "truck" (Braine, 1963).

Status. Status refers to the concepts young handicapped children can achieve. Since no one has systematically tried to find the limits to what disabled children can learn, exactly what they can be taught has been questioned (Blake, 1976). The question is further compounded by the nature and severity of the child's handicapping condition and his age.

Baroff (1974) suggested learning experiences in five areas to help the retarded child acquire knowledge about himself and his world. They include: (1) things related to himself, (2) common objects in his environment, (3) action words (verbs), (4) concepts, and (5) academic readiness skills. Using these five areas and the Learning Accomplishment Profile for Cognitive Skill Develop-

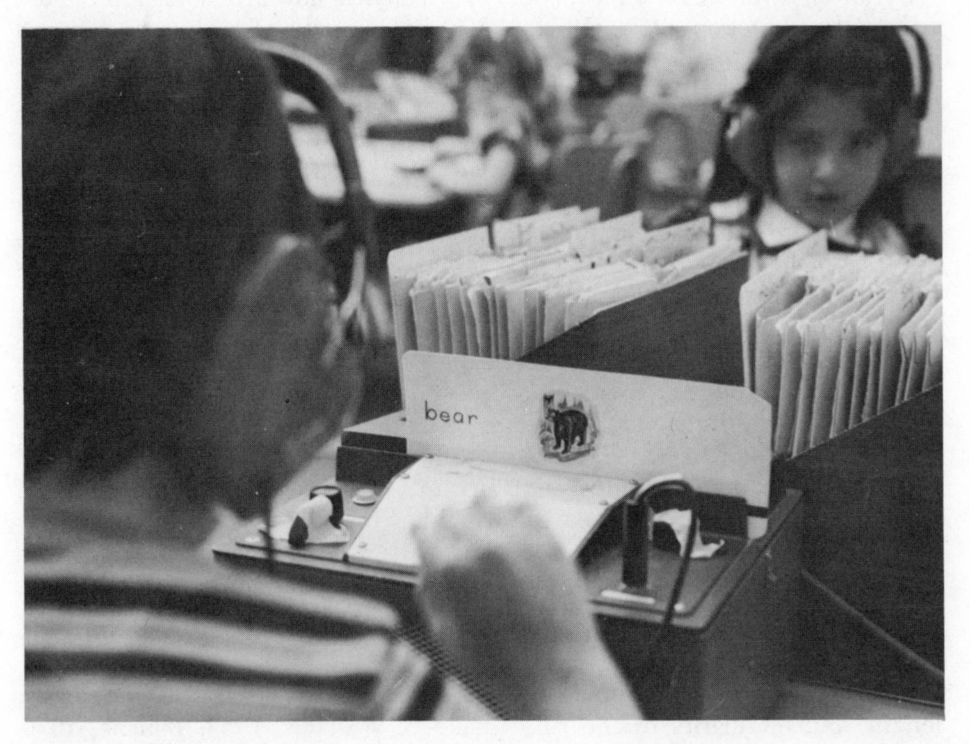

Children learn more efficiently when they are helped in verbalizing information presented in pictures and in other forms of verbal elaboration.

ment, Table 1 identifies selected skills expected to develop during one of the 5 years of preschool development. The chart clearly delineates those concepts which usually develop during the first 5 years of life. While the chart does not identify the limits of what can be taught, it does provide suggestions as to what achievement can be reasonably expected.

Conditions Affecting Concept Learning

A number of general conditions apply to all types of learning in the same way. They include conditions influencing acquisition, retention, and transfer. Criteria pertaining to the general conditions were presented in Chapter 3.

Seven specific conditions affect developmentally young and normal children's acquisition of concepts. Three of the seven pertain to the nature of the material: nature of rules, relevant and irrelevant dimensions, and taxonomic level. Four pertain to the methods of presenting the concepts to be learned: contiguity of instances, positive and negative instances, simultaneous and successive exposure, and expository and discovery methods. These seven specific conditions are discussed below.

Nature of Rules

Definitions. Rules define concepts by specifying how attributes are related or how they function. Blake (1974, p. 207) has described four frequently used rules:

1. *Simple affirmation* is the presence or absence of a single attribute. Naming a familiar object is an example. The child either names the object correctly or he doesn't.
2. *Conjunction* is the joint presence of two or more attributes. Associating use with the object is an example. The child drinks from a cup, combs his hair with a comb, reaches for his coat when outdoor playtime is announced.
3. *Disjunction* involves either one set of characteristics or another set. With disjunction, there are several sets of defining attributes, any one of which may be used. For example, when the young child can tell how many circles when shown a number of colored circles, he is ignoring the concept of color for the concept of numbers.
4. *Relations* involve comparative amount, size, distance, or position. When the child selects the heavier weight, which he can do invariably by approximately age 5, he is dealing with a larger than or smaller than relation even if he does not understand the concept or have the vocabulary to explain his choice. Counting four objects and answering correctly how many is an example of the equality relation.

Conceptual rules vary in difficulty. The difficulty depends on the complexity, length, and familiarity of the rule (Blake & Williams, 1963; Bourne, 1970; McLaughlin, 1976a, 1976b, 1976c). For example, it is easier for a child to learn the simple affirmation involved in naming objects than it is for him to learn the

Table 1

Selected Cognitive Skills Expected During Preschool Years

Age	Things That Relate to Himself	Common Objects	Action Words (Verbs)	Concepts	Academic Readiness
1–12 Months	Responds to name	Uncovers toy Turns head to look for dropped spoon	Plays pat-a-cake Waves bye-bye Rings bell purposively	Responds to sound of rattle Reacts to sight of toy	Responds to name
12–24 Months	Points to 1–3 body parts	Fetches & carries familiar objects Uses names of familiar objects	Understands & follows simple commands Responds to request "Give me"	Labels one object Discriminates 2 items; cup, box, plate	Imitates putting toys in box Follows one-step direction
24–36 Months	Recognizes own picture Shows & imitates names for hair, hands, feet, etc.	Labels mud, clay Names 6 common objects	Responds to request "Put ___ in the ___."	Comprehends another Knows sex	Repeats 2 digits Participates in story-telling, words or phrases
36–48 Months	Can point to tongue, neck, knee	Can name 10 of 18 objects	Tells action in pictures	Names all colors Compares textures Comprehends 3 prepositions	Can count 2 blocks Can tell how many
48–60 Months	Can respond correctly to: A hat goes on your head, Shoes go on your feet.	Names 14–18 pictures of common objects	Can follow 3 commands in proper order	Knows day and night Matches & names primary colors	"Reads" pictures When shown 3 circles, counts 3

Note: Compiled from *Learning Accomplishment Profile* by A. R. Sanford. Chapel Hill, N.C.: Training Outreach Project, 1973, and *Mental Retardation: Nature, Cause and Management* by G. Baroff. Washington, D.C.: Hemisphere Publishing Corp., 1974, p. 200. Reprinted with permission.

conjunction concept involved in associating use with objects. These two examples tend to indicate that conceptual rule learning may be developmental in nature (simple affirmation developing earlier than conjunction). In either case, the implications for instruction are clear.

Relevant and Irrelevant Dimensions

Relevant dimensions define the concept; they help make the instances of the concept alike. Irrelevant dimensions are present, but they do not define the concept; they help make the instances of the concept different. A child from 4 to 5 years of age may be expected to name and match the four primary colors illustrated in four objects. The relevant dimensions are the colors and their names, while the irrelevant dimensions are the forms of the objects or their names (circles, dolls, or cars).

When the number of relevant or irrelevant dimensions are increased, concept learning becomes harder. Increases in either dimension affect the amount and type of information the child has to consider (May, 1973). For young children these negative effects must be reduced by decreasing the number of dimensions (naming the four colors or matching and naming only two primary colors) or by making the relevant dimensions more obvious than the irrelevant dimensions, keeping the instruction concrete.

Taxonomic Level

A taxonomy is a hierarchical classification system. Taxonomic level refers to how many other concepts a concept includes under it. For example, the concept of threeness is at a low taxonomic level. In contrast, the concept of odd numbers is at a higher taxonomic level.

Higher-order concepts are harder to learn because they are further removed from concrete objects and events. They include a large number of disparate instances which show the subtle defining characteristics and differ on a large number of irrelevant attributes (Blake & Williams, 1968b). For example, it is easier for a child to learn the concept of threeness than it is for him to learn the concept of odd numbers.

Contiguity of Instances

Contiguity of instances refers to how closely together instances of a given concept are presented when several concepts are being taught (Blake, 1974). When the instances for only one concept are presented until the concept is learned, one has high contiguity. This is an unmixed presentation and the instances are close together or highly contiguous. There is low contiguity in a mixed presentation where instances of several concepts are presented together. As an example, if the concepts of fruit, vegetables, and meat were being taught, in an unmixed presentation instances of each concept would be presented separately until each was mastered. The types of fruit would be presented first, types of vegetables next, and meats last. In a mixed presentation, the concepts would be presented concurrently. Peaches, steak, carrots, beans, chicken, pears, pork chops, and apples would be presented at the same time until the three concepts—fruit, vegetable, and meat—were mastered.

The unmixed presentation with higher contiguity is easier. The mixed presentation, and thus lower contiguity, puts more of a strain on the child's memory since instances of any one concept are farther apart in time (Bourne & Jennings, 1963; Hurley, 1975a; Kurtz & Hovland, 1956).

Positive and Negative Instances

Positive instances are examples of the concept. Negative instances are not. For example, for the concept of fruit, positive instances are apples, oranges, pears, grapes, and negative instances are chairs, pens, shirts, dogs, hamburgers.

Positive instances help concept learning by showing what characteristics define the concept. Negative instances help by showing what characteristics do not define the concept. The child can learn in situations where there are only positive instances or only negative instances. However, a mixed sequence of positive and negative instances is best. The best mix is more positive than negative instances (Hurley, 1973, 1975b; Smoke, 1933). Blake (1974, p. 211) stated that the positive and negative instances should be of the same form; that is, either all verbal or all concrete rather than some of both.

Simultaneous and Successive Exposure

In successive exposure, the student sees only one instance at a time. After he responds and gets feedback, the instance is removed. In simultaneous exposure, the instances are kept in view after the pupil responds and gets feedback. Simultaneous exposure permits the child to look back at earlier instances.

Simultaneous exposure simplifies concept learning. It reduces memory load and increases ease of making inferences. As the amount of information the child is exposed to is increased, the time available for him to deal with it also needs to be increased (Bourne, Goldstein, & Link, 1964; Cahill & Hovland, 1969; McLaughlin, 1976d).

Expository and Discovery Methods

When the expository method is used, the children are given information about the concept—the relevant and irrelevant dimensions, attributes, rules, and other information. With a discovery method, they are given a question and allowed to discover the dimensions, attributes, rules, and other information. These methods have often been called deductive and inductive methods, respectively.

Concept learning is faster with expository methods. The children have more information, make fewer errors, and experience less failure and frustration (Blake & Williams, 1968a). However, with discovery methods, the children have to be more active, and this activity may lead to more attention.

Educational Applications

Concept learning is prevalent throughout the skills usually taught to both handicapped and nonhandicapped preschool children. In fact, children are more often called upon to use concept learning than any other type of learning. Table 2 lists concepts and topics which involve concept learning that are appropriate to teach handicapped preschool children.

Blake (1974, 1976) has been the trailblazer in applying information about concept learning to teaching. She has specified criteria for instructional procedures which reflect the results of research on how children respond to conditions which influence concept learning (1974, pp. 205–224). These criteria and teaching illustrations follow.

Table 2
Domains and Topics Involving Concept Learning
Appropriate to Teach Developmentally Disabled Preschool Children

Domain	Topic
Gross Motor	*People:* Participant player positions in many games (e.g., being "it," "chaser," "little Indians"). *Objects:* Types of games and manipulative toys, their names, and parts (e.g., tricycle, pedal). Body parts (e.g., arm, shoulder, legs, hands, fingers, toes). *Events:* Moving, crawling, walking, running, balancing, holding, carrying, hopping, skipping, jumping, hammering, catching, throwing, being strong, weak, tired.
Fine Motor	*People:* Participant player positions in many fine motor games (e.g., imitating majorette in a band, guitarist, pianist, seamstress). *Objects:* Shapes, forms, names and types of manipulative utensils and their parts, pencil, book, scissors, page. *Events:* drawing, copying, tracing, picking up, cutting, turning (on, off), coloring, touching, feeling.
Social–Emotional Adjustment	*People:* Mother, father, sister, brother, self, family, friend, neighbor, enemy, boy, girl, leader, follower, helper, bully, community workers (e.g., police officer, doctor, pastor, teacher). *Objects:* All concepts concerning home (e.g., rooms, toys, car), school (e.g., books, games, personal and community property), community (e.g., stores, offices, street lights). *Events:* Attending, approving, helping, requesting, accepting, offering, smiling, sharing, allowing, cooperating, insulting, disapproving, blaming, demanding, attacking, teasing, grabbing, refusing, rejecting, ignoring, interfering, frowning, yelling, whispering. Being afraid, honest, neat, happy, sad, "good."

Table 2

Domains and Topics Involving Concept Learning
Appropriate to Teach Developmentally Disabled Preschool Children *(cont.)*

Domain	Topic
Self-help	*People:* Self. *Objects:* Bathroom appliances and implements, kitchen utensils and appliances, clothing and its parts, food, body parts. *Events:* Toileting, washing, wiping, drying, dressing, eating, brushing, lacing, cutting, buttoning, zipping, cleaning (up), pouring, spreading, drinking.
Arithmetic	*People:* Teacher, all concepts and concept labels (e.g., people in the home, school, and community) already mentioned which involve sets, numbers, and numerals. *Objects:* All concepts and concept labels (e.g., objects in the home, school, and community) already mentioned which involve sets, numbers, and numerals. *Events:* Counting, grouping, writing, sequencing, naming.
Oral Language: Listening and Speech	*People:* All concepts and concept labels (e.g., people in the home, school, and community) already mentioned. *Objects:* All concepts and concept labels (e.g., objects in the home, school, and community) already mentioned. *Events:* All concepts and concept labels (e.g., events in the home, school, and community) already mentioned. Identifying and supplying nouns (people, places, things), verbs (action, existence), modifiers, connectives, pronouns, possessives.
Written Language: Reading and Writing	*People:* Correspondence between a few words and real people (e.g., self, mom, dad, etc.). *Objects:* Correspondence between a few grapheme combinations and real objects (e.g., dog, cat, etc.), letters. *Events:* Writing, reading.

Nature of Rules

Criteria:

> The instructional procedure should vary the amount of teaching and practice according to the difficulty of the rule. For example, more teaching and practice should be provided for disjunction rules than for simple affirmation rules. (p. 207)

Illustration: The nature of rules defines the complexity of a concept. The rule for the concept *number* is a simple affirmation rule. Elements are members of the concept (1,2,3,. . .,) or they are not. The concept *big* involves comparisons in terms of size or amount; therefore, it involves a relations rule. For instance, an object is big only in relation to some other object. The latter concept is the

Children in the preschool need substantial instructional assistance in order to learn what it is that they are supposed to learn.

more complex, and the teacher should spend more time presenting this concept and should allow the child more time to practice for ultimate mastery.

Relevant and Irrelevant Dimensions

Criteria:

> The number of relevant dimensions should be reduced to the minimum needed to define the concept. Similarly, the number of irrelevant dimensions should be reduced as much as possible. In addition, instructional procedures should be used to emphasize the differences between the relevant features and minimize the irrelevant features and to vary how much the relevant and irrelevant features differ from instance to instance; they also should include forms of instances which show fewer irrelevant features. (p. 208)

Illustration: For the concept *square* there is only one relevant dimension, form. All other dimensions vary with particular instances, but they are irrelevant. Such irrelevant dimensions are size, color, and orientation. Irrelevant dimensions should be held constant within each presentation, or confusion might result. For young children the use of concrete objects which they can manipulate is essential. The teacher's comments can help to avoid confusion in the learner. The following presentations in Figure 1 show varied size and orientation as well as form.

Children with cerebral palsy who have difficulty pointing with their fingers may be able to point with a straw held between the teeth or gesture in some way (nodding head, blinking eyes) to indicate the correct response.

Following instruction using a square block which the child has handled, ask:

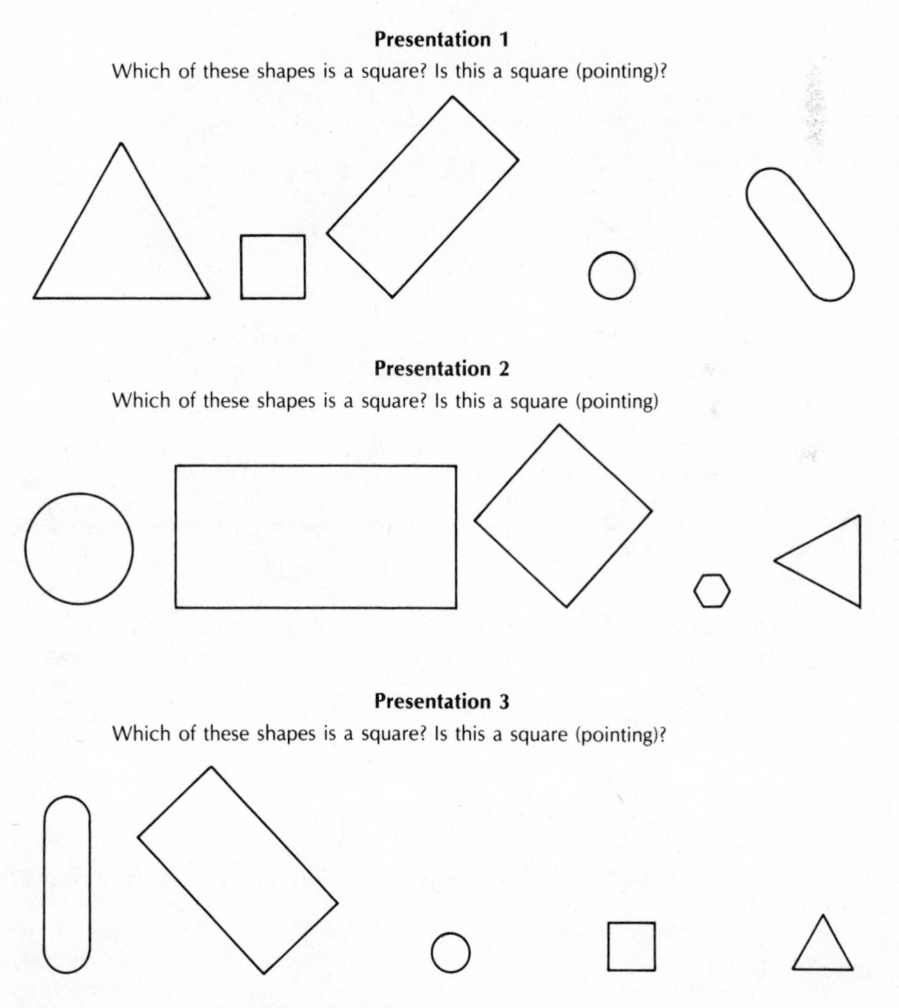

FIGURE 1. Relevant and irrelevant dimensions.

The following three presentations (Figure 2) maintain constancy for size and orientation within each presentation, but vary *across* presentations in order to introduce a variety of contexts. Confusion is reduced through the use of concrete objects and verbal clues which help the learner distinguish between relevant and irrelevant dimensions. Examination of other illustrations in this

Presentation 1

Instructions: A square is the shape that has four sides, all the same size. The four corners are like the corners of a page in a book. A square looks like this: (show a positive instance of a square as a model). Which of these shapes is square?

Is this a square (pointing)? Is this a square (pointing)? Is this a square (pointing)? Is this a square (pointing)? Is this a square (pointing)?

Presentation 2

Instructions: Remember that a square has four sides all the same size and its four corners are like the corners of a page of a book. Now, see if you can find a square when you look at these shapes that have been turned.

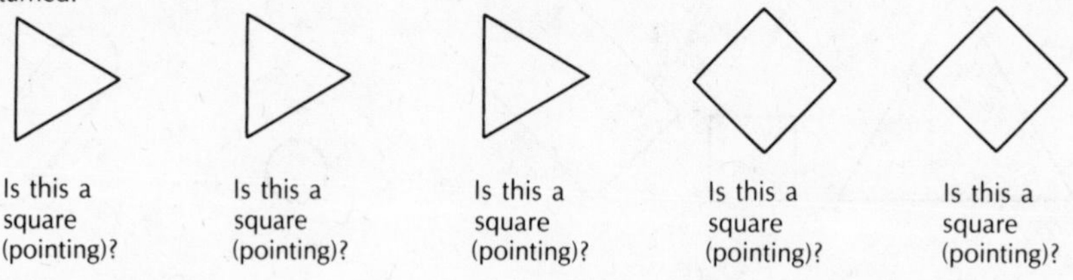

Is this a square (pointing)? Is this a square (pointing)? Is this a square (pointing)? Is this a square (pointing)? Is this a square (pointing)?

Now you can see that a square is the same whether it stands up straight or is turned. It is still a square.

Presentation 3

Instructions: You've found a square when it stands up straight and when it is turned. A square is always the same. It doesn't even matter if it is big or little, it is still a square. The special thing about a square is that it has four sides that are all the same size and its corners are like the pages of a book. See if you can find the square when the shapes are little.

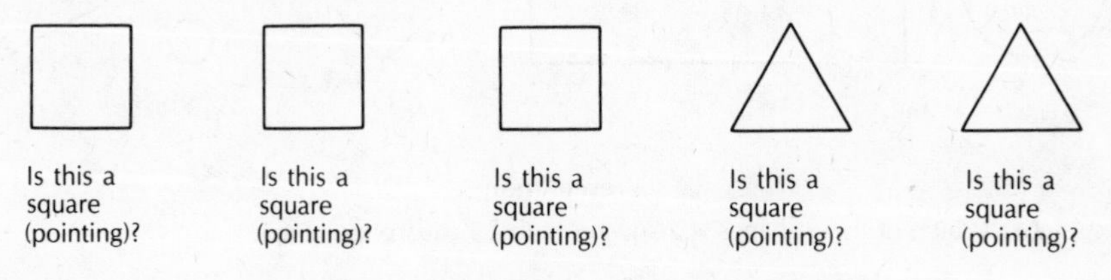

Is this a square (pointing)? Is this a square (pointing)? Is this a square (pointing)? Is this a square (pointing)? Is this a square (pointing)?

FIGURE 2. Educational application of relevant dimensions.

chapter to determine how well they control relevant and irrelevant dimensions may be helpful.

Taxonomic Level

Criteria:

> The instructional procedures should vary the amount of teaching and practice according to the hierarchical level of the concept, i.e., the number of lower order concepts it subsumes. In addition, instructional procedures should be used to identify the key relevant dimensions going through the hierarchy to define the higher order concepts. (pp. 216–217)

Illustration. The concepts *dog, pet,* and *animal* are all members of the same hierarchy. Dog is the lowest order concept, pet is second, and animal is the highest order concept. In this example and all others like it, the lowest order concept has the greatest number of relevant dimensions. As the concept progresses to higher orders, previously relevant dimensions become irrelevant and, therefore, the concept becomes harder to learn. For example, relevant dimensions of a dog are barking, wagging tail, sniffing. Because these dimensions are not true of all pets, they become irrelevant to the concept of pet. The dimensions of all pets become relevant. For the concept *animal* (the highest order concept in the example), one relevant dimension is locomotion. Animals move their bodies; nonanimals are stationary unless someone else moves them. This relevant dimension maintains throughout the hierarchy.

The teacher must continuously identify the dimensions that are relevant at the highest order, or confusion results. When teaching concepts, the teacher considers the number of lower order concepts they subsume and varies the amount of time and practice accordingly.

Contiguity of Instances

Criteria:

> When there are several concepts to be learned, the instructional procedures should include an unmixed presentation. Each concept should be learned separately rather than several concepts concomitantly. The instructional procedures should provide overlearning, verbal mediation, and similar methods to facilitate reversal shifts and learning sets. (pp. 217–218)

Illustration: Occasionally, several concepts which are related in some way must be taught. An example is the teaching of colors. It is not enough that the preschooler learn red. He must also learn green, yellow, blue, and so on. Although all these concepts can be (and have been) taught together, it is easier for the learner if the colors are learned separately. Examples of unmixed and mixed presentations of the concepts for red, green, and blue are provided in Figures 3, 4, 5, and 6. Such presentations would go on with more changes in materials (concrete objects if needed) and continued verbal clues until the material is overlearned.

Unmixed Presentations

Red

Red is the group of things that are the color of catsup. (The teacher must be sure the child is familiar with the color of catsup.) Look at each drawing and decide if it is the color of catsup. If it is the color of catsup, it is called red. When you find a red drawing, compare it with all the other drawings to see how they are alike and different. Let's start!

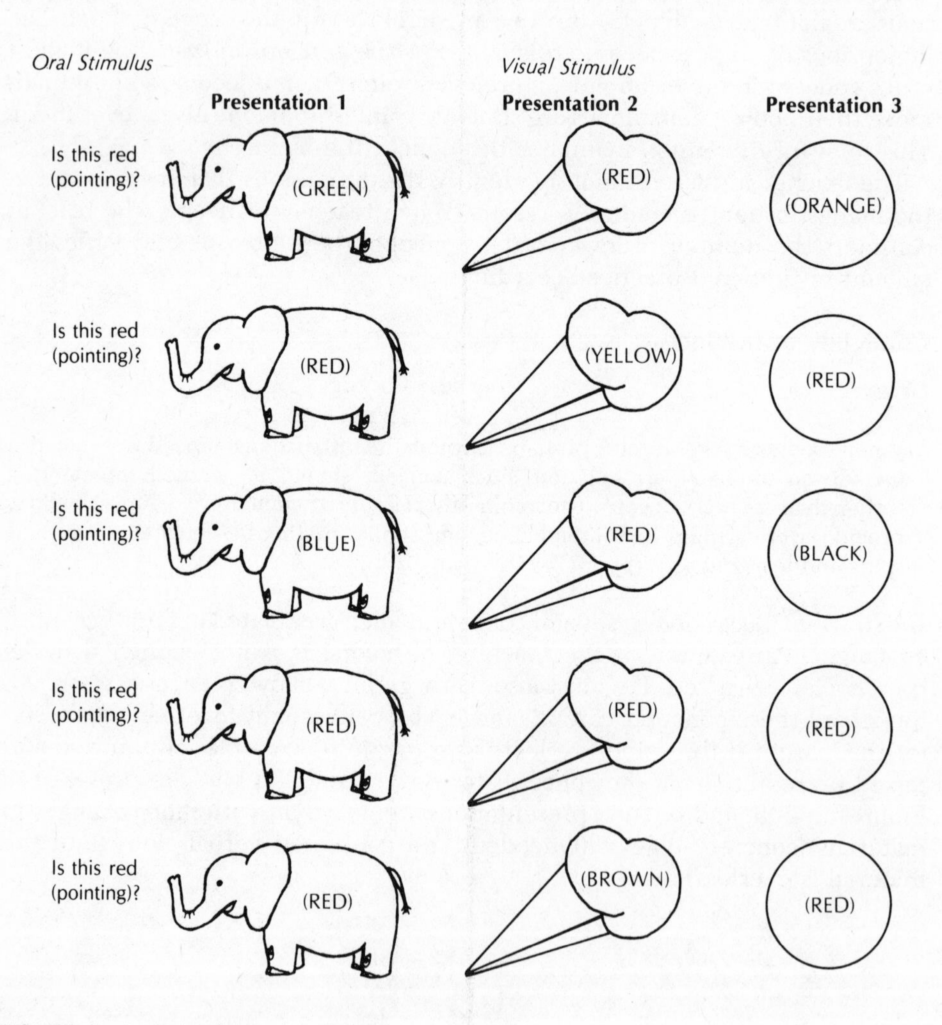

FIGURE 3. Red visual-stimulus diagram.

Green

Green is the group of things that are the color of grass. (The teacher must be sure the child can recognize green.) Remember that you are no longer looking for red things. Now when you see something red, don't mark it because it is wrong for this job. Mark only those drawings that are green, the color of grass. When you find a green drawing, compare it with the others and see how they are alike and different. Let's start!

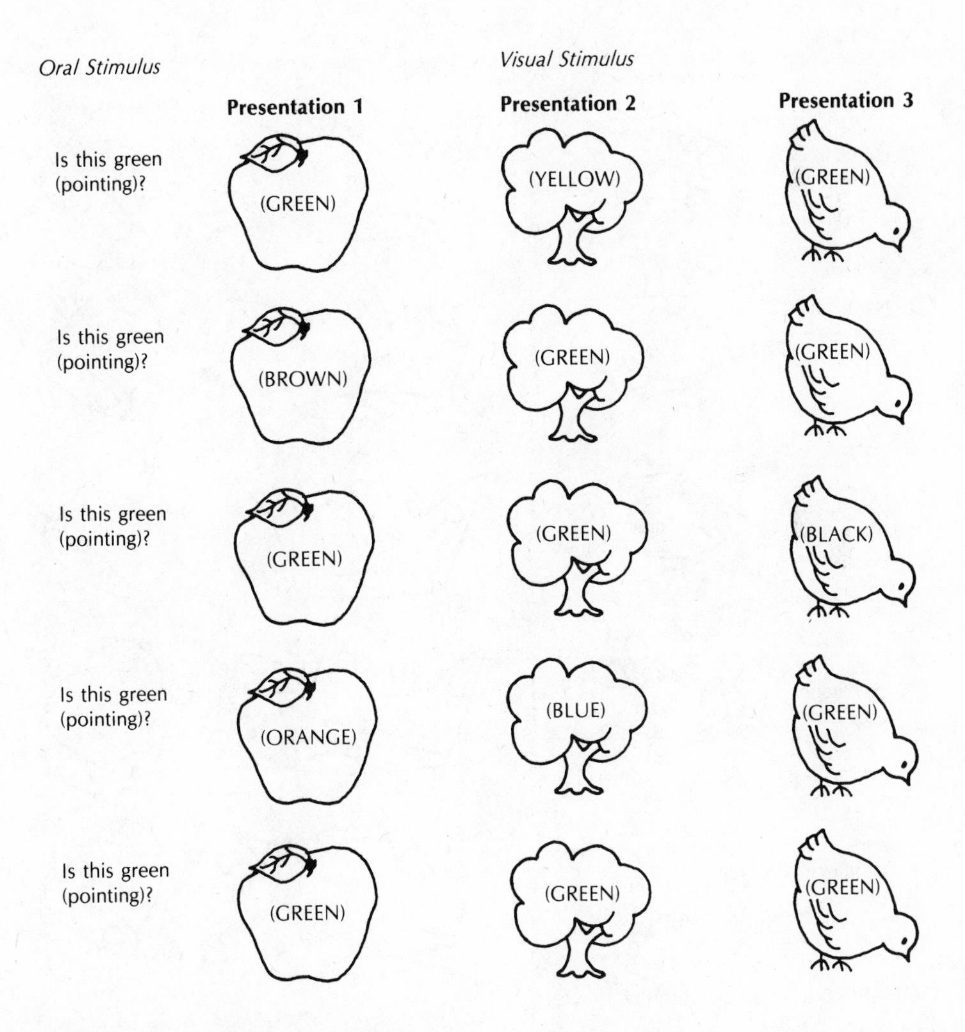

FIGURE 4. Green visual-stimulus diagram.

Blue

Blue is the group of things that are the color of the sky on a clear day. (The teacher must be sure the child can identify blue.) Remember that you are no longer looking for red things or green things. Now, when you see something red or green don't mark it because it is wrong for this job. Mark only those drawings that are blue, the color of the sky on a clear day. When you find a blue drawing, compare it with the others and see how they are alike and different. Okay, Let's start!

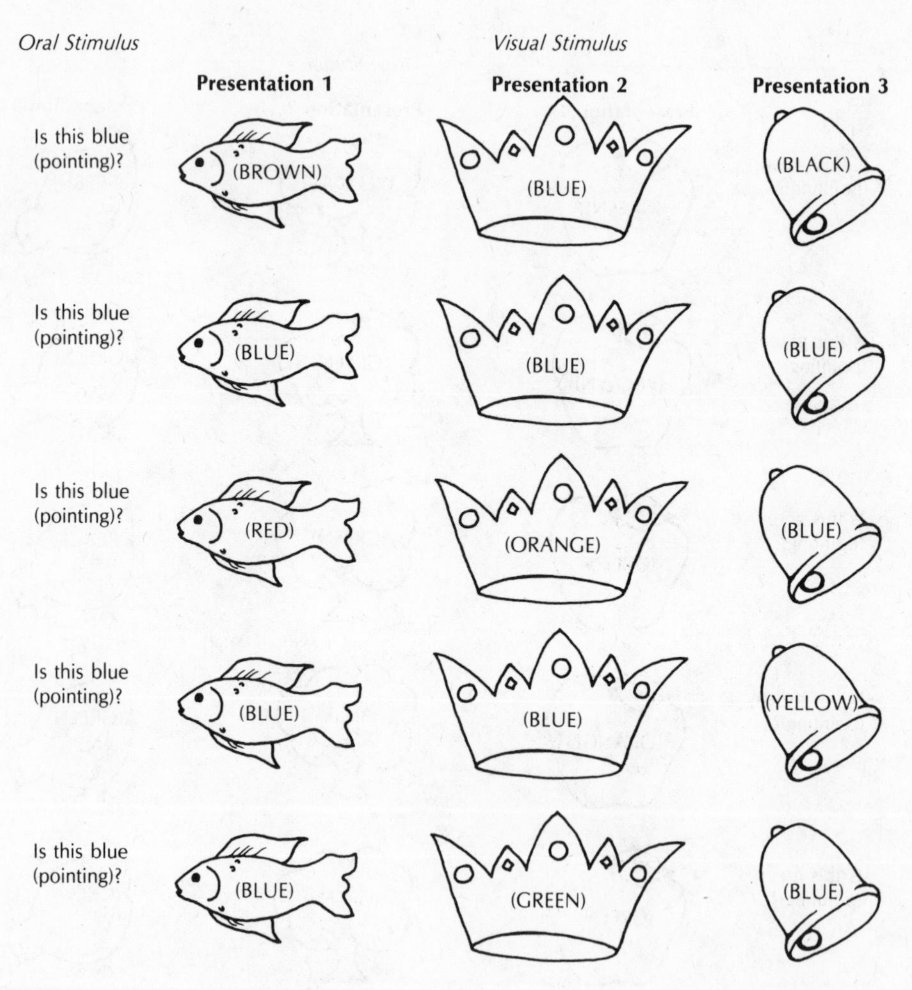

FIGURE 5. Blue visual-stimulus diagram.

In a mixed presentation, colors (and therefore concepts to be learned) are allowed to vary within and across presentations. The correctness of a response depends upon the color mentioned in the question ("Is this blue?" "Is this red?"), the stimulus (red, green), and the pupil's specific response (yes, no). Because instances of any given stimulus ("Is this blue?") are spread so far apart, it takes longer for the child to learn the colors both individually and collectively. Figure 6 shows a layout for three mixed presentations.

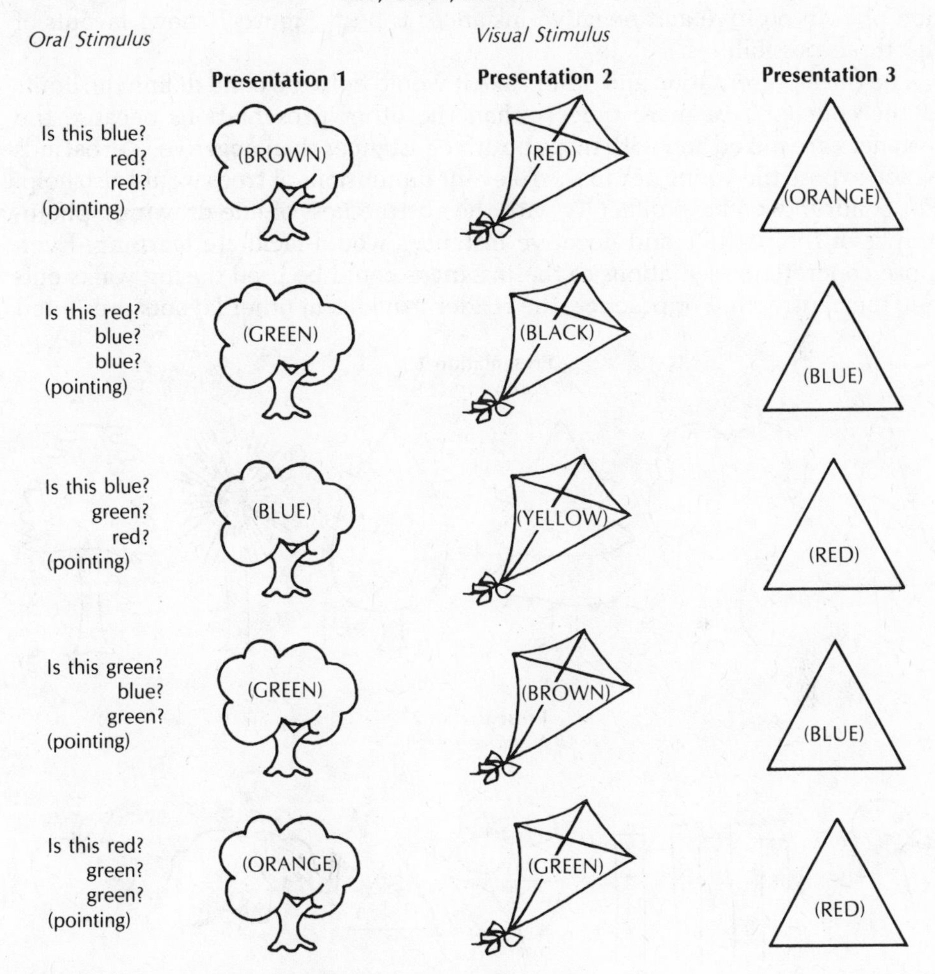

FIGURE 6. Red, green, and blue visual-stimulus diagram.

Because of the poor contiguity of instances, the preschooler would need a longer amount of time to learn these concepts.

Positive and Negative Instances

Criteria:

> The instructional procedures should include both positive and negative instances rather than positive or negative instances alone. In addition, they should include arranging positive and negative instances in a way to facilitate the pupils' identifying relevant attributes. There should be sequences in which negative instances are followed by positive instances. Positive and negative instances should be in the same form (all verbal, all objects, etc.). (p. 211)

Illustration: Although the concept *tree* can be taught in three ways (i.e., all positive instances, all negative instances, and a mixed series), a mixed presentation of both positive and negative instances is best. Figure 7 shows layouts of the three possibilities.

The third presentation and others like it would help the child define the limits of the concept *tree* more quickly than the other presentations because the instances are mixed and with more positive instances than negative. Verbal aids which expose the youngster to the relevant dimensions of trees would also help. For children who have difficulty with the abstractness of line drawings, photographs of the positive and negative instances would facilitate learning. Even more concrete presentations of the instances could be used during walks outside the classroom. For practice, the reader can look at other layouts presented

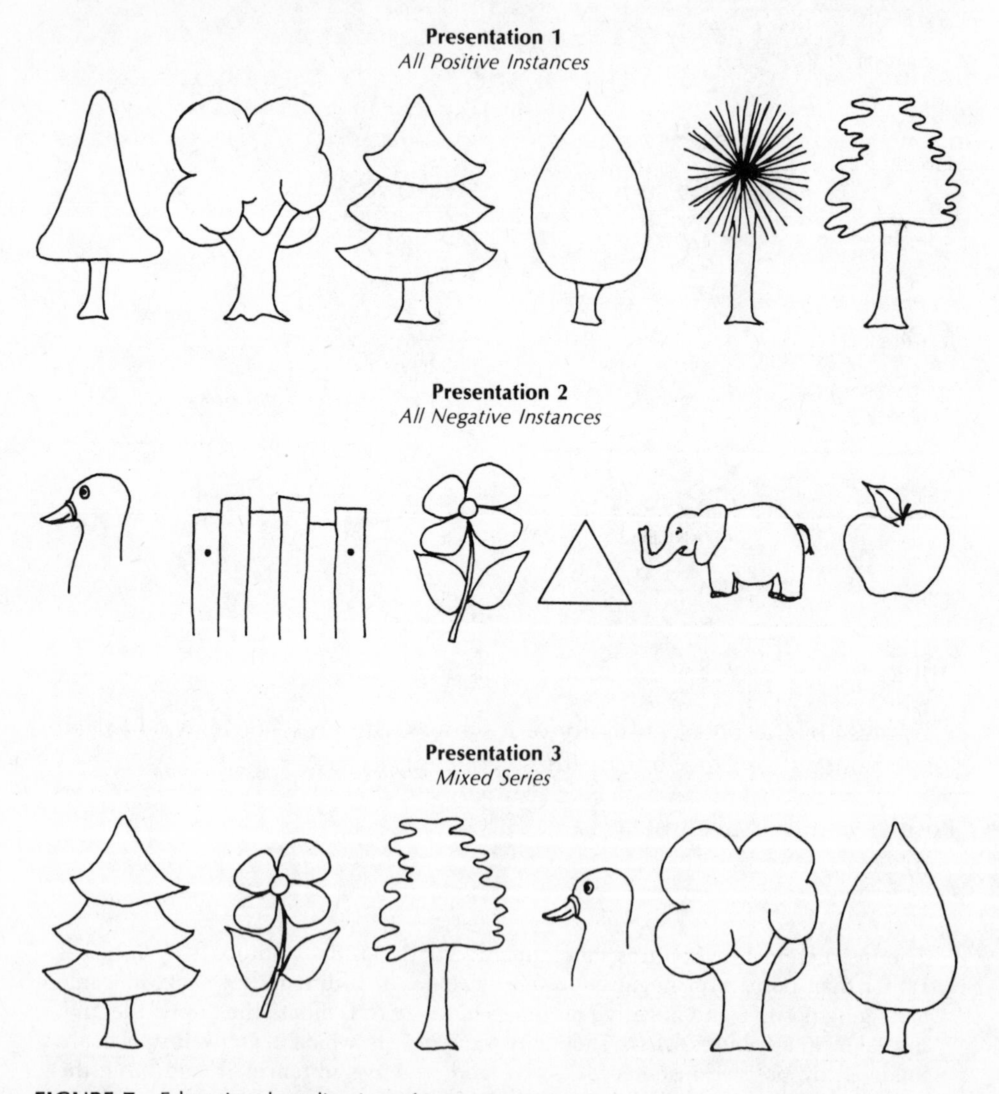

FIGURE 7. Educational application of instances.

in this chapter and determine how the ratio of positive and negative instances could have been improved.

Simultaneous and Successive Exposure

Criteria:

> The instructional procedures should include simultaneous exposure. After the pupil responds to a set of instances and gets feedback, that set of instances should be kept in view and he should be told not to try to rely on memory but to refer back to it as often as he needs to, to see what the positive instance was. As the pupil has more instances to refer to, the instructional procedures should allow more time for study. (p. 220)

Illustration: If the concept *number* were being taught, exposure of positive and negative instances of the concept could be made successively or simultaneously. In concept learning, simultaneous presentations are best. Figure 8 uses successive exposures and 3-by-5-inch cards as stimuli.

Number

Presentation 1

Put a check on every card that has number.

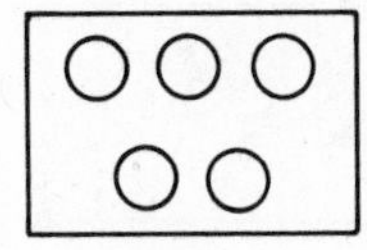
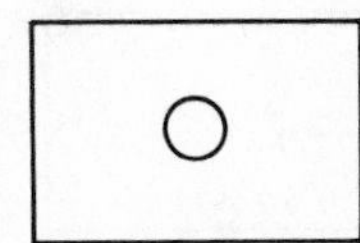

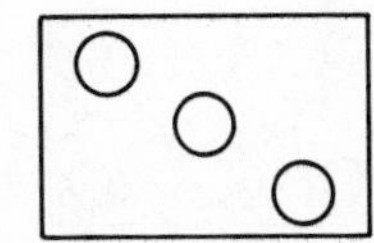

Give feedback and remove the stimulus from the pupil's view after each instance.

Presentation 2

Put a check on every card that has number.

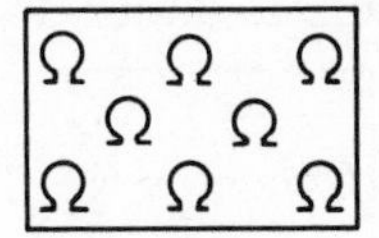
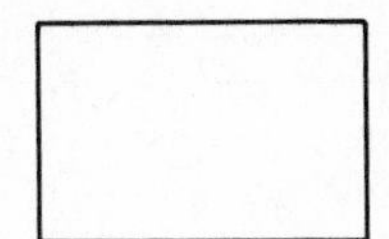
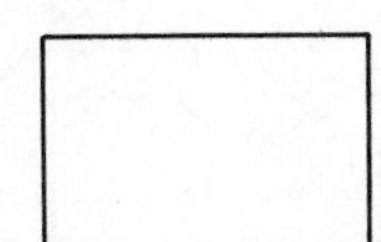
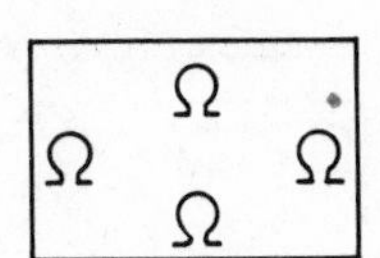

Give feedback and remove the stimulus from the pupil's view after each instance.

Presentation 3

Put a check on every card that has number.

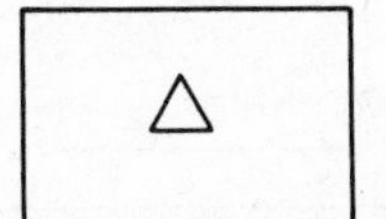
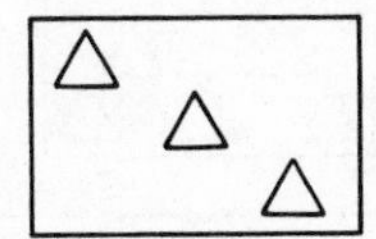
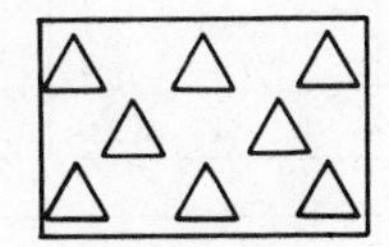
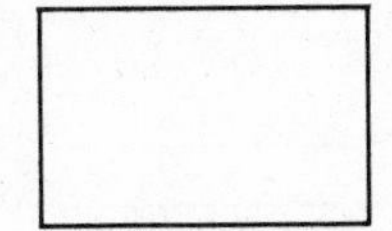

Give feedback and remove the stimulus from the pupil's view after each instance.

FIGURE 8. Successive presentation.

A child can learn the concept *number* using the successive presentation approach, but he will learn the concept more quickly if he is allowed to refer back to previous instances to which he has been exposed. Figure 9 illustrates a layout for teaching number as a concept when a simultaneous presentation is used. Again, 3-by-5-inch cards provide the stimuli.

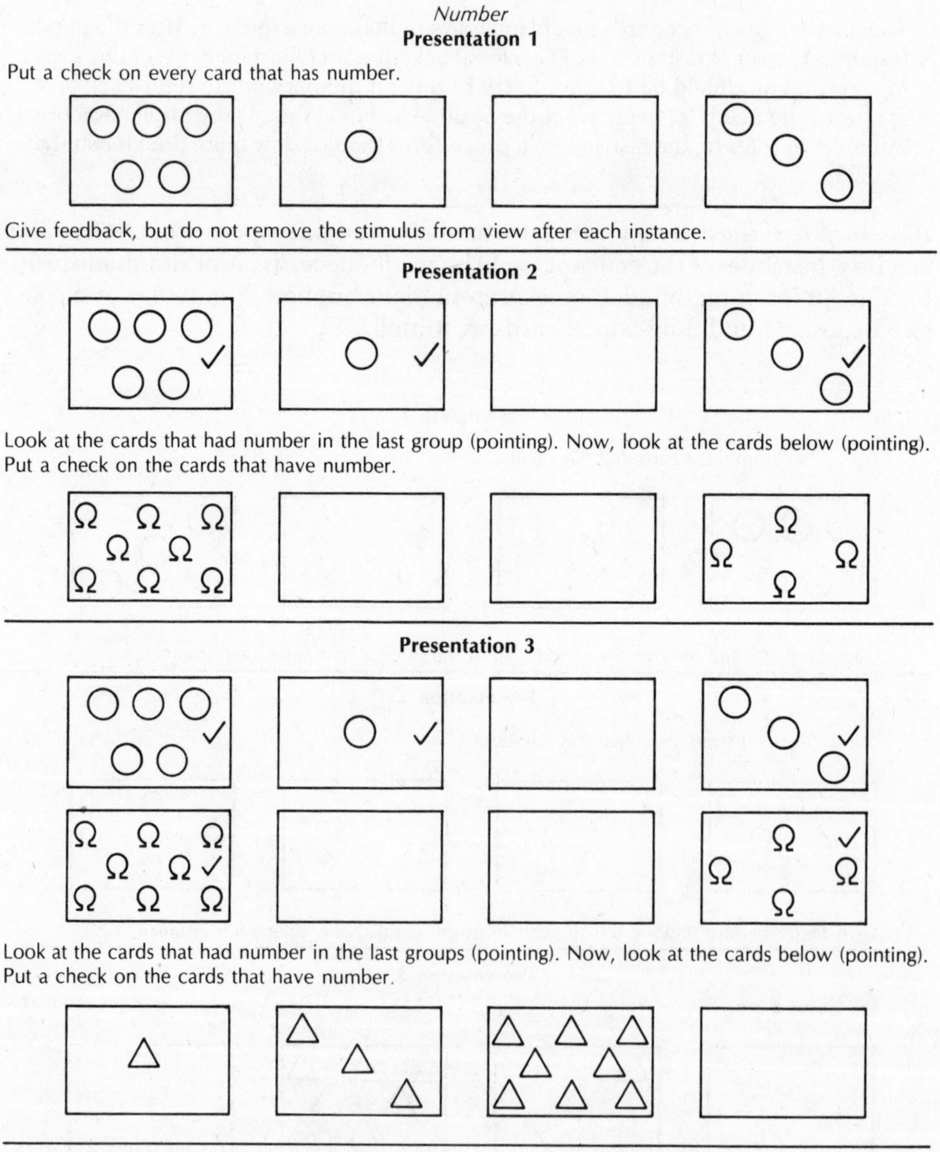

Number

Presentation 1

Put a check on every card that has number.

Give feedback, but do not remove the stimulus from view after each instance.

Presentation 2

Look at the cards that had number in the last group (pointing). Now, look at the cards below (pointing). Put a check on the cards that have number.

Presentation 3

Look at the cards that had number in the last groups (pointing). Now, look at the cards below (pointing). Put a check on the cards that have number.

FIGURE 9. Simultaneous presentation.

In this case, all prior instances to which the pupil has responded are left in full view so that he may use them as aids when necessary. In concept learning, the child will reach mastery more quickly if simultaneous presentation is used.

Expository and Discovery Methods

Criteria:

> When the goal is to teach a specific concept, instructional procedures should include an expository method. Pupils should be given information about rules, dimensions, relevant and irrelevant attributes, etc., and practice applying that information. When the goal is to give pupils practice trying out strategies and to teach pupils to tolerate frustration in dealing with concepts, instructional procedures should include a discovery method. (p. 222)

Illustration: With reference to the section on relevant and irrelevant dimensions, in the first three presentations (in which irrelevant dimensions were allowed to vary within each presentation), the pupil is told nothing about the concept (square). No information is given about rules, relevant dimensions, irrelevant dimensions, and no model is presented. It is left up to the child to *discover* this information on his own.

With reference to the second three presentations in the section on relevant and irrelevant dimensions, the pupil is told about the important dimension concerning the concept *square.* He is told the rules—"A square . . . has four sides, all the same size. The four corners are like the pages in a book." He is presented with a model square. He is given pertinent information about the irrelevant dimensions (orientation, size). In short, an *expository* method is used. In concept learning, expository methods lead to more efficient mastery.

In order to familiarize yourself with expository and discovery methods, you may wish to look over all of the illustrations presented in this chapter and classify each as applying an expository or discovery method. (For information concerning resources for teaching concepts, the reader is referred to Appendix B.)

Problem Solving and Reasoning

Problem-solving activity is present in all levels of development and can be observed in infants and young children. It is a kind of one trial learning in which the young child brings to a new situation his past experiences of similar situations. Elkind (1974) has provided the example of the young child who sees his mother put candy on a high shelf. Because he wants the candy, he looks around, finds a chair, and uses it to reach the candy. Although he had climbed on chairs before, he had never used one to accomplish a particular goal.

Because the young child has not yet developed symbolic thought and the ability to reverse the thinking process (reversibility), reasoning at this age is action oriented and unlike that of a later developmental period. Most children

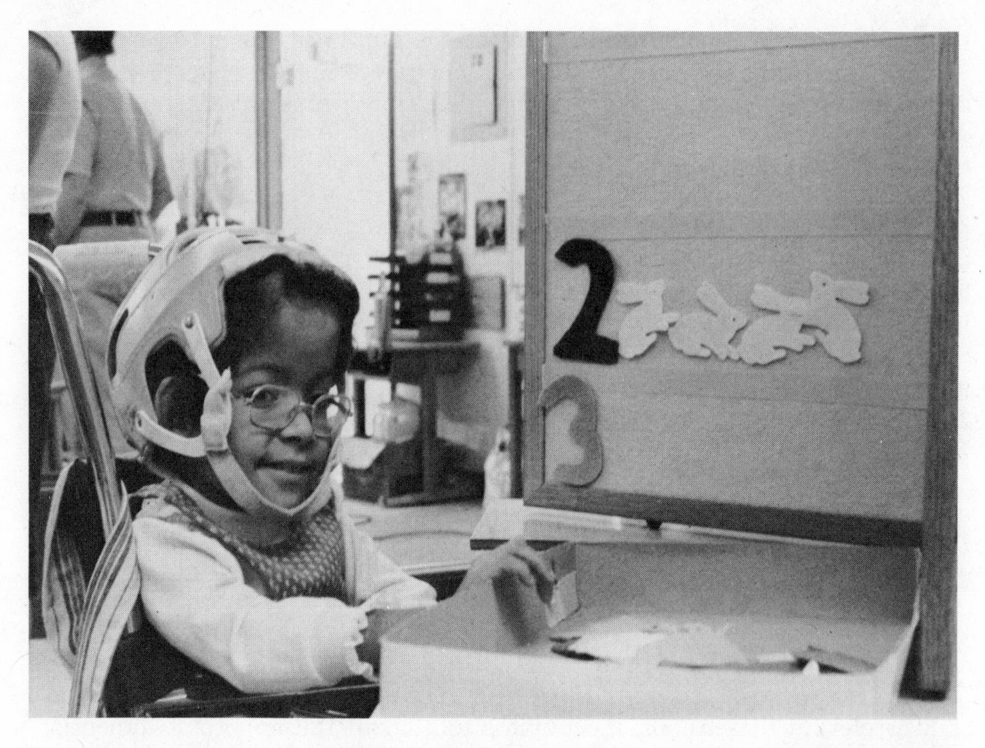

The child's attention span is affected by such factors as levels of difficulty, fear of failure, and content of the task.

just below 2 years of age begin to mentally perform activities before physically performing them. Piaget used the term *transducive reasoning* for this kind of mental activity in which the child links earlier learning. Banus (1971) said that such mental activity is neither induction nor deduction; it simply proceeds from particular to particular. It is likely that the young child will place the rings on the cone correctly just because they do not fit any other way; he will not reason that the task requires correct ordering of the largest to the smallest.

Much of the young child's cognition takes the form of what Piaget has called mental experiment which is the step-by-step mental replica of concrete actions and events as the child recalls them. Thus, thought during this period of development is concrete (Ausubel & Sullivan, 1970).

Deterrents to Cognitive Development

According to Rohwer (1976), much of the forgetting experienced by young children is caused by interference from prior learning or from material presented subsequent to the information in question. Kershner (1975) suggested that interference may result from other causes such as over-reliance on the perceptual features of stimuli. Although much research is needed to delineate the causes of interference, teachers need to be aware of its existence and exercise care in helping the child to distinguish clearly what he is expected to learn.

Closely related to the problem of interference is the characteristically short attention span of young children. It is well known that the capacity to sustain attention increases with mental age and is also affected by the child's personality. However, children who have difficulty sticking with a task have shown surprising persistence in activities appropriate to their levels of ability and interest (Baroff, 1974). The child's attention span is affected by such factors as level of difficulty, fear of failure, and content of the task; these factors subsequently affect the child's cognitive development. Simplification of the concept, measures to minimize distractions, and increased stimulus value of instructional materials are necessary to encourage attention (Peterson, 1974; Robinson & Robinson, 1965).

Negative Self-concept. A negative self-concept is a significant influence on the young child's cognitive development and should be the cause of grave concern.

A child's concept of himself includes his thoughts and feelings about his physical and psychological self-images. Like other concepts the child will acquire, the self-concept is an outgrowth of experiences. In this case, the experience comes from the child's relationship with other people and how he *thinks* they value him.

Physical self-images refer to the child's general appearance, sex, and "the importance of different parts of his body to his behavior and the prestige they give him the eyes of others" (Hurlock, 1972, p. 365). Psychological self-images refer to thoughts, feelings, and emotions in relation to abilities and other qualities such as honesty, confidence, and independence.

Primary self-concepts are the combined physical and psychological self-images resulting from the child's experiences at home. Secondary self-concepts are similar but result from experiences outside the home. Primary self-concepts greatly influence secondary self-concepts in that the child usually seeks companions and experiences which reinforce his primary self-concept.

Usually the primary self-concept is the more favorable one, and the child attempts to bring the two in harmony with one another. If there is a discrepancy, the child will have to adjust his primary self-concept to make it compatible with reality (Hurlock, 1972). If the primary self-concept is not favorable, feelings of self-consciousness and inferiority and a lack of confidence persist, limiting to some extent the child's ability to learn (Jersild, 1968).

A positive self-concept results from the satisfaction of needs, both physical and psychological. The physical needs of food, shelter, clothing, and bodily care are fairly well known and are usually provided. Less well-known are the psychological needs. According to Mouly (1968) those needs include the need for affection, belonging (security), achievement, independence, social recognition, and self-esteem. When needs are neglected or provided for in an unreliable manner, the child fails to develop basic trust in his caretakers and begins to distrust his own ability to cause things to happen. These feelings, expressed by

A child's concept of himself includes his thoughts and feelings about his physical and psychological self-images.

poor motivation and lack of persistence, are the foundations of a negative self-concept.

The young handicapped child is particularly vulnerable to the development of a negative self-concept. In spite of the fact that his family provides for all of his needs, an unaccepting or unsupportive society will foster feelings of self-doubt. His view of himself as "different" may erase the possibility of self-esteem. Rejection by peers could remove all hope of a positive self-concept. One of the effects of a negative self-concept is depressed ability to learn.

Overattachment. Overattachment is the result of prolonged dependency and overprotection. Because of the extra care required by the young handicapped child, prolonged dependency may result unless all of the family members share in the child's care. From time to time, other people can gradually become a part of the child's life by visiting in the home and assisting with his routine (Finnie, 1975).

Overprotection on the part of one or both parents can delay the child's interacting with other children in small group or nursery school activities. The longer the child is prevented from becoming part of a group, the more dependent he will become. Overattachment results in fewer opportunities for varied experiences and, therefore, fewer opportunities to learn.

Handicapping Conditions. The child's handicapping conditions can delay or depress cognitive development. With the sensory impaired (deaf or blind), the child receives partial if not distorted information. Specifically, the blind child or one who is visually impaired, according to Nolan (1976), is restricted by his handicap in the following ways: (1) range and variety of experience, (2) ability to get about, and (3) control of the environment and of self in relation to it.

The deaf child, "although potentially of normal intelligence is constrained by communication limitations" (Moores, 1976, p. 91). He too has difficulty interacting with his environment and learning from it. Without adequate help this child is doomed to impoverished communication skills that set limits on the development of other skills.

The problems of the retarded child are multifaceted, including, for many, both physical and mental problems. From a learning difficulties point of view, Peterson (1974) has suggested deficits in the following areas: (1) concept formation, (2) incidental learning, (3) short-term memory, and (4) generalizations and transfer. An additional problem is rigidity in learning strategies.

Children with learning disabilities have marked intraindividual differences. In spite of normal intelligence, children with learning disabilities have great difficulty performing in some areas. Their problems, stemming from processing information, generally center around language. While their cognitive development progresses, optimal development is limited by language deficiencies (Kirk, 1972).

Garfunkel (1976) has indicated that until the present time, preschool children with moderately disturbed behavior have been largely ignored. Confinement at home and in preschools which have little demands on the child prevent the disability from surfacing. On the other hand, the severe withdrawal tendencies of the autistic child are more readily identified. The effects of this disability on cognitive development are severe due, in part, to the absence of attention. The invisible curtain around the autistic child may prevent the child from receiving information; it certainly prevents the teacher from knowing how much information is received.

The motor problems of the child with cerebral palsy directly contribute to his limited ability to receive information. Also, the effects of the handicap are related to the location of affected areas and the severity of the disability. The effects on cognitive development are believed to be much greater when the child's ability to acquire language is involved. It is generally believed that organic or functional language disabilities may limit a child's access to information or the ability to make experience coherent.

Summary

The various components of cognitive development and their relevance to preschool education for young handicapped children have been presented. The emphasis has been on concept development because of its emergence during the early years and its amenability to instructional strategies. For purposes of understanding and the possibility of triggering ideas for new instructional approaches, deterrents to cognitive development have been presented.

REFERENCES

Ausubel, D., & Sullivan, E. *Theory and problems of child development.* New York: Grune & Stratton, 1970.

Banus, B. *The developmental therapist: A prototype of the pediatric occupational therapist.* Thorofare, N.J.: Charles B. Slack, 1971.

Baroff, G. *Mental retardation: Nature, cause and management.* Washington, D.C.: Hemisphere Publishing Corp., 1974.

Blake, K. *Teaching the retarded.* Englewood Cliffs, N.J.: Prentice-Hall, 1974.

Blake, K. *The mentally retarded: An educational psychology.* Englewood Cliffs, N.J.: Prentice-Hall, 1976.

Blake, K. A., & Williams, C. L. Induction and deduction in retarded, normal, and superior subjects' concept attainment. *American Journal of Mental Deficiency,* 1968, **73,** 226–231. (a)

Blake, K. A., & Williams, C. L. Retarded, normal, and superior subjects' attainment of verbal concepts at two levels of inclusiveness. *Psychological Reports,* 1968, **23,** 535–540. (b)

Blake, K. A., & Williams, C. L. *Studies of the effects of systematic variations of certain conditions related to learning. III. Task conditions.* Washington, D.C.: U.S. Office of Education, Cooperative Research Program, 1963.

Bourne, L. E., Jr. Knowing and using concepts. *Psychological Review,* 1970, **77,** 546–556.

Bourne, L. E., Jr., Goldstein, S., & Link, W. E. Concept learning as a function of availability of previously presented information. *Journal of Experimental Psychology,* 1964, **67,** 439–448.

Bourne, L. E., Jr., & Jennings, P. C. The relationship between contiguity and classification learning. *Journal of General Psychology,* 1963, **69,** 335–338.

Braine, M. D. The ontogeny of English phrase structure: The first phase. *Language,* 1963, **39,** 1–13.

Cahill, H. E., & Hovland, C. I. The role of memory in the acquisition of concepts. *Journal of Experimental Psychology,* 1969, **59,** 137–144.

DeCecco, J., & Crawford, W. *The Psychology of learning and instruction.* Englewood Cliffs, N.J.: Prentice-Hall, 1974.

Elkind, D. *A sympathetic understanding of the child: Birth to sixteen.* Boston: Allyn & Bacon, 1974.

Finnie, N. *Handling the young cerebral palsied child at home.* New York: E. P. Dutton & Co., 1975.

Flavell, J. *Cognitive development.* Englewood Cliffs, N.J.: Prentice-Hall, 1977.

Gagné, R. *The conditions of learning.* New York: Holt, Rinehart & Winston, 1970.

Gagné, R. The learning of principles. In H. J. Klausmeier & C. W. Harris (Eds.), *Analyses of concept learning.* New York: Academic Press, 1966.

Garfunkel, F. Early childhood special education for children with social and emotional disturbances. In H. Spieker, N. Anastasiow, & W. Hodges (Eds.), *Children with special needs: Early development and education.* Minneapolis: University of Minnesota, 1976.

Hurley, O. Learning concepts: Mixed and unmixed contiguity. *Journal of Research and Development in Education,* 1975, **8,** 59–61. (a)

Hurley, O. Learning concepts: Ratio of positive to negative instances. *Journal of Research and Development in Education,* 1975, **8,** 62–63. (b)

Hurley, O. Learning concepts: Positive to negative instances. *Journal of Research and Development in Education Monograph,* 1973, **6,** 131–137.

Hurlock, E. *Child development* (5th ed.). New York: McGraw-Hill, 1972.

Jersild, A. *Child psychology* (6th ed.). Englewood Cliffs, N.J.: Prentice-Hall, 1968.

Kershner, J. Visual-spatial organization and reading support for a cognitive developmental interpretation. *Journal of Learning Disabilities,* 1975, **8** (1), 30–36.

Kirk, S. *Educating exceptional children* (2nd ed.). Boston: Houghton Mifflin Co., 1972.

Kurtz, K. H., & Hovland, C. I. Concept learning with different sequences of instances. *Journal of Experimental Psychology,* 1956, **51,** 239–243.

May, W. The role of relevant and irrelevant dimensions in concept attainment among retardates and normals. *Journal of Research and Development in Education Monograph,* 1973, **6,** 144–149.

McLaughlin, P. Complete learning and retarded and normal pupils' learning phonics rules. *Journal of Research and Development in Education,* 1976, **9,** 37–39. (a)

McLaughlin, P. Identification of relevant attributes and retarded and normal pupils' learning phonics rules. *Journal of Research and Development in Education,* 1976, **9,** 35–37. (b)

McLaughlin, P. Identification of rules and retarded and normal pupils' learning phonics rules. *Journal of Research and Development in Education,* 1976, **9,** 33–35. (c)

McLaughlin, P. Simultaneous vs. successive exposure and retarded and normal pupils' learning phonics rules. *Journal of Research and Development in Education,* 1976, **9,** 43–44. (d)

Meier, J. Cognitive functioning: Normal development–mental retardation. In R. Johnston & P. Magrab (Eds.), *Developmental disorders.* Baltimore: University Park Press, 1976.

Moores, D. Early childhood special education for hearing handicapped children. In H. Spicker, N. Anastasiow, & W. Hodges (Eds.), *Children with special needs: Early development and education.* Minneapolis: University of Minnesota, 1976.

Mouly, G. *Psychology for effective teaching* (2nd ed.). New York: Holt, Rinehart & Winston, 1968.

Nolan, C. Implications from education of the visually handicapped for early childhood education. In H. Spicker, N. Anastasiow, & W. Hodges (Eds.), *Children with special needs: Early development and education.* Minneapolis: University of Minnesota, 1976.

Peterson, D. Educable mentally retarded. In N. Haring (Ed.), *Behavior of exceptional children: An introduction to special education.* Columbus, Ohio: Charles E. Merrill Publishing Co., 1974.

Robinson, H., & Robinson, N. *The mentally retarded child: A psychological approach.* New York: McGraw-Hill, 1965.

Rohwer, W. Cognitive and perceptual development in children. In H. Spicker, N. Anastasiow, & W. Hodges (Eds.), *Children with special needs: Early development and education.* Minneapolis: University of Minnesota, 1976.

Sanford, A. R. *Learning Accomplishment Profile.* Chapel Hill, N.C.: Training Outreach Project, 1973.

Sanford, A. R. (Ed.). *A manual for use of the Learning Accomplishment Profile (LAP).* Winston Salem, N.C.: Kaplan School Supply Corp., 1974.

Smoke, K. L. Negative instances in concept learning. *Journal of Experimental Psychology,* 1933, **16**, 583–588.

Triffler, N. Language function: Normal and abnormal development. In R. Johnston & P. Magrab (Eds.), *Developmental disorders.* Baltimore: University Park Press, 1976.

8

Language Skills

One unique aspect of human development is language. The ability to communicate by means of language and speech has been considered to be the principal characteristic that distinguishes the human species from all other animals. Different aspects of human development—learning, intelligence, cognitive development, and social development—are closely linked to language. Because normal language development seems to influence, in a significant way, other facets of an individual's development, it seems fair to suggest that abnormal language development adversely affects the development of a persons's abilities. It is appropriate, therefore, to examine normal language development and the ways a young special child may deviate from this pattern.

This chapter presents a discussion of the following topics: normal language development with respect to structure and sequence; language development of young children in terms of the ways in which language ability is affected by specific disabilities; procedures for identifying and assessing the language skills of young children; and strategies, techniques, and materials that may facilitate language skills development.

Normal Language Development

The two major features of language are *structure* and *sequence.* Before structure can be discussed, some of the terms that pertain to language must be defined.

1. *Language* is defined as a system of signs and symbols used for communication. The signs and symbols have commonly understood meanings.

Jill E. McGovern has combined her work with material by *Rizpah L. Welch* to form this chapter.

When the system is used in speaking or writing, humans are able to communicate with each other.

2. *Speech* is defined as "the production of the unique audible utterances which serve as the basic symbols for oral language" (Dunn, 1973, p. 302). While speech and language are closely related, a distinction needs to be made between them. Speech is one aspect of language development and derives its meaning from the complex system of grammatical rules known as language. Speech and language may occur independently.
3. *Phoneme* is defined as the basic unit of sound; as one of the smallest units of speech, it distinguishes one utterance or word from another. For example, the *c* in *cap* is the phoneme that distinguishes the word *cap* from other words like *map, nap,* or *tap.* It is generally agreed that there are approximately 45 phonemes in the English language. Some languages use as many as 85 phonemes and others as few as 15 (McCandless & Trotter, 1977).
4. *Morpheme* is defined as a combination of phonemes, or a linguistic unit, that cannot be divided into smaller meaningful units. Examples of morphemes are *cap, boy,* and *girl.* Prefixes and suffixes, as meaning-carrying units, are considered to be morphemes. For instance, *ish* and *ful* are morphemes, and they may be combined with *boy* and *cap,* respectively, to produce other morphemes, *boyish* and *capful*.
5. *Vocabulary* is defined as all the words of a language.
6. *Semantics* pertains to the meaning of words. In vocabulary development, children seem initially to attach the most obvious meanings to words, then later to assimilate the more complex and subtle meanings of words.
7. *Syntax* is defined as the way in which words are put together to form meaningful phrases and sentences.
8. *Grammar* is defined as "that aspect of language that includes all of the rules for the construction of words (morphology), the arrangement of words into phrases and sentences (syntax), the meanings of words (semantics), and the pronunciation of words (phonology)" (McCandless & Trotter, 1977, p. 324). Grammar incorporates all the elements of the structure of language.

Some of these same elements of structure, as well as other characteristics, seem to make human language unique and unlike any other form of animal communication. One apparently unique feature of human language is that it utilizes a small number of *phonemes* to produce a large number of meanings (Hockect & Altman, 1968). With the approximately 45 basic units of sound, the English language user can draw upon the more than 100,000 morphemes and produce an infinite variety of meaningful messages (Goldenson, 1970).

Another characteristic unique to human language is *displacement.* Displacement may be defined as the ability to communicate about persons, objects, and events not actually present in space or time (McCandless & Trotter, 1977). In contrast to humans, animals are only able to communicate about the environment in its present state. Infants experience this same limitation during their development of language but eventually add displacement to their language repertoire.

The ability to be *creative* with language is another unique aspect of human language. The creativity may be in the form of monumental literary works or insignificant fibs.

Two final characteristics unique to human language are *learnability* and *reflectiveness.* The first term refers to the ability of users of one human language to learn to use another language. The second quality, reflectiveness, may be described as the ability to think about the ideas and messages that are being communicated through language.

The structure of language is learned by the child in an orderly sequence. Normal language and speech development seems to occur within a certain specific time, that is, about the first 7 years of a child's life, and such development seems to be associated with normal development in other areas, such as physical and intellectual growth.

During a relatively short span of time, the child's language skills evolve from instinctive, undifferentiated crying to sophisticated speech. Although the parameters for normal language and speech acquisition seem to be fairly specific in terms of years, each of the various stages of development may be reached within a general range of months. Table 1 summarizes the normal speech and oral language developmental stages.

Initially, the infant is a passive participant in the language development process. Very early, however, there is a change from the passive to the active state, as the infant learns that her vocal actions directly affect her well-being. Undifferentiated crying, which is a random response, becomes alarm crying or cooing, depending on the infant's needs. The need for relief of a state of discomfort elicits alarm crying, while the expression of satisfaction results in cooing. When these early attempts at speech are reinforced, a simple but functional means of communication begins to develop.

After the first few months of random vocalizations, the child begins specific vocalizations. These vocal responses occur during the stages of babbling and lalling. Babbling may be defined as the stage in which the child makes all the sounds that are possible with the human speech apparatus. There is a universal aspect to babbling. Lalling refers to the stage of vocalization in which the child reduces her sound repertoire to those sounds which are peculiar to the language she hears. The refinement of general speech behaviors to specific speech patterns is the result of the reinforcement of the latter by the speech models of such persons as parents and family members.

By the end of one year, the normal child begins to utter single words. Often the first word refers to one of the parents because any speech attempt that approximates *mama* or *dada* probably has been strongly reinforced. During the next six months, the child uses one-word utterances as sentences, and at the same time, expands her vocabulary. Gradually, two and three words are strung together to communicate a message.

Oral language and speech develop at a phenomenal rate during the years from 2 to 4. The child's language skills grow significantly in terms of phonology, vocabulary, and syntax. In addition to the vowel sounds, the child adds about a dozen new consonant sounds to her speech repertoire. The child's vocabulary of approximately 25 words expands to one of more than 1,500 words. From the two-word sentence stage, the child evolves to a mastery of the basic syntax of

Table 1

Summary of Early Normal Speech and Oral Language Developmental Stages

Age	General Characteristics	Usable Speaking Vocabulary (Number of Words)	Adequate Speech Sound Production
Months			
1–3	Undifferentiated crying. Random vocalizations and cooing.		
4–6	Babbling. Specific vocalizations. Verbalizes in response to speech of others. Immediate responses approximate human intonational patterns.		
7–11	Tongue moves with vocalizations (lalling). Vocalizes recognition. Reduplicates sound. Echolalia (automatic repetition of words and phrases).		
12	First word.	1–3	All vowels
18	One-word sentence stage. Well-established jargon. Uses nouns primarily.	18–22	
Years			
2	Two-word sentence stage. Sentences functionally complete. Uses more pronouns and verbs.	270–300	
2.5	Three-word sentence stage. Telegraphic speech.	450	h, w, wh
3	Complete simple-active-sentence structure used. Uses sentences to tell stories which are understood by others.	900	p, b, m
3.5	Expanded grammatical forms. Concepts expressed with words. Speech disfluency is typical. Sentence length is 4–5 words.	1200	t, d, n
4	Excessive verbalizations. Imaginary speech.	1500	k, g, ng, j
5	Well-developed and complex syntax. Uses more complex forms to tell stories. Uses negation and inflexional form of verbs.	2000	f, v
6–8	Sophisticated speech. Skilled use of grammatical rules. Learns to read. Acceptable articulation by 8 years for males and females.	2600+	l, r, y, s, z, sh, ch, zh, th, consonant blends

Note: From *Exceptional children in the schools*, L. M. Dunn (Ed.). New York: Holt, Rinehart and Winston, 1973, p. 301. Reprinted by permission.

her language. Consequently, at about the age of 4, the normal child, by some unknown miracle, has acquired almost complete knowledge of the complex grammatical system of her home language.

The years from 4 to 7 are used by the child to refine her syntactical skills and to expand her phonological and morphological repertoire. Finally, by age 7, the child demonstrates appropriate articulation and skillful use of the rules of grammar. Subsequent language development is vertical in nature and predominantly an expansion of vocabulary.

The preceding discussion of the structure and sequence of language represents the widely held view of normal language development. Another view of the development of language was suggested by Myklebust (1964). He delineates five levels on his developmental hierarchy of man's language system: *inner auditory receptive, auditory expressive, visual receptive, and visual expressive language.* Figure 1 presents Myklebust's representation of these levels as well as the corresponding language skills. The first three levels are the most relevant

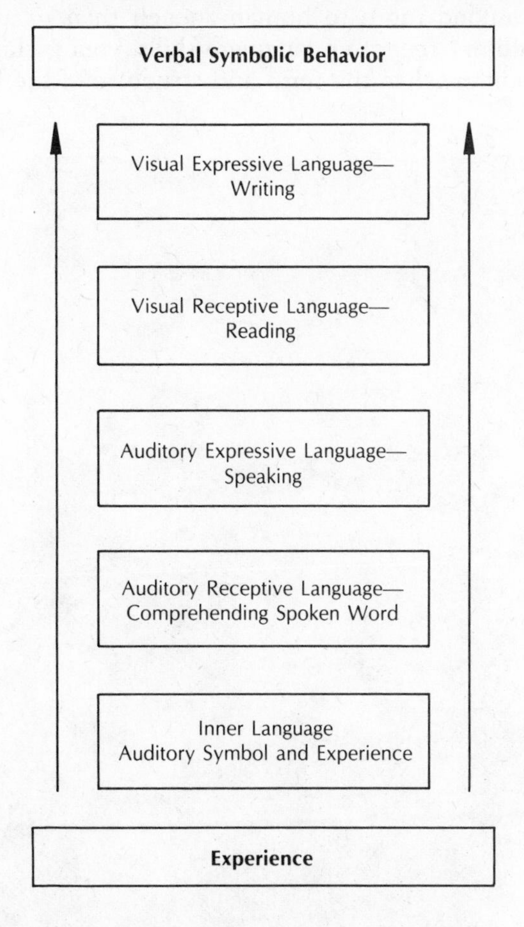

Figure 1. The developmental hierarchy of man's language system.

Note: From *The Psychology of Deafness* by H. R. Myklebust, p. 232. New York: Grune & Stratton, 1960. Reprinted by permission.

to our discussion of early childhood–special education because the skills that occur at each of these three levels are mastered by the normal child during the first 5 or 6 years of life.

According to Myklebust, the first kind of language acquired by the infant is *inner language.* Inner language is founded on a base of experience. Through the use of inner language, infants begin to grasp the meanings of their experiences. For a word to have meaning, it must represent a given unit of experience. Myklebust's first level of language development, inner language, is that process which permits the transformation of experience into symbols, initially spoken symbols, then written symbols.

The second facet of language to be acquired by the child is *auditory receptive language,* which is the ability to comprehend the spoken word. The auditory receptive language, or listening, skills develop from the moment of birth. Newborn infants have the ability to distinquish between pitches and the ability to locate the source of a sound (see Chapter 1). Although they have these abilities, infants tend to respond more to human speech than to any other sounds. Utilizing their auditory receptive language skills, young children begin, at a very early age, to internalize the form and structure of the language of their environment.

Auditory receptive language is the ability to comprehend the spoken word.

The third level in Myklebust's sequence of language development is *auditory expressive language* which is the ability to speak. When a child has acquired meaningful units of experience and when comprehension occurs, he is prepared to engage in auditory expression, or speech.

Myklebust suggests that each level of language skill in his hierarchy follows in the presented sequence. Inner language and the auditory language skills must precede the visual language skills of reading and writing. Each level provides a basis for the development of the succeeding language skill.

Theories of Language Development. Language development seems to occur in a similar manner for all normal children. There are several theories related to language development that attempt to explain the process of language acquisition. These deserve some consideration since they may enable early childhood–special educators to plan programs of intervention for children with inadequate language development.

One theory of language development, advocated by B. F. Skinner (1957), suggests that the processes involved in learning explain language development in children. According to Skinner's hypothesis, when children begin to make a variety of sounds, adult reinforcement of specific sounds used in the language causes them to learn to produce more meaningful sounds or words. Eventually, with continued reinforcement from adults and other children, children learn the syntax and the grammar of the language. Social learning also serves to reinforce language skills. Brown and Hanlon (1970) found that parents reinforced their children's language attempts through approval or disapproval. Corrections were made more often of socially inappropriate words than of faulty syntax.

Another theory of language proposes that biological connections or structures in the brain may control language ability. Lenneberg (1964), a proponent of the biological basis of language, offers four arguments in support of his position: (1) there are relationships between verbal behavior and sensory and cognitive behaviors; (2) there is an extremely regular sequence in the acquisition of the components of language (i.e., phonemes, morphemes, syntax, and grammar) which is unaffected by cultural or linguistic differences; (3) the ability to learn language may be impaired by brain lesions or damage in some cases, but in other cases may be unimpaired by disabilities such as neurological, hearing, or visual impairments; and (4) there is a presumption that language cannot be taught to subhuman forms (Frost & Kissinger, 1976). Lenneberg maintains that any human behavior that demonstrates these characteristics may be assumed to have a biological basis.

With similar logic, linguists suggest that certain structures in the brain may be programmed with some language abilities that need not be learned. Chomsky, one proponent of the fixed function of the language areas of the brain, suggests the possibility that language ability may be genetically determined and that language may have a partially determined structure as a matter of necessity (Trotter, 1975).

A final theory of language, closely related to Chomsky's theory, is that of generative grammar. This particular theory proposes that children are able to produce or generate original sentences after they have acquired certain basic rules of language. Brown (1973), a supporter of the generative grammar theory of language, suggests that it is virtually impossible to acquire a repertoire of sentences. Instead, children acquire a system of rules that enables them to generate an infinite variety of sentences. How the system is acquired, whether through the principles of learning or because of certain biological structures in the brain, is still unknown.

Even though the theories of language development just presented are inconclusive, they have relevance for this discussion of language skills development in handicapped children. Each theory—the learning theory, the biological and brain structures theories, and the generative grammar theory—contributes to a greater understanding of the ways in which an exceptional child may deviate from normal language development, and the ways in which she may be treated to ameliorate her language skills development.

Language Development of Exceptional Children

Adequate language development depends on normal physical, motor, sensory, cognitive, and social growth during the first 5 or 6 years of life. If the child's developmental systems are functioning, then language acquisition is accomplished by the time the child reaches school age, without any formal teaching. Any impairment to these developmental systems impedes, by varying degrees of severity, the child's language skills development, and presents her with problems when she faces formal schooling at the age of 6.

Normal language development allows the child to communicate with other humans about her experiences within her environment. The listening and speaking skills developed initially enable the child to interact with others and, at the same time, provide a strong foundation for the development of more complex language skills, those of reading and writing. The special child reflects the lack of adequate language skills twofold. First, her inability to communicate efficiently during the formative years has lasting detrimental effects on her life adjustment potential. Second, her inadequate listening and speaking skills often hinder the development of her reading and writing skills which seem to be essential to a successful school experience. It is appropriate, therefore, to examine the ways in which the language skills development of young, exceptional children may be impaired.

Mental Retardation. Dunn (1973) points out that the relation of language disabilities to mental retardation is a high one; the greater the degree of mental retardation, the greater the degree of language and speech disability. Language and special disabilities in mentally retarded children may be characterized as follows:

1. Language and speech acquisition are a function of intellectual ability; the profoundly retarded (IQ below 25) never learn to speak, the severely retarded (IQ 25 to 35) acquire elementary speech by the adolescent

years, the moderately retarded (IQ 35 to 50 or 60) acquire the equivalent of third-grade language skills, including speech, by adolescence, and the mildly retarded (IQ 50 or 60 to 75) are able to learn language skills as advanced as the sixth-grade level.

2. Among the mildly retarded, language and speech development is delayed but not to a degree that would warrant a diagnosis of mental retardation during the preschool years.
3. Although maturation accounts for improvement in the language development of mildly retarded children, as they grow older, their language skills, particularly oral language abilities, reach a plateau. The lack of ability to manipulate language becomes a serious problem for the mildly mentally retarded.
4. The prevalence of speech disabilities among the mentally retarded ranges from 8% to 37%, with articulation disorders occurring the most frequently (Dunn, 1973). Speech disabilities of all types, however, occur with greater frequency in the retarded population than in the total population.
5. For the mentally retarded, oral language stimulation is more essential than other language skills, such as reading or writing. Such a language development program should be implemented as early as possible during the preschool years in order to minimize the language disabilities of the mentally retarded.

The language disabilities of the child who is functioning as mentally retarded because of cultural and linguistic differences deserve further consideration. There seem to be two schools of thought regarding the language of the culturally different child. One suggests the weakness of a culturally different child is her verbal ability (Bromwich, 1968). Such a child is supposedly below average or retarded in every aspect of intellectual development because of her language deficiency or impoverishment (Bereiter & Engelmann, 1966; Lewis, 1967; Moore, 1965).

Stating the case of the other school of thought, Mukerji and Robison (1966) contend that this nonverbal label applied to a culturally different child is not supported by data. A child from a low socioeconomic environment is no more verbally destitute than her middle-class peers (Olsen, 1965). In fact, according to Labov (1969), a nonstandard English dialect like black English is a highly-developed, sophisticated, and adequate system of communication.

Differences between standard English and nonstandard English dialects, with respect to style and vocabulary, have been noted by a number of investigators. Riessmann (1962) studied the speaking styles of lower- and middle-class individuals and found that the former group used a restricted language. This style relied on implicit meanings and nonverbal forms of expression for communication. It was differentiated from the speaking style of middle-class individuals who employed a more formal, elaborated language. These differences between the restricted and elaborated language styles may be contributing factors to functional mental retardation since school success seems directly related to proficiency with elaborated language and standard English.

A culturally different child whose language is a nonstandard English dialect may be diagnosed as functionally mentally retarded when she enters formal schooling. Oral language stimulation based on the primary home language as well as standard English and stressed during the preschool years could enhance a child's language development and minimize the effects of cultural difference.

Cerebral Palsy. Children with cerebral palsy show a relatively high incidence of language and speech disabilities. Wilson (1973) estimates that as many as 50% of these children have speech and language deficiencies. Language skills in young cerebral palsied children may be impeded by a variety of associated conditions: neuromuscular disability may result in limited mobility which in turn restricts the experiences upon which language develops; the same kind of disability may interfere with efficient use of the speech apparatus; and perceptual disturbances accompanying cerebral palsy may impede the development of basic language concepts.

The speech disabilities which are often found in children with cerebral palsy are disorders of articulation and voice, and occasionally stuttering. Hearing disabilities associated with one kind of cerebral palsy, athetosis, affect the child's ability to discriminate sounds within the human speech range. Normal language acquisition is subsequently impaired.

Autism. McLean and McLean (1976) found that autistic children exhibited no language or severe language delay. The absence of communication skills is one of the most readily observed symptoms of autism, and this may be attributed to the lack of development of functional language. In some autistic children, speech may develop, but it is usually characterized by echolalia, repetition, distorted rhythm and intonation, and inappropriate articulation (McLean & McLean, 1976). Speech such as just described may not be considered as functioning as one of the skills of language.

Much research has been conducted on the subject of autism. For instance, Ornitz and Ritvo (1968) regard autism as a disorder of perceptual constancy. Rutter (1969) suggests that autism is a central language disorder; and Rimland (1964) views the autistic condition as one of cognitive dysfunction. Although the theories about the cause and nature of the condition vary greatly, the resulting behaviors include the lack of any functional language development.

Hearing Impairment. The young child whose hearing impairment has occurred with birth or at a very early age experiences the detrimental effects of sensory deprivation in her language development. The normal sequence of language acquisition relies initially on what the child hears. Myklebust (1964) stresses the importance of the first two levels in his hierarchy of language development (*auditory receptive* language and *auditory expressive* language) for building a strong base for later language learning. The hearing impaired child does not receive auditory input, so her language development is delayed and impaired significantly.

Although the early stages of language development, crying and babbling, seem to be normal in the hearing impaired child, the babbling stage never progresses to the lalling stage because the child is unable to receive auditory reinforcement from the environment. Without early speech training, the hearing impaired child seldom advances beyond the point of making the sounds in the repertoire of a 12- or 13-month-old hearing infant. Instead of developing oral communication skills, the hearing impaired child often learns a system of gestures, or informal manual communication skills, during the period from 18 months to 4 years of age (McLean & McLean, 1976). Such language is not proficient enough for the demands of the language-oriented environment in which the child must function.

Even with the stress on language development in educational programs for the hearing impaired, the language of hearing impaired children often uses nouns and verbs extensively while limiting phrase or sentence length, omitting function words such as auxiliary verbs, adverbs, adjectives, prepositions, and conjunctions, and confusing syntactical order (Brannon, 1968). Mastery of the grammar of the English language does occur in hearing impaired children but at a stage significantly later than it occurs for normal, hearing children. A delay in oral language skills causes a subsequent delay in the language skills of reading and writing.

The degree of hearing impairment directly affects the language and resultant educational retardation that may occur. In one survey, it was noted that partially hearing children were retarded ½ to 2 years in grade level, and severely hearing impaired children were retarded at least 3 to 4 years in grade level (Dunn, 1973). It is hoped that early identification and treatment of hearing impaired children will enable them to develop their language skills more expediently and more fully.

Visual Impairment. Of the two major categories of sensory disabilities, hearing impairment affects the language development of special children much more seriously than visual impairment. Nevertheless, visual impairment may cause oral language to be somewhat delayed. Normal children use visual as well as auditory cues in the process of imitating sounds but visually impaired children rely instead on the auditory and sometimes the tactual channels in learning to speak.

Speech disorders occur in the language of the visually impaired but not to any degree that is greater than in the total population. A more serious problem for the visually impaired in learning language is the acquisition of word concepts. Without visual stimuli, color concepts, dimensions, nonverbal gestures, and the like cause the visually impaired learner some difficulty when learning language.

A firm foundation in oral language skills is essential for the visually impaired child in preparation for the monumental task of learning to read. A major responsibility of early childhood–special educators is to provide visually impaired children with training in oral language skills.

Speech Impairment. The various speech impairments described in Chapter 1 interfere with the successful acquisition of language skills but not necessarily to a degree that communication is completely hindered. When a child with an articulation disorder or with a stuttering problem reaches the regular elementary program, her speech impairment may appear less significant in comparison to her mastery of the other language skills, reading and writing. But for a young speech-impaired child whose only form of expression is disabled, the problem of communication is much greater. Such impairment may be associated with several kinds of problems: delayed speech, cleft palate, hearing impairment, and aphasia.

Delayed speech is classified as a lack or retardation in speech development. A number of the conditions described in this section—mental retardation, hearing impairment, and behavioral disorders—may cause delayed speech. Other causes include cerebral dysfunction, glandular irregularities, and environmental deprivation (Kirk, 1972). A language-impoverished environment, which may exist in the affluent home as well as in the low-income home, may not provide adequate stimulation for language and speech development.

In some cases, the delayed onset of speech may establish a pattern of retardation that continues through the process of language acquisition. Mentally retarded children and children with hearing impairments, for instance, most often remain several grades behind their normal peers in language development. In other cases, delayed speech is a temporary kind of exceptionality and does not necessarily foreshadow significant delays in the development of other language skills.

The condition of *cleft palate* (described in Chapter 1) obviously presents problems in speech development. The structural defects in the palate, mouth, and lip cause speech disabilities of misarticulation, hypernasality, and nasal emission. Language skills development is further complicated by a high incidence of hearing impairment in children with cleft palate. Because of the structural deviations, there is a tendency for cleft palate children to contract middle ear infections (serous otitis media) which may result in hearing loss and subsequent language deficits.

The language development of children with *hearing impairment* has been presented earlier in this section. It is appropriate at this juncture, however, to delineate the specific speech disorders that may be associated with hearing disabilities. Besides generalized problems of language acquisition, the impaired child experiences difficulty in developing speech sounds. The difficulty increases with the severity of the hearing loss. For a child with a mild hearing disability, the pitch, rate, and inflectional patterns of speech may be normal, but the voice may be breathy and nasal and the sounds *s, sh, z, th, t, k, ch,* and *f* are most likely to be misarticulated (Dunn, 1973).

For a child with a more severe hearing impairment, speech usually develops only with training and even then it contains a great number of misarticulations, and abnormal breathing, voicing, rhythm, and rate (Dunn, 1973). Nevertheless, speech acquisition may be achieved and used as an effective means of communication by the child with hearing impairment.

Aphasia refers to the inability to use linguistic symbols for the purpose of communication. In young children, aphasia manifests itself as a disability in oral language. Depending on the time of onset, aphasia may be divided into two types: *congenital* or *developmental aphasia* is caused by damage to the central nervous system prior to the development of language; *childhood aphasia* results from central nervous system damage incurred from severe brain injury or extremely high fever after language development began.

Normal language development allows the child to communicate with others about her experiences within her environment.

Eisenson (1972) distinguishes between children with developmental aphasia and children with other conditions which may delay language. According to Eisenson, an aphasic child is not mentally retarded, hearing impaired, or emotionally disturbed, even though she may appear on occasion to display some of the characteristics of these disabilities.

The child with developmental aphasia may be identified by several linguistic deviations. Because spoken language may be meaningless or confusing to the child, she may seem to be hearing impaired or extremely inattentive. What speech she has may be characterized by misarticulations, limited or inappropriately used vocabulary, faulty syntactical patterns, and inadequate grammatical structures.

The linguistic aberrations may be further complicated by perceptual dysfunction, particularly in the areas of auditory and visual perception, and by maladaptive behaviors such as hyperactivity, perseveration, motor incoordination, and general behavioral disorders. The overriding problem, however, is the child's inability to process linguistic symbols. For a preschool child with aphasia, oral language skills must be strengthened by appropriate intervention so that the language tasks faced in a formal school setting are not overwhelming.

Learning Disabilities. The definition of learning disabilities in Chapter 1 indicates that this exceptionality is especially related to language development. The definition contains the following statement: "Children with special (specific) learning disabilities exhibit a disorder in one or more of the basic psychological processes involved in understanding or in using spoken or written language" (National Advisory Committee, 1969, p. 14). The inability to process language and to use language skills appropriately and efficiently constitutes the major problem for children with learning disabilities.

Some of the characteristics of learning disabilities include disturbances in the areas of auditory, visual, tactile, and kinesthetic perception, and disorders of symbolization such as deficient skills on any of the levels of Myklebust's (1964) hierarchy of language development: auditory receptive, auditory expressive, visual receptive, or visual expressive. Normal children are able to rely on their sensory channels for information which facilitates language development. For example, the auditory and visual cues from others' speech permit a normal child to imitate sounds with a great degree of accuracy. For a learning disabled child whose auditory or visual perceptual skills are in some way impaired or distorted, the auditory and visual channels are of limited usefulness in providing accurate sound models. The result of these perceptual disturbances is deficient language skills development.

The basic problem of language dysfunction associated with learning disabilities is compounded by a variety of other symptoms which often accompany the condition and further impede development. Some of these characteristics are

Educational intervention can help developmentally delayed children handle the multitude of language tasks they will encounter in formal schooling.

hyperactivity, inattention, distractibility, impulsivity, gross and fine motor incoordination, generalized behavioral disabilities, and disorders of sequencing and memory.

Because the deficiencies in the language skills may not manifest themselves until the child encounters the task of learning to read, early identification of learning disabilities is difficult. A cluster of some of the adjunct characteristics just cited in combination with even minimal language disabilities may alert the early childhood–special educator to the possibility of a learning disability.

Behavioral Disabilities. The behavioral disabilities described in Chapter 1 do not usually have any language or speech disabilities associated with them (Clarizio & McCoy, 1976). With regard to speech patterns, the pitch and loudness of the voice are sometimes related to specific behavioral disabilities. A loud voice may be characteristic of a child with conduct disorders, while a low, soft, weak voice may be typical of the immature, anxious child.

One exception to the generalization just suggested is the childhood psychosis of *childhood schizophrenia.* The use of language and speech in a deviant manner is one of the most widely observed characteristics of this behavioral disability. Some schizophrenic children appear to lack language or only to have a very restricted vocabulary of one or two words. Other young schizophrenics who do have speech skills do not use them for communication. Instead they employ techniques such as repetitions, language distortions, and the development of a private language where known words are assigned different, unrelated meanings, apparently in order to maintain their detachment from reality. Absorption in their fantasy world is also enhanced by word play with rhyming and alliterative but nonsensical speech (Clarizio & McCoy, 1976).

Speech disabilities are also present in the schizophrenic child, in addition to language disabilities. The most prevalent speech disorder seems to be related to voice quality. Schizophrenics seem to speak with a dull or wooden voice (Goldfarb, Braunstein, & Lorgo, 1956), devoid of inflections conveying emotion or mood. Other speech disorders that have been noted in schizophrenic children are nasality, denasality, breathiness, throatiness, and high-pitched voice (Clarizio & McCoy, 1976). Furthermore, there seems to be little relation between the meaning of the spoken words and the accompanying nonverbal gestures, such as facial and hand movements. Clarizio and McCoy conclude that "the individualized and sometimes bizarre patterns of language and speech in schizophrenic children result in an inability to use language for normal purposes of communication" (p. 338).

Identification and Assessment of Language Development

The process of identification and assessment of exceptional children was presented in some detail in Chapter 2. Such a critical procedure deserves further discussion as it relates to language development. Identification and accurate assessment of deficiencies in language skills development enables early childhood–special educators to maximize the early developmental potential of special children. Such intervention can help these children handle the multitude of language tasks they will encounter in formal schooling.

The key observer of the child's language development is the parent. Abnormal development noted by the parent may be brought to the attention of the medical practitioner who may refer the child to the appropriate specialist. The audiologist and otologist are the primary resource persons involved in identifying hearing disabilities. Other specialists may be the ophthalmologist who would identify severe visual disabilities; the speech pathologist who would pinpoint specific speech impairments caused by cerebral palsy, cleft palate, or aphasia; and the psychiatrist or the psychologist who would recognize behavioral disabilities such as autism and childhood schizophrenia.

There are a number of formal and informal screening and assessment instruments related to language development. Many formal tests of intelligence include sections which assess language abilities. Examples of these are the following:

1. *Denver Developmental Screening Test* (Frankenburg, Dodds, & Fandal, 1970). This test measures a number of abilities, including language in children from 2 weeks to 6 years of age.
2. *Detroit Tests of Learning Aptitude* (Baker & Leland, 1935). Appropriate for children 3 years of age and older, this battery of 19 subtests contains a number related to language abilities.
3. *A Developmental Screening Inventory* (Knobloch, Pasamanick, & Sherard, 1966). This inventory is based on selected items from the Gesell Developmental Schedules (Gesell, 1949). Children in the age range of one month to 18 months may be assessed on a variety of skills, including language.
4. *McCarthy Scales of Children's Abilities* (McCarthy, 1973). These scales measure verbal abilities, among others, in children 2½ years to 8½ years of age.
5. *Minnesota Child Development Inventory* (Ireton & Thwing, 1972). This inventory records observations made by the mother and assesses abilities in children from the ages of one year to 6 years. Expressive language is one of the abilities observed.
6. *Minnesota Preschool Scale* (Goodenough, Maurer, & Van Wagenen, 1970). This measure of intellectual capacity, in children ages 1½ to 6 years, assesses verbal ability in one of its subtests.
7. *Peabody Picture Vocabulary Test* (Dunn, 1965). This test relies primarily on auditory and visual receptive language skills to measure general intellectual abilities.
8. *Preschool Attainment Record* (Doll, 1967). Covering a range of 6 months to 7 years of age, this test measures young children's achievement in a variety of skill areas, including oral language.
9. *Quick Screening Scale of Mental Development* (Banham, 1963). This scale includes sections which assess speech and language abilities in children between the ages of 6 months and 10 years.

10. *Vane Kindergarten Test* (Vane, 1968). This test, intended for use by educational psychologists, contains a subtest which measures the vocabulary development of children in the kindergarten age range of 4 to 6 years old.

Finally, because intellectual development and language development are so closely linked, three of the most frequently used individual tests of intelligence contain subtests which measure language skills. The tests are the *Slosson Intelligence Test* (Slosson, 1963), the *Stanford-Binet Intelligence Scale* (Terman and Merrill, 1960), and the *Wechsler Preschool and Primary Scale of Intelligence* (Wechsler, 1967).

None of these formal assessment tools is a comprehensive measure of language development. Assessment of language skills development in young, special children may be accomplished more accurately and more precisely with instruments intended specifically for the evaluation of language development. Some of these tests follow:

1. *Ammons Full-Range Picture Vocabulary Test* (Ammons & Ammons, 1948). This test of receptive language vocabulary is designed for use with preschool children.
2. *Environmental Language Intervention Program* (MacDonald & Horstmeier, 1978). This program provides a rationale and methods for assessing and training the language delayed child on a developmental continuum. It establishes the child's natural environment as her primary language trainer. The program has at its core four major assessment batteries which are used to diagnose children who fail to exhibit language skills.
   a. *Oliver: Parent-Administered Communication Inventory* (MacDonald, 1978). This home-based assessment instrument is designed to be utilized for educational and diagnostic purposes before professional intervention. The family members become an essential part of the assessment and treatment process.
   b. *Environmental Prelanguage Battery* (EPB) (Horstmeier & MacDonald, 1978). This battery is a series of assessment and training or treatment procedures for developing prelinguistic behaviors that lead to communication and language skills. The training component focuses on preliminary skills (i.e., attending, sitting, and responding to task), the use of play activities, imitation of sounds and words, and production of meaningful nouns and verbs.
   c. *Environmental Language Inventory* (ELI) (MacDonald, 1978). This inventory assesses and trains expressive language based on meaningful language units found in natural linguistic environments. The goal of such training or intervention with language delayed children is to enable these special children to use language spontaneously for appropriate social interaction.
   d. *Ready Set Go: Talk to Me* (Horstmeier & MacDonald, 1978). This battery consists of several prescriptive training units for parents and caregivers under the direction of a professional. It incorporates the skills assessed in EPB and ELI.

3. *Houston Test of Language Development* (Crabtree, 1963). This test measures reception, conceptualization, and expression with two forms. One is appropriate for children from 6 months to 3 years of age, and the other form may be used with children between the ages of 3 and 6 years.
4. *Illinois Test of Psycholinguistic Abilities, Revised Edition* (Kirk, McCarthy, & Kirk, 1968). This test assesses specific dimensions of the process of communication, such as reception, association, and expression. It consists of twelve subtests which measure certain abilities:
   a. the ability to receive and understand using the auditory and visual channels;
   b. the ability to associate and understand relationships using the auditory and visual channels;
   c. the ability to express oneself through the auditory expressive and motor channels;
   d. the ability to complete auditory and visual patterns when only parts of the patterns are presented; and
   e. the ability to remember and repeat auditory and visual sequences of material.

   The test is appropriate for use with children ages 2 years, 4 months to 10 years, 3 months.
5. *Language Facility Test* (Dailey, 1968). This test assesses vocabulary, information, pronunciation, and grammar in the oral language of children 3 years of age and older.
6. *Northwestern Syntax Screening Test* (Lee, 1969). Appropriate for children between the ages of 3 and 7 years, this test assesses receptive and expressive language skills.
7. *Preschool Language Scale* (Zimmerman, Steiner, & Evatt, 1969). This scale includes measures of auditory comprehension, verbal ability, and articulation in children from the ages of 2 to 6 years.
8. *Reynell Development Language Scales, Experimental Edition* (Reynell, 1969). These scales are designed for children one to 5 years of age who display delayed or deviant language. They include measures of verbal comprehension and expressive language.
9. *Test for Auditory Comprehension of Language* (Carrow, 1973). Covering an age range of 3 years, 10 months to 6 years, 11 months, this test assesses a young child's understanding of language structure.
10. *Utah Test of Language Development* (Meacham, Jex, & Jones, 1959). This test measures language abilities and skills in children 1.5 to 14.5 years of age.
11. *Verbal Language Development Scale* (Meacham, 1959). This scale utilizes the communication items on the Vineland Social Maturity Scale (Doll, 1965), and extends and restandardizes them for use with children from birth to 15 years of age.

No one test presents a complete picture of the young child's language skills development. A battery of tests as well as informal assessment measures must be utilized to insure effective and appropriate intervention. Some of the informal evaluation techniques which may be employed are anecdotal records, measurements of behavior, inventories, and individual observation methods (see Chapter 2). For example, some of the inventories and rating scales have sections which pertain to language development:

1. *Developmental Checklists for 3-, 4-, and 5-year-olds* (Frost, 1972). This inventory contains sections on language, auditory and visual discrimination, and comprehension skills.
2. *Pupil Behavior Rating Scale* (Gearheart, 1973). This scale rates children in five areas including auditory comprehension and listening, and spoken language.
3. *The Pupil Rating Scale* (Myklebust, 1971). This scale measures areas such as auditory comprehension and spoken language.
4. *The Valett Developmental Survey of Basic Learning Abilities* (Valett, 1966). This survey measures language development in terms of vocabulary, fluency, and articulation in preschool and kindergarten children.

Consideration of all data gathered from the identification and assessment procedures is essential for planning and implementing an appropriate program of intervention to facilitate language skills development in young, special children.

Intervention in Language Skills Development

The intervention procedures presented in Chapter 2 (see pp. 53–57) as well as the principles of learning and instruction suggested in Chapter 3 have general application to the language development program for young handicapped children. There are several more specific strategies and techniques which deserve consideration.

Infant stimulation is a strategy for fostering overall development, including language development in young children. This approach is patterned after a model of mother-child interaction in a stimulation-rich environment. It is often associated with the kinds of sensory, physical, linguistic, and social experiences a middle-class mother tends to share with her child. These experiences provide her with the skills necessary for success in school.

An infant stimulation program usually attempts to accomplish two objectives: one is to enhance all aspects of the child's development; the other is to train parents to stimulate their children in the home. The efficacy of such a program is significantly diminished if stimulation is limited to a few hours a day in the educational setting. Cooperation between the teacher and the parent is essential.

Infant stimulation related to language development begins from the moment of birth. Newborns respond very early to the sounds of human speech. Exposure to auditory stimulation, including speech, during the child's first months, aids her in the process of learning the sounds and the structure of language. For the

The goal of language intervention programs is to help the child learn as many communication skills as possible.

normal child, this process occurs naturally. For the handicapped child, an intense program of stimulation is necessary during the first years of life to insure the development of language to the extent possible.

Several well-known intervention programs have been based on infant stimulation and have met with remarkable success in reducing the effects of environmental deprivation on children at risk for mental retardation. One of these, the Milwaukee Project, has had some notable results. The program, for children from an environment with a high degree of cultural mental retardation, had two primary emphases: training mothers in child-care skills development, and intervention and enrichment for newborn infants. After 6 years of intense training designed to develop the children's intellectual, cognitive, linguistic, physical, emotional, and social skills, significant differences were found between the experimental and control groups with respect to problem-solving ability and language development (Trotter, 1976). Such a program of infant stimulation may be an effective means of language skills development not only in children at risk for mental retardation but also in children with other developmental disabilities, sensory disabilities, and language disabilities.

Behavior Modification. Like infant stimulation, *behavior modification* is an intervention strategy that has general usefulness. It may be effectively employed with all kinds of handicapped children. Examples of the various ways behavior modification principles may be used for the development of language skills are to increase eye contact in autistic children; to increase the vocabulary of mentally retarded children; to increase the accuracy of sound production in children with cerebral palsy, hearing impairment, and cleft palate; to increase the task behavior of children with learning disabilities and associated hyperactivity; and to increase positive statements made by children with behavioral disabilities.

As presented in Chapter 2, behavior modification is based on several principles:

1. Acceptable behavior is clearly defined.
2. Appropriate behavior is reinforced immediately with an effective reinforcer.
3. Inappropriate behavior is ignored or punished when absolutely necessary.

These principles of behavior modification are actually in operation, though at an unconscious level, when normal children learn language. The parent provides the model of acceptable language behavior. When the child progresses from the babbling stage to the lalling stage and begins to approximate the sounds of the language in her environment, her parent reinforces her attempts with attention and displays of affection. The sounds made by the child that are not in the primary home language are simply ignored and eventually extinguished.

The same behavior modification techniques may be applied in a deliberate, systematic fashion to develop language skills in children with delayed or deviant language behaviors. For example, for an autistic child who exhibits no language, behavior modification may be implemented to elicit such elementary, prelanguage skills as making eye contact and attending to the task. The reinforcers that are effective initially may be ones related to the child's basic needs such as food; gradually, other reinforcers like praise, a smile, or tokens would be equally effective. The ultimate goal of behavior modification is for the learning process to become internalized and self-reinforcing. In the case of language skills development, the objective is for language also to become internalized and continually reinforced during the process of communication.

Teaching English as a Second Language (TESL). Another strategy for developing language skills in young, exceptional children, particularly in children at risk for functional mental retardation due to cultural and linguistic differences, is *Teaching English as a Second Language* (TESL). This approach regards the primary home language, often a nonstandard English dialect, as effective for communication within the home. At the same time, TESL presents standard English as another language that is appropriate for use in the school.

Because the phonemes are almost identical in all English dialects, emphasis is placed on the morphemes, syntax, and grammar of standard English. Basic grammatical patterns are established in the same sequence that language is normally acquired: auditory reception, auditory expression, visual reception, and visual expression. The first two levels are the concern of early childhood–special educators. Repetition and drill are used to present the language patterns. Variables within the patterns are controlled so that the chance for error is minimized. For example, a language pattern may be as follows:

Step I
Teacher: Where is the *book?*
Child: (The child points to the book.)
Teacher: Where is the *chair?*
Child: (The child points to the chair.)

The response required of the child is consistent, while only one variable, the object, changes.

Step II
Teacher: Where is the book?
Child: The *book* is over there. (She points to the book.)
Teacher: Where is the chair?
Child: The *chair* is over there. (She points to the chair.)

The response required of the child now includes a single verbal change patterned after the teacher's question, as well as a motor response, which changes only in direction.

Step III
Teacher: Where is the book?
Child: The book is on the table.
Teacher: Where is the chair?
Child: The chair is on the floor.

The responses required of the child at this point include two verbal changes in the pattern, one describing the object and one indicating the location. The patterns may become increasingly complex with the introduction of questions and negative grammatical structures. It is felt that once these auditory language patterns are internalized, the language skills of reading and writing will follow in a natural sequence. TESL techniques seem to be appropriate not only for culturally different children at risk for mental retardation, but also for children with autism or learning disabilities.

Total Communication. This approach, used primarily with children with hearing disabilities, attempts to develop all functioning sensory channels for the purposes of communication. Lip- or speech-reading, speech therapy, and the use of residual hearing are combined with finger spelling, American Sign Language (ASL), and Signing Exact English (SEE) to achieve the greatest efficiency in the handicapped child's language skills. Although total communication seems to have the most usefulness with hearing impaired children, it may also have effective application with autistic and aphasic children.

In addition to the intervention strategies presented in Chapter 2, these four techniques—infant stimulation, behavior modification, TESL, and total communication—may be utilized to develop the language skills of exceptional children. Some specific activities and materials that are appropriate for use with special children are suggested in Appendix B. Neither listing is intended to be inclusive but rather is intended to provide direction for early childhood–special educators.

Summary

This chapter has focused on language skills development. Normal language development was presented with respect to its structure and sequence. Several theories of language were discussed.

Language skills in special children may deviate from the normal language skills depending upon the disability. The ways in which mental retardation, cerebral palsy, autism, hearing impairment, visual impairment, cleft palate, delayed speech, aphasia, learning disabilities, and behavioral disabilities affect language skills development in young children were presented.

The importance of early identification and accurate assessment by means of formal and informal evaluation instruments was stressed. Finally, intervention strategies and techniques, such as infant stimulation, behavior modification, TESL (Teaching English as a Second Language), and total communication, were suggested in order to achieve the goal of adequate language skills development in young special children.

REFERENCES

Ammons, R. B., & Ammons, H. S. *Full-Range Picture Vocabulary Test.* Missoula, Mont.: Psychological Test Specialists, 1948.

Baker, H. J., & Leland, B. *Detroit Tests of Learning Aptitude.* Indianapolis: Bobbs Merrill, 1935.

Banham, K. M. *Quick Screening Scale of Mental Development.* Munster, Ind.: Psychometric Affiliates, 1963.

Bereiter, C., & Engelmann, S. *Teaching disadvantaged children in the preschool.* Englewood Cliffs, N.J.: Prentice-Hall, 1968.

Brannon, J. A. Comparison of syntactical structures in the speech of three and four-year-old children. *Language and Speech,* 1968, **11,** 171–181.

Bromwich, R. M. Developing the language of young disadvantaged children. *Education Digest,* 1968, **34**(1), 19–22.

Brown, R. Development of the first language in the human species. *American Psychologist,* 1973, **28,** 97–106.

Brown, R., & Hanlon, C. Derivational complexity and order of acquisition in child speech. In J. R. Hayes (Ed.), *Cognition and the development of language.* New York: John Wiley & Sons, 1970.

Carrow, E. *Tests for Auditory Comprehension of Language.* Austin, Tex.: Learning Concepts, 1973.

Clarizio, H. F., & McCoy, G. F. *Behavior disorders in children.* New York: Thomas Y. Crowell Co., 1976.

Crabtree, M. *Houston Test of Language Development.* Houston, Tex.: Houston Press, 1963.

Dailey, J. T. *Language Facility Test.* Alexandria, Va.: Allington Corp., 1968.

Doll, E. A. *Preschool Attainment Record.* Circle Pines, Minn.: American Guidance Service, 1966.

Doll, E. A. *Vineland Social Maturity Scale.* Circle Pines, Minn.: American Guidance Service, 1965.

Dunn, L. M. (Ed.). *Exceptional children in the schools.* New York: Holt, Rinehart & Winston, 1973.

Dunn, L. M. *Peabody Picture Vocabulary Test.* Minneapolis: American Guidance Service, 1965.

Eisenson, J. *Aphasia in children.* New York: Harper & Row, 1972.

Frankenburg, W. K., Dodds, J. B., & Fandal, A. W. *Denver Developmental Screening Test.* Denver: Ladoca Project and Publishing Foundation, 1970.

Frost, J. C. *Developmental checklists of 3-, 4-, and 5-Year-Olds.* Austin: University of Texas, 1972.

Frost, J. L., & Kissinger, J. B. *The young child and the educative process.* New York: Holt, Rinehart & Winston, 1976.

Gearheart, B. R. *The Pupil Behavior Rating Scale.* St. Louis: C. V. Mosby, 1973.

Gesell, A. *Gesell developmental schedules.* New York: Psychological Corp., 1949.

Goldenson, R. M. Language. In *The encyclopedia of human behavior.* New York: Doubleday, 1970.

Goldfarb, W., Braunstein, P., & Lorgo, I. A study of speech patterns in a group of schizophrenic children. *American Journal of Orthopsychiatry,* 1956, **26,** 544–555.

Goodenough, F. L., Mauer, K. M., & Van Wagenen, M. J. *Minnesota Preschool Scale.* Minneapolis: American Guidance Service, 1940.

Hockect, C. F., & Altman, S. A. A note on design features. In T. A. Sebok (Ed.), *Animal communication.* Bloomington: Indiana University Press, 1968.

Horstmeier, D., & MacDonald, J. D. *Environmental Prelanguage Battery* (EPB). Columbus, Ohio: Charles E. Merrill Publishing Co., 1978.

Ireton, H. R., & Thwing, E. J. *Minnesota Child Development Inventory.* Minneapolis: NCS Interpretive Scoring Systems, 1972.

Kirk, S. A. *Educating exceptional children.* Boston: Houghton Mifflin, 1972.

Kirk, S. A., McCarthy, J. J., & Kirk, W. O. *Illinois Test of Psycholinguistic Abilities* (Rev. ed.). Urbana: University of Illinois Press, 1968.

Knobloch, H., Pasamanick, B., & Sherard, E. S., Jr. *Developmental Screening Inventory.* New York: Psychological Corp., 1966.

Labov, W. The logic of nonstandard English. Paper presented at the Twentieth Annual Round Table Meeting on Linguistics and Language Studies, Washington, D.C., 1969.

Lee, L. *Northwestern Syntax Screening Test.* Evanston, Ill.: Northwestern University Press, 1969.

Lenneberg, E. H. A biological perspective of language. In E. H. Lenneberg (Ed.), *New directions in the study of language.* Cambridge, Mass.: M.I.T. Press, 1964.

Lewis, C. Language and literature in childhood. *Elementary English,* 1967, **44,** 518–522.

MacDonald, J. D. *Environmental Language Inventory* (ELI). Columbus, Ohio: Charles E. Merrill Publishing Co., 1978.

MacDonald, J. D. *Oliver: Parent-Administered Communication Inventory.* Columbus, Ohio: Charles E. Merrill Publishing Co., 1978.

MacDonald, J. D., & Horstmeier, D. *Environmental Language Intervention Program.* Columbus, Ohio: Charles E. Merrill Publishing Co., 1978.

McCandless, B. R., & Trotter, R. J. *Children: Behavior and development.* New York: Holt, Rinehart & Winston, 1977.

McCarthy, D. *The McCarthy Scales of Children's Abilities.* New York: Psychological Corp., 1973.

McLean, L. P., & McLean, J. E. Teaching autistic children. In F. B. Withrow & C. J. Nygren (Eds.), *Language, materials, and curriculum management for the handicapped learner.* Columbus, Ohio: Charles E. Merrill Publishing Co., 1976.

Meacham, M. J. *Verbal Language Development Scale.* Minneapolis: American Guidance Service, 1959.

Meacham, M. J., Jex, J. L., & Jones, J. D. *Utah Test of Language Development.* Salt Lake City: Communication Research Associates, 1959.

Moore, W. J. Compensatory language arts programs for disadvantaged children. *Teacher's College Journal,* 1965, **37**(2), 25–32.

Mukerji, R., & Robison, H. F. A head start in language. *Elementary English,* 1966, **43,** 460–463.

Myklebust, H. R. *The psychology of deafness.* New York: Grune & Stratton, 1964.

Myklebust, H. R. *The pupil rating scale.* New York: Grune & Stratton, 1971.

National Advisory Committee on Handicapped Children. *First annual report, Subcommittee on Education of the Committee on Labor and Public Welfare, U.S. Senate.* Washington, D.C.: U.S. Government Printing Office, 1968.

Olsen, J. The verbal ability of the culturally different. *The Reading Teacher,* 1965, **18,** 552–556.

Ornitz, E. M., & Ritvo, E. R. Neurophysiological mechanisms underlying perceptual inconstancy in autistic and schizophrenic children. *Archives of General Psychiatry,* 1968, **19,** (1), 22–27.

Pasanella, A. L., & Volkmor, C. B. *Coming back . . . or never leaving.* Columbus, Ohio: Charles E. Merrill Publishing Co., 1977.

Reynell, J. *Developmental Language Scales, Experimental Edition.* London: NFER Publishing Co., Ltd., 1969.

Riessman, F. *The culturally deprived child.* New York: Harper & Row, 1962.

Rimland, B. *Infantile autism.* New York: Appleton-Century-Crofts, 1964.

Rutter, M. Concepts of autism: A review of the research. In S. Chess and A. Thomas (Eds.), *Annual progress in child psychiatry and child development: 1969.* New York: Brunner/Mazel, 1969.

Skinner, B. F. *Verbal behavior.* New York: Appleton-Century-Crofts, 1957.

Slosson, R. L. *Slosson Intelligence Test.* E. Aurora, N.Y.: Slosson Educational Publications, 1963.

Smart, M. S., & Smart, R. C. *Children: Development and relationships.* New York: Macmillan Publishing Co., 1977.

Terman, L. M. & Merrill, M. A. *Stanford-Binet Intelligence Scale.* Boston: Houghton Mifflin Co., 1960.

Trotter, R. J. The Milwaukee Project. *APA Monitor,* September 1976.

Trotter, R. J. From language to linguistics and beyond. *Science News,* 1975, **109**(2), 332–334.

Valett, R. *The Valett Developmental Survey of Basic Learning Abilities.* Palo Alto, Calif.: Fearon Publishers, 1966.

Vane, J. R. *Vane Kindergarten Test.* Brandon, Vt.: Clinical Psychological Publishing Co., 1968.

Wechsler, D. *Wechsler Preschool and Primary Scale of Intelligence.* New York: Psychological Corp., 1967.

Wilson, M. I. Children with crippling and health disabilities. In L. M. Dunn (Ed.), *Exceptional children in the schools.* New York: Holt, Rinehart & Winston, 1973.

Withrow, F. B., & Nygren, C. J. *Language, materials, and curriculum management for the handicapped learner.* Columbus, Ohio: Charles E. Merrill Publishing Co., 1976.

Zimmerman, I. L., Steiner, V. G., & Evatt, R. L. *Preschool Language Scale.* Columbus, Ohio: Charles E. Merrill Publishing Co., 1969.

9

Emotional and Social Development

Under normal circumstances, from birth through age 5, the child evolves through a complex system of experiences into an emotionally and socially competent individual. Like other areas of development, emotional and social development are dependent upon available environmental opportunities (Kohlberg & Mayer, 1972). The expected average environment, according to White (1975), contains the majority of what most children need during the early months in order to move ahead as far as education is concerned. While the development of an emotional repertoire (person's ability to express different emotions) and the process of socialization are made more difficult when there is a disability, the ingredients which enhance personal and social adjustment are the same for all children. Children born without defects may become handicapped in social relationships by faulty early experiences (Read, 1976). Umsted (1975) was referring to visually handicapped children when he emphasized the need for an optimal climate throughout the early years for satisfactory personal and social adjustments, but the statement logically applies to all children.

This chapter is addressed primarily to factors which contribute to emotional and social development, with emphasis on practices which enhance personal adjustment in young children.

The content of this chapter has been developed from three manuscripts: "Mental Health" by *Walter Draper*, "Human Interaction in Parenting and Teaching" by *Howard Garner*, and "Social and Emotional Development" by *Robert J. Resnick*.

Emotional Development

Much of the basic quality of an individual's emotional life is determined by the interaction between the new born and the person who provides mothering during the first two years of life. The mothering one need not necessarily be the biological mother. The interaction between the mothering one and the young child produces an empathic bond which in time establishes a clear concept of self-identity in the child. The empathic bond is strengthened by the warmth of the mother's body and the other physical contacts the child has with her. These experiences, particularly during feeding, can have lifelong beneficial effects. Bottle feeding versus breast feeding is not the issue here; instead, it is a matter of the quality of the physical contact (caressing and touching) with the baby. The young child uses this emotional bond as a protective device in times of physical or emotional stress and as a source of strength to grow and mature with confidence.

To the degree that the bonding effect is denied the young child for any reason, his emotional development is impoverished and his ability to be affectionate is impaired. The effects of severe mothering deprivation in infancy are cumulative, resulting later in social ineptness and a narrow scope of adaptability (Knobloch & Pasamanick, 1974). Although severe deprivation is most often in evidence when children have been institutionalized early in life, the same effects may be found to some degree among children of socially disadvantaged homes as well as overly well-managed middle class homes which are emotionally sterile (p. 191).

The impaired child whose condition makes him unresponsive to his mother's caresses may inadvertently contribute to his deprivation. As indicated by Bromwich (1977) and others, not only does the mother have a clear effect on the infant's or young child's behavior, but the infant or young child significantly influences the mother's actions toward him. Nevertheless, the young child needs to be valued in the home "without proof" in order to develop the courage to prove his value on the outside (Read, 1976). Thus, the continued acceptance of the child by the mother with unconditional affection contributes greatly towards the child's normal development.

Emotional/Developmental Tasks

Erikson (1950) described the three emotional milestones during the first 5 years of life. In the first year, the milestone is the development of *trust* versus *mistrust* of the world. With an adequate empathic bond between mother and child, the child begins to place basic trust in others and in himself. The adequacy of the relationship also will affect the child's sensitivity and self-confidence. During this period, as in all periods, it is not the quantity of experience the child has with his mother but the quality that is critical (Bromwich, 1977).

In the second year, according to Erikson, the milestone is the development of *autonomy* versus *shame and doubt.* The sense of autonomy or control that can be acquired in this stage leads to a lasting sense of goodwill and personal pride. White (1975) has indicated that from 8 months of age the child needs freedom to explore his environment and to initiate his own activities. If this freedom is denied, and if the environment is restrictive, it is unlikely that autonomy will develop; the development of self-doubt is almost assured.

During the preschool years, the developmental goal may be described as *initiative* versus *guilt.* As the child matures, he develops an increasing awareness of his own power as an initiator of activity. He becomes more and more able to control his environment as he gains mastery over his own body. The child understands at this age that people have different motivations and perceptions, and he delights in his ability to figure things out, to use his initiative. The danger of this stage is that the child's newfound ability may lead him to act or wish to act in ways that will make him feel guilty, or he may be made to feel guilty for behavior which resulted from the exercise of initiative. Such feelings can be inhibiting and contribute later to a lack of initiative.

However, beneath these milestones is another significant development. At birth, the emotional repertoire is confined to excitement versus quiet. By the third month emotional expression has modified to include delight, distress, and excitement. Essentially, the infant is saying, "I feel good," "I feel bad," or "I feel something but I'm not sure what!" By 6 months of age fear, disgust, and anger have been added to the repertoire. In fact, many mothers correctly state that they can tell by the sound of the cry whether it is distress or anger or fear. By the end of the first year, elation and affection have been added, and by 18 months, jealousy. A distinction between affection for adults versus affection for children can be accurately seen about this time. Consequently, at the end of the second year, the toddler has all the emotional expressive potential of a fully matured adult.

What discriminates the toddler and a preschool child from older children is the triggering mechanism of the emotions. The 5-and-under group tend to be easily triggered. A child may move from tears to smiles in a matter of a few seconds. Expression may also be characterized as intense. When the child is emotionally aroused, he uses virtually every part of his body. A temper tantrum is an example of this characteristic. The younger child does not modulate his expressive reactions as well as older children. The ability to modify emotional expression comes with increasing age and increased accuracy in perceiving the world around him. To summarize, then, the range of emotional development in the early years is from a diffuse, poorly articulated feeling level at birth to a highly discriminated and well-differentiated system of feeling levels by the end of the second year.

Forms of Emotional Expression

The emotional expressions most frequently seen in young children are dependence, aggression, anxiety, and fears.

Dependence. Feelings are demonstrated quite early in a child's life. He becomes very affectionate as he tries to work through his dependence versus independence quandry. The young child feels secure when his dependency needs are met. This strong emotional attachment to the family continues into the preschool years. It is important that the child learn from his own experience, not only for survival but for his own emotional growth. The secure feelings of infancy must be tempered now by the independence and initiative of the toddler. As part of the striving for independence, self-discipline and self-reliance are necessary and demanded by the outside world. The child who has not adequately worked through his dependency needs or has not tackled the first problems of independence from the immediate family may have unwittingly placed himself in an emotionally unhealthy situation. If the child is forced to use immature behaviors such as whining and crying, he cannot develop the self-confidence that is a by-product of independent growth.

While overindulgence and overprotection are counterproductive to the development of independence, there are actions that parents and educators can take in the evolution of this characteristic. Very young children can be allowed to make decisions, for example, in the selection of their clothing. Asking the child whether he wants to wear a red shirt or a blue shirt allows him to make a decision and to see the consequence of that decision. Even though he may not know the colors red or blue, the child does seem to benefit from this kind of experience. Independence training is promoted when parents encourage the child to initiate activities. Children's games add to his early self-concept by exposing him to the consequences of his own behavior.

It is a natural course of growth that, as a child matures, he depends less on parents and more on other adults.

Aggression. As the child gains independence from the parents there seems to be a tendency to increase aggressive expression. Possessiveness, greed, and sibling rivalry are common causes of aggressive behavior. Tired children also tend to be impulsive and aggressive. With increasing age, however, physical aggressiveness gives ground to verbal aggressiveness.

In general, the expression of aggressive feelings during the preschool years may best be described as a rapid onset-offset situation. Aggressive behavior is easily triggered and expressed, and quickly turns off. At this age it is not uncommon to see children fighting with one another one minute and then playing cooperatively in a few minutes. Many aggressive episodes among preschool children erupt primarily because a child of this age is unable to discriminate intentional from nonintentional aggressive acts. Thus, when one child accidentally bumps into another child, the second child reacts with strong and intentional aggression.

Anxiety. Anxiety may be communicated to infants by their mothers or by the lack of immediate satisfaction of their needs to be fed, changed, or put to rest. Anxiety may be defined as inner tension without reason. As the child becomes older, anxiety can be generated by shame, doubt, guilt, aggression, or jealousy. Moreover, about half the infants between the fifth and eighth month of age show a decided fear of strangers or stranger anxiety. This appears to be an augmentation of reserve or wariness that a 3-month-old child shows towards strangers. Many visiting grandparents may feel rejected by a baby who does not have ample time to reacquaint himself with them. The wise stranger keeps his distance knowing that babies react to any novel stimulus with both fear and curiosity. Gradual reaquaintance would help to reduce, although not necessarily eliminate, stranger anxiety.

Experiencing anxiety is a part of the human condition. Studies have shown that humans function more efficiently under conditions of mild anxiety-arousing conditions. As anxiety increases, the efficiency begins to deteriorate. Thus, minimizing but not eliminating the anxiety of children would appear to be useful. With the young infant, parents should make efforts to satisfy the child's needs for love, safety, and esteem. Research has shown that punishment over any appreciable length of time has a deleterious effect on and increases the child's anxiety (Kessler, 1966). While short periods of withholding of parental support and love can have some disciplining effects, the extensive use of this as a punishment measure is unwise.

Fears. The development of fears seems to occur very early in a child's life, starting with the fear of strangers. With increasing age there is a decrease in the fear of noise, strange objects or persons, pain, falling, and loss of support. However, with increasing age the fear of imaginary creatures, the dark, animals, ridicule, harm, and dangerous situations increases. Forcing the child to confront the fearful object does not reduce his fear and may, indeed, increase it. Coercing a child to pet a dog can increase his fear of animals to an intolerable and traumatic level. Similarly, the child cannot be talked out of his concern nor will ridicule force the child's fear to alter. However, there are some things that parents can do to help the child live through this period unharmed.

If the parents explain the situation and pleasantly persuade the child to face the fearful object, he may be able to muster his courage. In the case of a feared dog, for example, gradually stepping closer to the dog with gentle, calm persuasion may help the child. An adult setting an example frequently is of benefit to a frightened child. Approaching the dog and petting it demonstrates, by example, that there is nothing to fear. In essence, what is being accomplished is a positive reconditioning of the child; the object of negative fear is being presented to the child as a positive object. Thus, the dog, instead of becoming a fearful object, becomes an object that can be played with and that does have some attraction. These techniques may help the child gain confidence in dealing with a fearful object and thereby reduce his discomfort.

A relatively common fear that develops among 4- or 5-year-old children is an intense fear of losing their mother. If this fear develops it can be extremely frightening to the parents as well. The loss, at a fantasy level, is usually through death. This fear is rarely verbalized but is deduced from the child's clinging behavior. Reassurances from the mother are usually effective on a short-term basis and allow the child to continue the growth process. By age 6, this fear has all but disappeared.

In summary, between birth and through age 5, the child has gradually developed an affective repertoire, complete by age 2 but further refined during the next few years. In the beginning, the child's orientation to the world is egocentric or self-centered; during the period from 14 to 24 months, his orientation becomes very negative. The child is often very stubborn and easily frustrated due to his inability to make his wishes known.

In the second year, any statement, including the offer of ice cream, may be met with a resounding no. Somewhere in the third year the child moves to a position where he likes to please others. More importantly, the child now has a capacity to be concerned about the feelings of others, to experience sympathy. This period ends about the age of 4 when the child becomes argumentative and impatient. In turn, the difficult 4-year-old becomes the receptive 5-year-old.

Social Development

Ambron (1975) defines *socialization* as a broad term for the process that guides the growth of one's social personality. It allows one to become a reasonably acceptable and effective member of society. Through socialization, discipline is acquired as well as the skills of knowledge, taste, and ambition that provide for participation in the life of the family and later in many larger groups. Socialization is not merely a matter of learning to avoid doing the things that are wrong; it also involves learning to take on responsibilities that are expected by parents and others in authority.

Social Milestones

The newborn is characteristically asocial. During the first week of life, he does not discriminate between "me" and "not me." Consequently, the baby is content to have all of his needs for food, warmth, and elimination met without defining any other person or object around him. As the baby's visual apparatus and maturation allow him to differentiate human and nonhuman parts of his environment, socialization begins. This usually occurs by the end of the second month. As indicated before, the primary bond between the mothering one and the baby takes on extreme importance since this is his first social contact. It establishes a one-to-one relationship with another person. The stranger anxiety seen at approximately 6 to 8 months of age is primarily due to the anxiety over separating from the mother. Mother has become so clearly defined to the infant that anyone who is not mother is a source of tension. The anxiety related to strangers appears because of the inability to comprehend or understand who or what a stranger is, and therefore, a stranger becomes a threat.

Nonanxious separation from the mother, the next step in the socialization change, usually occurs about the end of the first year. The nature of the mother-child relationship by now has been altered greatly by the baby's ability to crawl and creep about the house. The baby now has a world of his own and will go where his curiosity takes him. It also happens that social opportunities increase as he recognizes an ever-growing number of different faces. Also, he quickly learns society's first word, "No." Even if he does not want to stop, he is made to stop, and thus the association of stopping and "no" become connected. This may be the first attempt to teach the child obedience which is so important for effective socialization.

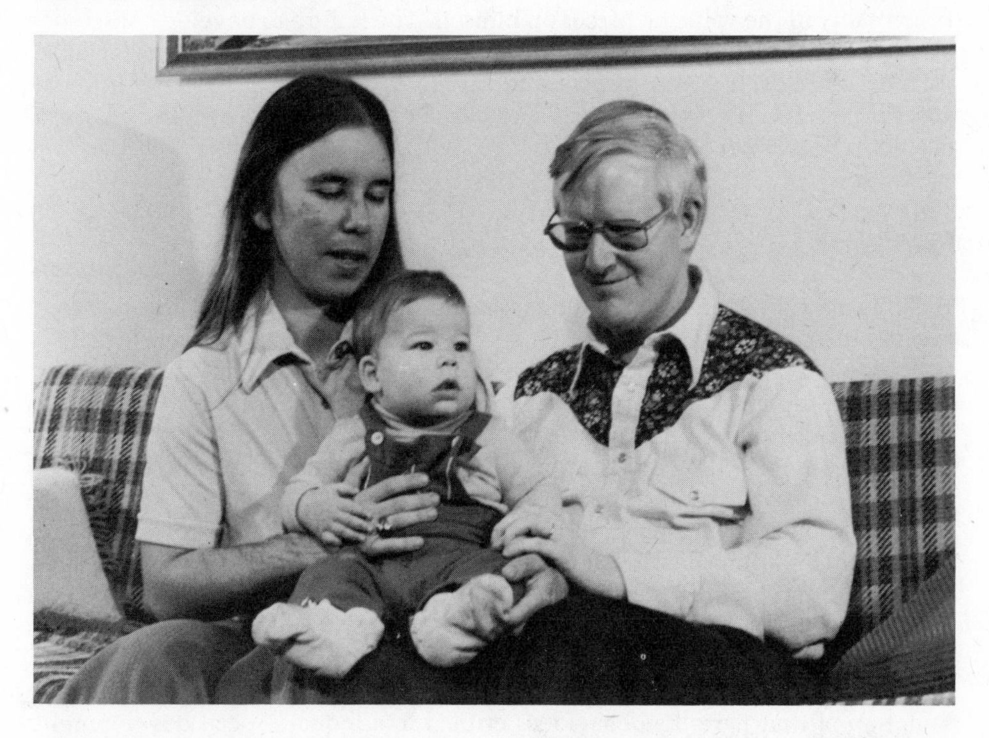

The prime variable for healthy social and emotional development is the nature of the child's past and present relationship with salient adults.

Toilet training becomes an important socializing phenomenon. It teaches the toddler autonomy and control over his own body functioning. Autonomy, it will be recalled, is followed by initiative, a trait which, if not understood, is seldom welcomed by the child's family. The results of initiative may lead to feelings of guilt when the child's throughts or actions are involved in a situation that he recognizes as "bad." An example of this predicament is when a toddler "steals" a lollipop. The initiative taken is labeled by a previous experience as bad. Pangs of guilt may develop, sometimes leading to confusion. From this situation, it is apparent that the 2½- or 3-year-old child already has built into his social system a very necessary ingredient for successful adjustment, a primitive version of morality or conscience.

Two characteristics of the adequately socialized preschooler may be described as a sense of autonomy and a sense of conscience. It is extremely important for adequate adjustment in society that both of these characteristics be taught well. Autonomy can be taught early in a child's life by providing him with experiences that reinforce independent thinking. Overprotective and overindulgent parents may prevent the child from becoming self-reliant. It is a natural course of growth that as a child matures he depends less on parents and more on other adults and other children. The failure to develop conscience often leads to unrealistic self-perceptions. If a child is rarely disciplined or corrected, the probability of his developing grandiose ideas about himself increases. As Read (1976) has pointed out, the undisciplined child is removed from reality in the value he places on himself. The failure to develop conscience also leads to antisocial behavior, the extreme example of failure to socialize. Antisocial children are impulsive and highly egocentric. They have little respect for others and their property and a lack of guilt about engaging in antisocial acts (Banus, 1971).

Forms of Social Expression

By kindergarten age, socialization is well underway. Children at this age tend to chose friends who are similar. Thus, the child's closest friends are usually of the same sex and approximately the same age. Friendship is an important socializing step in that it demonstrates the child's awareness of other people as separate and unique individuals.

The preschooler uses imitation of his parents in games and fantasy. In this manner, society's expectations for behaviors of adult men and women are learned. About now, the child also begins to learn his sex role as society rewards conformity and punishes deviance. To a great extent the child is influenced by the sex stereotype he observes in life and from TV and movies which show a man as strong and aggressive and a woman as passive and nurturant. It is also during this age span that boys have a strong identification with the father and girls with their mother. The identification with the same sex parent and the imitation of that parent's behavior is critical in adequate social development.

Role playing is another common form of socialization. It is a play activity in which children model their behavior after policemen, cowboys, nurses, mothers, and so forth. It may be described as a series of trial identifications as the child becomes increasingly aware of the multiple roles in society. Role playing or modeling also becomes an avenue by which a child can explore various life-styles.

There are sex differences in the expression of social behaviors. For example, since society continues to frown on aggressive preschool girls, they develop more covert ways of expressing their aggressiveness. Where a boy might strike back, a girl would be more likely to tattle.

While jealousy is experienced by babies and toddlers, competitiveness is not usually seen until age 3. Sibling rivalry is mutually profound once the younger or youngest has reached his third year. Competition with peers is also quite prevalent. A child may show varying degrees of competition depending on the situation. The difference in his behavior is caused by the extent to which he is interested in a person, object, or game.

Another socialization behavior seen in the preschooler is cooperation. Fundamentally, children seek approval. A child may be willing to help in order to obtain merit, but also he recognizes that older children and adults receive social approval when they do things for one another. When a child is uncooperative, more than likely there is a plausible reason. The job may be too difficult, or he does not understand what he is to do or how he is to complete the task. Often, the new task is not as enticing as the one immediately occupying the child's attention. Under such conditions, the child will be antagonistic and disobedient.

Interaction of Emotional and Social Development

It is extremely difficult to separate the areas of emotional and social development and discuss them independently because of the strong interrelationship between them. Competence in one area is almost predicated on competence in the other. Accordingly, weakness in one area usually has a commensurate weakness in the other.

The emotion-arousing nature of many of the child's perceptions in his environment exerts a powerful influence upon the development of social values. Since no two children have identical backgrounds, similar situations do not necessarily arouse similar emotions in two children at the same time. However, in many situations the emotional quality of a child's experience is the direct result of those experienced by his parents and others around him. Emotional and social development interact strongly. By observation and imitation, especially of the child's heroes, he is motivated to express himself in ways that would be acceptable to the heroes. In this way, social values are achieved, largely by the example of others.

The Child with Special Needs

Although the emotional and social needs of both handicapped and nonhandicapped children are the same, the handicap may create special problems that affect the course of development. Autistic children do not imitate the behavior of the parental figures and peers. Emotional and social development are difficult because these children either demonstrate little interest in their surroundings or are so acutely aware of their surroundings that they cannot tolerate change. With other children, the disability may not be as severe, but because the parents do not know how to provide meaningful experiences or how to make experiences meaningful, the child becomes vulnerable to deprivation or other experiencing problems. This fact applies to all handicapping conditions in young children. The multiply handicapped child's problems in social and emotional development are commensurately compounded.

The residual effects of disabilities often cause negative emotions in the child. The aspects of loneliness have been described by Kronick (1974). Negative body image is common because the child often feels he cannot live up to his parents' expectations and is overcome with shame and guilt. Even by ages 4 and 5 there is a significant amount of self-pity. The child's social roles are impaired particularly with his peer group: the more debilitating the disability, the greater degree of the social impairment. Because of the parents' concern and perhaps overprotection, these children are often severely dependent on the parents, particularly the mother. Unfortunately many parents become guilt ridden because they feel they have produced an imperfect child. Other parents completely deny the existence of the child's special needs and place unreal expectations upon him. The inability to meet these unrealistic demands increases the self-pity and frustration imposed upon the child by the disability.

Society imposes a strong penalty on a child with special needs. The disabled child may have limited social contacts (Baroff, 1974) and this, in turn, impairs normal social and emotional development. Consequently, many disabled children have difficulty expressing anger, hostility, guilt, and frustration appropriately. In the face of inadequate socialization, children with special needs become highly introverted and fearful. Fearfulness is often reinforced by a shortened attention span that results from the disability. Restrictions placed on a young child (whether by the handicap, society, or his parents) interfere with the pleasure that is normally obtained from achievement and increased independence. A confounding variable, too, is that many parents believe that normalcy will be achieved with training. As a consequence, the child does not receive the support he needs.

To promote social and emotional development, the young child with special needs should not be denied awareness of his own disability. As Wright (1960) pointed out, the negative aspects of disability, along with the coping aspects, must be brought to the young person's awareness by those who know and love him. If not, the child may be first brought face-to-face with his shortcomings in a hostile or rejecting environment. This can be such a devastating experience that precaution must be taken to avoid it. If parents, as well as teachers, can accept a child with his limitations and maximize whatever potential and abilities he has, the child is then placed in a position where he can develop emotionally and socially. Positive acceptance of the child with a disability is the first necessary strategy for the parents and those people responsible for the home environment. Frequent social activities with the peer group should be strongly encouraged. Lastly, the reality that this child will never be completely normal must be integrated into the parents' and child's belief system.

Preschool Instructional Programs

Literature concerning early intervention programs support the preschool concept as a facilitator of the emotional and social development in young children with special needs. Four different factors or reasons contribute to such support: (1) the preschool experience, (2) significant adults, (3) peer relationships, and (4) curriculum and methods.

The Preschool Experience

Many writers express the view of Allen (1974) who found that the homes and neighborhoods of young handicapped children do not always provide opportunities for the children to learn the necessary social responses. For this reason, a good preschool program is seen as essential. Baroff (1974) sees the preschool experience as vital to the young retarded child because it provides opportunities to overcome the effects of developmental immaturity which tend to isolate the child from interpersonal experiences outside the home. Although his reference is limited to the young retarded child, it is equally applicable to youngsters with other handicapping conditions. Strain and Wiegerink (1976) reviewed studies which showed that the preschool environment could be arranged to provide occasions for positive social interaction.

Significant Adults

The need for good models to foster healthy emotional and social development is described repeatedly in the literature. A study by Strain and Wiegerink (1975) clearly demonstrated that teacher attention increases the social play of preschool children with behavioral disorders. In a review of studies, Strain and Shores (1977) found support for the notion that adults can effectively bring about reinforcing social interactions between young children who tend to be withdrawn. Social responses, according to Allen (1974), are learned responses. For the young child with special needs, these responses can be taught by the significant adults in the environment. Heinicke (1976) has stated that the prime variable for healthy social and emotional development is the nature of the child's past and present relationship with salient adults in the environment.

Peer Relationships

Positive emotional and social development in young handicapped children is fostered by peer interaction. According to Snyder, Apolloni, and Cooke (1977) peer imitation, one of the justifications used for early intervention programs, may be increased by having the handicapped child observe peer models and receive rewards for desired behavior. In a series of studies, Strain and associates (1970, 1976a, 1977) trained nonhandicapped preschool children as effective behavioral models and used them to initiate appropriate social responses in young handicapped children. The integration of handicapped children with nonhandicapped children in day-care centers and nursery schools is viewed as beneficial to both groups (Read, 1976). This thought is supported by many others including Allen (1974) who said that segregating young handicapped children from their normal peers seems only to increase their atypical behaviors, especially in the realm of social development.

> Early integration, given appropriate structure and instruction, may result in the development of an early attitude of acceptance and understanding by nonretarded children for those different from themselves while offering retarded children an environment that maximally facilitates their behavioral development. (Snyder, Apolloni & Cooke, 1977, p. 265)

Curriculum and Materials

Social development was viewed by Lickona (1969) as a special case of learning in general. It entails the learning of concepts that enable the child to cope with the interpersonal part of the world, to handle the stimuli from his social environment, to anticipate and interpret the behaviors of other people. Instruction for social concepts is not unlike that needed for other concepts. Allen (1974) indicated that while adult and peer models are important in social development, specific intervention is also required. Early learning programs must concentrate on helping children acquire appropriate social skills. Heinicke (1976) viewed the child's task orientation as the most important social-emotional variable in the effective teaching of the young child. The optimal manner in which to enhance this aspect of functioning is through the development of positive adult-caretaking relationships with the child. While Strain (1975) saw play and dramatic activities as vehicles for acquiring social skills, he and his associates (Strain, Cooke, & Apolloni, 1976a) indicated the need for specific methodology for teaching young children to share, to smile, and to control their own behavior. Effective methods for increasing positive social behavior and decreasing negative social behavior (Strain, Shores, & Kerr, 1976) include prompting and reinforcement. Strain and his associates (1976a) have emphasized, also, the child's need to have affective educational procedures structured around his appropriate social-emotional developmental level.

Mental Health

Instead of striving to formulate a concise definition of the term *mental health,* it seems more profitable to consider the essential ingredients, a predominance of which seem to insure a state of mental healthiness. Included are the capacity for happiness, and the ability to love, to work, and to initiate, maintain, and enjoy interpersonal relationships. A sense of humor, neither malicious nor sadistic, is very helpful. The ability to recognize, to identify, and to express one's inner feelings and emotions in an adequate, socially acceptable way is also essential. Most outstanding in mentally healthy people is a consistent, reality-based, firm sense of self-identity. The resilient permanency of self-identity permits one a certain degree of self-reliance and independence. It enables one to assume responsiblity and to have the self-discipline necessary to undertake and complete tasks, even unpleasant ones. Adequate self-image and self-identity include a positive, built-in set of moral standards of thought and behavior. Positive standards are essential because it is not sufficient to know only what one is against, but one must also know what one is for. Real inner convictions are demonstrated not so much by pronouncement as by observable behavior.

Mental health implies the ability to assess reality even when it hurts. The ability to make good judgments concerning one's self and behavior, undistorted by irrational fears or unsocialized primitive urges, is necessary. There must be a realistic, good-humored tolerance toward self and others without desertion, or compromise, of ethical standards. Finally, the mentally healthy person is able to maintain reasonable optimistic attitudes and expectations even in the face of ever-present uncertainties. Mental health, then, is the result as well as the goal of procedures that foster emotional and social development.

Surprisingly, most discussions about mental health are actually concerned with "mental unhealth." The mentally healthy ordinarily do not consult anyone about their healthy state. Only during periods of discomfort or disorder is the lost state of health truly appreciated. This state of "unhealth" will be referred to in this chapter as *emotional disturbance.* The term indicates a state of mental, emotional, and perhaps social unrest, sufficient to impede, delay, or halt the child's development and maturation, or to institute a state of regression to a less mature, more primitive level. An emotional disorder may be brief, transient and self-limiting, or may progress in time to a severe, totally incapacitating, untreatable mental disease.

Levels of Intervention

Before the problem of identification of emotional disturbances in children can be addressed, there is another basic conceptual area that may be considered. There are three levels of intervention in the identification and fostering of mental health. At the first level, one must have knowledge of, and concern with, all those conditions and techniques of child rearing most conducive to the realization of the child's potential for physical, emotional, intellectual, and social development, as well as the biologically and genetically determined maturation. The second level is concerned with interventions motivated by a recognition of loss of mental health and is designed to restore health and to prevent the development of more serious emotional disturbance. The third level of intervention includes those techniques and methods that have evolved to modify or eliminate disorder-producing conditions and that enable the child to make up developmental time lost during the disorder and to continue his development and maturation in a normal fashion. These three levels must be kept in mind as specific techniques of intervention are discussed.

Assessment of Mental Health

In assessing the degree of mental health, or the presence and extent of emotional disturbance, there are three basic areas of observation:

1. The observer must know the kinds of behaviors which are age-appropriate. During a portion of the observation, the observer temporarily disregards the child's chronological age and body size and estimates the behavior purely in terms of the question, At what age would this behavior be considered normal? The answer to this question frequently gives excellent clues as to the developmental level at which the tasks were not adequately accomplished and at which the child has fixated or regressed.
2. If the observer knows the typical problems faced by a child at this age, the observer has clues to the sort of stresses or traumas which may have precipitated a regression. If it is determined that the child has fixated at a particular level, knowing the developmental tasks to be accomplished at the estimated age of functioning, clues can be obtained as to the causes of the possible fixation.
3. Finally, a knowledge of the usual coping mechanisms available to the child at his particular developmental level allows one to assess the effectiveness of defense measures being used by the child.

The estimation of the success or failure of these measures will, to some degree, suggest the need for emergency intervention and the kind of intervention required. The younger the child, the more important will be the support

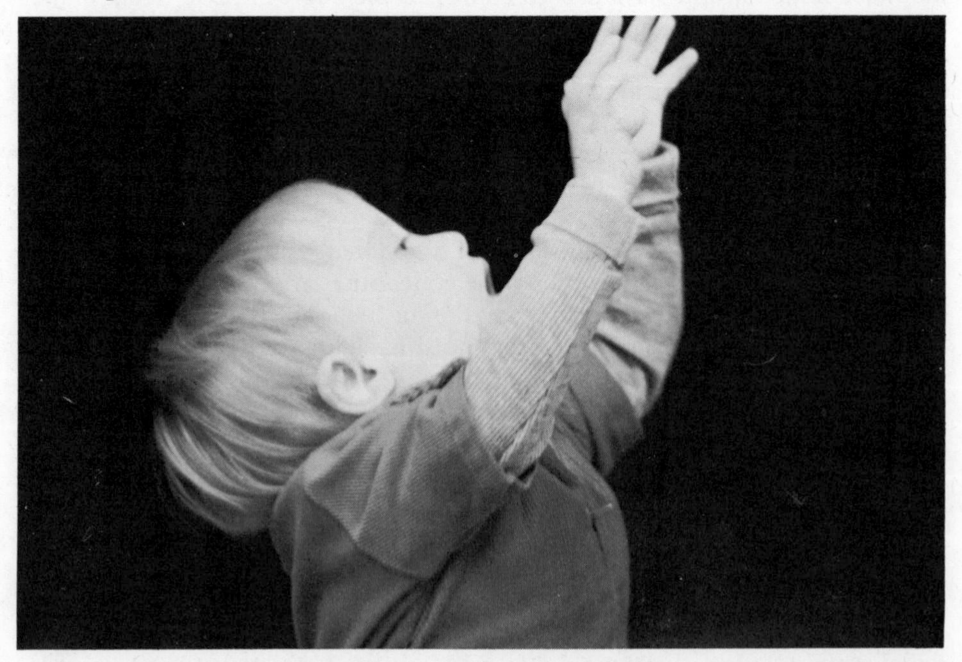

If a child has never learned to play, he may experience feelings of failure and rejection.

and guidance of parents and other important adults. An assessment of the availability to the child of this kind of support is essential to understanding the complete situation.

From this discussion it can be seen that the child-care specialist of whatever discipline is obligated to know an extensive amount about child development. Particularly recommended is the developmental chart summarizing normal and pathological behaviors in the preschool child (see Table 1).

Assessment of Child Behavior

Behaviors are stimulated from two directions. They are stimulated by environmental occurrences and can be purely reactive in nature. An example of this would be the knee-jerk reflex elicited by the neurologist's rubber hammer. Other behaviors appear to be motivated almost completely by internal stimuli which have to do with all those internal states discussed under the consideration of the term *mental health.* In actuality, behaviors are seldom clear-cut. The young child's reactions to external stimuli are usually modified considerably by his internal state. Even the perception of environmental events is extensively modified by expectations, fears, mental set, attention, and emotional state. A clinical or educational assessment of a child's behavior must take these considerations into account.

From infancy through the fifth year, the assessment procedures must be adjusted according to the chronological age, the general physical and mental condition of the child, and his social circumstances, including the integrity and soundness of the family in which he is developing. It is to be remembered that the repertoire of human responses is not unlimited but rather is circumscribed. There is an economy of expression in emotions. Developmentally, then, in identifying and assessing emotional disorders in young children, one must ask, What are the usual responses and patterns of behavior available to the child? What are the developmental tasks to be accomplished? And What are the supportive systems available to the child in terms of family, material supplies, and cultural and social institutions?

The newborn has as his basic task the establishment of the biological systems and functions essential to physical survival. Supportive systems include an attentive, competent mother, an ample supply of food and shelter, and opportunities to begin experiencing and discovering the world. Possible responses to stress are quite limited for the infant. He must manifest inner tension and discomfort through such behaviors as interruptions of sleep and feeding patterns, excessive crying, irritability, and failure to thrive. As the infant matures and develops, his repertoire of responses also expands, especially with the emergence of communicative skills, to the point where he may one day stamp his foot, pout, and verbally express his opposition.

As the child's understanding of himself in relationship to the world increases, he gradually finds it possible, and learns the skills, to manipulate the environment to his own advantage and purpose. It becomes helpful to think of the child's arenas of operations as consisting of three primary areas: the home, the

Table 1

Developmental Schema Chart

THE NEWBORN AND YOUNG INFANT (Birth to 6 months)

Tasks in Process

INFANT	MOTHER
To adjust physiologically to extra-uterine life.	To sustain baby and self physically and pleasurably.
To develop appropriate psychologic response.	To give and get emotional gratification from nurturing baby.
To assimilate experientially, with increasing capacity to postpone and accept substitutes.	To foster and integrate baby's development.

Acceptable Behavioral Characteristics

INFANT	MOTHER
Copes with mechanics of life (eating, sleeping, etc.)	Provides favorable feeding and handling. Gets to "know" baby.
Body needs urgent.	Develops good working relationship with baby.
Reflexes dominate.	Has tolerance for baby.
Has biologic unity with mother.	Promotes sense of trust.
Establishes symbiotic relationship to mother.	Learns baby's cues.
Sucking behavior prominent.	Applies learning to management of baby.
Cries when distressed.	Interacts emotionally with baby.
Responds to mouth, skin, sense modalities.	Encourages baby's development.
Is unstable physiologically.	Has reasonable expectations of baby.
Functions egocentrically.	
Is completely dependent.	
Has low patience tolerance.	
Is non-cognitive; expresses needs instinctually.	
Develops trust in ministering adult.	
Begins to "expect."	

Minimal Psychopathology

INFANT	MOTHER
Feeding and digestive problems.	Indifference to baby.
Sleep disturbances.	Ambivalence towards baby and its needs.
Excessive sucking activity.	Self-doubt and anxiety.
Excessive motor discharge.	Intolerance of baby's characteristics.
Excessive crying.	Over- or under-responds to baby.
Excessive irritability.	Premature or inappropriate expectations.
Hypertonicity.	Dissatisfaction with role of motherhood.
Difficult to comfort.	

Extreme Psychopathology

INFANT	MOTHER
Lethargy (depression).	Alienation from baby.
Marasmus.	Severe depression.
Cannot be comforted.	Excessive guilt.
Unresponsive.	Complete inability to function in maternal role.
Infantile autism.	Overwhelming and incapacitating anxiety.
Developmental arrest.	Denies or tries to control baby's needs.
	Severe clashes with baby.
	Vents life's dissatisfactions on baby.

THE OLDER INFANT (6 to 18 months)

Tasks in Process

INFANT	MOTHER
To develop more reliance and self-control.	To provide a healthy emotional and physical climate.
To differentiate self from mother.	To foster weaning, training, habits.
To make developmental progress.	To understand, appreciate and accept baby.

Acceptable Behavioral Characteristics

INFANT	MOTHER
More stable physiologically.	Derives satisfaction from serving baby well.
Heightened voluntary motor activity and exploration.	Responds appropriately to baby's signs of distress.
Higher level of patience tolerance.	Aware of baby's inborn reaction pattern.
Instinctual needs in better control.	Has more confidence in own ability.
Strong selective tie to mother.	Gives positive psychologic reassurance (fondling, talking, comforting).
Stranger differentiation.	Shows pleasure in baby.
Increased verbality, play and sensori-motor behavior.	Keeps pace with baby's advances.
Discernible social responses; joyful in play.	Is accepting of baby's idosyncracies.
Outbursts of negativism and anger.	
Sensory modalities important.	
Emergence of isosyncratic patterns.	
Demonstrates memory and anticipation.	
Begins to imitate.	

Minimal Psychopathology

INFANT	MOTHER
Excessive crying, anger and irritability.	Disappointed in and unaccepting of baby.
Low frustration tolerance.	Misses baby's cues.
Excessive negativism.	Infancy unappealing.
Finicky eater, sleep disturbances.	Impersonal management.
Digestive and elimination problems.	Attempts to coerce to desired behavior.
Noticeable motility patterns (fingering, rocking, etc).	Over-anxious or over-protective.
Delayed development.	Mildly depressed and apathetic.

Extreme Psychopathology

INFANT	MOTHER
Tantrums and convulsive disorders.	Neglect or abuse of baby.
Apathy, immobility and withdrawal.	Rejection of the maternal role.
Extreme and obsessive finger-sucking, rocking, head-banging.	Severe hostility reactions.
No interest in objects, environment or play.	No attempt to understand or gratify baby.
Anorexia.	Deliberately thwarts infant.
Megacolon.	Complete withdrawal and separation from baby.
Inexpressive of feeling.	
No social discrimination.	
No tie to mother; wary of all adults.	
Infantile autism.	
Failure to thrive.	
Arrested development.	

Table 1
Developmental Schema Chart (cont.)

THE TODDLER AND PRE-SCHOOL AGE (Under 5 years)

Tasks in Process

CHILD

To reach physiologic plateaus (motor action, toilet training).
To differentiate self and secure sense of autonomy.
To tolerate separations from mother.
To develop conceptual understandings and "ethical" values.
To master instinctual psychologic impulses (oedipal, sexual, guilt, shame).
To assimilate and handle socialization and acculturation (aggression, relationships, activities, feelings).
To learn sex distinctions.

MOTHER

To promote training, habits and phsiologic progression.
To aid in family and group socialization of child.
To encourage speech and other learning.
To reinforce child's sense of autonomy and identity.
To set a model for "ethical" conduct.
To delineate male and female roles.

Acceptable Behavioral Characteristics

CHILD

Gratification from exercise of neuromotor skills.
Investigative, imitative, imaginative play.
Actions somewhat modulated by thought; memory good; animistic and original thinking.
Exercises autonomy with body (sphincter control, eating).
Feelings of dependence on mother and separation fears.
Behavior identification with parents, siblings, peers.
Learns speech for communication.
Awareness of own motives, beginnings of conscience.
Intense feelings of shame, guilt, joy, love, desire to please.
Internalized standards of "bad," "good"; beginning of reality testing.
Broader sex curiosity and differentiation.
Ambivalence towards dependence and independence.
Questions birth and death.

MOTHER

Is moderate and flexible in training.
Shows pleasure and praise for child's advances.
Encourages and participates with child in learning and in play.
Sets reasonable standards and controls.
Paces herself to child's capacities at a given time.
Consistent in own behavior, conduct and ethics.
Provides emotional reassurance to child.
Promotes peer play and guided group activity.
Reinforces child's cognition of male and female roles.

Minimal Psychopathology

CHILD

Poor motor coordination.
Persistent speech problems (stammering, loss of words).
Timidity towards people and experiences.
Fears and night terrors.
Problems with eating, sleeping, elimination, toileting, weaning.
Irritability, crying, temper tantrums.
Partial return to infantile manners.
Inability to leave mother without panic.
Fear of strangers.
Breathholding spells.
Lack of interest in other children.

MOTHER

Premature, coercive or censuring training.
Exacting standards above child's ability
Transmits anxiety and apprehension.
Unaccepting of child's efforts; intolerant towards failures.
Over-reacts, over-protective, overanxious.
Despondent, apathetic.

Extreme Psychopathology

CHILD

Extreme lethargy, passivity or hypermotility.
Little or no speech; non-communicative.
No response or relationship to people, symbiotic clinging to mother.
Somatic ills: vomiting, constipation, diarrhea, megacolon, rash, tics.
Autism, childhood psychosis.
Excessive enuresis, soiling, fears.
Completely infantile behavior.
Play inhibited and non-conceptualized; absence or excess of auto-erotic activity.
Obsessive-compulsive behavior; "ritual" bound mannerisms.
Impulsive destructive behavior.

MOTHER

Severely coercive and punitive.
Totally critical and rejecting.
Over-identification with or overly submissive to child.
Inability to accept child's sex; fosters opposite.
Substitutes child for spouse; sexual expression via child.
Severe repression of child's need for gratification.
Deprivation of all stimulations, freedoms and pleasures.
Extreme anger and displeasure with child.
Child assault and brutality.
Severe depression and withdrawal.

Note: From *Problems in Child Behavior and Development* by M. J. E. Senn and A. J. Solnit, Philadelphia: Lea & Febiger, 1968. Copyright 1968 by Lea & Febiger. Reprinted by permission.

play yard, and school. In order to assess the level of mental health or the intensity of emotional disturbance, his behavior in each of these areas must be known.

It is commonplace for a child to show disturbance in one area and to make an apparently good adjustment in the other two. An assessment of home must include interpersonal relationships and quality of care from parents and other family members. Play yard considerations focus primarily on relatively independent peer interactions in which the child must establish his place in the peer group and learn to interact with children cooperatively, competitively, and often defensively. Peer activities in this arena differ in certain respects from those more dominated by adults.

In preschool, the child has to contend with, and relate to, authority figures who do not have the intense emotional investment in him that he experienced from his family. The teacher also demands social behaviors which are more restrictive and conforming. The child, often for the first time, is assigned tasks to complete. His activities are assigned values which affect his status with his parents, with the teacher, with peers, and, most importantly, in his own eyes. In school, his peer relationships must conform in the classroom to certain imposed behavioral standards. He must solve the problem of relating adequately to his teacher without losing status in the eyes of his peers.

The opportunities for conflict from all of these various interpersonal relationships are obviously many, and it is no surprise that emotional disturbances often seem to arise with the beginning of school.

Recognition of Emotional Disturbance

There are several practical general principles for recognizing emotional disturbance in children. There may be an accentuation or intensification of certain aspects of behavior which make them stand out as unusual or unexpected. This includes such behaviors as overreactions to stimuli, excessive quietness, preoccupation or daydreaming, a persistent sadness and pessimism, excessive hostility, excessive aggressiveness, and excessive anxiety, tension, or fearfulness.

Social and interpersonal difficulties may be noticed first. More careful observation will usually reveal accompanying personality changes. Of importance are increased peer difficulties; lack of development of good peer relationships (especially the child who is picked on or mistreated by peers); poor or deteriorated relations with the teacher and other adults; increased social misbehavior, such as destructiveness, stealing, lying, assaultiveness; and inappropriate expressions of sexuality.

Abrupt or rapid changes in a child's usual behavior that are more than transient and often seem to be an overreaction, or an excessively prolonged reaction, to relatively minor traumatic occurrences may be seen. These behaviors are usually viewed as deteriorated to some extent but they may also be episodes of inappropriate cheerfulness with or without increased motor activity. Generally, the emotionally healthy child will have a relatively uniform personality with only expectable reactive interruptions, which can often be attributed to specific events. If the child is normally emotionally volatile, the outbursts are usually predictable and seem to fit the child so that his behavior seems to be falling within the limits of the expectable. The emotionally disturbed child has an uneven temperament in which there is usually the element of unpredictability and often with no apparent relationship to environmental occurrences.

Fixations, manifested by an apparent reluctance to move on to more mature, appropriate behaviors, or regression to infantile, primitive behavior patterns, unless temporary and related to identifiable external traumas, are evidences of emotional disturbances. Clinging, whining, and transient enuresis may occur about the time of the birth of a sibling. This indicates the child's anxiety is related to his own status with his parents. The same behaviors, in the absence of such strong provocation, would be viewed with more alarm and would be of much more serious importance.

The child's patterns of behaviors and responses are learned through daily interactions with members of his family, friends, and other adults responsible for his care. The quality of these interpersonal relationships is significant to his emotional and social development, and thus to his mental health. It is critical that those who work with young handicapped children and their parents have guidelines for increasing effective interaction.

Human Interaction in Parenting and Teaching

Among parents and teachers, the desire for self-control in children seems to be universal. While the need for external controls (laws, traffic lights, and mother's rules) is acknowledged, these controls do not negate the child's need to control his impulses and make decisions about his own behavior. However, children are not born with self-control. It must be learned in much the same way as learning to talk, eating with a spoon, and accomplishments of childhood. Similar to other learning, certain procedures contribute to mastery of the skill. The following guidelines are suggested for the development of self-control in young children.

Teaching Self-control

1. Build a Trusting Relationship. Teaching self-control depends on a positive, caring, and trusting relationship between the child and the adult. When children do not trust the adults in their lives, they must constantly test the adult to find out where the relationship stands. A positive relationship eliminates the need for much of the testing behavior which irritates and frustrates adults.

A child's capacity for trusting personal relationsips is determined soon after birth. The child's mother is the central person during this stage of development as she responds to the child's physical needs. Basic trust at the infant stage provides the foundation for the interpersonal relationships that will be the primary means for the child's learning self-control. Three factors characterize good adult-child relationships: affection, spending time together, and sharing personal feelings.

Relationships are built on affection. Human beings need love. Children need to experience unconditional acceptance. This implies acceptance of appearance, behavior, and for the young child with special needs, the handicapping condition. Most parents feel this kind of unconditional love for their children, but many do not know how to show it. A child needs to hear the words, "I love you." A child needs to hear the words, "I don't like what you did, but I still love you."

Affection is shown in ways other than words. Touching, hugging, and kissing are important nonverbal ways of showing love. Research has shown that infants who do not receive physical affection develop both emotional and physical disabilities that, in extreme cases, lead to serious illness and even death. In a caring relationship, a long hug can communicate the unconditional love which lies beneath the surface behavior. Boys and girls alike need the affection of both parents.

Relationships are built while spending time together. Adults who want to build positive relationships with children must spend time with them. They must engage in activities with the children. Because young children communicate through play more than through words, adults must learn to play with them.

A good relationship is satisfying to both people; therefore, it is important for both adult and child to participate in choosing shared activities. Shared decision

Three factors characterize good adult-child relationships: affection, spending time together, and sharing personal feelings.

making also builds the relationship because it communicates respect and concern for both people's feelings.

Relationships are built by sharing personal feelings. Parent-child and teacher-child relationships need to include the sharing of personal feelings. When feelings are shared with a child, the adult communicates to him deep personal trust and commitment. Adults expect children to express their feelings in socially acceptable ways, but then too often, keep a close guard on their own feelings. Such an environment can produce disturbed feelings in children because the adults they admire do not seem to have any of the feelings they experience constantly. Or it may communicate to the child that he is not big enough or trustworthy enough to know what goes on inside adult heads and hearts.

Simple statements of feelings by adults provide models and build the interpersonal relationship. For example:

> "Our vacation plans make me feel excited."
> "I am bored from watching so much television today."
> "Our dog's accident makes me feel sad."

Parents and teachers who share their feelings with children in this manner are building a strong relationship that will help each child accept himself and use his feelings in exercising self-control. Children who are impulsive and acting out frequently have not learned to be aware of their feelings and therefore become the victims of, rather than the masters of, their feelings and desires.

2. Practice Self-control. Children imitate or model the behavior of adults with whom they live. An adult who lives the life of self-control will be teaching the quality through their every action. Many adults, however, do not control themselves and rely on external factors. When children observe adults playing "cat and mouse" with authority figures, they learn to play the same game with their parents and teachers. "Do as I say, not as I do", sounds good, but it does not work with children.

Thus, if children are to be orderly, adult models must be orderly. If children are to show respect for others, adult models must be respectful. If a child is to be honest, each adult model must tell the truth. Adult interactions with children model the behaviors they will learn.

3. Nurture and Support a Positive Self-concept in the Child. Much has been written about the relationship between self-concept and behavior. Self-concept refers to how worthy, capable, effective, and lovable a person feels he or she is. Harris (1967) in his book *I'm OK - You're OK* talks about the not-OK feelings children experience. He states that these not-OK feelings follow one throughout life because they are recorded in our deepest memory. All children experience not-OK feelings because adults are bigger, stronger, and smarter than they are. A young child with a handicapping condition experiences these same feelings due to the inability to master developmental tasks. Parents and teachers need to become sensitive to the internal feelings of children in order to minimize the number of not-OK feelings the child experiences. Adults can build a positive self-concept and minimize negative feelings toward self through the following activities:

a. Praise children for things they do well.
b. Encourage the child's efforts to learn new skills.
c. Provide opportunities for children to learn and to feel independent. For example, allow a child to walk instead of carrying him.
d. Play with the child in a way that allows the child to direct the activity. It feels good to be in charge.
e. Avoid statements that are critical of a child's play. Don't evaluate his drawings, block castles, or imaginary friends.
f. Show interest in the things the child cares about. Taking time to watch a butterfly that the child points out confirms the child's belief that his own feelings are important.

The self-concept of a child is constantly being shaped. It is changed to some degree by every event in their lives. A positive self-concept is built by being trusted, by being allowed independence, by successfully completing a task, by making a choice, by helping others, and by receiving affection. A negative self-concept is built by being overprotected, by being constantly corrected, by being constantly supervised, and by always receiving help. Moreover, adults who sorrowfully discuss the child's handicap in his presence greatly damage his self-concept.

A child develops a positive or negative self-concept through interactions with other people. Those attitudes toward self are internal factors that control how the child behaves. Children with positive self-concepts achieve better in learning skills, show more appropriate social behavior, are liked by their peers, and are more likely to enjoy mental health.

4. Allow Children to Learn Self-control from the Natural Environment. Parents of young children certainly must protect them from running and playing in the street, from drinking poisonous liquids, from using sharp objects as toys, and from playing close to deep water. They cannot allow the natural consequences of these behaviors to teach their dangers. However, many parents are overprotective and attempt to protect their child from any pain or discomfort. In the process, the parent takes the responsibility for every experience the child has rather than allowing the child to learn self-control.

Children can learn self-control through their day-to-day encounters with the world. Parents who allow this learning to take place increase the child's sense of ability in decision making and self-management. The child feels the adult trusts him to choose wisely, and he feels grown-up to be in charge of self. Internal control of behavior will be enhanced by the child learning to rely on his own feelings to make judgments about what is best for self. To the degree that adults are required to set limits and make decisions for the child, external control prevails.

5. Build Self-control by Responding Consistently to the Child's Behavior. Internal control is increased when the child can remember the consequences of similar situations that have occurred in the past. Parents and teachers who want children to develop controls from within need to provide an environment that allows children to predict accurately whether their behavior will be acceptable or unacceptable. Self-control is greatly enhanced when one's memory provides a guide for present and future behaviors. Inconsistency in adult responses makes it difficult for the child to exercise self-control because the child cannot predict what the consequences of his behavior will be.

Consistency in responding to behavior is important for another reason. Children need to learn cause and effect in interpersonal relationships. A child learns very early that if you hold an ice cream cone upside down, the ice cream will fall out. Cause and effect are more difficult to teach in human behavior because people are inconsistent in how they respond to the same behavior. When adult responses are confusing and misunderstood, children do not relate their own behavior to the effects in their environment.

6. Provide Opportunities for Children to Exercise Self-control. Children enjoy the experience of being in control of self. It makes them feel important, trusted, and strong. If parents and teachers want children to learn self-control, they must provide opportunities for the children to exercise self-control. The following are examples of planned experiences for children in learning self-control:

a. Crawling: In the park or on the large playground, a child can be allowed to crawl around within the sight of the parents. If the child crawls too far away, he will begin to feel anxiety and will return to the adults or will cry for help. The experience of returning to one's parents in response to a feeling of insecurity is an example of self-control. In this same situation, external control would occur if the adults retrieve the child every time the youngster wanders only a short distance away before the child experiences any anxiety at all. Children who are constantly rescued learn to rely on adults to come get them and seem to develop a complete absence of anxiety in wandering long distances away.

b. Playing: Children can be allowed to play without adult supervision. A fenced-in backyard is a means of allowing a child to play outside without an adult hovering nearby. Young children need the security of knowing that a parent figure is within calling distance, yet they enjoy the sense of independence with their internal controls as the guiding force. If the adult reappears periodically, the child will be reassured. Gradually the child will develop the self-control to manage longer periods of time alone in self-directed play.

c. Choosing: Children can be given choices at an early age. Choosing between an apple and a banana allows the child to make a small decision that requires a low level of self-direction. Adults can suggest that the child select a toy to share in play with the adult. Statements such as "You made a good choice" reinforce the child's self-concept as a competent person.

d. Failing: Constant failure is debilitating, but occasional failure, when the consequences are not severe, helps the child to learn realistically. Some parents try to protect their children from failure and thereby rob them

If parents and teachers want children to learn self-control, they must provide opportunities for the children to exercise self-control.

of their chance at trial-and-error learning. Children should have a "right to fail" in an environment that supports efforts to be independent, creative, industrious, and decisive. One of the greatest barriers to learning self-control is the fear of the external consequences if failure should occur. At early ages children do not expect themselves to be perfect and therefore approach new tasks with a sense of adventure and excitement. Exposure to adults who are intolerant of failure quickly develops within children a self-critical attitude which may lead to greater dependence on the adults rather than self-directed behavior.

The Use of External Controls

A legitimate concern of parents and teachers is the need for external controls of various degrees while the child is learning self-management. External controls and structure are essential ingredients in a healthy environment. The degree of control and structure is the central issue in determining whether the child will become dependent on external controls or will become independent with positive self-control. The following sections will focus on the types of external controls that can facilitate or impede the development of controls from within.

1. Structuring the Child's Environment. Adults provide many of the external controls for children's behavior. These include the arrangement of the physical environment, rules, planned activities, rewards, and punishments. Many adults concentrate only on the rewards and punishments that follow behavior and fail to pay adequate attention to the factors that come before the child acts. The environment of a child can be structured to produce positive behavior and to avoid undesirable behavior by providing behaviors cues, establishing limits, and including children in thinking through the rules for behavior.

Giving cues that signal appropriate behavior. Parents and teachers can teach children social skills by providing consistent environmental cues. For example, toys should be stored in the areas of the home or classroom where they are to be used. It would be confusing to keep a toy on the shelf in the den if the parents insist that the child use it only in the kitchen. The location of objects can signal the child to behave in desirable or undesirable ways.

The mother who leaves a china bowl on the coffee table when there is a toddler around has designed the environment for trouble. Not only will the china bowl be broken and the mother emotionally upset, but also the toddler will experience a sense of wrongdoing and guilt for having explored his environment. In this case, the parent should recognize that the child does not have the self-control to resist handling objects nor the cognitive understanding to recognize which objects are breakable. Parents must structure the environment to allow the child to explore tables and shelves as a natural reward for having learned to pull up and to crawl around the room. Later, the parent can teach the child to discriminate the objects that are off-limits. This can be done systematically by returning one breakable item at a time when the parent can verbally reward the child for exercising self-restraint in looking at the china bowl without using it as a toy.

Another example of an environmental cue is the type of activity that precedes bedtime or rest time in nursery school. Quiet activities such as reading a story or listening to a record can be helpful cues for children to begin unwinding for a time of rest. Loud, active games prior to a rest period serve to stimulate the children and make it difficult for them to exercise self-control when naptime is announced. The planned use of one activity to prepare children for the next event in the day can facilitate the development of self-control. Failure to provide environmental cues for children makes the adult responsible for enforcing the desired behavior and builds dependence on external controls.

Making the limits clear and consistent. Setting limits with appropriate discipline develops self-control and understanding, and also provides an environment in which the child can freely explore and successfully experience living within established guidelines. The child can then act with some degree of confidence because he is protected from himself. The following are general guidelines that may help to establish limits.

Do not place limitations on a child that he cannot follow. Limits should match the stage of development and the individual needs of the child. A 2-year-old child would have difficulty stopping himself from touching things around the house no matter how insistent or forceful the parent is. By 5 years of age there is sufficient maturation to reasonably expect the child to follow a rule against touching objects.

Limitations that are imposed should be necessary. Sometimes it is difficult to know whether a limit is imposed for the child's own well-being or for adult comfort. The child must understand the limitation in order to follow it.

The language used must be one that the child will understand. Thus, to tell a child, "I want you to be reasonably well adjusted" does not tell the child what he is supposed to do. In the establishment of limits there is a tendency to offer only negatives—don't do this or that. Negatives should be incorporated with direction or a positive statement. An example of the negative is, "Stop making so much noise." A positive addition is, "Why don't you play with your puzzles?"

A healthy child will not always conform passively to limitations. In fact, the testing of limits is necessary for a child. If he is to acquire independence and emotional strength he must occasionally assert himself. Adults must be comfortable with this resistance and should accept the child's right to *informed resistance* without feeling threatened by it. Informed resistance may be described as resistance to limits that the parent has explained. Parents should be prepared to provide adequate answers, not just, "Because I said so." Parents should also be prepared to enforce the limit while acknowledging the child's right to resist.

Parents should avoid the use of shame, fear, or ridicule. This type of corrective measure tends to make the child think that parents do not care about how he feels. Consequently, the child will reason that he should not listen to someone who does not care about him.

2. Minimizing the Use of Punishment. In limit setting, the parent must consider punishment or discipline when limits are broken. Discipline should be prompt. Delay causes the child to be confused about what he has done wrong, and delay may cause one to inflict punishment at a time when the child's behavior is good. The punishment should fit the crime. Minor infractions should receive minor punishments and major crimes should receive major punishments.

Punishment must take into account the child's age, personality, and development. Long sermons, talks, logic, or reasoning should be avoided. They are ineffective because the child's attention span is usually short, and furthermore, the child may be too upset to comprehend what is said. One minute or two of brief, to-the-point statements about the misbehavior is about all the child will understand.

Discriminate quite clearly between the bad behavior and the child. It is the bad behavior of the child and not the child himself that is intolerable. After the punishment has been imposed and the child is calm, it is important that the child comprehend the reason he was punished.

Threats of punishment with no follow-through have very little effect and cause the child to learn quite easily that all threats are not carried out. If corporal punishment is to be used, it is unwise to spank a child more than two or three times. After that, there is a ventilating of parental anger without any corrective value for the child. Shouting matches with the child are of little value. A firm, low voice is much more beneficial. The parent should remember that rewarding desired behavior is just as important as punishing undesirable behavior.

3. Maximizing the Use of Positive Reinforcement. Positive reinforcement, the process of rewarding behavior, is one of the adult's most powerful tools in socializing children. However, adults whose long-range goal is to develop self-control in children will select those reinforcers that can teach the child eventually to reinforce himself. Self-reinforcement takes the form of feelings of pride, effectiveness, and mastery. The sense of a "job well done" is a powerful reinforcer. It feels good to be successful and effective. Positive feelings about one's self are reinforcing events that maintain positive behavior from within.

The lists below divide positive reinforcers into three categories that have implications for internal control.

Tangible Reinforcers	**Social Reinforcers**	**Self-reinforcers**
things to eat	praise	feelings of: pride,
toys	attention	mastery,
special privileges	smiles	effectiveness,
getting one's way	compliments	strength,
staying up late	status	satisfaction,
a party	affection	privileges granted to self

The self-reinforcers listed above are primarily good feelings about one's self. These feelings are based on values that have been learned through significant human interactions. It is reasonable to assume that for most individuals social reinforcers are more likely to develop internal control than are tangible reinforcers. However, tangible controls may be needed for those children whose level of awareness is such that social reinforcers may have no meaning.

It is important to note that some children have experienced such painful and inconsistent responses from adults that they cease to value social reinforcers. In such cases it may be necessary to use tangible reinforcers such as candy or cereal bits that can be paried with praise, attention, and affection until the youngster learns that the social reinforcers are real, valuable, and worthy of trust. When tangible reinforcers are needed to change behavior, they should be used only as long as necessary. Social reinforcers should be substituted gradually and as soon as possible. Successful performance followed by meaningful social reinforcers builds a positive self-concept and leads to self-management and internal control.

Like all other children, the child with handicapping conditions needs to feel good about himself to develop close trusting relationships with others, to value honesty and productivity, and to exercise self-control. These important behaviors and others valued by most people are learned through interactions with other human beings. Parents, teachers, siblings, and friends are the people who will gradually mold the developing child, reward the behavior, and shape the self-concept. Exceptional children are normal in their need for unconditional love, positive adult models, opportunities to grow, discipline, and social reinforcement. The nurturing environment for these children is one in which the adults care enough to grow and change themselves.

WHAT EVERY CHILD NEEDS FOR GOOD MENTAL HEALTH

To grow healthy and strong, children should have good food, plenty of sleep, exercise and fresh air. Children have emotional needs too. To have perfect health – to be both healthy and happy – all children require . . .

LOVE

Every child needs to feel

. . . that his parents love, want and enjoy him

. . . that he matters very much to someone

. . . that there are people near him who care what happens to him

ACCEPTANCE

Every child needs to believe

. . . that his parents like him for himself, just the way he is

. . . that they like him all the time, and not only when he acts according to their ideas of the way a child should act

. . . that they *always* accept him, even though often they may not approve of the things he does

. . . that they will let him grow and develop in his own way

SECURITY

Every child needs to know

. . . that his home is a good safe place he can feel sure about

. . . that his parents will always be on hand, especially in times of crisis when he needs them most

. . . that he *belongs* to a family or group; that there is a place where he fits in

PROTECTION

Every child needs to feel

. . . that his parents will keep him safe from harm

. . . that they will help him when he must face strange, unknown and frightening situations

INDEPENDENCE

Every child needs to know

. . . that his parents want him to grow up and that they encourage him to try new things

. . . that they have confidence in him and in his ability to do things for himself and by himself

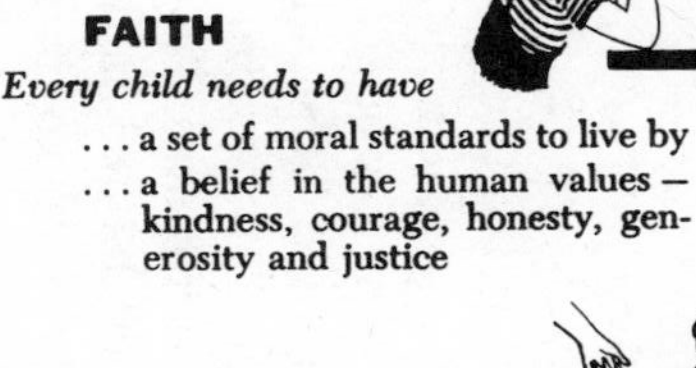

FAITH

Every child needs to have

. . . a set of moral standards to live by

. . . a belief in the human values – kindness, courage, honesty, generosity and justice

GUIDANCE

Every child needs to have

. . . friendly help in learning how to behave toward persons and things

. . . grown-ups around him who show him by example how to get along with others

CONTROL

Every child needs to know

. . . that there are limits to what he is permitted to do and that his parents will hold him to these limits

. . . that though it is all right to feel jealous or angry, he will not be allowed to hurt himself or others when he has these feelings

Children whose basic needs are satisfied have a better chance to grow up in good mental health and to become mentally healthy adults – people who are good parents, good mates, good workers, good neighbors, good citizens.

FIGURE 1.

Note: Reprinted by permission of the Mental Health Association, 1800 N. Kent, Rosslyn Station, Arlington, Va. 22209.

Summary

Social and emotional development do not occur independently of one another. A disability will affect this development. The more severe the disability, the greater will be the potential impairment of normal development. In normal development, increasing age naturally results in more accurate awareness of the environment and differentiation of the emotions. By age 2, there is a complete differentiation of all emotions found in adults. From this point on, social experiences and development, primarily through play in the first 5 years, influence the way the child will express his emotional repertoire.

Since each child's background is different, children will show individual ways of reacting to the same emotionally arousing stimuli. At other times, there will be a remarkable similarity in the reaction to the same stimulus. The young child with special needs faces not only all the difficulties of the normally developing child, but in addition, the negative value society places on an imperfect child. It becomes the task of his parents and professionals to negate the undesirable aspect of disability by providing an open and caring environment which helps him maximize his abilities and to enjoy positive interpersonal relationships (see Figure 1). Realistic expectations are the keynote for the developing child.

REFERENCES

Allen, K. The acquisition of social skills in the young child. In N. Haring (Ed.), *Behavior of exceptional children: An introduction to special education.* Columbus, Ohio: Charles E. Merrill Publishing Co., 1974.

Ambron, S. *Child development.* San Francisco: Rinehart Press/Holt & Winston, 1975.

Banus, B. *The developmental therapist: A prototype of the pediatric occupational therapist.* Thorofare, N.J.: Charles B. Slack, 1971.

Baroff, G. *Mental retardation: Nature, cause and management.* Washington, D.C.: Hemisphere Publishing Co., 1974.

Bromwich, R. Stimulation in the first year of life: A perspective on infant development. *Young Children,* 1977, **32**(2), 71–82.

Erikson, E. *Childhood and society.* New York: W. W. Norton & Co., 1950.

Harris, T. *I'm ok—you're ok.* New York: Harper & Row, 1967.

Heinicke, C. Early childhood social and emotional development: Relationships and task orientation. In H. Spicker, N. Anastasiow, & W. Hodges (Eds.), *Children with special needs: Early development and Education.* Minneapolis: University of Minnesota, 1976.

Kessler, J. *Psychopathology in children.* Englewood Cliffs, N.J.: Prentice-Hall, 1966.

Knobloch, H., & Pasamanick, B. (Eds.). *Gesell's and Amatruda's developmental diagnosis: The evaluation and management of normal and abnormal neuropsychologic development in infancy and early childhood.* Hagerstown, Md.: Harper & Row, 1974.

Kohlberg, L., & Mayer, R. Development as the arm of education. *Harvard Educational Review,* 1972, **42**, 449–456.

Kronick, D. Some thoughts on group identification: Social needs. *Journal of Learning Disabilities,* 1974, **7**(3), 144–147.

Lickona, T. *The early social development of children: Implications for a preschool program.* Paper presented to the Early Childhood Teachers of the Courtland College Campus. Courtland, N.Y., April 1969.

Read, K. *The nursery school: Human relationships and learning* (6th ed.). Philadelphia: W. B. Saunders, 1976.

Sears, R., Maccoby, E., & Levin, H. *Patterns of child rearing.* Evanston, Ill.: Row Peterson, 1957.

Snyder, L., Apolloni, T., & Cooke, T. Integrated settings at the early childhood level: The role of nonretarded peers. *Exceptional Children,* 1977, **43**(5), 262–266.

Strain, P. Increasing social play of severely retarded preschoolers with socio-dramatic activities. *Mental Retardation,* 1975, **13**(6), 7–9.

Strain, P., Cooke, T., & Apolloni, T. Teaching exceptional children: Assessing and modifying social behavior. New York: *Academic Press,* 1976. (a)

Strain, P., Cooke, T., & Apolloni, T. The role of peers in modifying classmates social behavior: A review. *Journal of Special Education,* 1976, **10**(4), 351–356.

Strain, P., & Shores, R. Social reciprocity: A review of research and educational implications. *Exceptional Children,* 1977, **43**(8), 526–529.

Strain, P., Shores, R., & Kerr, M. An experimental analysis of spillover effects on the social interaction of behaviorally handicapped preschool children. *Journal of Applied Behavior Analysis,* 1976, **9**(1), 31–40. (b)

Strain, P., & Trimm, M. An experimental analysis of social interaction between a behaviorally disordered pre-school child and her classroom peers. *Journal of Applied Behavior Analysis,* 1970, **7**(4), 583–590.

Strain, P., & Wiegerink, R. The social play of two behaviorally disordered preschool children during four activities. *Journal of Abnormal Child Psychology,* 1975, **3**(1), 61–69.

Strain, P., & Wiegerink, R. The effects of socio-dramatic activities on social interaction among behaviorally disordered preschool children. *Journal of Special Education,* 1976, **10**(1), 71–75.

Umsted, R. Children with visual handicaps. In J. Gallagher (Ed.), *The application of child development research to exceptional children.* Reston, Va.: The Council for Exceptional Children, 1975.

White, B. *The first three years of life.* Englewood Cliffs, N.J.: Prentice-Hall, 1975.

Wright, B. *Physical disability: A psychological approach.* New York: Harper & Brothers, 1960.

10

Play Skill Development

The play of handicapped children has received an increasing amount of attention in recent years (Knapczyk & Yoppi, 1975; Wehman, 1977). Through the special education movement, deinstitutionalization, and increased parent training, handicapped children have a greater opportunity to learn appropriate play behavior. Development of play skills in children with developmental delays may increase their proficiency in language, motor, cognitive, and social skills (Strain, Cooke, & Apolloni, 1976; Wehman, 1977a, b). Furthermore, games and related recreational activities which are integrated into other areas of instructional programming provide functional tasks which are conducive to establishing a positive learning environment (e.g., Thiagarajan, 1976).

The purpose of this chapter is to describe the specific functions and relationships of assessment, methods, materials, and generalization in the context of play skill development. The importance of play, specific play problems encountered by handicapped children, and representative learning characteristics of the developmentally disabled are also discussed. Learning and behavior characteristics of young delayed children are directly related to selection of methods and play materials. Those readers specifically interested in a discussion of different theoretical approaches to play of exceptional children are referred to work by Ellis (1973) and Wehman and Abramson (1976).

Paul Wehman is the author of this chapter, portions of which have been adapted from *Helping the Mentally Retarded Acquire Play Skills: A Behavioral Approach* by P. Wehman. Springfield, Ill.: Charles C Thomas, 1976. Used with permission.

The Importance of Play

Play as a Facilitator of Behavior Development. A major reason for encouraging play is the positive effect which it may have on adaptive behavior. While the concept of play as an intensive programming technique for general behavior development in handicapped children has not been fully explored (Bradtke, Rosenblatt, & Kirkpatrick, 1972), it is well documented that the play of normal children fosters cognitive development and motor skills (Wenar, 1971). It would appear that a play program which is consistent with the present needs and functioning of the developmentally delayed child would enhance the acquisition of collateral skills as well. The play research literature with handicapped children is of limited value on this critical issue. Studies performed by Mehlman (1953) and Leland, Walker and Taboada (1959) reported correlated increases in personality adjustment, social behavior, and intelligence in mildly retarded children. These increases were small and do not indicate a cause-effect relationship. More recent work, however, suggests the positive effect which a systematically developed play repertoire can have on the development of fine motor skills, personal-social behavior, and language skills in handicapped children (Morrison & Newcomer, 1975; Newcomer & Morrison, 1974).

The development of play skills in delayed children should facilitate gross motor and fine motor skills. By acquiring a variety of play skills which require fine motor or gross motor movements, the child's physical development should be enhanced as she gains a play behavior repertoire. A good example of this is the child who learns how to use a slide board, a tricycle, or a trampoline in a

Play is the natural activity of children, and children need to play.

recreation setting; although she is learning play behaviors, gross motor skills are also being acquired and strengthened at the same time.

Development of Social Behavior Through Play. Social behavior is also directly influenced through the development of cooperative and competitive play behavior (Knapcyzk & Yoppi, 1975). Cooperative play between children leads to learning acceptable modes of socialization such as sharing, learning to take turns, and so forth. This is an area in which handicapped children are commonly deficient. Young delayed children may play independently and consistently for long periods of time but often fail to act cooperatively with peers unless given verbal encouragement or physical guidance (Whitman, Mercurio, & Caponigri, 1970).

The role of play as a mediator of social development has been summarized by Luckey and Shapiro (1974):

> Games with increasingly complex rules and social demands further enhance children's social adaption as they grow older, and participation in clubs and organizations takes on increasing social importance during the school years. (p. 33)

These social traits are mandatory for social-emotional adjustment and for successful learning experiences in school. While the precise effects which involvement in games and sports have on handicapped children are unclear, it is likely that participation in games is helpful in establishing appropriate social behavior patterns in other avenues of life and in providing opportunities for more positive learning experiences.

The Adaptability of Play. Another positive aspect of play experiences is the facility with which they may be adapted to a number of different learning situations and settings. Play skills learned in the classroom can also be used at home, on the playground, or in community settings. Play may be used to encourage other neighborhood children or siblings to interact more freely with handicapped children. It may break down barriers of stigma or uneasiness which many people feel toward children with disabilities and thus promote normalization (Nesbitt, Neal, & Hillman, 1974).

Play may be used in academic learning situations, either as a reward or privilege for good work or as an instructional method. Children who have already acquired certain play skills might be allowed to go to the play area of the classroom for free time contingent on academic performance or good behavior. Play also facilitates the development of physical education skills, music abilities, and artistic qualities. The strong influence of play on physical development has been aptly noted by the Council for Exceptional Children and the American Association for Health and Physical Education (1966):

> Many retarded children are clumsy and weak, lack endurance, and are poorly coordinated. This condition is usually caused by hour after hour of sitting with no activity. Biologically vigorous activity is as much a necessity for the human body as food and oxygen, rest and sleep, and elimination of wastes. To meet this need for activity, it is necessary for all children, including all levels of the retarded, to participate in a variety of activities involving large and small muscle groups. Mastery of fundamental motor skills—such as walking, running, jumping, grasping, carrying, pulling, and bending—stimulates development of the large muscles of the

> body. Skills which are involved in low organized games, lead-up games, relays, stunts, and self-testing activities, and which are fundamental to most of our sports are combinations of the basic large muscle movements with refinements brought about by use of the appropriate small muscles. (p. 17)

Children who have developed play behaviors do not require constant supervision and may need only limited amounts of play materials, provided they are selected appropriately. If a child has some ability to play and interact socially, her chances for developing friendships will be increased. With increased contacts and friendships, the probability of eventual exclusion is minimized.

Play as an Alternative to Inappropriate Social Behavior. Play also inhibits unacceptable social behavior. Children who are engaging in playful activities or constructive use of leisure time rarely display aggressive behavior. Furthermore, stereotypic rocking behavior and bizarre vocal sounds which are characteristic of the severely handicapped child may be decreased or eliminated during play.

The research literature in this area is quite clear. Studies have demonstrated a significant reduction in self-stimulatory behavior through acquisition of play skills (Berkson & Davenport, 1962; Flavell, 1973; Wehman, Karan, & Rettie, 1976). Other research has shown play to be an effective alternative behavior to self-inflicted aggression (Whaley & Tough, 1968). Socially withdrawn behavior has also been overcome by engaging the delayed child in play activities (Morris & Dolker, 1974; Paloutzian, Hazazi, Streifel, & Edgar, 1971).

Pleasure Aspects of Play. People of all ages enjoy leisure-time activities which are a diversion from daily routines. Handicapped children are no different and may, in fact, have a stronger need for diversion due to living conditions which provide little joy. An example of this was described by Benoit (1955) who found that mentally retarded residents in extremely drab state institutions had much time for play, but little guidance for more enjoyable use of this time.

Many handicapped children have not learned how to play or use free time for activities. The handicapped are often denied the pleasure of playing with toys and games because of inadequate instruction and limited availability of materials and funds. Frequently, play during recreational periods becomes a task or chore. This is particularly true with severely disabled children. For them the joy or pleasure of jumping rope, playing house, or even throwing a ball is an emotion which does not occur unless these play skills can be taught. For the mildly disabled child, the pleasurable aspects of independently attending community entertainments such as movie theaters, sporting events, and carnivals cannot be enjoyed without previous training and direction.

In summary, play has at least four major functions which are of value for young handicapped children:

1. The potential development of collateral behaviors such as gross or fine motor skills, language, or higher-level social behavior.
2. A reinforcer of instructional activity.
3. Inhibitor of socially inappropriate behaviors.
4. Pleasure or joy.

Play Problems of Young Handicapped Children

Few Program Guidelines for Teaching Play. There is only a limited amount of play research which delineates teaching procedures and methods for handicapped children. The lack of guidelines for developing play programs has worked a hardship on practitioners in the field of special education.

Specific training methods and appropriate materials are critical areas in program development. They must be considered in terms of the varied functioning levels and learning characteristics typical of a broad range of developmentally delayed children. Training methods refer to the principles and procedures used to develop play skills. Appropriate materials are toys and play materials, recreational equipment, and environmental settings (gymnasiums, playgrounds) for different levels and ages of children.

There is presently a growing body of research literature that examines the exploratory and play behavior of intellectually average infants and preschool children (Hutt, 1966, 1970; Nunnally & Lemond, 1973). One of the more interesting findings is that certain properties of toys—complexity of form, sound or sound potential, and plasticity—seem to promote play and exploratory activity in nonretarded infants (McCall, 1974). Exploratory research on the play of intellectually average children from developmental and experimental child psychology may be of value in determining the best learning conditions for disabled children. Unfortunately, this work has not, as yet, become widely applied or used in special education. Ultimately, it may be useful to identify the critical interaction of materials, methods, and learning characteristics of the individual.

Shortage of Qualified Recreation Leaders. Another problem in helping the handicapped child acquire play skills is the lack of expertise in precise teaching procedures by many recreation therapists. Many of those knowledgeable in the different types of recreation activities available to special populations have not experienced the unique behavior and learning characteristics of developmentally delayed preschoolers. It comes as a shock to these workers when they are faced with handicapped children who refuse eye contact or who destroy toys. Often the therapist develops a "set" or "expectancy" that children with handicapping conditions cannot learn to play and that they are best avoided.

The recent movement in therapeutic recreation (Nesbitt, Neal, & Hillman, 1974) may be the most logical outlet for training recreation professionals with strategies and methods to deal with handicapped children of all ages and degrees of severity. While the number of certified therapeutic recreation specialists is limited (approximately 1,000), these individuals may be able to serve as resource personnel for special educators and therapists. What is required is an integration of behavior modification technology with recreation programming expertise. This includes a thorough understanding and working knowledge of task analysis, skill sequencing, prompting and fading, modeling, demonstration techniques, and methods of behavior recording.

Lack of Spontaneity in Play. A crucial difference between the play of normal children and developmentally delayed children is the latter group's failure to play spontaneously. This has been documented by several writers (Hillman, 1966; Paloutzian, Hasazi, Streifel, & Edgar, 1971). This difference becomes increasingly obvious as the functioning level is more depressed.

Severely developmentally delayed children rarely act on play materials in any constructive or spontaneous manner without some form of external cue, supervision, or instruction. This may be due to not having previously experienced the reinforcing and pleasurable aspects of play, or it may be a lack of sensory awareness of the play materials presented. Also, free play behavior may not occur simply because of faulty arrangement of the recreation area by the teacher or activity therapist.

The question of why the developmentally delayed fail to act spontaneously on play materials or do not take the initiative in constructive use of leisure time is not relatively important. What is critical is providing answers which ameliorate this problem. What is required is a set of play program guidelines with teaching procedures which outline optimal conditions for learning.

Inappropriate Toys and Play Materials. Many of the toys which are used by recreation professionals and activity therapists in play with disabled children are woefully inadequate for promoting and stimulating play behavior. Usually, these play materials have been designed for use by nonretarded preschoolers.

Cooperative play between children leads to learning acceptable modes of socialization such as sharing and taking turns.

This presents at least two difficulties. First, the toys are not durable and fail to hold up over time. Slowly emerging skills require repetitive use for longer periods of time than that required by the normal child. Before the skill is mastered, the handicapped child may have grown larger and have more strength than the toy can accommodate. Second, many of the toys are designed for the purpose of facilitating symbolic and imaginative play, that is, playing house or with dolls. With rare exceptions (Domnie, 1974), this usually works a hardship on the majority of handicapped children who demonstrate limited symbolic play. The net result of using these toys during recreation periods is that the children do not act on them and usually ignore them.

A similar problem can be seen with many of the playgrounds and much of the field equipment available to handicapped children. Ellis (1973) aptly notes the static quality of playgrounds in the following manner:

> Playgrounds are no more than a combination of large playthings placed together in one location. There is no reason that playgrounds have to be outside but the tradition that has imposed this unnecessary constraint is strong, and few playgrounds are built indoors. Tradition has also decreed that a playground be designed to provide opportunities for gross motor activity by simulating, in galvanized steel, some primitive jungle setting. If the statements about playthings are applied to the average traditional playground, it can be seen to be a travesty. (p. 137)

Effects of Learning and Behavior Characteristics on Handicapped Children's Play

Handicapped infants and toddlers differ from normal children in several behaviors. They do not show the same rate of motor development, language is grossly impaired, self-care skills are usually deficient, and little positive emotion is displayed. While intellectually average preschoolers display social and cognitive growth through extended exploration of their environment and surroundings, the intellectually subnormal child rarely explores spontaneously.

Minimal social interaction with peers and siblings is observed in many young handicapped children. Attending skills may not be well developed with only loud sounds or gross changes in visual stimuli resulting in brief orienting responses.

This general lack of sensory awareness and the limitations in exploratory behavior are most notable in severely handicapped preschoolers and reduce the emergence of play activity. Through exploring the environment, the nonretarded child acquires knowledge which allows her to develop behaviors that are necessary for human development.

Paying attention to relevant cues in the environment is the initial step in sensory awareness and responsiveness. It is also crucial in the development of visual tracking and searching skills, and imitative behavior. A behavioral analysis of play behavior deficits of handicapped young children reveals the following dilemma. If a child does not attend, or is unaware of the surroundings, the opportunity to gather new information about the environment cannot occur, therefore inhibiting the development of more sophisticated play activity.

For example, the child who watches another child playing with a new toy that makes pleasant sounds may be able to imitate the play behavior when given the same toy at a later time. Moreover, attending to a wide assortment of sounds, sights, and tactile stimuli assists a child to physically cope with the environment.

It is known that handicapped children do not attend well nor imitate readily and thus do not display the social awareness typical of normal children. Another equally important behavioral characteristic of the handicapped child is the limited number of events which are reinforcing. Many developmentally disabled children require greater amounts of reinforcement, more frequently, and with reinforcement contingencies which are clearly labeled. Frequently, social reinforcement, or approval, is not a sufficient motivator to encourage exploration on the part of severely retarded preschoolers, and tangible reinforcers may have to be used initially.

This presents an inherent difficulty in developing play skills in the severely delayed child. Noted writers in the area of play (Ellis, 1973) and leisure (Neulinger, 1974) have observed that play should be pursued for the joy of engaging in an activity without external consequence. Play behavior ought to occur as a result of the intrinsic reinforcement derived from the activity. However, without external reinforcement presented contingent on play activity or exploratory behavior, severely handicapped preschoolers may display little sustained activity.

Once a child has begun to explore the environment and act on a variety of different objects, at least two broad categories of play should then be encouraged: (a) more sophisticated and sustained toy play and (b) greater frequency of social interaction patterns. While the nonretarded child readily displays these behaviors with little instruction, many of the children with developmental difficulties are deficit in skills which are critical to these behaviors. Limitations in visual tracking and searching skills, and a general failure to learn in other than intentional learning situations, that is, incidental learning, create serious problems in the development of play behavior. Equally troublesome is the characteristic lack of spontaneity with toys observed in many handicapped children. What frequently occurs when young handicapped children are introduced to a roomful of toys is repetitive and nonfunctional actions with the playthings. In similar situations, a normal child will beat the drum, blow a horn, and bounce a ball playfully; however, the developmentally delayed child may hit the horn repetitively on the floor until it breaks.

It has been noted earlier that a major reason for inappropriate play is that the child has not been taught appropriate behavioral alternatives with play or has not learned the reinforcing value of certain toys. This is not to imply that no attempt has been made at instruction; rather, the issue is what combination of teaching procedures and materials have been used and how carefully they match the learning characteristics of the child.

Limited cooperative play and social interaction between peers are also regularly observed with handicapped children. Independent or isolated play may be noted frequently (Paloutzian, Hasazi, Streifel, & Edgar, 1971). The child may play well alone and be able to amuse himself appropriately for a short period of time. However, the duration of play activity is usually brief when there is no supervision or assistance.

When there is little or no peer interaction during play sessions, children fail to develop higher-level social behaviors such as cooperative and competitive play. In short, independent play is a lower stage of social development which may only provide sensory input from inanimate objects. Affective feedback cannot be gained until children begin to interact.

Lack of social interaction is a dominant characteristic of young disabled children. This limitation grossly impedes the development of language and communication skills and, unfortunately, minimizes the effects of play as a potent medium of social development. Moreover, it is generally accepted that if social interaction is not encouraged at a young age, the long-range outlook for competent social behavior is not bright.

Play Assessment: Determining Where to Start a Play Program

The initial step in devising recreation programs for the young handicapped child is to assess the general level of behavioral functioning (Wehman, 1975). This requires a thorough analysis of behavioral strengths as well as deficits. A child with a very short attention span, limited visual tracking skills, and inability to imitate would not be a good candidate for a lengthy program but instead might function better in two to three brief play sessions during the day.

Physical and sensory deficits should also be evaluated and considered when planning an individualized program. Prosthetic devices may have to be introduced as a means of helping the child engage in play activities (Abramson, 1977).

Once a careful behavioral assessment of general adaptive behavior level is completed, target play skills may be selected. Typically, recreational activities are arranged for severely and multihandicapped youngsters according to the following criteria:

1. Any activity in which the child might show an interest.
2. Any activity in which the child cannot get hurt or hurt someone else.

Leisure time activities are not always selected for the purpose of developing social, cognitive, motor, or language skills. Acquiring such behaviors is seen as a collateral benefit, but generally the idea is to find an activity in which everybody can have a good time. This is, of course, one of the avowed goals of recreation and is most admirable. However, it falls short of maximizing the effects which intensive play experiences may have on developing adaptive behavior in the severely retarded (Bradtke, Rosenblatt, & Kirkpatrick, 1972). The position taken here is that assessment, or the selection of appropriate play skills for training, is a critical aspect of devising a play program which meets the pleasure needs of the severely handicapped as well as accelerating behavioral development.

A Multidimensional Approach to Leisure Time Activity

A multidimensional assessment strategy for categorizing the leisure time activity of developmentally delayed children is proposed here. Four basic levels of recreation skill development are shown in Figure 1: (1) exploratory play, (2) toy play, (3) social play, and (4) structured game play. Assessment of the adaptive behavior of the handicapped child reveals that functioning levels range from a most primitive level of exploration (e.g., orienting response) to following multiple instructions, which is prerequisite to learning table games. Therefore, in devising an assessment strategy for play, a logical sequence of behaviors which features upward movement and cumulative growth is required. Placement into a certain level of play sequence is contingent on the functioning level and play development of the child.

There will be considerable overlap and transition between levels of play noted in Figure 1. This is a natural characteristic of normal development and is expected in the acquisition of play behavior. Each of the four levels is subdivided into smaller behavioral components or segments. These subdivisions are made to facilitate program planning and evaluation of play skill development.

While the segments in exploratory, toy, and social play may be viewed as hierarchical, this is not essential for programming purposes. The proposed multiple-level skill hierarchy is an effort to create a logical scope and sequence in the selection of categories of play behavior.

With little or no peer interaction during play sessions, children fail to develop social behaviors such as cooperation.

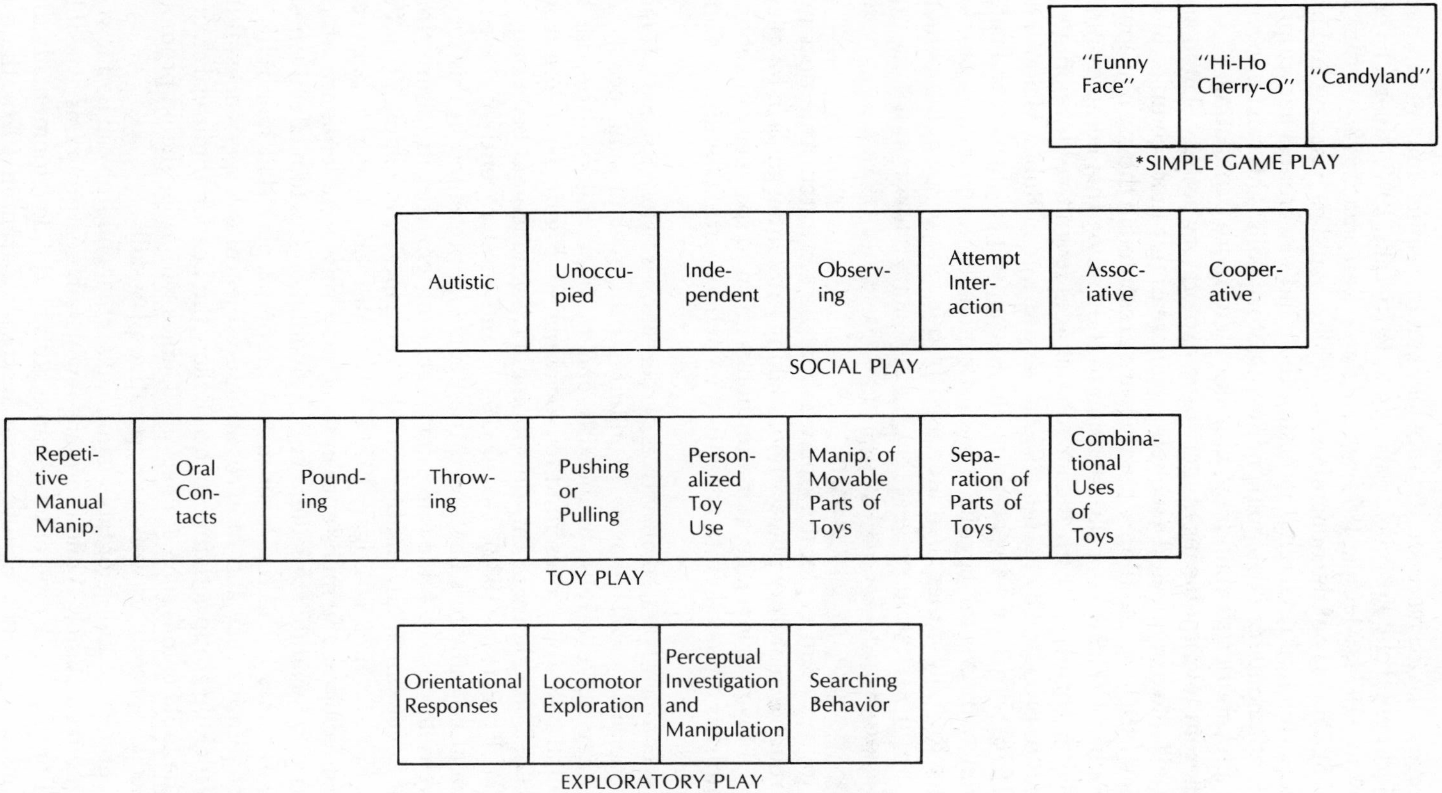

"Funny Face"	"Hi-Ho Cherry-O"	"Candyland"

*SIMPLE GAME PLAY

Autistic	Unoccupied	Independent	Observing	Attempt Interaction	Associative	Cooperative

SOCIAL PLAY

Repetitive Manual Manip.	Oral Contacts	Pounding	Throwing	Pushing or Pulling	Personalized Toy Use	Manip. of Movable Parts of Toys	Separation of Parts of Toys	Combinational Uses of Toys

TOY PLAY

Orientational Responses	Locomotor Exploration	Perceptual Investigation and Manipulation	Searching Behavior

EXPLORATORY PLAY

FIGURE 1. A play skill hierarchy for young handicapped children.

*These games represent only samples of some of the many games available for the developmentally delayed.

Note: From *Helping the Mentally Retarded Acquire Play Skills: A Behavioral Approach* by P. Wehman. Springfield, Ill.: Charles C Thomas, 1976. Copyright 1976 by Charles C Thomas. Reprinted by permission.

Exploratory behavior has been the subject of an increasing amount of attention by experimental child psychologists (Bijou, 1975; Ellis, 1973; Moore, Evertson, & Brophy, 1974; McCall, 1974; Nunnally & Lemond, 1973; Weisler & McCall, 1976). The play of the nonambulatory child should be based on findings from this experimental research. Increasing the child's awareness and responsiveness is fundamental to developing her exploratory skills. This can be accomplished by altering her surroundings to make them more stimulating.

Using different toys is a means of increasing exploratory activity. Tilton and Ottinger (1964) have delineated a sequence of increasingly more complex independent play with toys, and these categories are presented in the toy play levels shown in Figure 1. This level calls attention to the finding that complex independent play is correlated with higher mental ages (cognitive development) than was earlier proposed by Parten (1932). The research of Rubin, Maioni, and Hornung (1976) with 3- and 4-year-old nonhandicapped preschoolers indicates that children with greater cognitive sophistication displayed more complex independent toy play rather than increased frequencies of social interaction. Results of this investigation suggest that the developmentally young may acquire simple problem-solving behaviors, in addition to increased sensory responsiveness, through toy play activity.

Clearly, toy play and exploratory play cannot be separated. One does not proceed through exploratory play without making substantial gains in toy play. However, at a toy play level, greater attention is given to specificity of actions. Greater emphasis is placed on the creativity of actions with different toys and play materials.

One of the commonly stated objectives of recreation is to foster social interaction and cooperative social behavior. In children with developmental problems, social play may not evolve spontaneously and must be trained. The use of developmental milestones presented for social play in Figure 1 is taken from Parten (1932). The validity of this developmental sequence has been empirically verified by Parten (1932), Gesell (1940), and most recently by Barnes (1971). Several investigators have used the behaviors presented in this social play hierarchy as response measures for evaluating changes in leisure time behavior of developmentally disabled children (Knapczyk & Yoppi, 1975; Paloutzian, Hasazi, Streifel, & Edgar, 1971). Although there is overlap between each of the developmental milestones in social play, this is one sequence which might be used to facilitate assessment and evaluation of program effectiveness.

Games with rules is the top level in the proposed play skill hierarchy. It includes cooperative play and requires structured learning experiences. Rule games may include group activities such as Follow the Leader or musical chairs. They may be table games such as checkers. Games with rules should promote cognitive social behavior as well as cooperative play skills.

One advantage to training for table-game skills is that children can be allowed to select preferred games. While there are few data-based programs available demonstrating the acquisition of table-game skills by the developmentally disabled (Wehman, Renzaglia, Schutz, Gray, James, & Karen, in 1976), there is some evidence to indicate that these behaviors may be learned and generalized (Rankin, Bates, Baldwin, Kelly, & Hannah, 1975).

The skills required in a typical table game (e.g., rolling dice, simple recognition and matching, taking turns) should be relatively easy to generalize across similar table games. Many table games and toys are easily modified and adapted to the functioning level of the individual (Cleland, Swartz, & Chasey, 1970).

Once the severely handicapped display advanced toy play skills in conjunction with social play, a simple group or table game may be introduced for instruction. Games should not be complex and only a limited number of steps should be required to understand the rules.

Assessment of the game level should be based on where the child's learning breaks down. Most games can be presented in a task analysis or an easy-to-hard, step-by-step approach. The child can be evaluated on her ability to perform each of the component skills in the sequence. At the point where performance to criterion cannot be met, training must be initiated.

Assessment: A Five-Part Process

Determining where to begin a play program for the severely handicapped becomes a five-part process. This process includes:

1. Assessment of general behavior functioning level, either formally through instruments or anecdotally through observation.
2. Exposure to different levels of play activity for purposes of gaining an approximate index of recreational skills.
3. Identification of target behaviors which may be realistically attained.
4. Selection of target behaviors according to weaknesses in or absence of general adaptive behavior.
5. Selection of target behaviors which are observable and easily measured.

Variables which can be used to make target behaviors observable and measurable are frequency (number of different toys used), length of time engaged in appropriate play, and latency of response (time between presentation of toy and action with the toy).

Measurement of task-analyzed games may be done in the following way: each component in the behavioral chain is taught individually, and a certain criterion of success must be met before teaching of the next response begins. Response measures may be coded by using a Self-Initiated (SI), Verbal (V), Gestural (G), or Physical Prompt (P) system. Plus or minus may be recorded by the trainer according to the level of assistance required at each step in the task analysis.

Specific Training Methods to Facilitate Play Skills

When target behaviors are identified and assessed, training strategies and procedures can be chosen. As a general instructional model, a continuum is provided in Figure 2 which describes a sequence of training that may be followed in developing play skills with young handicapped children. One goal of this sequence is to emphasize that different students require varied degrees of instruction.

The more proficient child may play appropriately with little assistance or supervision, and require only variations in play materials periodically. Other children may require musical background (Zine, Ferolo, Hass, & Hass, 1975) or certain types of social play materials (Quilitch & Risley, 1973) before engaging in sustained play. Frequently, however, developmentally delayed children must have individualized assistance and instruction which lead them through a sequence of simple and consistent instructions, verbal prompting, modeling, and even physical guidance. The less able a child is to independently initiate play, the more she will need instructional supervision by a trainer.

In this section, several techniques and procedures are discussed which will help children acquire play skills. The organization of this section initially involves methods of arranging the recreation environment and, secondly, procedures which would be classified as consequences that follow leisure time activity.

Recreation Environment

Different materials, instructions, types of models, and toy arrangements are among the types of conditions which may facilitate leisure time activity. Providing appropriate space and the removal of distractions are implied in environmental arrangement or control. An advantage to judicious arrangement of the recreation environment is that play may be more spontaneous and not be under complete control of external reinforcement contingencies.

Toy Proximity. One factor which contributes to development of increased play activity is the proximity of recreation materials to children. Placing several materials near a student may elicit greater activity and allow for greater spontaneity in recreation sessions. Several reports are available which stress the critical aspects of ecological arrangement and space utilization (Cataldo & Risley, 1974; Twardosz, Cataldo, & Risley, 1974).

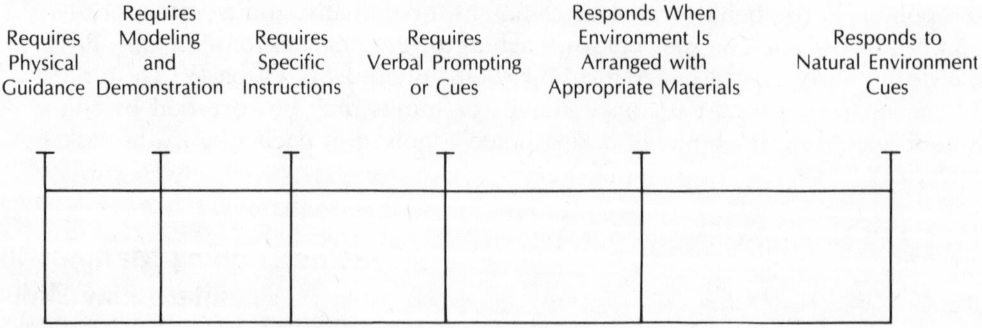

Requires Physical Guidance
Requires Modeling and Demonstration
Requires Specific Instructions
Requires Verbal Prompting or Cues
Responds When Environment Is Arranged with Appropriate Materials
Responds to Natural Environment Cues

FIGURE 2. An instructional sequence for developing play skills.

Note: From *Helping the Mentally Retarded Acquire Play Skills: A Behavioral Approach* by P. Wehman. Springfield, Ill.: Charles C Thomas, 1976. Copyright 1976 by Charles C Thomas. Reprinted by permission.

Appropriate leisure time activity is best developed and maintained if play activities are intrinsically reinforcing.

Recent research indicates that proximity of toys to severely developmentally disabled adolescents and adults increased physical action on objects from a mean baseline level of approximately 20% to almost 70% (Wehman, 1976b). An adult trainer placed two different toys near individuals who had not previously played appropriately for 30 consecutive seconds. An untested hypothesis is that young handicapped children will respond similarly.

Selection of Play Materials. A critical feature of any recreation environment is the play materials which are employed. The specific problems in selection of appropriate toys and suggestions for overcoming these difficulties has been discussed previously (Wehman, 1976a). Many of the recommended guidelines for play materials were based on the experimental research performed by child psychologists with nonhandicapped infants and preschoolers (e.g., McCall, 1974). While there is little doubt that reactive materials influence exploratory actions or that socially oriented materials such as table games (Quilitch & Risley, 1973) influence level of social interactions, greater attention must be given to empirically verifying the effectiveness of different materials with the young handicapped children.

Some support may be given to the value of balls, paddleballs, bubble blowers, Lincoln Logs, and viewmasters with the severely handicapped (Wehman, 1976b; Williams, Pumpian, McDaniel, Hamre-Nietupski, & Wheeler, 1975). In Table 1 are displayed the rank order preferences of play materials which were acted on across 50 training and baseline sessions by three profoundly retarded individuals (Wehman, 1976b). Unfortunately, these findings are confounded by the lack of control of toy selection by each trainer. Each trainer was instructed to select different leisure time materials and present them according to the guidelines given in each experimental condition. However, no provision was made for collecting data on which materials were presented to which individuals most frequently.

Instructions. Verbal cues and instructions may also be factors in eliciting increased levels of leisure time activity, promoting social play, and training games which require rules. Instructions have been consistently influential in behavior development of the developmentally young (Cooke & Apolloni, 1976; Kazdin, Silverman, & Sittler, 1975). When instructions have been paired with demonstration of appropriate leisure time activity (Wehman, 1976b) or with appropriate social behavior such as smiling or saying "Hello" (Nelson, Gibson, & Cutting, 1973) by a model, substantial increases in the target behavior were observed. Instructions should be given consistently and with a minimum of extraneous language cues.

Modeling. Specific effects of modeling during play periods have not been closely examined and bear greater investigation. The influential role of modeling is well documented with a nonretarded population (Bandura, 1969), and there is increasing evidence to suggest that observational learning processes are a major means through which the retarded acquire new information (Baer,

Table 1

Rank Order of Toy Preference

Subject 1	Subject 2	Subject 3
1. Balls	1. Lincoln Logs	1. Balls
2. Marble Shaker	2. Coloring Books	2. Paddleballs
3. Paddleballs	3. Paddleballs	3. Bubble Blower
4. Movie Viewer	4. Balls	4. Coloring Books
5. Lincoln Logs	5. Bubble Blower	5. Silly String
6. Bowling Kit	6. Silly String	6. Movie Viewer
7. Life Preserver	7. Hockey Game	7. Frisbee
8. Slinkies	8. Yo-Yo	8. Music Box
9. Music Box	9. Bowling Kit	9. Marble Shaker
10. Yo-Yo	10. Slinkies	10. Yo-Yo
11. Coloring Books/Crayons	11. Scooters	11. Scooters
12. Bubble Blower	12. Movie Viewer	12. Bowling Kit
13. Pinball Machine	13. Life Preserver	13. Slinkies
14. Hockey Game	14. Marble Shaker	14. Lincoln Logs
15. Silly String	15. Frisbee	15. Pinball Machine
16. Scooters	16. Pinball Machine	16. Hockey Game
17. Frisbee	17. Music Box	17. Life Preserver

Peterson, & Sherman, 1967; Wehman, 1976c). The positive implications of integrating handicapped children into physical education and recreation classes with nonhandicapped children should be apparent if modeling effects occur.

Some attempts at pairing higher-functioning peer models and adult models with the mentally retarded have been performed successfully in developing social play (Kazdin & Erickson, 1975; Morris & Dolker, 1974) and independent play (Paloutzian, Hasazi, Streifel, & Edgar, 1971; Wehman, 1976b; Wehman, Karan, & Rettie, 1976). Nonretarded 8-year-olds have also been integrated into a playroom with trainable-level retarded children and encouraged to interact with each other through cooperative play (Knapczyk & Peterson, 1975). It was discovered that substantially increased rates of cooperative play occurred in the trainable-level retarded children when normal models were present. This was empirically evaluated in a reversal design and indicated that contingent on the removal of these models cooperative play levels decreased to baseline rates.

Physical Prompting and Fading. Frequently, the severely handicapped do not follow instructions, often because they do not understand commands. When this occurs, the teacher is faced with how to get a desired behavior to occur. If the behavior is not demonstrated, little opportunity is present for reinforcement. Only when the desired response occurs and is followed with positive reinforcement can the behavior become stronger.

When developing new play skills in the severely handicapped child, the teacher may have to physically guide the individual through the desired skill or response (Whitman, Mercurio, & Caponigri, 1970). In order to encourage a young handicapped child to pull a wagon or roll a ball, the teacher may have to manually guide the child, providing praise and affection contingent on successful approximations of the behavior. Whenever manual guidance is used, the process of fading (Chapter 3) must be an integral part of the program. In play activities such as pulling a wagon the teacher must decide when to gradually remove his hand from the child's hand on the wagon tongue. Removal of physical prompts must be gradual (releasing pressure on the child's hand in small increments until no support remains). If, during the fading process, it becomes apparent that the child's ability to pull the toy is still dependent upon external physical support, fading should be postponed temporarily.

Task Analysis and Skill Sequencing. The method in which learning material is presented to the severely handicapped plays a critical role in the acquisition of skills and also in the rate at which new behavior is acquired. While a task analysis approach has been used in several different areas of programming for the developmentally disabled (Anderson, Hodson, & Jones, 1974; Brown, Williams, & Crowner, 1974; Knapczyk, 1975), it has rarely been employed in play programs. This may be due to an assumption that play must be spontaneous and should not be trained. Furthermore, many professionals responsible for initiating therapeutic recreation efforts have not been exposed to the efficacy of a task analysis methodology. Therefore, play skills have not been presented in a systematic step-by-step approach. If sequences have been established, they may not have been task analyzed into the smallest possible behavioral components.

When applied to recreation training efforts, task analysis and skill sequencing are most appropriately used in training specific play skills such as holding a rattle, riding a tricycle (Peterson & McIntosh, 1973), learning to play a table game (Bates & Rankin, 1975; Wehman, Abramson, & Norman, 1977), or engaging in group activities which require a certain amount of structure and understanding of rules. Tables 2 and 3 show a task analysis of Candyland and Checkers, respectively.

Reinforcer Sampling. Reinforcer sampling involves the presentation of new types of stimuli and events (Ayllon & Azrin, 1968). For example, a different toy whose function is unfamiliar to children is demonstrated by a trainer, thus displaying the toy's potentially attractive qualities. Reinforcer sampling is most applicable to encouraging exploratory activity in severely handicapped youngsters who are withdrawn and unresponsive to environmental stimulation. Toys and play materials are frequently strange stimuli which the handicapped have not previously experienced; therefore, their reinforcing value has not been established.

Consequence Conditions. The development of play skills may also be influenced according to different types of reinforcement conditions. Although negative reinforcement (Whaley & Tough, 1968) and punishment (Koegel, Firestone, Kramme, & Dunlop, 1974) have been employed to decrease nonfunctional behaviors and increase play skills, this discussion is limited to positive reinforcement conditions.

Edibles, points, and pennies have been used to develop ball rolling, cooperative play, and ball throwing skills in developmentally disabled individuals. Although tangible reinforcers can be effective in shaping new leisure time skills, they are recommended with these cautions: it may be difficult to reduce the amount of reinforcers given, and self-initiated play behavior does not occur when under control of artificial reinforcers such as tokens and edibles.

Praise, attention, and approval from peers, parents, teachers, and others are potent consequences available for developing and strengthening leisure time activity. Praise and physical affection were given in two studies which demonstrated development of independent play and social play in six institutionalized, severely handicapped individuals (Wehman, 1977d). Controlled studies which assess the effects of peer reinforcement versus adult reinforcement and specific learning characteristics of influential peers are lacking but are required if one is to understand how to develop more natural reinforcement conditions in recreation sessions.

The best reinforcers may be the toys, play materials, and games used in play skill development. That is, appropriate leisure time activity is best developed and maintained if play materials are intrinsically reinforcing. Few studies are available which demonstrate the effective transfer of stimulus control from trainer cues to toys in the play area (Hopper & Wambold, in press). Use of the Premack principle, or the contingent access to a high-preference leisure activity if a low-preference activity is performed, may also be implemented in

Table 2

Task Analysis of Candyland

Consists of: a game board with a winding path, moving pieces, a deck of cards (consisting of single colored cards, double colored cards and pictured cards).

Playing procedures: Student draws a card, moves his man/lady to indicated space. The first player to reach the gingerbread house wins.

Steps Used

1. Picks a man/lady.
2. Puts man/lady on START.
3. Draws one card. (You want the student to draw just one card, not 3 or 4.)
4. Moves man to correct color. (This is the step where you should start stacking the deck.) In this step, use only the cards with one colored square on them. If needed, you can break this down further by using specific colors that you want to work on. NOTE: A student need not know his colors to play this game. Matching is all that is needed. When the student learns to play this game you might want to work on *recognizing* colors. Don't combine the learning of the game and color recognition.
5. Moves man to double colors. In this second deck, use only the cards that have 2 colored squares on them. With this deck the student learns that 2 colored squares on the card allows him to move 2 of those colored spaces. With these 2 decks, the student learns when to move 1 space or 2 spaces.
6. Identifies pictured cards to game board. Hold up the pictured cards and ask the student to show you where the gingerbread man is, where the gumdrops are, etc.
7. Moves man to pictured spaces. Require the student to specifically put his man/lady on the pictured space indicated on the path. Once the student has played the entire game a few times, he soon learns that a pictured card either allows him to move up or makes him move back. Without any printed instructions, this game familiarizes the student with gaining territory or losing it.
8. Plays an entire game with the teacher.
9. Plays game with teacher and another student.
10. Plays game with others.

Adaptions

1. The path to be followed is in such an indirect route that many students had problems in going forward. Arrows were put on the yellow spaces to indicate to the student which direction he should move his man. This didn't work. Using moving pieces that showed a walking movement was successful. When the students come to a curve on the path, remind them to turn their man around. Try to make sure that the extended foot on the man or lady is pointed in the right direction for the next play.
2. Refer to the path as a "sidewalk" with the students. The students are probably better familiarized with what a sidewalk is as opposed to what a path is. "Keep your man on the sidewalk."
3. Cheating occurred with this game. (a) After the students had learned to move to the space indicated on the cards, there wasn't any reason to look at their drawn card. The students found that by laying their cards face down, they could move to whatever space they wanted. Enforce the rule: all cards up. (b) Moving two red squares instead of one was another popular form of cheating. This trick was managed whenever lack of supervision permitted it. After sessions of two to four students playing with each other, they began to watch each other's moves. Cheating became embarrassing when their opponents pointed it out.
4. Remember to make the finish of the game very obvious. Rule—require students to land on the last space to win.

Note: From *Table Games for Institutionalized Severely Retarded Adolescents* by C. Rankin, P. Bates, D. Baldwin, T. Kelly, and S. Hannah. Lincoln, Ill.: Lincoln Developmental Center, 1975. Copyright 1975 by the Lincoln Developmental Center. Reprinted by permission.

Table 3

Task Analysis of Checkers

Materials: Commercial Game—Checkers

Step 1:	*S* identifies black from red.	Cue_1: "Point to the black." Cue_2: "Point to the red."
Step 2:	*S* identifies 1 color as being his man.	Cue: "Point to your man."
Step 3:	*S* places pieces correctly in preparation for game.	Cue: "Show me how you set your side of the board."
Step 4a:	*S* moves piece diagonally.	Cue: "Show me how you move your man."
4b:	*S* moves piece on same color.	
4c:	*S* moves piece forward.	
Step 5:	*S* single jumps opposition.	Cue: "Show me how you jump the other man."
Step 6:	*S* takes the other man after jumping him.	Cue: "Show me what you do when you jump the other man."
Step 7:	*S* avoids being jumped.	Cue: "Show me what happens if you get jumped."
Step 8:	*S* double jumps opposition.	Cue: "Show me how you jump 2 men."
Step 9:	*S* takes both men after jumping them.	Cue: "Show me what you do when you jump 2 men."
Step 10:	*S* moves his piece to other side of board to receive king.	Cue: "Show me what happens when you get to the other side of the board."
Step 11:	*S* crowns opposition by placing checker on top of opposition checker when opposition reaches other side of board.	Cue: "Show me what happens when the other man gets to the other side of the board."
Step 12:	*S* identifies physical difference between king and single checkers.	Cue: "Point to the king."
Step 13:	*S* moves king in forward and backward direction.	Cue: "Show me how the king moves."
Step 14:	*S* plays game with no procedural mistakes.	Cue: "Let's play checkers."

Note: From *Helping the Mentally Retarded Acquire Play Skills: A Behavioral Approach* by P. Wehman. Springfield, Ill.: Charles C Thomas, 1976. Copyright 1976 by Charles C Thomas. Reprinted by permission.

recreation sessions if students play with the same material for long periods of time.

Of course, these techniques are best used in conjunction and should not be considered as being comprehensive. An attempt has been made here to delineate techniques which are relevant to ameliorating the play problems of the young handicapped child. What is required is specific assessment of which

The early years are critical years.

antecedent conditions and types of reinforcing conditions are best with children who exhibit a certain level of play skill, learning and behavior characteristics.

In a study of three severely developmentally disabled individuals (Wehman, 1976b), the comparative effects of toy proximity, modeling, and instructions plus modeling on independent play actions were evaluated. Results indicated that toy proximity and modeling were functionally related to substantial increases in responding over an initially low baseline level. Instructions plus modeling by adult trainers led to almost 90% physical action on objects. No physical assistance was given.

Transfer of Training and Response Maintenance Strategies

Several strategies are available in generalizing and maintaining results of leisure time programs (Wehman, Abramson, & Norman, 1977). One study which demonstrates how trainer instruction can be gradually faded was performed by Hopper and Wambold (in press). In this program, four profoundly retarded children were trained to increase independent play actions and decrease inappropriate self-abusive behaviors. The study was performed in a school classroom by three practicum students under the teacher's supervision.

Once successful increases were gained in appropriate play actions, the number of trainers was gradually reduced from three to two to one, and finally no trainers were present. At this time, the children were still able to maintain independent play skills.

Fading in peers is another method of programming generalization and this has been demonstrated in the development of ball rolling skills in severely retarded children (Whitman, Mercurio, & Caponigri, 1970). Another strategy which has not been attempted, but which might also be effective would be that of fading in higher-functioning peers who already have a well-developed play repertoire. These peers might then serve as multiple models for generalization.

One technique which has not been documented and that might also prove worthwhile in developing maintenance of leisure time skills would be gradually decreasing the amount of time which a trainer spends with students. Presumably, continual supervision and assistance would be required initially when training social play to a pair of children. As the children become more spontaneous and acquire a greater number of appropriate play skills, the trainer can systematically reduce the training time and involvement.

Situation-specific learning is a common problem with the developmentally disabled and refers to the limited ability to display newly acquired behaviors in settings other than the original training environment. One way of overcoming this deficit is in practicing play skills in different places such as the home, the playground, and the school. Play materials, games, and toys should become cues for play to occur, not different types of buildings and environments.

Another method of achieving play skills across environments is through continued involvement of parents, relatives, and siblings. By including the child's family in leisure time training, greater maintenance and generalization may be attained. This may also have positive effects on the way other family members view the handicapped child.

Play skills which are performed only in gym class, in the classroom, or on Saturday morning have limited value. There must be ample opportunity for the child to participate in play activities in community facilities such as parks, camps, clubs, and other local recreation centers. The development of play skills should be community based with a major direction toward integration with nonhandicapped individuals. The frequent use of segregated recreation settings in the community should be discouraged and planned integration experiences targeted in selected recreational skills.

Future Research in Recreational Programming

A number of research topics in play skill development for the developmentally disabled have been briefly alluded to in this chapter. Therefore, in this final section a list of research ideas is presented which addresses certain critical issues in recreation programming for the young handicapped child. Specifically, these include:

1. What are the specific effects which different play activities have on behavior and cognitive development of the developmentally disabled? Can intensive play activities facilitate the acceleration of developmentally stagnant behavior in the severely delayed child?

2. Can research findings involving the exploratory activity and social behavior of nonretarded developmentally young children and infants be generalized for use with severely delayed children with similar mental ages?
3. What are the toys and play materials which facilitate development of recreation skills and social behavior of the preschool handicapped child?
4. What are the games and activities which can be used to facilitate the development of searching skills, visual tracking, and other sensorimotor skills?
5. What methods can be used to encourage spontaneous free play, that is, play with minimal intervention?
6. What are the different table games and structured activities which are within the skill level of most developmentally disabled children? Also, what are the specific teacher characteristics which allow for "fun" to enter into task analysis based recreation training?
7. What are the optimal behavioral and learning characteristics in peer models which are potent reinforcers in play sessions?

Summary

The primary purpose of this chapter has been to provide a systematic approach to developing play programs and recreational skills for young handicapped children. An assessment skill hierarchy was delineated and a number of specific behavioral techniques were discussed in the context of recreational programming. A number of generalization and response maintenance strategies were also identified. Finally, several areas for future research in recreation with the preschool severely and profoundly handicapped were suggested.

REFERENCES

Abramson, M. Helping the multihandicapped retarded learn to play. In P. Wehman (Ed.), *Helping the mentally retarded acquire play skills: A behavioral approach.* Springfield, Ill.: Charles C Thomas, 1977.

Anderson, G., Hodson, R., & Jones, W. *Instructional programming for the handicapped student.* Springfield, Ill.: Charles C Thomas, 1974.

Ayllon, T., & Azrin, N. H. Reinforcer sampling: A technique for increasing the behavior of mental patients. *Journal of Applied Behavior Analysis,* 1968, **1**, 13–20.

Baer, D., Peterson, R., & Sherman, J. The development of imitation by reinforcing behavioral similarity to a model. *Journal of Experimental Analysis of Behavior,* 1967, **10**, 405–416.

Bandura, A. *Principles of behavior modification.* New York: Holt, Rinehart & Winston, 1969.

Barnes, K. Preschool play norms: A replication. *Developmental Psychology,* 1971, **5**, 99–103.

Bates, P., & Rankin, C. *Teaching severely retarded adolescents to play Candyland.* Unpublished paper, Lincoln State School, Lincoln, Ill. 1975.

Benoit, E. P. The play problem of retarded children. *American Journal of Mental Deficiency,* 1955, **60,** 41–55.

Berkson, G., & Davenport, R. K. Stereotyped movements of mental defectives: I. initial survey. *American Journal of Mental Deficiency,* 1962, **66,** 849–852.

Bijou, S. W. *Symposium: Functional analysis of complex behavior.* Paper presented at the Society for Research in Child Development, Denver, April 1975.

Bradtke, L., Rosenblatt, W., & Kirkpatrick, K. Intensive play—a technique for building affective behaviors in profoundly mentally retarded children. *Education and Training of the Mentally Retarded,* 1972, **7,** 8–13.

Brown, L., Bellamy, T., and Sontag, E. *The development and implementation of a public school prevocational training program for trainable retarded and severely emotionally disturbed children.* Madison, Wis.: Madison Public Schools, 1971.

Brown, L., Williams, W., & Crowner, T. *A collection of papers and programs related to public school services for severely handicapped students.* Madison, Wis.: Madison Public Schools, 1974.

Cataldo, M., & Risley, T. Infant day care. In R. Ulrich, T. Stachnik, & R. Mabry (Eds.), *Control of human behavior.* Glenview, Ill.: Scott, Foresman & Co., 1974.

Cleland, C., Swartz, J., & Chasey, W. The role of play games and toys in recreation programming for the moderately and profoundly retarded. *Therapeutic Recreation Journal,* Fourth Quarter, 1970, 152–155.

Cooke, T. P., & Apolloni, T. The development of positive social-emotional behaviors: A study of training and generalization effects, *Journal of Applied Behavior Analysis,* 1976, **9,** 65–78.

Council for Exceptional Children and American Association for Health and Physical Education. *Recreation and physical activity for the mentally retarded.* Washington, D.C., 1966.

Domnie, M. *Teaching severely handicapped children to enact an imaginary event.* Unpublished manuscript, Madison, Wis.: Madison Public Schools, 1974.

Ellis, M. J. *Why people play.* Englewood Cliffs, N.J.: Prentice-Hall, 1973.

Flavell, J. Reduction of stereotypes by reinforcement of toy play. *Mental Retardation,* 1973, **11,** 21–23.

Gesell, A. *The first five years of life.* New York: Harper, 1940.

Hillman, W. A. Therapeutic recreation with the profoundly retarded. *Recreation for the Ill and Handicapped,* 1966.

Hopper, C., & Wambold, C. Improving the independent play of severely mentally retarded children. *Education and Training of the Mentally Retarded,* in press.

Hutt, C. Exploration and play in children. *Symposium of the Zoological Society of London,* 1966, **18,** 61–81.

Hutt, C. Specific and diversive exploration. In H. W. Reese & L. P. Lauton (Eds.), *Advances in child development and behavior.* New York: Academic Press, 1970.

Kazdin, A. E., & Erickson, B. Developing responsiveness to instructions in severely and profoundly retarded residents. *Journal of Behavior Therapy and Experimental Psychiatry,* 1975, **6,** 17–21.

Kazdin, A. E., Silverman, N., & Sittler, J. The use of prompts to enhance vicarious effects of nonverbal approval. *Journal of Applied Behavior Analysis,* 1975, **8,** 279–286.

Knapczyk, D. Task analytic assessment of severe learning problems. *Education and Training of the Mentally Retarded,* 1975, **10,** 74–77.

Knapczyk, D., & Peterson, N. *Social play interaction of retarded children in an integrated classroom environment.* Unpublished paper, Developmental Training Center, University of Indiana, Bloomington, 1975.

Knapczyk, D., & Yoppi, N. Development of cooperative and competitive play responses in developmentally disabled children. *American Journal of Mental Deficiency,* 1975, **80**, 245–255.

Koegel, R., Firestone, P., Kramme, K., & Dunlop, G. Increasing spontaneous play by suppressing self-stimulation in autistic children. *Journal of Applied Behavior Analysis,* 1974, **7**, 521–528.

Leland H., Walker, D., & Taboada, A. Group play therapy with a group of post-nursery male retardates. *American Journal of Mental Deficiency,* 1959, **63**, 848–851.

Luckey, R., & Shapiro, I. Recreation: An essential aspect of habilitative programming. *Mental Retardation,* 1974, **12**, 33–35.

McCall, R. Exploratory manipulation and play in the human infant. *Monograph of the Society for Research in Child Development.* Chicago: University of Chicago Press, 1974.

Mehlman, B. Group play therapy with mentally retarded children. *Journal of Abnormal and Social Psychology,* 1953, **48**, 53–60.

Moore, N. V., Evertson, C. M., & Brophy, J. Solitary play: Some functional reconsiderations. *Developmental Psychology,* 1974, **10**, 830–834.

Morris, R., & Dolker, M. Developing cooperative play in socially withdrawn retarded children. *Mental Retardation,* 1974, **12**, 24–27.

Morrison, B., & Newcomer, T. Effects of directive vs. nondirective play therapy with institutionalized retarded children. *American Journal of Mental Deficiency,* 1975, **79**, 666–669.

Nelson, R., Gibson, R., & Cutting, D. Videotaped modeling: The development of three appropriate social responses in a mildly retarded child. *Mental Retardation,* 1973, **11**, 24–27.

Nesbitt, J., Neal, L., & Hillman, W. Recreation for exceptional children and youth. *Focus on Exceptional Children,* 1974, **6**(3), 1–12.

Neulinger, J. *The psychology of leisure.* Springfield, Ill.: Charles C Thomas, 1974.

Newcomer, B., & Morrison, T. Play therapy with institutionalized mentally retarded children. *American Journal of Mental Deficiency,* 1974, **78**, 727–733.

Nunnally, J. C., & Lemond, L. C. Exploratory behavior and human development. In H. W. Reese (Ed.), *Advances in child development and behavior,* Vol. 8, New York: Academic Press, 1973.

Paloutzian, R., Hasazi, J., Streifel, J., & Edgar, C. Promotion of positive social interaction in severely retarded young children. *American Journal of Mental Deficiency,* 1971, **75**, 519–524.

Parten, M. Social play among preschool children. *Journal of Abnormal Psychology,* 1932, **28**, 136–147.

Peterson, R., & McIntosh, E. Teaching tricycle riding. *Mental Retardation,* 1973, **11**, 32–34.

Piaget, J. *Play, dreams and imitation in childhood.* New York: W. W. Norton, 1962.

Quilitch, H. R., & Risley, T. The effects of play materials on social play. *Journal of Applied Behavior Analysis,* 1973, **6**, 573–578.

Rankin, C., Bates, P., Baldwin, D., Kelly, T., & Hannah, S. *Table games for institutionalized severely retarded adolescents.* Lincoln, Ill.: Lincoln Developmental Center, 1975.

Rubin, K., Maioni, T., & Hornung, M. Free play behaviors in middle and lower class preschoolers: Parten and Piaget revisited. *Child Development,* 1976, **47**, 414–419.

Strain, P. S. Increasing social play of severely retarded preschoolers through sociodramatic activities. *Mental Retardation,* 1975, **13**, 7–9.

Strain, P. S., Cooke, T., & Apolloni, T. *Teaching exceptional children: Assessment and modification of social behavior.* New York: Academic Press, 1976.

Thiagarajan, S. Designing instructional games for handicapped learners. *Focus on Exceptional Children,* 1976, 7(9), 1–11.

Tilton, J., & Ottinger, D. Comparison of toy play behavior of autistic, retarded, and normal children. *Psychological Reports,* 1964, **15,** 967–975.

Twardosz, S., Cataldo, M., & Risley, T. An open environment design for infant and toddler day care. *Journal of Applied Behavior Analysis,* 1974, **7,** 529–546.

Webb, R. Sensory-motor training of the profoundly retarded. *American Journal of Mental Deficiency,* 1969, **14**(2), 283–295.

Wehman, P. Establishing play behaviors in mentally retarded youth. *Rehabilitation Literature,* 1975, **36,** 238–246.

Wehman, P. Selection of play materials for the severely handicapped: A continuing dilemma. *Education and Training of the Mentally Retarded,* 1976, **11,** 46–51. (a)

Wehman, P. *The role of different environmental conditions on leisure time activity of the severely developmentally disabled.* Unpublished doctoral dissertation. University of Wisconsin-Madison, 1976. (b)

Wehman, P. Imitation as a facilitator of treatment with the mentally retarded. *Rehabilitation Literature,* 1976, **37,** 41–48.

Wehman, P. *Helping the mentally retarded acquire play skills: A behavioral approach.* Springfield, Ill.: Charles C Thomas, 1977.

Wehman, P. Recreation programs with the mentally retarded: A review of the research: Part I. *Journal of Leisurability,* 1977, **4**(1), 23–30. (a)

Wehman, P. Recreation programs with the mentally retarded: a review of the research: Part II. *Journal of Leisurability,* 1977, **4**(2), 18–25. (b)

Wehman, P. Direct training of reading skills. *Academic Therapy,* 1977, **12**(4), 463–470. (c)

Wehman, P. Research on leisure time and the severely developmentally disabled. *Rehabilitation Literature,* 1977, **38**(4), 98–105. (d)

Wehman, P., & Abramson, M. Three theoretical approaches to play: Applications for exceptional children. *American Journal of Occupational Therapy,* 1976, **10,** 551–559.

Wehman, P., Abramson, M., & Norman, C. Transfer of training in behavior modification programs: An evaluative review. *Journal of Special Education,* 1977, **11**(2), 217–231.

Wehman, P., Karan, O. C., & Rettie, C. Developing independent play in three severely retarded women. *Psychological Reports,* 1976, **39,** 995–998.

Wehman, P., Renzaglia, A., Schutz, R., Gray, J., James, S., & Karan, O. C. Training leisure time skills in the severely and profoundly handicapped: Three recreational programs. In O. C. Karan, P. Wehman, A. Renzaglia, & R. Schutz (Eds.), *Habilitation practices with the severely developmentally disabled.* Madison, Wis.: University of Wisconsin, Research and Training Center in Mental Retardation, 1976.

Weisler, A., & McCall, R. Exploration and play: Resumé and redirection. *American Psychologist,* 1976, **31**(7), 492–508.

Wenar, C. *Personality development.* Columbus, Ohio: Charles E. Merrill Publishing Co., 1971.

Whaley, D., & Tough, J. Treatment of a self-injuring mongoloid with shock-induced suppression and avoidance. *Michigan Mental Health Bulletin,* 1968, **4,** 18–28.

Whitman, T. L., Mercurio, V., & Caponigri, J. Development of social responses in the severely retarded children. *Journal of Applied Behavior Analysis,* 1970, **3,** 133–138.

Williams, W. Procedures of task analysis as related to developing instructional programs for the severely handicapped. In L. Brown, T. Crowner, W. Williams, & R. York (Eds.), *Madison's alternative for zero exclusion: A book of readings.* Madison, Wis.: Madison Public Schools, 1975.

Williams, W., Pumpian, I., McDaniel, J., Hamre-Nietupski, S., & Wheeler, J. Social interaction. In L. Brown, T. Crowner, W. Williams, & R. York (Eds.), *Madison's alternative for zero exclusion: A book of readings.* Madison, Wis.: Madison Public Schools, 1975.

Zine, B., Ferolo, M., Hass, S., & Hass, W. Free play responses of profoundly retarded children to pre-recorded broadcast of children's songs. *Journal of Developmental Disabilities,* 1975, **1,** 17–22.

11

Working with the Parents

This chapter focuses on the special needs of the handicapped child's family. Its purpose is to examine the factors which contribute to effectiveness in the parent-professional partnership. The suggestions presented here are directed to both the professional and paraprofessional. Although for the sake of brevity the statements generally refer to the professional, they apply equally well to both in most cases. Indeed, research has found that programs developed by a professional staff can be delivered by a paraprofessional staff under supervision without any loss of effectiveness (Karnes & Teska, 1975).

Stages of Parental Reaction

To work effectively with the parents of young handicapped children, the professional and paraprofessional must understand the emotional climate in the home. Because parental attitudes largely determine the home atmosphere, professionals need to be aware of what happens to parents when they learn that their child is handicapped and how they adjust to this fact over time.

Numerous writers have discussed the stages of parental reaction to the realization that a serious problem exists in their child's development. The following

---

This chapter was developed with the help of material from *George A. Giacobbe, Bonnie S. Carlton, Elsie H. Blanton, Anita S. Fallen,* and *Bernadine S. Clark.*

Parents often need support and encouragement as they struggle to cope with the problems and frustrations of raising a handicapped child.

model is a synthesis of many complementary points of view including those of Baroff (1974), Gardner (1973), Keith (1973), Bryant (1971), Kessler (1966), and the American Medical Association (1965).

I. Acute Initial Reactions
  1. Shock
  2. Denial and disbelief
  3. Anger
  4. Bitterness and shame
  5. Inappropriate guilt
  6. Blame

II. Chronic Adaptive Reactions
  1. Masochistic reaction
  2. Overprotection
  3. Withdrawal
  4. Unhealthy parent-child relationship
    a. Rejection
    b. Compensation
  5. Doctor shopping
    a. Searching for a cause
    b. Searching for a cure

III. Mature Adaptations
   1. Behavior organized and directed toward maximizing the child's potential
   2. Healthy and productive motivation toward welfare of family
   3. Cooperative attitudes and interactions with others

Parental reactions may not occur precisely in this order, and they may not occur separately. Several of the stages may be worked through simultaneously. In many cases a stage that appeared to have been completed may later require a time of reworking with or without professional help.

The acute reactions are attempts to adapt to a tragic fact and are in most cases temporary. Most people would agree with Keesler's (1966) statement that it is impossible for parents to accept the diagnosis of a handicapping condition without reacting strongly. Reactions will vary according to personalities, but it is unrealistic to expect passive acceptance. It is equally unrealistic to expect parental reactions to conform to a time table. According to Olshansky (1962) all reactions may be intertwined with chronic sorrow.

Chronic adaptive reactions may be prolongations of the acute reaction phase, or they may develop at a later time. These reactions are viewed as more serious than the initial reactions of shock and disbelief and may persist for years, even a lifetime. Acute reactions may be resolved without treatment while chronic adaptive reactions may become deep-seated and require psychotherapy.

Mature adaptations are those actions which enable the parents to direct their concerns to each other and to the welfare of the whole family. In some cases this stage is never fully attained.

Each of the different reaction stages is described briefly here.

Acute Initial Reactions

Shock. Parents are particularly vulnerable to reactions of shock when the handicap is obvious at birth. If the parents have looked forward to the new baby with anticipation, their emotional reaction is completely opposed to what had been planned. Even if the child's birth had not been anticipated with joy, an abnormal baby conjures up a variety of different emotions. Temporarily, at least, the impaired infant is a threat to the parents' self-esteem no matter how they anticipated its arrival.

It is generally agreed by parents of handicapped children that there is no best time to learn that the child is impaired. Yet, their views on how the news should be handled are confusing. In a famous study (Kramm, 1963) of 100 parents with handicapped offspring, 84 expressed a clear opinion about the way they had learned the child was handicapped. Of those who commented favorably, one-third appreciated the doctor's soft, evasive manner, two-thirds liked his blunt, harsh treatment. Of those who disapproved, one-third complained about his soft, evasive treatment, while two-thirds complained about his blunt, harsh treatment.

Gradual Awareness. For many parents, the realization that their child is handicapped comes gradually. For example, delayed speech may, at first, cause little concern to the parents, and they may become aware of the problem only as the child's development continues to lag. However, many mothers who learned of a handicapping condition over time admitted to earlier suspicions that something was wrong with the young child.

Denial and Disbelief. A common parental reaction to the diagnosis of a handicap is to disbelieve that the problem exists. The family may doubt the physician's competence and begin consulting one expert and then another. Those who confirm the original diagnosis are frequently rejected. Underlying this initial reaction is a desperate hope that the diagnosis is wrong. However, the consequences to the child may be severe. Prolonged delay in accepting the diagnosis may deprive the child of treatment and intervention at critical times. On the other hand, Olshansky (1962) has expressed the view that delay in identification for two years allows the child to find his place in the family.

Anger. Anger is a normal reaction in the early stages of acceptance, according to Gardner (1973). It stems from feelings of helplessness and frustration toward a child with special needs. It may color all interpersonal relationships or be directed toward specific persons such as the physician or other professionals concerned with the child's care. The anger reaction is abnormal, however, when it is prolonged and if it replaces positive action. It may never disappear completely, but it can be directed into useful channels, such as working within organizations to benefit other children with similar handicaps. Anger, for some parents, is totally justified. They have been frustrated by professionals who have advised them from a viewpoint of ignorance or who have been less than honest in other ways. Anger also results from the proneness of professionals to refer the child unnecessarily, adding to the parents' already overwhelming financial burden.

Bitterness and Shame. Bitterness stems from sheer disappointment over the birth of an impaired child and from the prospect of limitations his birth places on the parent. Shame is based on anticipated disapproval from others, particularly from persons important to the child's parents. Because they believe the child will be judged as inferior, the parents feel ashamed of what they think will be perceived as poor performance in reproduction.

Inappropriate Guilt. Inappropriate guilt is a common reaction after the parents learn that their child is handicapped. In many cases, according to Gardner (1973), it takes the form of preoccupation with parental transgressions or mistakes that the parents believe may have caused the problem. Guilt of this sort is a futile attempt to control an uncontrollable situation. The parent, by attributing the cause to herself, puts into her own hands the power to control what is otherwise beyond her control. Such guilt is often used by human beings as a defense mechanism against anxiety over calamities.

Blame. The blame reaction seeks to place responsibility on others and cushions the feelings of helplessness that are common in parents of young children with special needs. Recipients of blame reactions are frequently professionals

—doctors, teachers, or therapists. This parental attitude can affect the child and undermine his acceptance of professionals and their services.

Chronic Adaptive Reactions

Masochistic Reaction. The person who reacts as a masochist, according to Gardner (1973), measures the depth of her love by the pain she will suffer for the handicapped child. The child may be used by his parents to further their masochistic gratification. The more severely handicapped the child is, the more gratification his condition provides. Such parents inhibit efforts to help the child and are themselves unable to follow through on recommendations to help him. They may talk about their efforts to help and even act as though they are trying.

Masochism may be used against the child. Through subtle expressions or overt actions, the parents may make him aware of how much trouble he is and how much pain he has caused. In this way, the child is made to feel guilty and ashamed of himself for the burden he has caused.

Overprotection. Gardner sees overprotection as an initial reaction as well as chronic, indicating that prolonged overprotection must be viewed as serious. This reaction is characterized by the parent's denying the child opportunities to play with other children. The child is not allowed to run for fear that he will fall; the weather is too hot, too cold, too wet, or too dry for the child to play outside. By denying the child the right to be a child, the parent further handicaps him by keeping him dependent. Bryant (1971) has indicated that the overprotected child is unlikely to benefit from programs designed to help him.

Withdrawal. Many parents of young handicapped children speak of their sense of isolation. On the other hand, there is evidence that some parents use the child's condition as an excuse to terminate relationships outside the home and to withhold expressions of affection for other members of the family. Temporary withdrawal as an expression of grief is natural; its intensity and the span of time it covers determine the critical nature of this reaction.

Rejection and Compensation. The behavior of the mother who rejects her impaired child is characterized as indifferent, careless, selfish, or cruel. Such behavior adversely influences the child's adjustment. Bryant (1971) states that the rejecting mother is easily identified by professionals. "She does not keep appointments and generally fails to follow through on recommendations" (p. 41).

A more subtle parent-child relationship involves the parent's compensation for her true feelings toward the child. This reaction may be conscious, unconscious, or both. In truth, the parent rejects the child but knows that the child needs to be accepted; therefore, the parent attempts to act out accepting behaviors. Bryant prepared the following table to demonstrate how compensation emerges from a combination of acceptance and rejection behaviors (p. 42). The compensating attitudes mirror both acceptance and rejection which are shown in behavior which is harmful to the child's emotional stability.

Table 1

Compensation from Acceptance and Rejection

Acceptance		Rejection		Compensation
love	+	indifference	=	possessiveness
empathy	+	selfishness	=	sympathy
forgiveness	+	fault finding	=	overpermissiveness
gentleness	+	cruelty	=	smothering
caution	+	carelessness	=	suspicion
activity	+	fear	=	withdrawal
involvement	+	resentment of others	=	hostility towards others
anticipation	+	disillusionment	=	resentment and distrust

Note: From "Parent-Child Relationships: Their Effect on Rehabilitation" by J. Bryant, *Journal of Learning Disabilities*, 1971, 4 (6), 42. Copyright 1971 by Professional Press. Reprinted by special permission of Professional Press, Inc.

The mother who is compensating for her child's disability is easily recognized. She is overly concerned about the child's progress, and suspicious about the program's quality and the professionals' qualifications. She appears to be physically and emotionally exhausted but continues to push for further accomplishment before the day's end.

Doctor Shopping. Doctor shopping initially occurs during the acute reaction stage while the parents are working through the denial of the original diagnosis. At that time the search is for a doctor who will say that the earlier diagnosis was erroneous. Once the diagnosis is accepted, doctor shopping may continue in search of a cure. As the parents' frustrations increase, they become vulnerable "to every quack and charlatan who offers a miraculous cure" (Gardner, 1973, p. 45). After a series of disillusions, it is not unusual for the parents to develop attitudes of bitterness and distrust toward even the most competent of doctors. Since the child's reactions to the professional so often mirror those of his parents, cycles of extreme optimism and subsequent disillusion make it extremely difficult for a working relationship to be established between the professional and the child.

Mature Adaptations

The third stage, mature adaptations, is one of adjustment. It should not be viewed as a time that is free of difficulties or even crisis periods, but rather as a level of adjustment which allows the parents to have positive attitudes towards themselves, accept the child, and show love for him. "The most obvious thing about this successful relationship is that the child is treated as a child, not a handicapped child" (Bryant, 1971, p. 41). These accomplishments with the special needs child occur concomitant to equal treatment for each child in the family. When the parents recognize the value of their own experiences and can use them in efforts which benefit children with similar problems, they have, at least in part, reached this stage of reaction. The swiftness with which this can occur is dependent in some measure upon the availability, knowledge, and sensitivity of professionals concerned with the care of the child and his family (Ditkoff, 1975).

Crisis Periods

Throughout the life of the impaired individual, certain events are particularly upsetting to his parents. Two of these crisis periods occur during the period of early childhood. The first happens when the parents first learn about or suspect a handicap. Baroff (1974) has emphasized the need for emotional support during the postdiagnostic period. This takes two forms: (1) activities designed to encourage the infant's development and (2) continued counseling of the parents. While continuous emotional support enables the parents to gradually assimilate what has occurred, the most helpful thing for the parents is to provide some direct services to the child. This includes prescriptive programs in skill areas designed to move the child to a particular milestone. This approach is not only beneficial to the child but also provides his family with specific activities on which to focus their attention.

The second crisis period occurs when the child's educational program changes from a home-based one to a center-based or school program. This event carries the same emotional factors as those in any family when a young child enters school. For the parents of a handicapped child, additional concern for the child's age (he may be only 2 or 3) and his limitations can be burdensome. Although the move will provide contact with other children, the mother especially may find life difficult when her handicapped child begins school at such a young age.

It is important that those who work with the child be alerted to potential crisis periods in order to be prepared to help the parents at this time. In times of crisis, parents may be more open to receiving helpful guidance (Keith, 1973). Parents will need long-term support as well. As the child develops, his needs change, and each change places new stress on the parents.

Meeting the Needs of Siblings

The lives of siblings are also affected by the birth of a handicapped child. Some mothers become so engrossed with the care of the disabled child that they have no time for the other children. The results have been similar to maternal deprivation, which can lead to defects in social relationships, in perception of reality, in cognitive development, and in conscience (Kessler, 1966). On the other hand, some families have been brought closer together by the handicapped child. The siblings loved the impaired child, petted him, and took pride in his accomplishments. The difference in the two extremes seems to depend on the integrity of the family before the handicapped child is born and the parents' abilities to manage during stressful events. The availability of knowledgeable and caring professionals has contributed to the family's ability to cope under stress (Kramm, 1963).

In a family brought closer together by the birth of a handicapped child, the siblings often take pride in the child's accomplishments.

Although he feels that most normal brothers and sisters have positive attitudes toward the handicapped child, Baroff (1974) has listed some of the problems resulting from their situation. Included are fear of embarrassment (loss of self-esteem) by the behavior of the disabled child, his accidental destructiveness and his excessive demands for attention. Siblings are also concerned with what their responsibilities will be when the parents can no longer take care of the impaired child. Three of the problems apply equally well to sibling problems with normal preschool children.

Problems identified by Murphy, Pueschel, Duffy, and Brady (1976) seem to be those peculiar to the siblings of handicapped children. The problems are (1) awareness, without understanding, of parental distress and preoccupation with the handicapped child; (2) lack of emotional support from the parents; (3) feelings of neglect and, at times, feelings of guilt fed by negative feelings toward the child; (4) embarrassment resulting from perceived negative attitudes toward children with handicaps similar to their sibling; (5) concern among older siblings about their vulnerability to bearing a handicapped child; and (6) reluctance or inability to talk to parents about the problem and reluctance or inability of the parents to answer questions concerning the child's condition.

Wolfensberger (1967) found no strong evidence that siblings of handicapped children are either better or worse adjusted than other children. Believing that the adjustment of children mirrors the adjustment of their parents, he suggested that efforts to support the parents will also benefit the siblings of an impaired child. A different viewpoint was expressed by Murphy, Pueschel,

Duffy, and Brady (1976). Recognizing that families are individual, they stated that "any program which seeks to help the handicapped child must also recognize the needs of all family members and take steps to meet them" (p. 23). Their suggestions, emerging from a program designed to be of assistance to all members of the family, follow:

1. At the time of the initial visit, the professionals should inquire about the adjustment of the other children. This calls attention to a possible need and encourages the parents to discuss any worries concerning the rest of the family.
2. Professionals should help the parents devise ways of talking and planning with their other children.
3. Parents should be encouraged to bring their other children with them to clinics or other programs in which the child is involved.
4. Saturday appointments will provide an opportunity for the whole family to attend the clinic or center together.
5. When the children come with their parents, they should be given a tour of the facilities, slide shows that explain their sibling's problem, and demonstrations of ways they can provide learning experiences for the handicapped child. At this time, with the help of the parents, the siblings may be assigned management functions in the home.

The Chapel Hill Training Outreach Project (Cansler & Martin, undated) emphasizes the sibling as an important person in his own right; his role as a sibling of a handicapped child is only one of his roles in life. To provide for assistance to siblings, this project provides a variety of activities including play days, workshops, games, movies, and other opportunities to meet and know other siblings of handicapped children.

Not all young handicapped children will live at home. Bullington, Sexton, and White (1976) have described a program for families of multihandicapped children in a residential institution. The program has four objectives which apply to all the family members: (1) to improve their knowledge and understanding of an institutionalized child; (2) to increase their acceptance of the child; (3) to increase family contacts with the child at the institution and to increase the number and length of home visits; and (4) to help family members learn the skills needed to teach and to communicate with the child or to improve existing skills.

In addition to family visits to the institution, support is provided through mail, phone calls, and a bimonthly newsletter. The authors have found that the participating families are a significantly helpful and unique resource to other families with handicapped children.

Parent Reaction to Professionals

Parents and professionals have not always worked harmoniously together, according to Roos (1977). In spite of recent parent alliance with professional organizations, successful efforts to secure legislation for the handicapped, and parent education programs across the nation, years of poor relationships left feelings of distrust particularly among the parents. Bitterness toward professionals is not likely to be erased unless professional practices change significantly.

Writing from the viewpoint of the Association for Retarded Citizens, a parent organization created in part because of professional apathy, neglect, and indifference, what Roos has to say should be of interest to each professional working with handicapped children, their parents, and the members of their family. From Roos's article, parents perceive the following types of professional mishandling:

Professional Ignorance. Some professionals in the medical and behavioral sciences have little knowledge of handicapping conditions. Some dispense misinformation. Parents continue to report that they have been told by professionals that the child will outgrow the condition; that there is nothing that can be done for the child; and that institutionalization is the only answer.

Professional Hopelessness. Professionals who view handicapping conditions as hopeless create a self-fulfilling prophecy. Hopeless conditions receive limited services; therefore, treatment and developmental experiences are not provided for the child. The child becomes what the professional predicted he would become.

Referral Ad Infinitum. While parents have been accused of shopping for information they want to hear, professionals have been guilty of referring the child and his family for unnecessary services to avoid facing the parents with the truth about the child's condition. The misuse of time and the added financial burdens have caused bitter resentment.

Veil of Secrecy. Some professionals have withheld information on the grounds that it was too uncomfortable, threatening, or destructive for the parents to hear. Thus, information which could have given direction to treatment has been kept secret.

Deaf Ear Syndrome. Parents' requests and suggestions are often ignored. Roos believes that this practice has contributed heavily to the distrust and resentment of parents towards professionals.

Professional Omniscience. While some professionals admit to their lack of knowledge concerning handicapping conditions, others profess to have greater knowledge than they possess. This type of professional often talks in professional jargon so that little useful information is given to the parent.

Professional Omnipotence. Professional omnipotence refers to the assumption that professionals have the wisdom to make decisions affecting the lives of other people. Even members of multidisciplinary teams have excluded parents from their decision-making sessions. The practice has been to inform parents after conclusions have been reached.

Parents as Patients. Instead of acknowledging the necessity of the grieving process and "allowing much time and space for emotions to run their natural course" (Ditkoff, 1975), professionals have tended to judge all parents of handicapped children as emotionally disturbed and prime candidates for psychotherapy. Instead of providing much needed information and services for the child, time has been spent exploring marital problems and other areas of maladjustment.

Suggested Professional Responses

Part of the problem between parents and professionals has been created by the professional's failure to explain her area of training and experience to the child's parents. Areas of specialty and how each contributes to the young child's development are often not provided to lay people.

Contributing to the problem is the professional's reluctance or inability to define her role. In many cases, this is not a human weakness but a situational problem. The scarcity of professional services in many parts of the nation has put heavy demands on professionals. As additional services have been created, professionals have not always been willing to relinquish roles, and parents have not always been willing to make appropriate changes.

The professional educator and the paraprofessional working with her are concerned with what the child needs to learn (curriculum), how to teach this particular child (instruction), and what devices are needed to teach (materials). These three areas have been discussed in other parts of this text.

The educator's responsibility includes not only the child but his parents and siblings as well. Professional service to them enhances the young child's chances for optimal development. Consequently, the creation of an effective parent-professional partnership must not be left to chance.

In the same article mentioned previously, Roos (1977) recommended procedures which, if implemented, should ameliorate many of the problems described. While his points are discussed here from the educator's viewpoint, there are implications for all other professionals. The following recommendations are designed to foster constructive and cooperative parent-professional relationships.

Parents should be considered as full participating members of the educational team. Recent laws have made the involvement of parents in the decision-making process mandatory. They are a much needed source of information concerning their child to every other member of the team. For this reason their position on the team is unique. The contributions of parents to deliberations should be considered priority information and respected. This is seen as a main prerequisite for successful work with the child.

Blodgett and Warfield (1959) have cautioned that work with parents should be more than conferences and reports. It should be a long-term working relationship that encourages confidence and freedom to discuss problems and plans pertaining to the child and the family.

Disagreements should be expected in any team effort. Conflicts between parents and professionals may arise because of differences in values, disagreements about timing, and other factors relative to programming. The professional needs to determine early what the parent expects the program to accomplish. When parents' goals are not compatible with program goals, professional honesty requires that the differences be explained. Usually such explanations followed by statements of what may be accomplished under what conditions help the parents to adjust their expectations. *Professionals are warned not to promise more than can be accomplished.* To do so would be unfair to the young child, to his parents, and to the professional and program as well.

Parents tend not to be future-oriented as are most professionals. They are more likely to emphasize immediate objectives which may appear relatively unimportant to professionals. As with any good relationship, compromise is the answer. However, the professional needs to remember that it is the parent who must cope with the young child's behavior on a day-to-day basis. Eliminating immediate frustrations may be more important than building toward some distant goal (Roos, 1977).

Professionals should try to accept parents where they are and learn to listen and to encourage full disclosure. The attitudes of teachers toward parents are prime determinants of the success of the program. The teacher must show faith in parents' ability to develop skills in working with their exceptional child. Although the child is the primary concern, parents also want to be understood and do not want to be considered merely a part of the child's environment (Kessler, 1966). Parents of handicapped children have the same strengths and weaknesses and the same desires for themselves and for their children as the general population. However, their reactions to having a handicapped child vary, and approaches for dealing with them should be individualized. Each family reacts according to its personality and situation. Professionals will need

Teacher effectiveness increases when the parents become involved.

to be prepared to work with individuals of many differing attitudes, characteristics, and needs. To look at these parents as a homogenous group simply because they are parents of young handicapped children would prevent effective functioning of the professional.

Roos (1977) said that professional criticism of parents' attitudes and beliefs tends to discourage parents from fully expressing their feelings and to diminish their self-esteem. To relate to the professional, the parent must feel free to speak comfortably, expecting that what is said will be accepted without judgment, disbelief, or scoffing. The professional must also learn to recognize nonverbal messages sent by movement, inflection, facial expression, and other cues. Some parents will not always express their true feelings for fear the professional will be critical. They need to know that it is not unusual nor wrong to sometimes wish to be free of the responsibility of the handicapped child. Sometimes the greatest help to the parent is to have a willing listener.

All parents should feel there is an understanding person who will be available for consulting purposes well after the initial assessment. Parents should have a chance to express their feelings to this team member.

Professionals should share all relevant information with parents. Federal and state legislation supports parents' rights to information concerning their child. Furthermore, it seems a matter of common sense that such information be available to them. Professionals recognize the need for complete information as a working basis for themselves. It is unrealistic to expect parents to arrive at conclusions similar to those of the professional if the parents are working with limited information. Professional responsibility also requires interpreting the information in terms parents will understand. For purposes of decision making, interpretation followed by suggestions of alternative courses of action are not only helpful but give expression to the professional's care and concern for the parents.

Concern is also expressed when professionals encourage parents to keep their own set of records for future reference. Parents need to be encouraged to request copies of the child's report in order to accurately recall what has been explained to them in conference. Speaking to parents on this matter, Gorham (1975) has stated:

> As soon as you know that you have a child with a problem, start a notebook. Make entries of names, addresses, phone numbers, dates of visits, the persons present during the visits, and as much of what was said as you can remember. Record the questions you asked and the answers you received. Record any recommendations made. Make records of phone calls, too; include the dates, the purpose, and the result. It is best to make important requests by letter. Keep a copy for your notebook. Such documentation for every step of your efforts to get your child the services he needs can be the evidence which finally persuades a program director to give him what he needs. Without concise records of whom you spoke to, when you spoke to him, what he promised, and how long you waited between the request and the response, you will be handicapped. No one can be held accountable for conversations or meetings with persons whose names and titles you do not remember, on dates you cannot recall, or about topics which you cannot clearly discuss. (p. 524)

Professionals should have the major responsibility for selecting methodology and technology; parents should have the principal responsibility for selecting goals and objectives. While Roos sees this area as one of potential conflict, differences in objectives and priorities between parents and professionals need not be inevitable. If parents are provided with sufficient information concerning the sequence of development and the concept of prerequisite skills, differences should be minor. For example, the priority objective for the professional may be to teach the child to drink from a cup. If the parent's priority is to teach the child to walk, professional responsibility requires that a reasonable explanation be given as to why the child is ready for cup drinking and not for walking. Otherwise, concentrated efforts should be directed toward helping the child achieve the milestone of walking, or instruction on both skills could proceed simultaneously.

If, however, the parent's priority is to teach the child to drink from a cup without spilling the liquid, an explanation that this is the refinement of the skill the child is learning should help the parent to adjust her priorities.

If a working parent-professional partnership has been firmly established, differences in priorities can be resolved by furnishing the parents with relevant information including descriptions of possible alternatives. Roos (1977) has stated:

> In cases where professional members of the team seriously question the soundness of a parental decision on the basis that it is not in the best interest of the [child], the matter should be referred to an independent committee charged with review of ethical and legal issues. (p. 80)

Since clear communication is vital, professional jargon should be minimized. Parents have a right to know what professionals know about the child, and the professional has an obligation to present the information in a manner that insures understanding (Kroth, 1975). This means avoiding terms like *mental retardation, multihandicapped,* or *hyperactive* which do not describe behavior. Acronyms like ADL (activities of daily living), MBD (minimal brain dysfunction), and TMR (trainable mentally retarded) should not be used in reports or conversations. Reports should be written in everyday language. When technical terminology cannot be avoided, it should be explained in carefully chosen words. After the parent has read a report, the professional should check with the parent to be sure the report's message was clear and that its points were meaningful.

Parents often need support and encouragement as they struggle to cope with the problems and frustrations of raising a handicapped child. The tone of any professional relationship with the parents of a young handicapped child should be one of support and encouragement. It is important that the parent be made to feel that someone is interested in the child and his family and is sufficiently well informed to be of assistance to them.

A much used form of parent-professional interaction is the conference, whether it be on a one-to-one or group basis. Basically there are two types of conferences, but they differ more by stated purpose than by their content. For example, parents and professionals may come together to share information and find that a problem exists which needs their mutual attention. Likewise, a conference may be called by either for the purpose of resolving a problem only to find that it requires a sharing of information (Kroth, 1975). Basic considerations apply to both situations. Because the quality of parent-professional interactions is critical to the success of the handicapped child and because the conference is a primary vehicle for such interaction, its form and content should be given much thought and attention.

Basic Considerations for Parent Conferences

In all contacts with the parents, educators must be careful not to lecture. They must respect parents as knowledgeable persons about their child and encourage them to share their opinions. Several procedures are recommended. It is always best to start by giving the more positive aspects of the child's performance. His more outstanding strengths and potentials should be outlined clearly and concisely. Many parents seem to be amazed that anyone could find anything good about their child. After outlining the positive aspects of the child's performance, the educator can then point out the problem areas that must be discussed. If this procedure is followed, the parents' anxiety will be relieved to some degree, and they will begin to perceive the educator as a warm, concerned, truly interested, and helpful person. Parents must have a positive attitude toward the teacher if they are to receive the information they need. It is the educator's responsibility to enhance this relationship in every way possible.

Once the parents' anxiety is at a reasonable level, or reasonable attempts have been made to bring anxiety to this level, it is often helpful to say something like, "I'm going to tell you some things that we have observed about Johnny, but first, I would like for you to tell me what you think you're going to hear." This procedure often gets the parents involved very quickly in a discussion. It focuses the discussion immediately upon the child, and it gives the educator an opportunity to learn some of the parents' expectations, attitudes, feelings, and fears about the child.

Whether the parents say mostly negative or mostly positive things is of great importance. The child who is reared in a family that expects little of him, that is constantly critical and seldom praising, brings these attitudes to the school and to his relationship with the teacher. The educator should always be careful to tell the parents that she is going to give them information after the parents have first speculated as to what they will hear.

When parents come up with mostly positive statements about their child, and accurately identify some of the problem areas that the teacher, too, has experienced, the teacher is then in a position to praise the parents for their knowledge of the child, their interest in him, and their attention to his functioning. In so doing, the teacher presents herself as a supporter and ally to the parents. When the parents come up with predominantly negative remarks, the educator may suggest ways in which they might take a more positive attitude toward their child and might be of more help and support to him. If the problem cannot be handled in a single conference, or in a series of conferences, the teacher may suggest consulting with mental health specialists.

Communications to the parents regarding the child's behaviors should deal with actual, observed behavior, not with subjective interpretations of these behaviors. It is not sufficient to note that the child "misbehaves." In what ways does he misbehave? With whom does he misbehave? In relation to what circumstances, events, and situations does he misbehave? The greater the specificity in describing the behaviors and the circumstances, the greater the possibility that the parents and the educator will be able to discover why the behaviors are occurring and to provide some possible interventions to modify these undesirable behaviors.

Before scheduling a conference, the teacher should have a plan. She must have all the facts on hand. For example, the teacher will not recommend an expensive special education program or facility if she knows that the family cannot afford it. She should not burden a family with criticisms about their child's performance and adjustment without being able to make any recommendations for improving the situation. The educator is obligated to know what resources are available within the community and school system, and the proper method of referral to each resource. Mental health clinics and social services organizations often have resource files from which information about state or out-of-state special children's facilities, and their specific referral requirements and procedures, can be obtained (see Chapter 12).

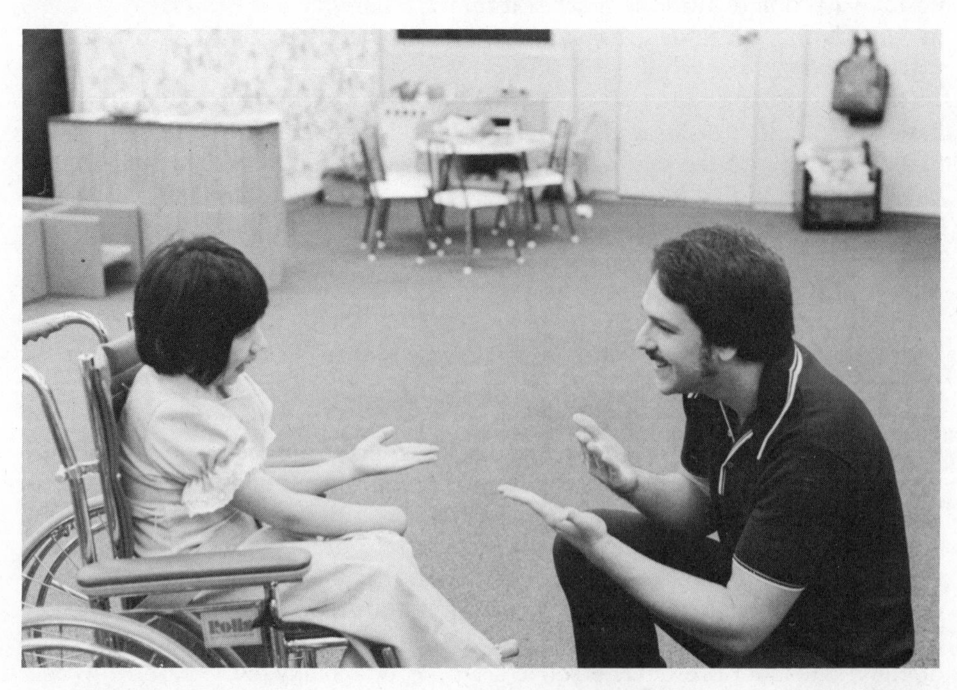

Professionals become important members of the child's extended family.

The services required by the child should be fully described to the parent, and procedures for obtaining the service should be outlined. It is equally important to review what is not available or necessary, such as certain drugs, types of surgery, or particular educational programs (Kessler, 1966).

Recommendations should always start with the simplest, most obvious procedures, which are also usually the most available. The educator should think out in advance the steps that ought to be followed in more clearly defining the difficulty to be dealt with, the special procedures that might be required, such as psychological tests, and what steps will probably be followed should the procedures meet with either success or failure. The plan is shared *selectively* with the parents in order not to anticipate difficulties that might never arise. Once again, the parents ought not to be burdened unnecessarily. The educator should maintain, when it is realistic, an optimistic, supportive attitude.

The parents should be given something to do which will make them feel active in their child's behalf. Whenever possible, the educator should be careful not to foster inappropriate, unrealistic, and unnecessary dependence on herself or the program. The more active the parents can be in their child's behalf, the more motivated they will usually be to do the right things and to cooperate with recommendations.

As Ditkoff (1975) has indicated, professionals need support services, also. It is highly recommended that those who work with handicapped children and their families have counseling services available to them. The professional may need to come to grips with his own feelings and attitudes about handicapping conditions and their manifestations in young children. Also, there will be times of failure. While optimism and tenacity are admirable and desirable, no human being, no matter how well trained, is omniscient or omnipotent. There comes a time when one is brought to the inescapable conclusion that there is no available answer to a problem. The inevitable failures should not result in irrational guilt for the professional. The professional loses her effectiveness if her own perspective becomes less than reality oriented. The educator, too, has the ultimate responsibility to know herself first.

Professionals should guard against entering into covert competition with parents. The educator should emphasize to herself, as well as to the parents, that the child belongs to the parents and not to herself or to the educational system. Parents are of more importance to the child than is the educator and, in most cases, are the most powerful influence in helping their child to a better adjustment and a better academic performance. If the parents are not allies, the educator will soon find himself partially or completely blocked in her efforts to help the child.

Speaking to a similar parent-professional situation, Bromwich (1977), emphasized that infant intervention programs must take care not to interfere with the mothering-infant attachment by either causing the mother to feel inadequate in the mothering role or dependent on the specialist for dealing with her baby. The infant specialist must support the mother's responsiveness. The mutually satisfying interaction may do more to promote development in the infant than any other factor.

Additional Needs of Parents

Parents' needs are numerous. In addition to instructional programs for their children, parents look to the professional community for information which will help them be more effective. Gordon (1977) stated that parents need "services delivered to them rather than services they have to mobilize for themselves" (p. 62). Neither the list of services nor the information which follows here is considered complete. It is presented to call attention to the needs and to provide guidance for further study.

Due Process Procedures

By law (P.L. 94–142) all handicapped children, 3 years of age or older, are entitled to a free and appropriate education in the least restrictive alternative setting with certain support services provided. If these provisions are not met, parents have a recourse in the due process procedures established by the department of education in their state. Parents need to be informed of their rights and the child's rights, and professionals working with young disabled children have an obligation to provide such information to them.

Although due process procedures vary among the states, certain minimum standards in identification, evaluation, and educational placement of handicapped children must be provided.

1. Written notification before evaluation [Parents whose primary language is not English have the right to an interpreter/translator.]
2. Written notification before change in educational placement.
3. Periodic review of educational placement.
4. Opportunity for an impartial hearing including the right to:
   Receive timely and specific notice of such hearing.
   Review all records.
   Obtain an independent evaluation.
   Be represented by counsel.
   Cross examine.
   Bring witnesses.
   Present evidence.
   Receive a complete and accurate record of proceedings.
   Appeal the decision.
5. Assignment of a surrogate parent for children when:
   The child's parent or guardian is not known.
   The child's parents are unavailable.
   The child is a ward of the state.
6. Access to educational records.

In order to administer these minimums, the state, in adopting its procedures, must provide for:

Enforcement of the requirements.
Training of state and local education agency personnel.

Identification, training, and monitoring of hearing officers.
Recruitment, training, and monitoring of surrogate parents. (Abeson, Bolick, & Hass, 1975, pp. 20–21)

Professional responsibility for due process procedures includes: (1) knowing the due process procedures of the state; (2) disseminating this information to parents; (3) encouraging parents, when appropriate, to exercise their rights to due process of law; and (4) helping parents find resource personnel who can provide needed services.

A significant point concerning due process is its potential as a safeguard against unnecessary labeling and classification of children by those who are providing services for children with special learning needs. It is especially important to the young child who, because of early intervention programming, outgrows his need for special education and can enter the mainstream of regular education. A label carried over from the early years could persist and taint the child's acceptance by teachers and peers.

Parent Organizations

Parent groups supply a different kind of support to parents of young handicapped children. Made up of people much like themselves and bonded together by similar problems, they have created programs for their children, secured services, and sponsored legislation to protect their rights and to identify the rights of their children. Generally, parent programs are addressed to the following objectives:

1. To develop public awareness of handicapping conditions and services needed.
2. To represent children's rights.
3. To disseminate information to other parents and professional personnel on a variety of issues including legal issues, institutionalization, programs, and school placement.
4. To create needed programs including recreational and vocational as well as educational.
5. To support state and national associations.

Professionals should inform parents of young handicapped children of local organizations and encourage parents' participation.

Health Care

Although health care is beyond the scope of an educator's responsibilities, it is appropriate for the educator to be sensitive to conditions within the family. The added financial burden of raising a handicapped child may create problems related to nutrition, dental care, immunization, and adequate care of other family members.

Public health services are available to assist families in need. In metropolitan areas, the educator can compile lists of resources for health care and directions for securing services. Specific information such as dates of screening clinics or immunization programs should be provided.

Information on daily nutritional needs, low cost foods, and preparation methods may be secured from the National Dairy Council and health departments. In many health facilities, nutritionists are available for consultation with the parents as well as evaluation of the child's nutritional status.

Educators involved in home programs can be alert to potential safety hazards. Also, information concerning toy safety may be provided to the parents.

Counseling

Many writers have expressed the need for continuing and adequate counseling services to the families of young handicapped children. Such services will be needed at various stages of the child's life. If the educator has not been trained to be of service in this area, referral of the parents to university centers, social workers, and mental health centers will be helpful. If this is done, the name of a contact person and a telephone number will make it easier for an appointment to be made.

Closer Look (1976), the newsletter of the National Information Center for the Handicapped, has stated that if adequate counseling services are ever to be provided for parents of children with handicaps, universities and colleges must design programs to train graduates in special education to meet this need. What

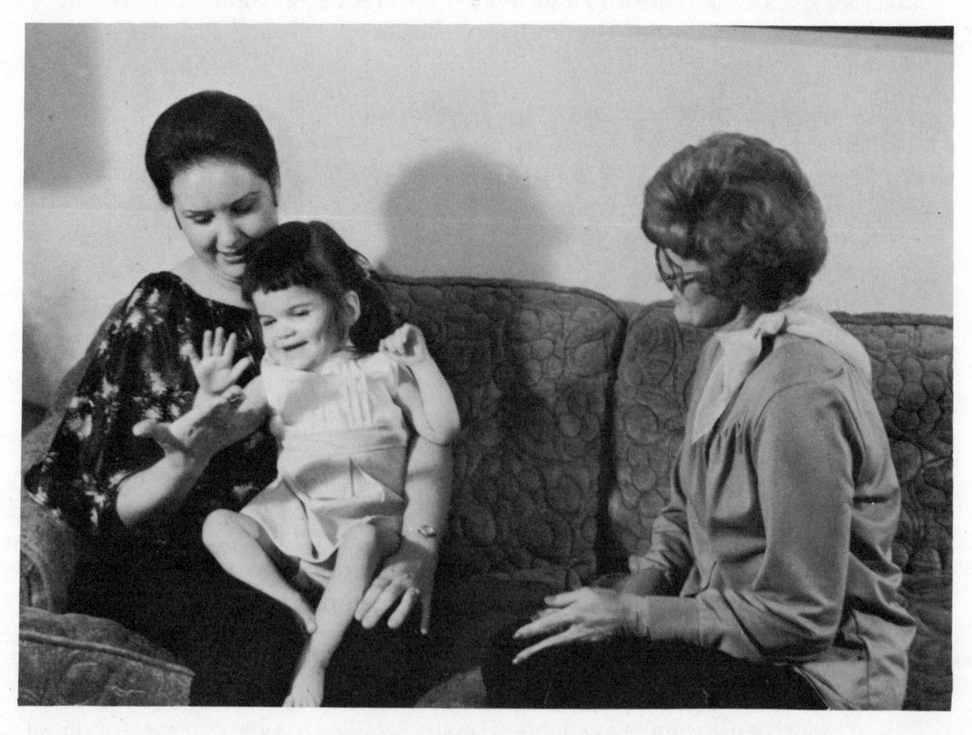

Professionals must not allow the mother to become dependent on them or to feel inadequate in her mothering role.

is needed in the meantime, according to the newsletter, is "a change in the attitudes that are communicated" (p. 10). The professional can create by his own feelings, "an atmosphere of sharing, of willingness to help find ways of handling difficult human problems" (p. 10).

Schild (1964) suggested that counseling should be properly spaced and educationally focused to help the parents with practical problems of daily living with the handicapped child. "Such help is often crucial in determining if the child can live in his home and in strengthening and sustaining the mental health of the total family unit" (p. 9).

Respite Care

Although respite care facilities are increasing throughout the nation, the need for the service is great and the resources are few. These programs provide temporary care of the handicapped child in order to relieve the family of the heavy responsibility for awhile. This service, when available, may be in the form of nursing help, babysitting, or homemaker services in the home. It may include a temporary foster home or nursing home placement. The program is viewed as one way of keeping the child at home instead of being placed in an institution. Local parent organizations are good sources concerning respite care facilities available in the community.

Separation from the Program

Separation is unavoidable in early childhood education programs for handicapped children. A teacher may leave the program, the child's family may move, or the child may be placed in a more advanced educational setting. This can be a crisis period for the child and his family. The time of separation should be planned to avoid, as much as possible, any disruption in the child's program and to provide as much emotional support as may be needed. To this end, Ditkoff (1975) has provided the following suggestions:

1. Staff members should give advance notice of their intentions to leave the program. In this way the remaining staff can carefully select a replacement and introduce the new person gradually into the program. This will provide time for the new staff member to establish rapport with the child and his family.
2. If the child moves or graduates, provide several periods for the ventilation of feelings and to discuss with the parents any anxieties they harbor concerning finding new programs. A going-away party may help.
3. Attempt to determine if the family has a person (neighbor, minister, friend, relative) with whom they will have contact after they leave the program. Try to find someone who can give support after the school's support is terminated.
4. When appropriate, maintain contact with each family by phone calls or letters.

When termination from the program is prompted by the family moving to another location, try to supply names of contact persons in the new community. This may be a special education supervisor, superintendent of schools, or a public health nurse. Such consideration for the child and his family will assist in the early resumption of his educational program and help to fill the gap caused by the termination of support.

The following list, adapted from a similar one prepared by the Home-School Institute (1974), summarizes specific guidelines for teachers and others who work with young handicapped children.

10 TIPS FOR TEACHERS

**Recognize that all parents are a significant force in their child's education.* Call on parents for advice, help, support, and critical evaluation.

**Project for parents a realistic picture of what the child's program is designed to accomplish.* It has limited but achievable goals and objectives.

**Keep parents informed* about their child's progress, parent organizations, due process procedures, and other relevant matters. Provide as much information as possible in readable written material for distribution to parents.

**Offer a variety of parent education activities and materials* whose aim is to build educational partnership. Don't expect all parents to attend. Find ways to reach parents without their having to come to school or the center.

**Show parents you care about their child.* Make a phone call now and then, write a note, and always be on time for a home visit.

**Show parents how they can help their child at home.* Provide clearly written home-teaching activities that supplement your work with the child but stay within the limits of your training. Keep looking for a variety of ways to involve parents as educational partners.

**Tap the resources of the home.* Use the materials, ideas, expertise that all parents have and have time to use for their child's development. Send a questionnaire, make calls, set up a parent-teaching idea bank. In this way, you will be building up the self-esteem that parents themselves need in order to fulfill their role as home teachers.

**Expect parents to question, to give advice, to look over your shoulder.* Listen to parents at conferences; if necessary, encourage them to talk. Let them know that you need feedback from them and respect their opinions.

**Hold school or center doors open to parents* for visiting, for conferring. Know your community and its resources well enough so that you can refer parents to other social institutions when the help that is needed for the child and his family is the kind you cannot give.

**Trust yourself and your common sense.* Show respect for your parents by being yourself, not some superhuman model of a teacher who knows all and never makes a mistake.

Read (1976) has summarized the goal of working with parents as follows:

1. To help parents grow in confidence.
   a. They will be better able to enjoy their children.
   b. They will be better able to make creative use of experience.
   c. They will be able to learn about the needs of children and to use this knowledge effectively.
2. To help parents gain insights and knowledge that may improve their contribution to the child's development.

"The teacher who helps a parent feel more confident has achieved an important goal in her work" (p. 377).

Summary

To provide a basis for understanding of parents' needs, information concerning their reactions to the diagnosis of handicapping conditions in their child have been reviewed as well as periods of family crisis faced by parents of handicapped children and ways of working with siblings. The need for a working parent-professional partnership was established by examining parent accusations of professional mishandling. These have provided the foundation for the recommendations designed to foster constructive and cooperative parent-professional relationships. Additional needs of parents have been identified with brief indications as to how these may be met. The purpose of this presentation has been to provide guidelines for effective service to the professional and paraprofessional concerned with the education and care of the young handicapped child and his family.

REFERENCES

Abeson, A., Bolick, N., & Hass, J. *A primer on due process: Education discussions for handicapped children.* Reston, Va.: The Council for Exceptional Children, 1975.

American Medical Association. Mental retardation: A handbook for the primary physician. *JAMA,* 1965, **191**(3), 183–232.

Arend, P. New directions in special education: Federal, state and local roles in mainstreaming. In G. Taylor & S. Jackson (Eds.), *Educational strategies and services for exceptional children.* Springfield, Ill.: Charles C Thomas, 1976.

Baroff, G. *Mental retardation: Nature, causes and management.* Washington, D.C.: Hemisphere Publishing Corp., 1974.

Blodgett, H., & Warfield, G. *Understanding mentally retarded children.* New York: Appleton-Century-Crofts, 1959.

Bromwich, R. Stimulation in the first year of life: A perspective on infant development. *Young Children,* 1977, **32**(2), 71–82.

Bryant, J. Parent-child relationships: Their effect on rehabilitation. *Journal of Learning Disabilities,* 1971, **4**(6), 40–44.

Bullington, B., Sexton, D., & White, P. Working with families of multihandicapped children in a residential institution. *Children Today,* 1976, **5**(5), 13–17.

Cansler, D. P., and Martin, G. H. *Working with families: A manual for developmental centers.* Winston-Salem, N.C.: Kaplan School Supply Corp., undated.

Closer Look, Winter 1976, pp. 1, 9–11. National Information Center for the Handicapped, Box 1492, Washington, D.C. 20013.

Ditkoff, M. *Guidelines for working with parents of handicapped infants.* Charlottesville, Va.: EMI, Department of Pediatrics, University of Virginia Medical Center, 1975.

Gardner, R. *MBD: The family book about minimal brain dysfunction.* New York: Jason Arason, 1973.

Gordon, R. Special needs of multihandicapped children under six and their families: One opinion. In E. Sontag, J. Smith, & N. Certo (Eds.), *Educational programming for the severely and profoundly handicapped.* Reston, Va.: The Council for Exceptional Children, Division on Mental Retardation, 1977.

Gorham, K. A lost generation of parents. *Exceptional Children,* 1975, **41,** 521–525.

Hayden, A., & McGinness. Basis for early intervention. In E. Sontag, J. Smith, & N. Certo, (Eds.), *Educational programming for the severely and profoundly handicapped.* Reston, Va.: The Council for Exceptional Children, Division on Mental Retardation, 1977.

The Home and School Institute, Inc. *10 tips for teachers: School and community.* Washington, D.C.: Author, Trinity College, 1974.

Hunter, M., Schucman, H., & Friedlander, G. *The retarded child from birth to five: A multidisciplinary program for the child and the family.* New York: John Day Co., 1972.

Karnes, M., & Teska, J. Children's response to intervention programs. In J. Gallagher (Ed.), *Application of child development research to exceptional children.* Reston, Va.: The Council for Exceptional Children, 1975.

Keith, R. The feelings and behavior of parents of handicapped children. *Developmental Medicine and Child Neurology,* 1973, **15,** 524–527.

Kessler, J. *Psychopathology of childhood.* Englewood Cliffs, N.J.: Prentice-Hall, 1966.

Kramm, E. *Families of mongoloid children.* Washington, D.C.: U.S. Department of Health, Education and Welfare, Children's Bureau, Pub. No. 401, 1963.

Kroth, R. Facilitating educational progress by improving parent conferences. In E. Meyer, G. Vergason, & R. Whelan, (Eds.), *Alternatives for teaching exceptional children.* Denver: Love Publishing Co., 1975.

Murphy, A., Pueschel, S., Duffy, T., & Brady, E. Meeting the brothers and sisters of children with Down's syndrome. *Children Today,* 1976, **5**(2), 20–23.

Olshansky, S. Chronic sorrow: A response to having a mentally retarded child. *Social Casework,* 1962, **43,** 190–193.

Read, K. *The nursery school: Human relationships and learning* (6th. ed.). Philadelphia: W. B. Saunders Co., 1976.

Roos, P. A parent's view of what public education should accomplish. In E. Sontag, J. Smith, & N. Certo (Eds.), *Educational programming for the severely and profoundly handicapped.* Reston, Va.: The Council for Exceptional Children, Division on Mental Retardation, 1977.

Schild, S. *Counselling with parents of retarded children living at home.* Arlington, Tex.: National Association for Retarded Citizens, 1964.

Wolfensberger, W. Counselling parents of the retarded. In A. Baumeister (Ed.), *Mental retardation: Appraisal, education and Rehabilitation.* Chicago: Aldine Publishing Co., 1967.

12

Who Can Help?

The need for treatment and specialized services will continue throughout the handicapped child's life span. Because the child's needs are also the needs of her family, parents too will continue to need information resources and supportive services.

What is known about parent-professional relationships in the past has not been complimentary to either group. Generally, it can be summarized in two statements: (1) professionals have accused parents of shopping for answers they want to hear; and (2) parents have found professionals to be secretive and condescending (see Chapter 11).

No doubt, the mistakes of the past have been caused by a lack of understanding on both sides. Parents have expressed the need to know the roles of different professionals and the services available to parents (Gorham, 1975, p. 523). Professionals have failed to fully explain the reasons for additional referrals and, at times, their referrals have reflected a lack of knowledge (Roos, 1977, pp. 72–73).

The purpose of this chapter is to promote understanding through general information which can provide improved communications among professionals and paraprofessionals, parents, families, neighbors—anyone concerned with the care and welfare of young handicapped children. The information provided deals first with professionals and paraprofessionals in the various disciplines—

Ellen Bynum, Ardella M. Curtis, and *Maureen Larkin* contributed material for this chapter, with additional information provided by the senior author.

who they are and how they provide help for the child and his family. The second portion of the chapter presents organizations, agencies, and resources which provide programs and information for those working with young children and for parents.

The information presented is intended for use as a reference for those (1) making referrals, (2) studying professional reports, (3) attempting to coordinate information for parents, and (4) determining community needs for new programs and services. Such information can promote understanding and improve communications which, in turn, should result in cooperation built on mutual trust.

Personnel Providing Support Services

The Habilitation Team

The habilitation team is a group of individuals in the health, education, and social services whose training ranges from that of a volunteer to high levels of professional preparation. Their responsibilities interlock and their roles are interdependent (Hayden & Gotts, 1977, p. 247).

The habilitation team concept implies a working relationship based on mutual interest and concern between the disciplines and the family of the handi-

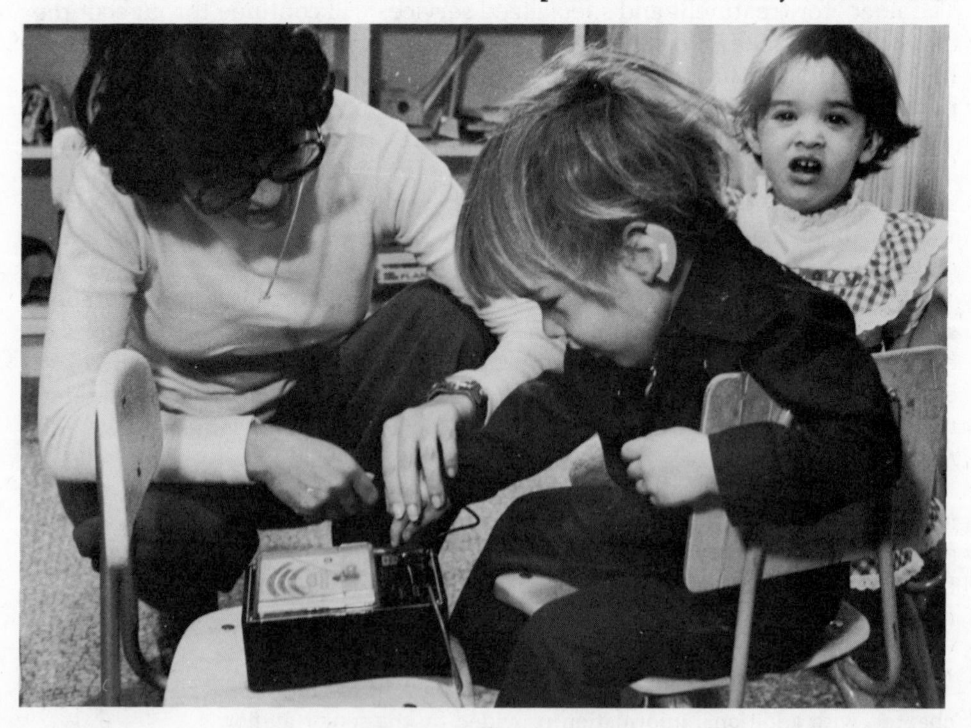

Instruction is based on the assessed needs of the child and follows an individualized educational plan.

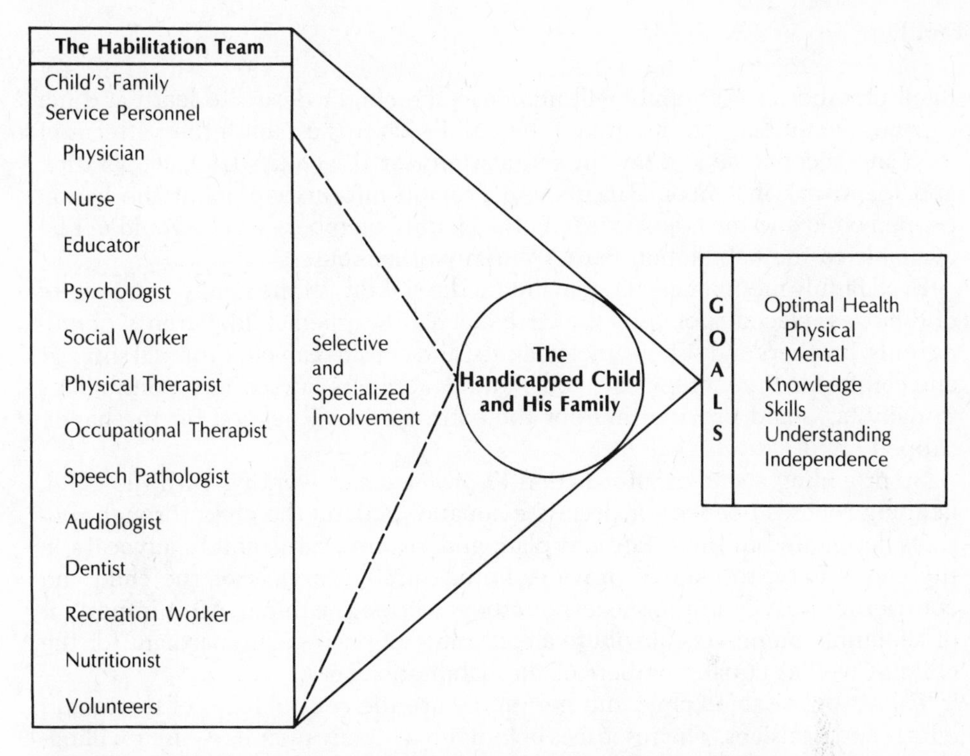

FIGURE 1. Habilitative Services for the Young Handicapped Child and His Family.

capped child. Team members work in partnership to foster the child's opportunities for normal development and life experiences.

When all services work in conjunction with one another, the child and her family are better served. This implies the need for shared information and open discussion concerning not only what needs to be done for the child, but also how the task can be accomplished and which discipline, even which person, can best serve the identified needs. As Barnard and Erickson have indicated, every professional skill is not required in every case; it is the selection and integration of all important ones from which effective planning and implementation proceed (1976, p. 24).

The nature of the partnership remains constant in spite of the fact that the situation changes. The special needs of the young handicapped child will change with the passage of time. Professional and paraprofessional members of the team may change as old problems are resolved and new ones arise. Specialists may be consulted, offer their contributions, and then leave the team. Communities, responding to obvious needs, may develop new services. Families move, and new partnerships are formed. Professionals change jobs and new team members take their places. Thus, the membership of the habilitation team changes, but the working relationship based on mutual interest and concern remains.

The composition of the habilitation team and responsibilities of its members are described here:

The Family

Each member of the family will influence the child's desire to learn and her capacity for subsequent learning. The child's parents establish the patterns of love and acceptance and lay the foundations for the child's later cooperation and teamwork in school. Parents also provide information about the handicapped child and the adjustment of other family members which would not be available to the habilitation team from any other source.

Each family member can help maintain the stability of the family unit in spite of the stress placed upon it by the birth of a handicapped child. Parents, grandparents, brothers and sisters, uncles, aunts, and cousins can offer mutual support and comfort in times of special need. Family members can share responsibilities in daily tasks and provide time for the extra attention needed for the handicapped child.

By providing accurate information to professionals working with the child, keeping records needed for precise evaluation, taking the child through routines designated in the treatment plan, and becoming the child's advocate in the community, the family provides immeasurable service for the child and contributes heavily to the success of others working with her. Most important of all, family members contribute a continuity of purpose as guardians for the child as well as equal members of the habilitation team.

The young disabled child and her family are the central focus of the team's efforts and decisions. The resources of individual family members, their willingness to learn, their commitment to the goals of the treatment program, and their ability to implement plans are significant considerations. Professional and paraprofessional services offered without regard for the welfare of other family members may be counterproductive. At the same time, if the family is unwilling to accept a measure of dependency on external services and to trust the judgment reflected in professional decisions, more than likely the child's opportunities for sequential and optimal development will be minimized.

Physician

The physician is probably the best known professional to the family of a handicapped child. In many ways, he is the most influential. Whether the physician is the family doctor, a clinic doctor, or a medical specialist, the patients rarely make such discriminations, referring to him as simply "the doctor."

The physician is frequently the first professional to see the young handicapped child. He may be the *obstetrician,* or the *neonatologist* or *pediatrician* called in when abnormalities are observed or suspected. Early verification of abnormalities may require the services of a *geneticist* or a *perinatologist.* Problems which later become apparent may require the attention of a *pediatric neurologist.*

The nature and extent of the child's problems will determine the number and variety of services required. Cleft lip or cleft palate requires a team of surgeons and perhaps assistance from the field of dentistry. At times a full array of medical treatment is needed. Each child's problem is unique; similar problems in different children are never exactly the same. Parents of handicapped children may need assistance in understanding the areas of medical specialization and the reason one doctor may not be able to provide all of the needed medical services.

Medical treatment is individualized and follows a routine which includes a medical examination, laboratory tests if indicated, and a study of the child's medical history. Physician reports and hospital records detailing prenatal care, birth events, postnatal problems, and records of family illnesses are included in the medical history. Diagnosis follows study and leads to a treatment plan which may take the form of medication, home care, hospitalization and surgery if needed, or therapy. Periodically evaluating treatment of effectiveness, seeking and providing information to the child's parents and to the habilitation team, and referring the child and her family for additional assistance are all important components of the physician's professional responsibility.

The *child psychiatrist* is a physician who specializes in the diagnosis and treatment of developmental and behavior disorders in children. When serious problems relative to the mental health of the disabled child or members of her family arise, and in cases of poor parent-child relationships, the child psychiatrist can provide valuable insights and recommendations. Also, a psychiatrist may be needed to help family members understand the handicapped child's problems. Other medical specialists offering services required for the habilitation of young handicapped children include *ophthalmologists, orthopedists,* and *otolaryngologists.* (See Glossary.)

Nurse

Nurses, like physicians, receive different levels of professional preparation and are qualified to work in various aspects of health care. As members of the habilitation team, they may be found in a variety of settings including the hospital, out-patient clinics, schools, doctors' offices, special diagnostic clinics, health departments, and homes.

Unless the handicapped child spends much of her time in a hospital, a *clinic nurse* or the *public health nurse* is the one most likely to be involved in her long-term care and in service to her family. Both the clinic nurse and the public health nurse are registered nurses trained to work with handicapped children and their families. Frequently the nurse is the key person to assist the parents in acknowledging special needs and in directing them to the proper resources for complete medical, social, and psychological assessment.

Barnard and Erickson (1976) identified three major areas of responsibility for nurses working within the field of childhood handicapping conditions: (1) in the area of primary prevention, nurses are responsible for programs in nutrition, immunization, and environmental modification; (2) nursing responsibility includes case finding; and (3) the major responsibility of the nurse is management, working directly with children and their families.

In the area of prevention, the nurse is concerned with the mother's general health and nutrition before and during her pregnancy. She monitors the dietary needs of inactive and hyperactive babies to assure proper weight control and makes changes in feeding practices when needed. Nurses assume responsibility for getting adequate food supplies for those who do not have them.

Disabling childhood infections can be prevented through immunization programs. Through health teaching, environmental conditions such as sanitation are improved and homes are made safe. Through case-finding efforts, nurses discover developmental problems among young children that otherwise might have gone undetected until much learning time had been lost. Because of a background in growth and development, the nurse can be a key resource to parents coping with difficult child behaviors. One of her major responsibilities is teaching parents principles of child care and ways of using this knowledge effectively in their own homes.

Within the hospital setting, often it is the nurse who assists the family in coping with the diagnosis and in beginning to plan for the long-term care of the handicapped child. In community settings, the nurse plans with parents and other members of the habilitation team for coordination of treatment plans, schedules return appointments for evaluations, and offers continued support in specific behavioral management.

In some sparsely settled areas of the United States, the public health nurse is the only readily available person trained to provide professional service to young handicapped children. Elsewhere in the nation, the public health nurse is a reliable resource and one that can put families in touch with other services provided locally and regionally.

Educator

Educators concerned with young handicapped children and their families include a variety of teachers known by different names. Their work is multifaceted but includes program planning, implementation, and evaluation, and their goals include skill acquisition and development for the young child. Teachers, like nurses and physicians, are trained at different levels and work in a variety of settings including the child's home, child development clinics, hospitals, day care centers, nursery schools, kindergartens, regular, special, and private schools, and state institutions. They are essential to early childhood education for the handicapped.

Labels used to identify different kinds of educators working with young disabled children and their parents are dependent more on local whim than on the responsibilities assumed. In general, services in early childhood education for the handicapped may be classified as professional or paraprofessional, each with several different positions included. The labels used for each position are not the same throughout the nation; however, the labels are relatively unimportant compared to the services offered.

Professional. The *child development specialist* (known also as the child development associate, the educational child development specialist, and by the initials CDS) is highly trained in child development practices. The duties of the child development specialist vary according to the needs of the local school system but the major duties include: (1) identification of children below age 5

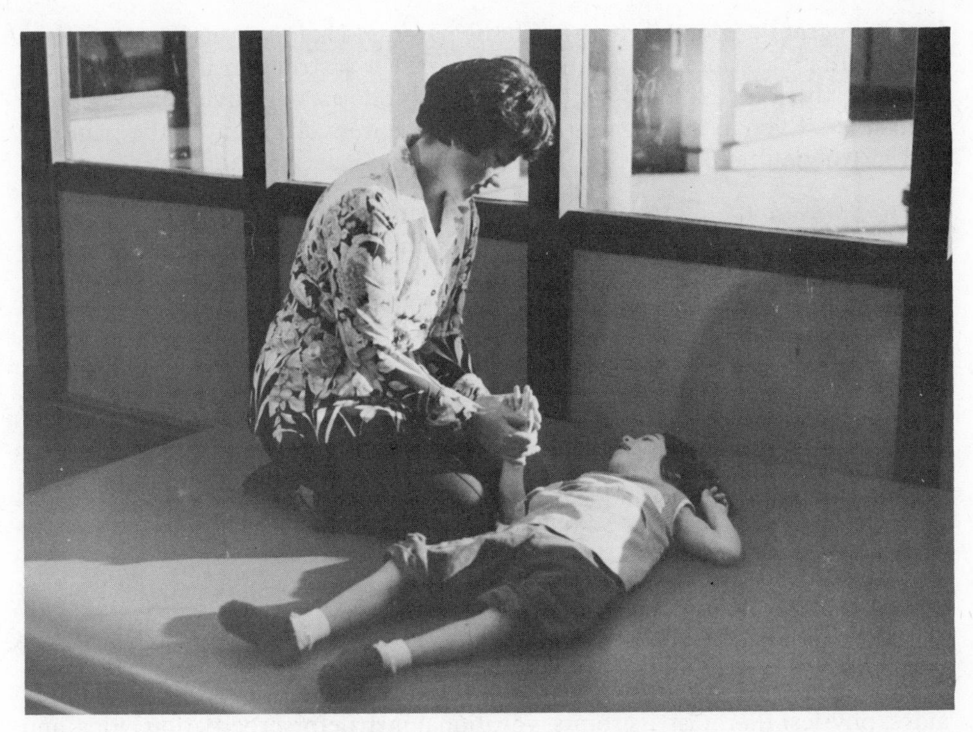

Programs for young handicapped children and their parents are designed to teach the child's first teacher to be the child's best teacher.

in need of special education services; (2) determination of the educational needs of these children; and (3) implementation of a home-based or center-based program of instruction for each child.

The CDS also acts as a linking agent between home, school, and community agencies, facilitates the procurement of other appropriate services for the child, and serves as an advocate for young handicapped children.

In sparsely populated areas, the child development specialist may be the key person in delivery of services working directly with a parent of the handicapped child. In heavily populated areas, the CDS may be a coordinator of many different services with other educators working under his supervision.

The *educational consultant* is a certified teacher with graduate training in special education who is employed by the local public schools to work in a school, clinic, or hospital setting. Educational consultants in private schools work as resources to the regular classroom teachers.

Using available information from records, standardized tests, interviews, and observations, the consultant assesses each child's developmental level and makes his recommendations accordingly. Contact is established with the child's educational program, and information is exchanged. The educational consultant also assists the child's family in locating other appropriate facilities.

Preschool teachers may be classroom teachers in a preschool center, day care center, nursery school, kindergarten, hospital, or institution where they work directly with the handicapped children, or they may be teachers in a home-based program working directly with the parents. Their instruction takes place in both the classroom and the home. Wherever instruction is provided, it is based on the assessed needs of the child and follows an individualized educational plan. Even in the classroom setting, parent involvement in the planning and instruction helps to insure effective educational programming.

Paraprofessional. In the literature, the term *paraprofessional,* as applied to special education programs for preschool handicapped children, is applied to many different people giving assistance in many different ways. In practice, however, the paraprofessional is easily identified. They are the teaching associates or the teacher's aides. They are nonprofessional, but before assignment to an educational setting, they receive training usually in public school or community college programs, or in the case of a special project, in staff development programs.

Paraprofessionals may perform nonteaching duties to free the professional educator for other responsibilities, or may be further trained by the professional to work directly with the child and her parent. Teaching associates and teacher's aides are salaried employees.

Associate teaching personnel is the name given by the journal *Education and Training of the Mentally Retarded* to a new department addressed to the needs of a population which includes cottage parents, ward aides, teacher's aides, special training instructors, house parents, foster parents, occupational therapy aides, physical therapist assistants, vocational instructors, recreation aides, and the child's parents. Many of these people work directly with the young handicapped child.

In announcing the beginning of the new department, editors Galloway and Larsen (1976) congratulated the journal for its recognition of other than professionals in the provision of full service to the handicapped and emphasized the value of these paraprofessionals in the care, education, and habilitation of handicapped individuals.

The significance of the new term is that it encompasses roles which, in the past, have not been considered a part of the educational process. The creation of this department is one indication of the growing trend which recognizes paraprofessionals as contributing members of the habilitation team.

The Child's Mother: First Teacher

The role of the child's mother as a teacher is significant. This fact applies to all children, but its importance in the life of the handicapped child cannot be overemphasized. As with all infants, the mother is responsible for laying the foundations which influence all subsequent learning (Finnie, 1975).

The child's mother controls stimulus events by creating or withholding appropriate learning experiences. Because she is the major person to respond to the behavior of the infant, she also controls the reward system (Gray, 1971).

Activities like talking to the child, smiling, touching, and feeding catch her attention and teach concentration rather than vague scanning of the environment. Continuing to provide experiences of increasing complexity helps the child to continue learning. Neglect, indifference, or impersonal care creates no stimulation; loud, raucous environments overstimulate. The end result of either situation is the child learning how not to learn.

The young handicapped child may respond so slowly to the mothering overtures that the mother becomes discouraged and ceases to caress and play with her baby. The baby, receiving no stimulation, no longer seeks stimulation. Little useful learning will then be possible (Finnie, 1975, p. 19).

Programs for young handicapped children and their parents are designed to teach the child's first teacher to be the child's best teacher.

Psychologists

Members of the habilitation team look to the psychologist for information concerning the child's intellectual functioning and personality assessment and for interpretation of certain behaviors. Extensive training in child development, personality dynamics, and the use of tests contribute heavily to this professional's competence. Keen observation skills are necessary tools for the psychologist working with young children.

To assess intellectual functioning, the psychologist working with young handicapped children will select appropriate measures of mental abilities (see Chapter 2), administer and score the tests, and interpret the findings. Because the child's condition may not allow her to give responses in the usual way, the psychologist must know how to improvise the testing program in ways that do not invalidate the test results. For example, if a child cannot speak, other means of communication must be established such as pointing or blinking the eyes. Such procedures are crucial when a child's intellectual functioning is being assessed.

In personality assessment, the psychologist will consider the child's temperament, emotionality, and character (Baroff, 1974, p. 140). Temperament includes the child's general mood and also her activity level (hyperactive, lethargic). Emotionality focuses upon levels of irritability, stress tolerance, and impulse control. In character assessment, the psychologist is interested in the child's personal relationships, her capacity for affection, and levels of trust, dependency, and aggression. Also, tests of achievement in language and perceptual-motor development are used to provide dimensional information.

Because the diagnostic process includes not only understanding but also translating information into effective intervention, the habilitation team depends upon the psychologist to take an active but not dominant part in program planning for the child, to assist other team members to delineate relevant information, and to do individual or group counseling with the child's parents and with staff personnel working with the child.

Social Worker

The social worker provides a broad range of social services to the young handicapped child and to the members of her family. As a member of the habilitation team, the social worker assesses the family dynamics which could assure or prevent successful treatment and intervention.

Services provided by the social worker include: (1) helping each family member understand the child's condition, and working with the family to accept the child as an individual; (2) assisting parents to understand changes in the child's behavior at different developmental stages and to set realistic goals for the child and for themselves; (3) answering questions, explaining procedures, and providing counseling when it is needed; and (4) directing parents to community agencies and other resources which can provide assistance to them. (See Appendix.)

During an initial interview, the social worker seeks to obtain as much information concerning the family as possible from the child's parents. Since the social worker is specifically trained to understand feelings, it may be easier for the parents to talk about family concerns to this professional than to other team members.

The social worker's skills in interviewing, observing the child in the home, and evaluating the parents' intellectual, emotional, and financial resources will assist other team members in achieving an overall picture of the child. A sympathetic, sensitive, and warm relationship with family members can help to alleviate negative feelings and replace them with a sense of purpose.

If the social worker knows the family's financial situation, he can negotiate for reduced costs of professional service and make arrangements for the family to use less expensive service facilities. In some cases, direct financial assistance can be arranged.

The contributions of the social worker to the family and to the habilitation team are equally valuable. Through the efforts of this professional, family members learn to make adjustments and thus become more capable of working as a unit. Information provided by the social worker to members of the habilitation team assists them in planning realistically for both the child and her family.

Physical Therapist

A physical therapist is concerned with various types of paralysis, muscle weakness, fractures, and other orthopedic conditions resulting from disease, injury, or disability.

Physical therapists work as members of the habilitation team in hospitals, clinics, medical centers, institutions, and special schools. Also, they may serve as consultants to programs or engage in private practice. In each setting, physical therapists provide treatment according to the prescription of a physician.

The goal of a physical therapist is to make the child as independent as possible in movement. The work of this professional includes the following:

1. Exercises: used to strengthen muscle groups, to maintain or increase muscle tone, to stretch muscle groups, to increase range of motion, to

develop patterns of muscle movement, and to increase or decrease reflex actions.

2. Balance: practiced by the child while sitting, kneeling, standing, or walking. Through these activities young children learn to control head balance, trunk balance, and body balance. Mirrors, parallel bars, and mat activities are used to help children master balance control.
3. Movement: promoted as young children are taught to roll over, to creep, to crawl, to walk, to run, to hop, to skip, and to walk on stairs. Some children are instructed in crutch walking, wheelchair locomotion, or transfer activities.
4. Modalities: include heat, cold, light, massage, water, and exercise. Ultrasound and ultraviolet rays may also be used. Physical therapy modalities are used in such equipment as heating pads, ice packs, infra-ray lamps, and whirlpool baths, and in such activities as swimming.
5. Activities of daily living: taught to promote independent movement. Young children practice dressing skills, toileting activities, and bathing and grooming to learn to help themselves. When they are able, children are taught to care for braces, splints, and special appliances.
6. Parent education: to extend the work of the therapist. In some cases, parents receive instruction in a home treatment program of daily activities and exercises for the young child. They are also taught to use and protect expensive self-help aids.

Occupational Therapist

The primary focus of occupational therapy is the development of adaptive skills and performance capacities. Pediatric occupational therapists provide services to children whose abilities to cope with tasks of living are threatened or impaired by developmental deficits (Council on Standards and Executive Board, 1972, p. 204).

Pediatric occupational therapists participate as members of the habilitation team working under the referral and guidance of a physician.

> *Occupation* is the child's play, his developmental tasks, movement exploration, and all daily learning experiences. *Therapy,* based on definitive evaluation, is providing the individual child with specific activities that will help him develop more normally. (Virginia Occupational Therapy Association, 1976)

Prior to planning a therapeutic treatment program, the occupational therapist assesses the child's developmental achievement. Major treatment areas include the following:

1. Motor development. Instruction is given in gross motor skills and in fine motor coordination. The occupational therapist trains children in use of arm and hand skills emphasizing coordination.
2. Perceptual-motor development. Activities are planned to improve sensory integration, body concept, position in space, and spatial relationships.

3. Activities of daily living. The occupational therapist provides instruction in feeding—in straw drinking, mouth closure, chewing, sucking, swallowing, and drooling control. Children learn to use feeding utensils or adaptations in tableware designed by the occupational therapist. Dressing skills, grooming, bathing, and toileting are also taught in occupational therapy. Children learn to undress, to dress, and to manage fastenings on clothes. Parents learn tips on clothing selection, construction, care, and adaptations. The occupational therapist may use splints, slings, weights, sandbags, or special devices to help young handicapped children learn to master self-care skills and thus become more independent.
4. Personal-social development. Young children learn to work and to play with appropriate behavior control. In occupational therapy a preschooler may learn to increase her attention span, to improve her concentration, and to develop socially acceptable frustration controls.
5. Language development. The occupational therapist encourages language development with instruction in listening, thinking, speaking, and interacting with others.

Speech Pathologist

The speech pathologist is the member of the habilitation team concerned with the evaluation, diagnosis, and treatment of speech and language disorders.

The language development specialist focuses on helping the child to comprehend speech and to use language effectively in communication.

The work of this professional with very young children includes speech and language stimulation in a cooperative effort with the child's mother.

Speech and language problems range from mild to profound and include anomalies such as lisping, stuttering, inability to make certain sounds, and the inability to use language. The problems may result from deafness, developmental delay, mental retardation, emotional disorders, brain injury or variations, or combinations of these disorders. They can exist for no apparent reason. Some speech and language problems develop because the child has never heard well-articulated speech. The speech pathologist is concerned with the nature and extent of the disability, its cause as well as its treatment.

Evaluation includes assessment of the child's achievement in speech and language development with reference to quantity, quality, age, and normal expectations. Because deafness and hearing impairments are possible causes of speech and language problems, auditory assessment is essential.

Evaluation is individual and may be informal. Initial observation by the speech pathologist of the child in the waiting room can yield as much information as the child's performance during the testing situation. From such observation in an unstructured setting, formal testing can be verified or disproven.

Diagnosis is accomplished through individual study of the child. The speech pathologist will make a routine examination to determine any abnormalities of the oral speech mechanism including the tongue, teeth arrangement, and the palate. Further examination is necessary to determine functional adequacy and the need for further referral.

The selection of standardized tests used in the diagnostic process will vary according to the child's age and problems. Typically, an articulation test, language assessment test, a discrimination test, and a sample of speech would be included. From these and additional selected procedures, the speech pathologist determines the child's language competence, her language processing capabilities, and performance.

Accurate diagnosis gives direction for the treatment program which the speech pathologist designs and administers. Remedial programs in speech and language have the long-range objective of bringing the child to her maximum potential for communication as soon as possible. Careful monitoring and adjustments in the child's program will be necessary during the treatment period.

Speech pathologists work in medical centers, child study centers, school divisions, child development clinics, and health departments. They make an invaluable contribution to the habilitation team by discussing what effect the child's speech and language problems will have on other test results and diagnostic procedures.

Language Development Specialist. The language development specialist works with children on a regular basis in ways similar to those of a speech pathologist. This professional may have training as a speech therapist or pathologist or as an educator concerned with how language develops and how it can be stimulated. The focus of the language development specialist is helping the child to comprehend speech and to use language effectively in communication.

Audiologist

The audiologist is the professional trained in the science of hearing measurement. The work of an audiologist includes audiometric testing to determine hearing ability, recommending procedures for the remediation of hearing loss, and parent counseling. As a member of the habilitation team, the audiologist discusses the effects of the child's disability on other diagnostic procedures and recommends appropriate methods for communicating with the child.

The audiologist uses a soundproof room and special equipment including loudspeakers and earphones, but exact testing procedures will depend upon the child's age and ability.

The audiologist begins with the most sensitive test available and proceeds according to the child's capabilities, revising the procedure as necessary. Signals used to test the hearing sensitivity of infants and children are classified as gross sounds or electronically produced signals. Gross sounds, referred to as noisemakers, are items such as toy crickets, whistles, bells, and drums. In spite of their limitations, noisemakers are simple, inexpensive devices that a competent audiologist can use productively. A quick estimate of hearing sensitivity can be made from them to indicate the type of testing needed and the level of response anticipated. When the audiologist has some indication of the level of response, he is better prepared to begin formal testing.

The conventional audiometric measures include air conduction, bone conduction, speech reception, and speech discrimination tests, all of which are electronically produced signals. Results of the tests are recorded in terms of loudness and frequency on an audiogram. Hearing may be normal or hearing loss may be judged as mild, moderate, moderately severe, severe, or profound.

As part of the child's treatment program, the audiologist will determine the need for a hearing aid and assume responsibility for making a specific choice. The child's treatment plan will also include speech reading, auditory training, and speech conservation. A few children will need sign language and finger spelling.

The audiologist may refer the child to a speech pathologist for some aspects of the treatment program. Throughout the treatment program, parents are encouraged to learn techniques which will maximize the child's hearing capability and communication skills.

Dentist

A pediatric dentist is the specialist responsible for the comprehensive dental health care of children. In addition to dental training, this professional has received training in child psychology qualifying him to care for the special problems of young handicapped children.

The pediatric dentist has two major responsibilities: (1) examination and restoration and (2) prevention and education. The dentist will examine the child's head, neck, and mouth to insure that all areas are developing normally. X-rays will be taken to determine if the correct number of teeth are developing and if they are in the proper position. X-rays will be used also to detect decay in those teeth already in the mouth.

Following a review of the child's health history and a study of clinical and X-ray examinations, the pediatric dentist will provide treatment to correct problem areas and to help the child's mouth develop normally. Through an educational program, parents and the child learn measures for preventing dental problems. Prevention is considered part of the total dental health program.

The orthodontist is a specialist trained to correct deformities of the mouth. This professional's work includes the correction of malocclusions, a condition which occurs when the lower and upper teeth do not meet properly, and as a team member in the treatment of cleft lips and cleft palates when the gums are involved.

As members of the habilitation team, these dentists are information resources, especially to other team members concerned with the child's speech and language development problems.

Recreation Workers

Included in this group of professionals are therapists from the field of music, art, and recreation who plan activity programs which are instructional but, more importantly, improve the quality of life for the handicapped child. The focus of their work is to provide opportunities for the disabled child to learn the appreciation of art and music and to find satisfying uses of time away from instruction and environmental stimulation.

Professionals in these three fields have learned techniques to use in the area of their speciality for remediation of disorders and social adjustment. As an example, the rhythm of music often helps a cerebral palsied youngster to relax and use her arms and legs in a purposeful fashion. Singing often helps alleviate the sound blockage of the stutterer. Clay manipulation in art strengthens finger muscles too underdeveloped to hold a crayon. Finger painting is an enjoyable method of exercising arms and hands. Using colored chalk on the chalkboard teaches basic strokes needed for handwriting skills. Playing catch with a bean bag and a scoop will develop eye-hand coordination.

Recreation workers are employed by a few hospitals, special schools, and special project programs. The information they can provide to the habilitation team comes entirely from their observations of the child, usually in informal settings. Such information gives added dimension to the deliberations of the team.

The traditional referral process is inappropriate in securing this service. It is only available in settings which have employed recreation workers. However, it is a type of service an organization or community can develop to provide full service to its handicapped children.

Nutritionist

A nutritionist is a professional concerned with dietary habits and the body's use of food elements. Unlike other members of the habilitation team, this professional usually works behind the scenes and rarely has direct contact with the young handicapped child over a period of time. Nevertheless, the nutritionist is an influential member of the habilitation team.

Nutritionists are employed in hospitals, day care centers, schools, and camps. When physicians and other professionals distribute information on the proper use of food, more than likely it originated in the office of a nutritionist. This professional's service is available indirectly through any of the members of the habilitation team. The child's eating habits and problems such as constipation or the child's refusal of important foods should be discussed with a physician or public health nurse.

Volunteers

A distinguishing trait of volunteers is that they are not monetarily compensated for their work. In spite of this fact, they have made their presence available in a variety of settings (Azarnoff, 1974) and their contributions have been effective (Marcovich, 1974). The extensive needs of young handicapped children and their parents have attracted volunteers to varied programs in hospitals, clinics, day care centers, Head Start programs, preschool classes, Sunday schools, and community playgrounds.

Volunteers come from varied backgrounds. Some may be professionals who have retired or parents who have raised their families but want to be involved with children, while others may have neither training nor experience with handicapped youngsters. Their ages range from early teens to senior citizens. Their activities range from those concerned only with recruiting other volunteers to providing sophisticated training for the young handicapped child. Volunteers work in infant stimulation programs, counsel with parents in times of crisis, and work for children's rights. Perhaps their greatest contribution is that of friendship to both the child and her parents.

The nature of their activities with handicapped children provides them with insights which might escape others who are working in more formal settings. Because of this, volunteers can provide valuable information to the habilitation team.

Active inservice training programs conducted by professional staff serve to develop understanding of handicapping conditions and to sharpen the volunteer's observation skills. The overall effect is increased effectiveness and efficient use of the volunteer's time.

Organizations, Agencies, and Other Resources

The kinds of services provided for young children with special needs vary according to where they live and a number of other factors. As a general rule, the number of services increases with the size of the community; the more heavily populated areas having the most, the sparsely populated areas having few or none at all. In rural areas, it is not uncommon for the one available service to be located in the county courthouse with the family being unable to use the service due to lack of transportation. A lack of family physicians and hospitals in these areas has left the child's parents with almost no support except that provided by relatives and friends.

In large metropolitan areas where a variety of services exist, the situation for parents of handicapped children has not been much better. The array of services has been confusing, and locating them has been frustrating. Examples of parents not knowing where to go or what to look for appear repeatedly. In many cases, they have not known that anything could be done for a handicapped child.

Generally, the professional community has not assumed responsibility for informing parents of services for their handicapped children. Ethical standards have limited advertising, and a general attitude of hopelessness toward handicapping conditions has suppressed the notion that services could make a difference (Roos, 1977, p. 72).

The facts of the past, however, are no longer universally true. Parent organizations have effectively demonstrated that early intervention can make a difference in the life of a handicapped individual. Their sophisticated legislative activities at the state and national levels have resulted in laws which establish the rights of handicapped children. Such legislation has received active support from professional organizations and leaders in the field of special education.

The consequence has been a nationwide movement toward the creation of new resources and the reshaping, strengthening, and coordination of traditional ones. Because of increased public sensitivity to the problems accompanying handicapping conditions, the need for vital services has been recognized. New programs are being developed and made available where they are needed.

Her special need is to be cared for by people who accept her limitations.

For the purpose of providing a reference of resources the following information has been compiled. It should be noted that the material presented is not considered comprehensive; it was selected to show types of services available, to indicate how they can provide assistance, and to encourage further exploration. Also, a purpose of the references is to stimulate creative ideas for ways in which preschool handicapped children and their families everywhere can receive full service with at least a measure of convenience. (Addresses of agencies and organizations are listed alphabetically in Appendix A.)

Health Care Services

Handicapping conditions rarely exist in isolation. When two or more disabilities are present, one may be a barrier to the amelioration of the other. An uncorrected physical condition may prevent the child from learning. In such cases, the best of educational treatments will fail. Also, some conditions recognized early can be corrected or ameliorated to the extent that the child's ability to learn is affected to a far lesser degree. Health care is provided through the following types of programs of funding (President's Committee on Mental Retardation, 1976):

Public mental retardation or mental health agencies—such as residential institutions, community mental health centers, and day care centers.

Medicaid—federally assisted, state programs for financing health care of public assistance recipients and certain others.

Medicare—federal Social Security program for persons 65 years of age and older or their children permanently handicapped prior to age 22.

Head Start—federally supported preschool, health, nutrition, and parent education program.

Follow Through—early school follow-up of Head Start children.

Public schools—health services for children and youth with special needs.

Maternal and child health services clinics—federally supported "well-baby" clinics.

Crippled children's services—federally supported, state-operated clinics for children and youth with a wide range of physical and mental impairments.

Maternal and infant care projects—federally financed prenatal care, delivery, and postpartum services for women in high-risk groups, such as the poor and uneducated.

Children and youth projects—federally financed comprehensive health care for children and youth in high-risk groups.

Developmental and evaluation clinics—federally financed special projects for the diagnosis and evaluation of mentally retarded persons.

Private practitioners—such as physicians, dentists, psychologists, social workers, nurses, and counselors.

Information concerning these services may be secured from the state or city health department or the public health service located in each county or parish throughout the nation.

Social Services

Social services apply to programs and services designed to guide families, individuals, and groups and to assist them in solving complex problems of daily living. Of particular interest to parents of handicapped children are the foster family programs and adoption services available through the department of social services located in each county or parish. Income support may be provided through the following types of services:

Supplemental security income—federal and state financial assistance on the basis of need for persons who are permanently and totally disabled, blind, or aged. Eligibility for this program is restricted and determined by family income for children under age 18.

Public welfare—general assistance available in some states, and federal Aid to Families with Dependent Children program which exists in all states, granted on the basis of need.

Social Security and railroad retirement—federal retirement income guarantee programs based on contributions by employees and employers, covering retired and disabled persons and survivors of the beneficiary.

Veteran's benefits—benefits to veterans and their children; varies from state to state.

Food stamp, school lunch, and school breakfast programs—administered through the U.S. Department of Agriculture for recipients of public assistance and other low-income persons.

Medical assistance (Medicaid)—federal and state payment for residents of hospitals, skilled nursing facilities, and intermediate care facilities.

Medicare—Social Security program to pay costs of hospital and nursing home care for Social Security beneficiaries.

Federal black lung disease benefits—provided for survivors of the disease.

Public mental retardation or mental health residential institutions—total care is provided through these facilities.

Public mental retardation programs—located throughout the community.

Guardianship—management of the retarded person's own income and resources.

Interim support or the provision for special needs may be provided from the agencies listed above as well as the following:

Private voluntary agencies—provide a variety of specific benefits for which the handicapped child may be eligible.

Emergency assistance grant—provided by public or private agencies in such forms as food allotments, temporary housing, and cash for other living expenses.

Educational Services

Educational programs for preschool handicapped children are increasing rapidly in the wake of federal legislation recognizing the need for early intervention and providing support funding for program implementation.

First Chance Projects. New programs currently being developed will benefit from the reports of First Chance Projects which have been funded by the Bureau of Education for the Handicapped (BEH), Department of Health, Education and Welfare, since 1968 when Congress established the Handicapped Children's Early Education Program. The purpose of the program has been stated as follows:

> to develop experimental projects to serve as demonstration models for public schools and other agencies who need information on how to provide a variety of kinds of special help to handicapped children and their families. (DeWeerd, 1977, p. 3)

The program called for projects which would (1) offer well-rounded programs for children; (2) be designed to meet local needs; (3) call for parent involvement; (4) coordinate the program with public schools and other local programs; (5) provide inservice training; and (6) evaluate the program and children's progress.

First Chance Projects have been reviewed in *Early Childhood Education for Exceptional Children: A Handbook of Ideas and Exemplary Practices,* published by the Council for Exceptional Children. Coordinators of new programs will find tested and refined practices described and the names of instructional materials developed for use in the projects. The Directory of BEH First Chance Projects, included as an appendix, provides addresses and phone numbers that facilitate direct communication with each project (Jordan, Hayden, Karnes, & Wood, 1977).

Head Start Programs. Head Start programs are federally funded programs, originally designed for young children likely to experience later educational difficulties because of economic deprivation. In recent years, the program has changed to include "not less than 10 percentum of the total enrollment" handicapped children (LaVor & Harvey, 1976, p. 227). Information concerning local Head Start personnel or the location of programs may be secured from the national office.

Public School Programs. Public school programs for young children with special needs vary according to community needs. However, a common element among them is that the responsibility for such programs is assigned to the superintendent of schools in each school system, thus making the school board office a key resource for information concerning local programs.

The same responsibility at the state level has been assigned to the director of special education in the state department of education. Information concerning programs throughout the state may be obtained from that office (Schipper, Wilson, & Wolf, 1977, p. 7).

Special schools, such as those found in cerebral palsy centers, resulting from cooperative efforts between school systems and parent organizations may be found through the office of the superintendent of schools. As a general rule, these are found in urban areas, usually serving as regional programs.

Community facilities for handicapped children may be increased at little cost by making minor modifications in existing programs for nonhandicapped children. The addition of one staff member trained in special education may be all that is required.

Other types of education programs for children include private kindergartens, nursery schools, child care centers, university or college special projects, and child study centers.

Parent Education Programs. Parent education programs have been integral parts of Head Start and First Chance programs. Increasingly, educational programs for parents whose handicapped children have not been served by these programs are being developed by public schools and universities. One such program focused on behavior management and skills development techniques in language, motor, sensorimotor and social areas (Bricker & Bricker, 1977). Another parent education program was designed to provide information, mutual support, and improved communication among parents. While the parents were attending class, recreation was provided for their handicapped and nonhandicapped children (Flint & DeLoach, 1975). The expressed needs of the parents provide direction for the program.

Parent Organizations

Parent groups first developed informally as gatherings of individuals sharing a common problem. Their primary purpose was to help their children and themselves by providing mutual support to cope with immediate needs and social pressures. In spite of their accomplishments in securing educational programs and other services for their children, the basic purpose of the organizations have not changed (Cain, 1976).

Parent organizations are a vital resource in relaying information regarding various services in the community. It is possible for these groups to provide workshops, speakers, and seminars by qualified professionals. Parent groups also compile necessary data to give a realistic picture of the number of children with special needs who reside within their community. These statistics can provide the necessary impact for initiating special services and classes for their children at community, state, and federal levels.

Parent groups have been and show promise of continuing to be significant instruments in improving the quality of life for them and each member of their

Parent organizations are a vital resource in relaying information regarding various services in the community.

families. (Names and addresses of national parent organizations serving the needs of handicapped children and their families are included in Appendix A.)

Informational Organizations

Federal and state agencies provide information concerning handicapped individuals. Of special interest to parents with young handicapped children is the National Information Center for the Handicapped. Its publication and service program, *Closer Look,* disseminates information on services available for the handicapped child, her parents, and people who work with them. Information is sent upon request to students seeking career information, parents asking for advice on how to make their organization work, and those looking for specific services for their children. *Closer Look* provides referral information to state and local resources. Other services include (1) literature to help parents understand their child's condition and to suggest ways of coping with the challenges of a handicapped child; (2) emotional support through contact with other parents; (3) information concerning their state's special education laws and due process steps for obtaining their rights; and (4) conference planning for the organization of coalitions.

Requests for information from *Closer Look* should be specific, identifying the child's age and the handicapping condition for which service is desired. This enables the center to provide helpful responses (Dean, 1975).

State Councils on Developmental Disabilities (DD). Each state council for developmental disabilities is a public–private partnership which determines the nature and scope of its program based on the needs of the state it serves. Contributions of individual state councils have included advocacy activities, client tracking systems, program evaluation models, and progressive legislation on behalf of handicapped individuals. State DD council offices provide information concerning services and contact personnel (Stedman, 1976).

Other informational resources include the following:

Council for Exceptional Children (CEC) Information Center

National Hotline, National Blindness Information Center

ERIC (Educational Research Information Center) Clearinghouse on the Handicapped and Gifted

Office of Child Development

Parenting Materials Information Center

National Instructional Materials Information Center

Miscellaneous Services and Resources

Transportation. Greyhound Bus Company and some local transit systems provide free transportation for young handicapped children traveling with an adult. The service, Helping Hand, includes assistance with nonmotorized wheel chairs, crutches, walkers, and similar devices. Application forms are available from Greyhound Bus depots.

Advice and Legal Assistance. Steps in the process of registering dissatisfaction with an educational program or exclusion from a program include (1) contact with the local superintendent of public schools; (2) contact with the director of special education in the department of special education; and (3) contact with the superintendent of public instruction. Most problems will be resolved at the first step, making the second and third unnecessary. Time between contacts is needed to give each officer time to study the problem.

Legal advocacy services are often available through the local bar association or the American Civil Liberties Union. Particular legal needs may be met through contact with the National Center for Law and the Handicapped, or the Mental Health Law Project.

Area Service Phone Numbers. Many newspapers across the nation print a list of services available in the area daily. Each entry carries a brief description of the service provided. In a metropolitan area with a population of approximately 240,000, 45% of the area service phone numbers are for services concerned with young handicapped children and their parents or with the prevention of handicapping conditions.

Telephone Directory. The telephone directory should not be overlooked as a resource for information. A single telephone call to a local parent organization or school board office may supply enough information to begin providing full service to a handicapped child and her family.

The services for handicapped children are constantly changing. Old programs adopt new procedures emerging from model programs and exemplary practices. Federal and state legislation provide funds from which new programs are created, but personnel changes and relocation of program sites add to the frustrations of people looking for assistance.

Information concerning available services has not been complete enough to match families with appropriate agencies. Adding to the problem is the fact that in the past too many professionals have not known about existing services other than their own. At the same time, parents have not always requested specific information (Gorham, 1975). Consequently, time has been lost for both parents and professionals with little yield except added expense for the parents.

One solution to the problem is the systematic collection of information about available resources within a given area as it becomes known. Organization of the information may be facilitated by developing an index file. The use of 5-by-8-inch file cards will provide enough space; using one card for each service will simplify the task of keeping the information current.

It is suggested that the following information be collected and filed alphabetically according to the name of the agency or organization.

Name of the service: (i.e., Child Study Center)

Name of contact person: (Dr. Jane E. Doe)

Age range of persons served: (Birth to 8 years old)

Services provided: (use back of card if necessary) (Psychological and educational testing; medical examination; family history; speech and hearing screening; dental examination; educational program)

Who provides service: (Professional and paraprofessional personnel)

Location:

Report: Oral _____ Written _____
To Whom: _____
Information service needs from parents of the child:
(use back of card if necessary)

Access to a file of current, indexed information or resources can be equally beneficial to parents and the professionals working with young disabled children. Parents can save time and effort by preparing an additional card containing the following information:

Name of child

Birthday

Services received (check and add dates)
Medical
Public Health Nurse
Occupational Therapy
Physical Therapy
Other (list, using back of card)

Who may be contacted for records:

Name: _____
Address: _____
Post Office: _____
(be sure to give the state)

Phone Number: _____

Updating the card each year will keep the information relatively current. Copies of the card which contain basic information needed by many agencies are easily made for distribution. The chore of collecting information repeatedly will have been eliminated.

Summary

Movement on the national, state, and local levels is directed toward providing resources to the parents of handicapped children. The need for corrective assistance as early as possible in the child's life has been recognized and supported by legislation. Professional groups and organizations are making their presence known, and cooperative action between agencies is in evidence more than ever before. These are positive trends which seem to indicate that past frustrations caused by services being unavailable, or late arriving, will be lessened, and more importantly, that parents of handicapped infants will have some assurance of opportunity for their child's development. The effective use of resources begins with knowledge of what is available, not only among parents but among professionals who work with them. Such knowledge, freely shared, is evidence of professional commitment of the highest order.

An implied thought of this chapter has been that the parents of young children with special needs do not have to face their problems alone, nor is it necessary for them to be plagued with the frustrations of not knowing where to go for what kind of help. Kinds of personnel serving the needs of young handicapped children were described, with information concerning the work they do. In the closing portion of the chapter, resources for services and other useful information for parents have been listed with brief descriptions provided. To add to the usefulness of this information, a plan for organizing community service data has been included and addresses of the resources named have been listed in Appendix A.

REFERENCES

Azarnoff, P. Mediating the trauma of serious illness and hospitalization in children. *Children Today,* 1974, 3(4), 12–17.

Barnard, K., & Erickson, M. *Teaching children with developmental problems: A family care approach.* St. Louis: C. V. Mosby Co., 1976.

Baroff, G. *Mental retardation: Nature, cause and management.* Washington, D.C.: Hemisphere Publishing Corp., 1974.

Bricker, D., & Bricker, W. A developmentally integrated approach to early intervention. *Education and Training of the Mentally Retarded,* 1977, **12**(2), 100–108.

Cain, L. Parent groups: Their role in a better life for the handicapped. *Exceptional Children,* 1976, **42**(8), 432–437.

Council on Standards and Executive Board. Occupational therapy: Its definition and functions. *American Journal of Occupational Therapy,* 1972, **26**(4), 204–205.

Dean, D. Closer Look: A parent information service. *Exceptional Children,* 1975, **41**(8), 527–530.

DeWeerd, J. Introduction. In J. Jordan, A. Hayden, M. Karnes & M. Wood (Eds.), *Early education for exceptional children: A handbook of ideas and exemplary practices.* Reston, Va.: The Council for Exceptional Children, 1977.

Finnie, N. *Handling the young cerebral palsied child at home* (2nd ed.). New York: E. P. Dutton & Co., 1975.

Flint, W., & DeLoach, C. A parent involvement program model for handicapped children and their parents. *Exceptional Children,* 1975, **41**(8), 556–557.

Galloway, C., & Larsen, L. Associate teaching personnel. *Education and Training of the Mentally Retarded,* 1976, **11**(3), 273.

Gorham, K. A lost generation of parents. *Exceptional Children,* 1975, **41**(8), 521–525.

Gray, S. The child's first teacher. *Childhood Education,* 1971, **48**(3), 127.

Hayden, A., & Gotts, E. Multi-staffing patterns. In J. Jordan, A. Hayden, M. Karnes & M. Wood (Eds.), *Early childhood education for exceptional children: A handbook of ideas and exemplary practices.* Reston, Va.: The Council for Exceptional Children, 1977.

Jordan, J., Hayden, A., Karnes, M., & Wood, M. (Eds.) *Early education for exceptional children: A handbook of ideas and exemplary practices.* Reston, Va.: The Council for Exceptional Children, 1977.

LaVor, M., & Harvey, J. Head start economic opportunity, community partnership act of 1974. *Exceptional Children,* 1976, **42**(4), 227–230.

Marcovich, S. Dale and his teacher-mom. *American Education,* 1974, **10**(7), 29–33.

President's Committee on Mental Retardation. *Mental retardation: The known and unknown.* Washington, D.C.: DHEW Publication No. (OHD) 76-21008, 1976.

Roos, P. A parent's view of what public education should accomplish. In E. Sontag (Ed.), *Educational programming for the severely and profoundly handicapped.* Reston, Va.: The Council for Exceptional Children, 1977.

Schipper, W., Wilson, W., & Wolf, J. Public education of the handicapped. In E. Sontag (Ed.), *Educational programming for the severely and profoundly handicapped.* Reston, Va.: The Council for Exceptional Children, 1977.

Stedman, D. State councils in developmental disabilities. *Exceptional Children,* 1976, **42**(4), 186–192.

Virginia Occupational Therapy Association. *Occupational therapy in pediatrics.* Richmond, Va.: Author, 1976.

Appendix A

Resources for Services and Information

Education/Training

Local School Superintendents
- Infant stimulation programs
- Preschool programs
- Special education classes, including kindergarten

University Child Study Centers

Regional Centers for Blind/Deaf Children

Special Programs for Handicapped Children (DHEW-funded)
- Parent education
- Head Start programs

Handicapped Physical Education and Recreation
- Training—local Department of Parks and Recreation
- Therapeutic recreation—college or university programs

Library of Congress—Division for Blind and Physically Handicapped
- Information through local libraries

Health and Medical

Social Security Administration
- Medicaid
- Early and Periodic Screening, Diagnosis and Treatment (EPSDT)
- Medicare
- Supplemental Security Income (SSI)

Food Stamps

Special Food Service Programs for Children
- (Nonschool programs)—may include women and infant care programs (WIC)

School Breakfast Program

Summer Feeding

Crippled Children's Hospitals

Public Health Service
- Crippled children's services
- Family planning services
- Maternal and child services

Colleges and University Hospitals
- Genetic counseling
- Evaluation and diagnosis
- General health care
- Child study center

Department of Agriculture–Extension Services
- Home economics for the handicapped

Dental Association

Housing and Residential Information

County–City Child Welfare Departments
- Foster care information
- Respite care information
- Nursing home care
- (these may also be under Social Services, Human Resources, or other divisions of local governments)

ARENA (Adoption Resource Exchange of North America)

Division of Mental Retardation
- State institutions
- Regional centers
- Day care information
- Other community programs

Recreational and Social

Foster Grandparent Program—ACTION

Families Play to Grow—The Joseph P. Kennedy, Jr., Foundation

Advocacy Programs

Toy Lending Library—Public Library System

Youth Association for Retarded Citizens

Transportation

Greyhound Bus Company (and some local companies)—Helping Hand Service

Addresses

Alexander Graham Bell Association for the Deaf
1537 35th Street, NW
Washington, D.C. 20007

American Academy for Cerebral Palsy
University Hospital School
Iowa City, Iowa 52240

American Academy of Pediatrics
1801 Hinman Avenue
Evanston, Illinois 60204

American Alliance for Health, Physical Education and Recreation
Programs for the Handicapped
1201 16th Street, NW
Washington, D.C. 20036

American Association on Mental Deficiency
5101 Wisconsin Avenue, NW
Suite 405
Washington, D.C. 20016

American Association of Psychiatric Clinics for Children
250 West 57th Street
Room 1032
New York, New York 10019

American Association for Workers for the Blind, Inc.
1151 K Street, NW
Suite 637
Washington, D.C. 20005

American Foundation for the Blind, Inc.
15 West 16th Street
New York, New York 10011

American Medical Association
535 North Dearborn Street
Chicago, Illinois 60610

American National Red Cross
17th and D Streets, NW
Washington, D.C. 20006

American Occupational Therapy Association
6000 Executive Boulevard
Rockville, Maryland 20952

American Orthopsychiatric Association, Inc.
7790 Broadway
New York, New York 10019

American Physical Therapy Association, Inc.
1970 Broadway
New York, New York 10019

American Printing House for the Blind, Inc.
1839 Frankfort Avenue
Louisville, Kentucky 40206

American Psychiatric Association
1700 18th Street, NW
Washington, D.C. 20009

American Psychological Association
1200 17th Street, NW
Washington, D.C. 20036

American Speech and Hearing Association
10801 Rockville Pike
Rockville, Maryland 20852

Association for Education of the Visually Handicapped
711 14th Street, NW
Washington, D.C. 20005

Association for Mentally Ill Children
12 West 12th Street
New York, New York 10003

Association of University Affiliated Programs for the Developmentally Disabled
2033 M Street, NW
Suite 908
Washington, D.C. 20036

Bureau of Education for the Handicapped (BEH)
U. S. Office of Education
400 Maryland Avenue, SW
Washington, D.C. 20202

CHAP (Children Have a Potential)
AF/SGPC - CHAP
Forrestal Building
1000 Independence Avenue, SW
Washington, D.C. 20314

Child Study Association of America—Wel-Met, Inc.
50 Madison Avenue
New York, New York 10010

Child Welfare League of America
67 Irving Place
New York, New York 10003

Closer Look
National Information Center for the Handicapped
P. O. Box 1492
Washington, D.C. 20013

Conference of Executives of American Schools for the Deaf and Convention of American Instructors of the Deaf
5034 Wisconsin Avenue, NW
Washington, D.C. 20016

Council on Education of the Deaf
Clarke School for the Deaf
Northampton, Massachusetts 01060

Council for Exceptional Children
1920 Association Drive
Reston, Virginia 22091

Council of Organizations Serving the Deaf
4201 Connecticut Avenue, NW
Suite 210
Washington, D.C. 20008

Day Care and Child Development Council of America, Inc.
1401 K Street, NW
Washington, D.C. 20005

Deafness Research Foundation
366 Madison Avenue
New York, New York 10017

Developmental Disabilities
330 C Street, South
Room 3070
U.S. Department of Health, Education and Welfare
South Building
Washington, D.C. 20201

Dystonia Foundation, Inc.
425 Broad Hollow Road
Melville, New York 11746

Epilepsy Foundation of America
1828 L Street, NW
Washington, D.C. 20036

ERIC (Educational Resource Information Center)
Clearinghouse on the Handicapped and Gifted
1920 Association Drive
Reston, Virginia 22091

Family Service Association of America
44 East 23rd Street
New York, New York 10010

Head Start
U. S. Department of Health, Education and Welfare
Office of Child Development
P. O. Box 1182
Washington, D.C. 20201

International Association of Parents of the Deaf
814 Thayer Avenue
Silver Spring, Maryland 20910

The International Reading Association
800 Barksdale Road
Newark, Delaware 19711

Joseph P. Kennedy, Jr., Foundation
719 13th Street, NW
Suite 510
Washington, D.C. 20005

The Library of Congress
Division for the Blind and Physically Handicapped
Washington, D.C. 20542

Medic Alert Foundation International
P. O. Box 1009
Turlock, California 95380

Mental Health Association
1800 North Kent Street
Arlington, Virginia 22209

Muscular Dystrophy Association
810 7th Avenue
New York, New York 10019

National Association for Children with Learning Disabilities (ACLD)
4156 Library Road
Pittsburgh, Pennsylvania 15234

National Association of Coordinators of State Programs for the Mentally Retarded, Inc.
2001 Jefferson Davis Highway
Arlington, Virginia 22202

National Association of the Deaf
814 Thayer Avenue
Silver Spring, Maryland 20910

National Association of Hearing and Speech Agencies
919 18th Street, NW
Washington, D.C. 20006

National Association for Mental Health, Inc.
1800 North 10th Street
Rossalyn Station
Arlington, Virginia 22209

National Association for Retarded Citizens, Inc.
2709 Avenue E, East
P. O. Box 6109
Arlington, Texas 76011

National Blindness Information Center
1346 Connecticut Avenue, NW
Room 212
Washington, D.C. 20036

National Children's Center, Inc.
6200 2nd Street, NW
Washington, D.C. 20011

National Committee for Multi-Handicapped Children
239 14th Street
Niagara Falls, New York 14303

National Easter Seal Society for Crippled Children and Adults, Inc.
2023 West Ogden Avenue
Chicago, Illinois 60612

National Epilepsy League, Inc.
203 Wabash Avenue
Room 2200
Chicago, Illinois 60601

National Foundation March of Dimes
1275 Marmaroneck Avenue
White Plains, New York 10605

National Information Center for the Handicapped
Box 1492
Washington, D.C. 20013

National Instructional Materials Information System
Ohio State University
Columbus, Ohio 43210

National Society for Autistic Children
169 Tampa Avenue
Albany, New York 12208

National Society for Autistic Children
Information and Referral Service
101 Richmond Street
Huntington, West Virginia 25702

National Society for Low Vision People, Inc.
2346 Clermont
Denver, Colorado 80207

National Society for the Prevention of Blindness, Inc.
79 Madison Avenue
New York, New York 10016

National Therapeutic Recreation Society
1601 North Kent Street
Arlington, Virginia 22209

Office of Child Development
U. S. Department of Health, Education and Welfare
P. O. Box 1182
Washington, D.C. 20013

Office for Handicapped Individuals
Clearinghouse on the Handicapped
Office of Human Development
U. S. Department of Health, Education and Welfare
Washington, D.C. 20201

The Orton Society
8415 Bellona Lane
Towson, Maryland 21204

Parenting Materials Information Center
Southeast Educational Development Laboratory
211 East 7th Street
Austin, Texas 78701

Parents of Down's Syndrome Children
3358 Annandale Road
Falls Church, Virginia 22042

Planned Parenthood Federation of America
810 7th Avenue
New York, New York 10019

Prader-Willis Syndrome Association
Box 392
Long Lake, Minnesota 55356

President's Committee on Mental Retardation
ROB Building, #3
7th and D Streets, SW
Washington, D.C. 20201

Recordings for the Blind, Inc.
215 East 58th Street
New York, New York 10022

Science for the Blind
221 Rock Hill Road
Bala-Cynwyd, Pennsylvania 19004

Spina Bifida Association of America
343 South Dearborn
Chicago, Illinois 60604

United Cerebral Palsy Association, Inc.
66 East 34th Street
New York, New York 10016

U. S. Public Health Service
Health Services and Mental Health Administration
National Institute of Mental Health
5454 Wisconsin Avenue
Chevy Chase, Maryland 20015

USDA
Director of Child Nutrition
Food & Nutrition Service
Auditors Building, Room 3405
Washington, D.C. 20250

USDA
Program Manager, School Breakfast/Lunch
Food & Nutrition Service CND
Auditors Building, Room 3405
Washington, D.C. 20250

Western Institute for the Deaf
215 East 18th Avenue
Vancouver 10, British Columbia
Canada

Appendix B

Resources for Curriculum Materials and Instructional Aids

Books/Booklets

American Association for Health, Physical Education and Recreation. *Promising practices in elementary school physical education.* Washington, D.C.: author, 1969.

Bergen, A. *Selected equipment for pediatric rehabilitation.* Blythedale Children's Hospital, Bradhurst Avenue, Valhalla, N.Y., 1974.

Bill Wilkerson Hearing and Speech Center. *Listen, talk, do: Activity cards.* Nashville, Tenn.: author, Language Development Programs, 1975.

Blanton, E. *A helpful guide in the training of a mentally retarded child.* Richmond, Va.: Virginia State Department of Health, Bureau of Child Health, 1971.

Bryant, J. C. *Movement activities, motor ability and the education of children.* Springfield, Ill.: Charles C Thomas, 1970.

Cansler, D., & Martin, G. *Working with families: A manual for developmental centers.* Winston-Salem, N.C.: Kaplan School Supply Corp. (undated).

Chaney, C. M., & Kephart, C. *Motoric aids to perceptual training.* Columbus, Ohio: Charles E. Merrill, 1968.

Cochran, N., Wilkinson, L., & Furlow, J. *Learning on the move.* Dubuque, Iowa: Kendall/Hunt Publishing Co., 1975.

Finnie, R. *Handling the young cerebral palsied child at home.* New York: E. P. Dutton & Co., 1975.

Hackett, L. C., & Jenson, R. G. *A guide to movement exploration.* Palo Alto, Calif.: Peek Publications, 1967.

John Tracy Clinic. *Correspondence learning program for parents of preschool deaf-blind children.* Los Angeles: author, 1973.

Jordan, J., Hayden, A., Karnes, M., & Wood, M. (Eds.). *Early childhood education for exceptional children: A handbook of ideas and exemplary practices.* Reston, Va.: The Council for Exceptional Children, 1977.

Kephart, N. V. *Slow learner in the classroom* (2nd ed.). Columbus, Ohio: Charles E. Merrill, 1971.

Pearson, R. *Homemade innovative play equipment.* Reston, Va.: The Council for Exceptional Children, 1974.

Pennsylvania Department of Education. *Initial COMPET document: Commonwealth plan for education and training of mentally retarded children.* Harrisburg, Pa.: Pennsylvania Departments of Education and Public Welfare, 1972.

Quick, A. D., Little, T. L., & Cambell, A. A. *The training of foster children and their foster parents: Enhancing developmental progress and parent effectiveness.* Memphis, Tenn.: Memphis State University, Project MEMPHIS, 1973.

Robinault, I. P. *Functional aids for the multiply handicapped.* Hagerstown, Md.: Medical Department, Harper & Row, 1973.

Rosenberg, C. *Assistive devices for the handicapped.* Atlanta, Ga.: Stein Printing Co., 1968.

Sanford, A. R., Bailey, D., Johnson, W. C., Leonard, J., & O'Connor, P. D. *A manual for use of the learning accomplishment profile.* Chapel Hill, N.C.: Chapel Hill Training-Outreach Project, 1974.

Schloss, P. J., & Milliren, A. P. *Learning aids: Teacher-made instructional devices.* Springfield, Ill.: Charles C Thomas, 1975.

United Cerebral Palsy of Central Indiana, Inc. *Please help us help ourselves.* Indianapolis: author, undated.

University of the State of New York, The State Education Department. *Teaching aids for children with cerebral palsy.* Albany, N.Y.: author, 1966.

Valett, R. C. *The remediation of learning disabilities: A handbook of psychoeducational resource programs.* Palo Alto, Calif.: Fearon, 1967.

Wallace, G., & Kauffman, J. M. *Teaching children with learning problems* (2nd ed.). Columbus, Ohio: Charles E. Merrill, 1978.

Curriculum Guides

Badger, E. *Infant learning program.* Paoli, Pa.: The Instructo Corporation, 1971.

Board of Education, School District of Philadelphia. *Curriculum guide for the early years: Ages 3 and 4.* Philadelphia: Philadelphia Public Schools, 1970.

Johnson, V., & Werner, R. *A step-by-step learning guide for retarded infants and children.* Syracuse, N.Y.: Syracuse University Press, 1975.

Learning activities of the young handicapped child. Winston-Salem, N.C.: Kaplan School Supply Corp., 1977.

Massachusetts Department of Mental Health: Division of Mental Retardation. *Home stimulation for the young developmentally disabled child.* Waltham, Mass.: author, Media Resource Center, undated.

Montgomery County Easter Seal Treatment Center. *Language-related activities.* Rockville, Md.: author, 1973.

Norfolk State College. *Tentative curriculum guide for teachers of preschool handicapped children.* Norfolk, Va.: author, Department of Special Education, 1973.

Northcott, W. (Ed.). *Curriculum guide: Hearing impaired children (0-3 years) and their parents.* Washington, D.C.: The Alexander Graham Bell Association for the Deaf, Inc., 1977.

Parent-Child Early Education Program. *Shaping a curriculum for early education: A developmental sequence of skills for diagnostic teaching.* Ferguson, Mo.: author, Ferguson-Florissant School District, undated.

Project MORE (University of Kansas). *Daily living skills.* Bellevue, Wash.: Edmark Associates, 1975.

Quick, A., & Campbell, A. *Lesson plans for enhancing preschool developmental progress.* Dubuque, Iowa: Kendall/Hunt Publishing Co., 1976.

Whittington, P. *Early childhood education: A handbook for developing preschool programs.* New Albany, Miss.: New Albany Municipal Separate School District, 1973.

Directories of Resources

ERIC Clearinghouse on the Handicapped and Gifted, 1920 Association Drive, Reston, Virginia 22091.

Evans, J. *Parenting in 1975: A listing from PMIC.* Austin, Tex.: Southwest Educational Development Laboratory, 1975.

TADS. *First chance products.* Chapel Hill, N.C.: Technical Assistant Development Systems, University of North Carolina, 1974.

Equipment Sources and Catalogs

ABC School Equipment Company
437 Armour Circle, NE
Atlanta, Georgia 30324

Achievement Products, Inc.
P. O. Box 547
Mineola, New York 11501

Adaptive Therapeutic Systems, Inc.
162 Ridge Road
Madison, Connecticut 06443
(Mancine Chair, feeders, writers, communication and positioning aids)

American Guidance Service
Publishers Building
Circle Pines, Minnesota 55041
(Language development materials)

Ann Arbor Publishers
P. O. Box 1446
Ann Arbor, Michigan 48104
(Visual perception skill development materials)

Childcraft Education Corporation
20 Kilmer Road
Edison, New Jersey 08817
(Toys for classroom, fine-motor skill, conceptual development)

Cleo Learning Aids
3957 Mayfield Road
Cleveland, Ohio 44121

Community Playthings
Rifton, New York 12471
(Sturdy wooden toys)

Creative Playthings, Inc.
Princeton, New Jersey 08540
(Skills development equipment and materials)

Developmental Learning Materials
7440 Natches Avenue
Niles, Illinois 60648
(Toys and classroom aids for conceptual, perceptual, and fine-motor development)

Dexter and Westbrook, Ltd.
111 South Center Avenue
Rockville Center, New York 11571
(Auditory discrimination and language development materials)

Didax
P. O. Box 2258
Peabody, Massachusetts 01960

Early Learning—Special Education
Ideal School Supply Company
11000 South Lavergne Avenue
Oak Lawn, Illinois 60453

Edmark Associates
13241 Northrup Way
Bellevue, Washington 98005

Educational Activities, Inc.
P. O. Box 392
Freeport, New York 11520
(Basic Skills development activities on records)

Fearon Publishers, Inc.
2165 Park Blvd.
Palo Alto, California 94306
(Guide for task analysis)

Fred Sammons, Inc.
Box 32
Brookfield, Illinois 60513
(General equipment, feeding and dressing aids; Velcro; Dycem)

Functional Aids for the Multiply Handicapped
United Cerebral Palsy Association, Inc.
66 East 34th Street
New York, New York 10016
(A catalog of aids available for purchase with some patterns for making things at home)

Ideal School Supply Comapny
11000 South Lavergne Avenue
Oak Lawn, Illinois 60453

Information Resources
Stanford University
Stanford, California 94035

Instructor Publications, Inc.
Dansville, New York 14437

The Interstate - Printers and Publishers
19–27 N. Jackson St.
Danville, Illinois
(Materials for parents and teachers on sounds and language development)

Kaplan School Supply Corporation
600 Jamestown Road
Winston-Salem, North Carolina 27103
(Catalog of play, learning and growth)

Learning Concepts
2501 North Lamar
Austin, Texas 78705

Mafax Association, Inc.
90 Cherry Street
Box 519
Johnstown, Pennsylvania 15902
(Learning activities through use of games)

Markham Distributors, Inc.
507 Fifth Avenue
New York, New York 10017

Modern Education Corporation
P. O. Box 721
Tulsa, Oklahoma 74101

Nasco
901 Janesville Avenue
Fort Atkinson, Wisconsin 53538

Opportunities for Learning
5024 Lankershim Blvd.
Dept. B7
North Hollywood, California 91601

Playworld Systems
P. O. Box 227
New Berlin, Pennsylvania 17855

J. A. Preston Corporation
71 Fifth Avenue
New York, New York 10003
("Special Materials for Children" catalog; general equipment; special toys; feeding and dressing aids; Velcro)

Teaching Resources Corporation
100 Boylston Street
Boston, Massachusetts 02116
(Instructional materials in all skill areas)

Trend Enterprises, Inc.
Box 3073
St. Paul, Minnesota 55165
(Innovative instructional materials)

Glossary

Aberration. A deviation, usually regarded as abnormal.

Abortion. The ending of a pregnancy before the 24th week; may be spontaneous (occurs by itself) or induced (brought on intentionally).

Acquisition. (phase of learning) Includes the essential incident of learning; the coding of knowledge for its entry into storage in the central nervous system.

Acuity. Acuteness or clearness; amount of sensory perception, especially of vision.

Adaptive behavior. The standards of personal independence and social responsibility expected of a person at a given age and within a specific cultural group. The capacity to adjust to simple problem situations.

Amino acids. The end products of protein digestion; they are necessary for tissue repair and growth. If for some reason there is a breakdown in this digestive process, it can be detected through what is called an *amino acid screening.*

Amniocentesis. The withdrawal from the pregnant mother's womb of some amniotic fluid (usually between the 14th and 18th weeks of pregnancy) in order to chemically analyze cells from the baby. It is used to try to prevent handicaps by treating Rh problems and by allowing abortions of those fetuses which are discovered to be abnormal. It can also help parents who are afraid to take a chance that their baby might be born with some defect that is in their families. Because a chromosome study is part of this procedure, amniocentesis can also incidentally tell the sex of the baby before birth.

Amniotic fluid. The liquid, or "bag of waters," that surrounds the baby while it is in the mother's uterus (womb). Skin cells of the baby are sloughed off into the amniotic fluid and they are what are studied in amniocentesis.

Anomaly. Anything unusual or irregular or different from the general rule; usually refers to some physical characteristic. A congenital anomaly is one that happens to a baby before he is born and is usually diagnosed at birth.

Anoxia. The result of a decreased or insufficient amount of oxygen in the organs and tissues of the body. An anoxic person lacks enough oxygen, may turn purplish or bluish, and seems to struggle for air if conscious. Anoxia at the time of birth is a major cause of brain damage in babies.

Apgar score. A scale devised by Dr. Virginia Apgar to measure a newborn baby's vital signs at birth and right after birth.

Aphasia. A disorder of language learning; the loss of the ability to express or understand language symbols (the spoken or written word) as a result of some central nervous system dysfunction. It can be *expressive* (or "motor"), in which the person can understand but cannot give back appropriate responses; *receptive* (or "sensory"), in which the person cannot understand language he hears or sees; or both. *Congenital aphasia* means language did not develop at all, rather than that it was once developed and then lost.

Aphonia. Inability to utter vocal sounds, due to some structural or functional defect in the vocal cords.

Apprehending. (phase of learning) Consists of subject's attending and perceiving a stimulus.

Apraxia. A brain disorder characterized by loss of ability to manipulate and use common objects and to execute planned movements.

Articulation. The ability to enunciate speech sounds accurately.

Articulatory defects. Indistinct or confusing speech resulting from failure or inability to produce the commonly accepted speech sounds.

Ataxia. Muscle incoordination that shows itself, during a purposeful movement, by irregularity and lack of precision.

Athetoid. A type of cerebral palsy characterized by writhing, involuntary movements of the muscles, usually involving part of an arm or leg (hand or foot). Such movement stops during sleep.

Audiologist. The person who is trained to evaluate, diagnose, and treat hearing problems in children.

Audiometry. The measurement of hearing sensitivity and acuity; generally classified into pure tone audiometry and speech audiometry.

Autism. Severe emotional disturbance of childhood characterized by inability to form meaningful interpersonal relationships.

Behavior modification. An approach to changing behavior by understanding and manipulating the external, social, or behavioral forces that operate on a person. The belief is that a person is likely to repeat behavior that is followed by a pleasant or gratifying experience. Therefore, emphasis is placed on giving positive reinforcements (rewards) for desirable behavior; a form of operant conditioning.

Bilateral. Having two sides; pertaining to both sides.

Birth trauma. An injury to the infant received during or due to the process of birth.

Bonding. A shared and unifying relationship. Responsiveness between infant and family which promotes feelings of security and belonging in the young child.

Brain. The large, soft mass of tissue located inside the skull; the primary center for regulating and coordinating all body activities. Also, it is the center of awareness, thought, memory, reason, judgment, and feeling. Different parts of the brain control different functions; therefore, the results of brain injury or brain damage depend on which part or parts of the brain are affected.

Brain damage. The result of injury to, or lack of development of, brain cells. Also termed *brain injury.*

Breech delivery. Term given to the birth of an infant born feet first or buttocks first.

Capacity. A potential ability, or one largely inherited but not fully developed.

Central nervous system. Part of the total nervous system. It includes the brain and the spinal cord. (The nerve endings and fibers that go from the brain and spinal cord to all the parts of the body are called the *peripheral nervous system.*)

Cerebral palsy. Describes the effects of, or difficulty in, motor power and coordination resulting from damage to the brain.

Child Find Programs. Interagency activities associated with the early identification of handicapped infants and young children for the purpose of intervention with appropriate medical and educational treatment.

Chromosome. A microscopic part of the cell, containing thousands of genes (hereditary determiners, or traits that are passed from parents to their children). In humans, the normal number of chromosomes in each cell is 46 (or 23 pairs, including the sex chromosomes that determine whether a person will be a male or a female); one of each pair comes from each parent. Chromosomal abnormalities result in diseases or defects.

A chromosome study may be done on a baby to help diagnose a suspected condition. The study may be done on parents to see if they are carriers of an inheritable disease. A chromosome study is done through a special kind of examination of cells obtained through a blood sample. *Karyotype* is another name for chromosome study which shows the chromosomes arranged in pairs according to size and shape.

Chronological age. Sometimes referred to as CA, it means the actual number of years a person has lived.

Cleft lip. A congenital defect in which a fissure exists in the upper lip.

Cleft palate. A congenital defect in which a longitudinal fissure exists in the roof of the mouth.

Coma. An abnormally deep sleep, or state of unconsciousness, from which the person cannot be aroused (awakened). It may be due to injury to the head affecting the brain; to the effects of certain drugs or poisons; or to central nervous system illness or disease.

Compensation. A defense mechanism by which an individual covers up or counterbalances a real or imagined inferiority in an effort to reduce tension.

Competency based instruction. Instruction directed toward the development of specific skills composing a desired competence or ability.

Concept. Knowledge that is not directly perceived through the senses but is the result of the manipulation of sensory impressions. A concept requires both abstraction and generalization: the first to isolate the property, the second to recognize that it may be ascribed to many objects.

Conflict. A disagreement, dispute, or quarrel. Also refers to mental and spiritual struggles within a person.

Congenital. Any mental or physical trait or condition that exists at birth because of something that happened to the fetus during the time it was in the womb; it may or may not be hereditary.

Convulsion. Violent involuntary contracting and relaxing of the muscles; spasms.

Cranium. The skull; the bones of the head that are around the brain.

Cretinism. A type of mental deficiency resulting from a deficiency in thyroid secretion.

Criterion. An arbitrary decision as to the number of correct responses (i.e., six consecutive correct responses) a child must make before one assumes that learning has taken place and that the child is ready to learn the next task.

Criterion-referenced tests or tools. Instruments designed to identify the presence or absence of specific skills with regard for a predetermined quality of performance.

Crossing the midline. Ability to perform tasks requiring the eyes or hands to cross the midline of the body (i.e., touching the right ear with the left hand).

Cyanosis. The dark purple or bluish color of the skin and mucous membranes due to lack of oxygen (and too much carbon dioxide) in the blood; may be due to a severe reduction of blood moving through the body (very poor circulation).

Cystic fibrosis. A congenital metabolic disorder in which the body gives off certain abnormal secretions that are carried throughout the body in the blood. Symptoms usually appear in early childhood. The disease is chronic and degenerative, with no known cure. It is usually found only in Caucasians.

Development. Growth of the brain and body.

Developmental disabilities. Refers to individuals with a disability attributable to mental retardation, cerebral palsy, epilepsy, or autism, or who require treatment similar to that required for mentally retarded individuals. A developmental disability originates before the individual reaches an age of 18, and can be expected to continue indefinitely to such a degree that it constitutes a handicap.

Diagnosis. The determination, after studying the symptoms, of the nature and extent of a disease or condition.

Diplegia. Paralysis affecting like parts on both sides of the body; in bilateral paralysis—legs are more often affected than arms.

Directionality. Sense of direction.

Distractibility. Inability to attend to a given task for more than a few seconds.

Dominance. Refers to the more advanced development of one side of the brain than the other. Dominance determines which hand is used for writing, which eye is stronger, which foot is most likely to be used for kicking.

Drooling. Dripping or flowing of saliva from the mouth.

Dysfunction. Absence of complete normal function; differs from paralysis in which there is loss of function.

Dyslexia. A severe reading disability; an impairment, usually due to central nervous system dysfunction, associated with printed symbols. It is estimated that between 3% to 7% of the population of the United States has some dyslexia. Boys seem to outnumber girls almost 3 to 1.

The dyslexic child often sees letters or numbers reversed (this is normal in children of a certain age but then passes); he may not be able to tell differences between words he hears that sound somewhat alike; he may have problems with size and shape discriminations (big, small, a square, a circle). All of these factors affect the ability to learn to read.

ECG (or EKG). Stands for electrocardiogram; a "picture" of the heart action which results from a machine recording of the electrical currents originating in the heart.

Echolalia. The meaningless repetition of words; the involuntary repetition of a word or phrase just spoken by another person. It is common in the speech of very young children. At a later age, it may be associated with mental disorder.

Educational child development specialist. This professional is trained to provide services for young children with special needs and to coordinate those services which are outside the range of her training.

EEG. Stands for electroencephalogram; a record resulting from the use of a special machine to measure the electrical discharges of the brain. It is a painless examination in which electrodes from the machine are attached to the head with dabs of a glue-like substance. This examination, sometimes referred to as a "brain wave test" is often used as part of the diagnostic evaluation of a child suspected of having brain injury, brain damage, or epilepsy.

Encephalitis. An inflammation of the brain, usually caused by an infection. *Secondary encephalitis* is that which results from a disease or illness (such as mumps or measles). Encephalitis is sometimes referred to as sleeping sickness.

Encephalopathy. A general term for any disease of the brain.

Endocrinologist. A physician who specializes in the hormonal (glandular) system.

Endogenous. From within, often used to describe conditions arising from factors within the body such as an hereditary condition.

Enzyme. A substance in the body capable of causing chemical changes in other substances (food, for instance) without itself being changed. Enzymes are found particularly in the digestive juices, causing substances in food to break down into simpler compounds so the body can use them. Each enzyme can only work on one particular compound. The more common ones break down fats, starches, proteins, and sugar. The end products are amino acids.

Epilepsy. A chronic disease characterized by the appearance of convulsions or their equivalent.

Grand mal epilepsy. Major form of the disease in which the convulsions are generalized over the body with accompanying alterations of consciousness.

Petit mal epilepsy. A type of form of the disease characterized by a momentary loss of consciousness.

Psychomotor epilepsy. A type of epilepsy in which irrational reactions, such as temper tantrums, serve as substitutes for, or equivalents of, convulsions.

Etiology. The cause of an illness, disease, or condition.

Exogenous. From without, often used to describe a condition arising from factors outside the body such as a nonhereditary condition.

Extrinsic. Originating or operating from or on the outside of the body.

Feedback. Occurs through the reinforcement process. An act of learning requires either an automatic or a contrived feedback.

Fetus. Human embryo; baby before birth and while it is in the mother's uterus (womb).

Figure-ground difficulties. An inability to pay attention to a specific item or figure; instead, a person looks at all the stimuli in the background (visual). Also, inability to focus on a person's voice because of other sounds in the room (auditory).

Fissure. A narrow opening produced by cleavage or separation of parts.

Functional mental retardation. Term used to identify those people who are functioning at a significantly low level but who, according to a variety of indices, have the ability to function at a much more advanced level.

Gait. The way one walks. Many brain damaged children have what is called an "awkward gait."

Galactosemia. A metabolic disorder, starting in infancy, in which there are abnormal amounts of the enzyme galactose in the blood. The result can be physical and mental retardation, enlargement of the liver and spleen, and cataracts.

Generalization. Often referred to as *transfer of learning.*

Genes. Those parts of the body cell which hold the characteristics that parents pass on to their children (heredity). Genes are located in the chromosomes. A *dominant gene* is one that is inherited from both parents and that usually is visible in the child; a *recessive gene* is one that is inherited from one parent, and the chances of it being seen in the child are less.

Geneticist. Medical practitioner trained to study chromosomes and genes and how traits of parents are passed on to their children. She consults with parents concerning the risk of genetic-related problems in their offspring and performs amniocentesis.

Gestation. The period of pregnancy; the time from when the baby is conceived (conception) to delivery (birth). The "normal," or average, gestation is 280 days or about nine months.

Group therapy. Group psychotherapy; the treatment of several individuals as a group.

Habilitation. Process of developing individual skills which have never been learned or developed. Habilitation is developmental and, directly or indirectly, is always a part of the rehabilitation process with children.

Habituation. The method by which the nervous system reduces or prevents response to inconsequential repeated stimulation.

Hemiplegia. Paralysis of the arm and leg on one side of the body.

Hereditary resources. Innate abilities. Abilities the child is born with. (The ability to speak is an acquired skill.)

Heredity. The characteristics, conditions, or traits passed down in a family from parents to children.

Hydrocephaly. A condition of increased secretion of serum into the cranial spaces with a possible consequence of pressure to such a point that the brain may be damaged.

Hypertelorism. A congenital craniofacial deformity in which the distance between the eye sockets is abnormally great. Frequently associated manifestations are cleft lip and palate, malocclusion, congenital abnormalities of the fingers, hands, and ears, and mental retardation.

Hypertonia. Excessive muscle tone.

Hypotonia. Less than normal muscle tone.

IQ. Acronym for *intelligence quotient;* an index or measurement of a person's mental age, determined through the use of standard psychological tests. IQ scores between 90 and 110 are considered average, or normal.

Idiopathic. Of unknown cause.

Incidence. Range of occurrence or influence of a condition or disease.

Instructional materials. Equipment or devices used for the purpose of helping the learner gain in skill development and understanding. Included are optional types of environmental settings.

Intelligence test. A way of measuring the difference between people, or between the reactions of the same person on different occasions. It is used to determine the person's IQ.

Intrinsic. Originating or due to causes or factors within a body, organ, or part. Inherent.

Language development specialist. A professional who works with children in ways similar to those of a speech pathologist. She is concerned with how language develops and how it may be stimulated.

Language disorder. Any problem in using symbols for communication; may include problems in listening, speaking, writing, or reading.

Laterality. Sense of left and right. Complete awareness of the two sides of the body and the ability to use each separately or both sides together as required.

LEA. Local educational agency (district or division school board represented by the superintendent of schools).

Lesion. Change in tissue resulting from injury or disease.

Locomotion. Movement from one place to another.

Malocclusion. Irregular or faulty contact of the lower jaw teeth with corresponding teeth of the upper jaw when the jaws are closed.

Maturation. The process of achieving full development or growth.

Meningitis. Inflammation of the membranes around the brain or spinal cord.

Meningocele. A protrusion of the membranes of the brain or spinal cord through a defect in the skull or spinal column.

Mental age. A measure of mental development or general intelligence in terms of the average performance of normal individuals at various ages. It is determined by tests of intelligence.

Mental illness. A serious disorder of the mind characterized by a distorted mental outlook and behavior which is peculiar, bizarre, or different from what society considers normal.

Mental retardation. Subaverage general intellectual functioning that originates during the developmental period and is associated with impairment in adaptive behavior.

Borderline retardation. Intellectual functioning ranging from 70 to 84 IQ as measured by standardized testing materials.

Mild retardation. Intellectual functioning ranging from 55 to 69 IQ as measured by standardized testing materials.

Moderate retardation. Intellectual functioning ranging from 40 to 54 IQ as measured by standardized testing materials.

Severe retardation. Intellectual functioning ranging from 25 to 39 IQ as measured by standardized testing materials.

Profound retardation. Intellectually below 25 IQ as measured by standardized testing materials.

Metabolic disorder. A problem in the chemical changes of the body which result from converting food into body energy. Disorders of this nature are caused by abnormality in enzyme production.

Midline. The imaginary line that divides the body into right and left halves.

Mongolism. (Down's syndrome) A commonly recognized form of mental retardation caused by imperfect chromosome formation and characterized by low mentality and abnormal body features.

Multiple handicap. Term used to indicate the presence of two or more handicapping conditions.

Neonate. The newborn baby up to one month of age.

Neonatology. The study of disorders of the newborn (period immediately succeeding birth and continuing through the first month of life).

Nerves. Bundles of fibers which transmit impulses or "messages" from one part of the body to another.

Neurologist. A physician whose area is neurological problems, or problems of the central nervous system.

Neuromotor development. Concerned with the maturation of the nervous system and the parallel acquisition of control over the muscular system.

Neuromuscular organization. In the process of maturation, the nervous system and the muscular structure of the human body begin to work together, enabling the child to accomplish movement which was impossible before. As the process continues, the child gains control over his muscles and is able to make them work for him in activities such as holding a bottle or using a spoon. Practice facilitates neuromotor organization.

Neurosurgeon. A physician who specializes in performing operations that have to do with the central nervous system.

Nutritionist. A person who is trained especially in the use of food for growth and general health.

Obesity. The accumulation of fat that is detrimental to health.

Obstetrician. A physician who specializes in the medical care of women during pregnancy and childbirth.

Occupational therapist. A therapist concerned with the treatment of persons having physical or mental disabilities through specific types of activities to promote development or rehabilitation.

Ophthalmologist. The medical doctor whose specialty is the structure, functions, and diseases of the eye, including eye surgery.

Optometrist. The specialist in the scientific examination of the eyes to diagnose disease, and to treat vision problems through the use of lenses (glasses) or exercises but *not* through medication or surgery.

Orthodontist. A dentist who specializes in orthodontia, the branch of dentistry that deals with straightening and adjusting teeth.

Orthopedist. An orthopedist or orthopedic surgeon is concerned with the growth, repair, and care of muscles, tendons, joints, and bone.

Osteomyelitis. Inflammation of the bone marrow and adjacent bone and cartilage, usually caused by pus-forming microorganisms.

Otolaryngologist. An otolaryngologist is a physician specially trained in treatment of diseases of the ear, nose, and throat.

Otologist. A physician who specializes in diagnosis and treatment of ear problems.

Overlearning. Trials beyond criterion. Frequent errors in overlearning are indicative of a weak criterion. Overlearning tends to increase retention and to facilitate transfer of learning.

Paraplegia. Paralysis of the lower part of the body, including both legs.

Pathology. Condition produced by disease or injury.

Patterning. A method of training in which constantly repeated exercises are used in an effort to get other, healthy brain cells to take over the function of damaged brain cells.

Pediatric neurologist. Medical practitioner who specializes in the diseases and treatment of central nervous system disorders, including epilepsy and cerebral palsy, in children.

Pediatric psychiatrist. Medical practitioner concerned with children's mental health.

Pediatrician. (Pediatrist) Medical practitioner who specializes in children's diseases.

Performance. Observable behavior.

Perinatal medicine. Any diagnostic or therapeutic procedure upon the fetus in utero or in the immediate neonatal period.

Perinatalogy. The study of perinatal medicine.

Periodontist. A dentist who specializes in periodontics, the branch of dentistry concerned with the supporting tissues of the teeth.

Perservation. Inappropriate and purposeless repetition of a past experience (body rocking, repeating a word over and over again, waving the arms endlessly). Repetitive movements may be reflexive and may require control before more purposeful movement can be learned.

Physiatrist. The medical doctor who specializes in rehabilitation through other than surgical means.

Physical therapist. The person skilled and specially trained in treatment of the body by massage or exercise, as prescribed by the physiatrist.

Pica. A hunger to eat things that are not edible (things other than food).

PKU. Acronym for phenylketonuria, a congenital metabolic disorder in which abnormal amounts of the enzyme phenylalanine in the blood cause brain damage. This condition is now treated with a special diet.

Pneumoencephalogram. An X-ray picture of the brain taken by replacing the cerebrospinal fluid with air or gas; used to help diagnose brain injury, brain damage, or a tumor.

Postmaturity. When pregnancy goes well beyond term. A postmature baby begins to lose weight and can begin to suffer from anoxia.

Potential. Existing in possibility, not in actuality; the highest level at which a person could perform.

Premack principle. Using the child's most frequent (or high preference) activity, such as play, as a reinforcer for a less frequent (low preference) activity. The Premack Principle has the advantage of being a natural reinforcer requiring neither food nor liquid. Also, it is easily identified through careful observation of the child's daily activities.

Prematurity. When pregnancy ends before the ninth month. A premature baby weighs less than 5 pounds 8 ounces at birth.

Prenatal. Before birth.

Preoperational thought. A stage of intellectual development described by Piaget.

Profile chart. Graph or curve formed by uniting the points representing one's scores on each of several kinds of tests or performances.

Prognosis. A forecast of the probable course or outcome of a particular illness, disease, or condition.

Prosthesis. Addition of a false part (arm, leg) to the human body or the addition of a supporting device which enables the body part to function more efficiently, closer to normal.

Prosthetic device. A prosthesis.

Psychiatrist. A medical doctor who specializes in the treatment of mental illness and emotional disturbance.

Psychoanalyst. A specialist in treatment of mentally ill or emotionally disturbed people; her professional degree (educational background) may be medical, or she may be a certified psychologist or social worker.

Psychodynamic. Spontaneous activity of the mind, like a flashing thought, which is profound in nature.

Psychodynamics. The systematized study and theory of human behavior emphasizing unconscious motivation and the functional significance of emotion.

Psychologist. A person who is trained and certified to administer intelligence tests and who can also evaluate and treat people with emotional problems.

Psychotherapy. A treatment method for emotional disorders. It is based primarily on verbal (talking) or nonverbal (playing) communication, rather than on drug therapy or shock therapy.

Public health nurse. A registered nurse who is community based and who is especially trained to deal with community health problems or health problems in the home.

Quadriplegia. Paralysis or involvement of all four extremities.

Recall. Retrieval of previously learned information.

Recreational therapist. Person trained to plan and implement recreational activities for specific skill and/or attitude development.

Resuscitation. The stimulation of the breathing center in a person's brain to restore or improve breathing.

Retention. (phase of learning) Storage of memories in the nervous system.

Rubella. Commonly called German measles. Congenital anomalies including deafness, cataracts, cardiac malformations, and mental retardation may result in offspring of mothers contracting rubella in the first trimester of pregnancy.

Schizophrenia. A mental illness characterized by one's disassociation of himself with his environment and subsequent deterioration of character and personality.

Scoliosis. Lateral curvature of the spine, most commonly caused by an unsupported short leg.

SEA. State educational agency (State Department of Education represented by the superintendent of public instruction or the person carrying that responsibility).

SEE. Acronym for signing exact English. A type of sign language.

Sensorimotor. Motor responses to sensory stimuli (visual, auditory, tactile, etc.). As the child grows and develops, these responses become refined, less random, and thus skilled.

Sensory disabilities. The consequence of damage to some area of the brain or to the sense organs. These include serious impairments of vision, including blindness; hearing, including deafness; impairments of the senses of touch, smell, movement, and taste.

Sickle cell anemia. A genetic disease in which the red blood cells change to a shape resembling a sickle. These red blood cells then reduce the amount of oxygen going through the body, thus slowly causing damage to various parts of the body. Incidence is usually in black people. Although the symptoms may be treated, this disease is considered chronic and degenerative because there is no known cure.

Sign language. A system of communication in which motions and gestures stand for letters, words, and ideas. Used by those who are deaf or hearing impaired and by foreigners. The user is said to be "signing."

Social worker. A professional who is trained and certified to diagnose and treat social problems in the individual or in the family; works directly in the community for the improvement of social conditions which interfere with the mental and physical health of all people.

SQ. Acronym for social quotient; an index of a person's ability to look after his own needs and to take responsibility for himself. It provides an age at which the person is functioning socially (his social age) rather than how many years old he actually is.

Spasms. Alternate contracting and relaxing of muscles.

Spastic. The state of such increased muscle tone that there is exaggeration of all the reflexes; often found in people with cerebral palsy.

Speech pathologist. A professional who is trained and certified to evaluate, diagnose, and treat speech and language problems.

Spinal tap. A laboratory procedure in which fluid is withdrawn from the spinal canal for diagnostic purposes.

Stimulus. Something that excites an organ or part of the body to a specific activity or function. Examples of external stimuli are the sound of a bell, the touch of soft cotton, the smell of food cooking, the sight of a familiar face. Internal stimulus may be hunger, fear, or the feeling of confidence.

Successive approximations. Finely defined subtasks of a skill, carefully sequenced for instructional purposes.

Syndrome. A group or set of symptoms that together make up a certain disease or condition. A common example is mongolism, or Down's syndrome. *Chronic brain syndrome* is a term used to refer to a nonspecific disturbance of brain function that is of long duration.

Task analysis. The process of identifying and sequencing the subskills that compose a given task.

Tay-Sachs disease. A genetic disease that affects the central nervous system and leads to death in early childhood. It is found in children of Jewish ancestry.

Toxemia. A condition in which the blood contains toxic or poisonous substances.

Training methods. Principles and procedures used to develop skills and attitudes.

Trauma. A serious physical or emotional injury.

Traumatic experience. A sudden difficult situation that arouses a feeling of helplessness.

Tremor. An involuntary shaking or trembling in any part of the body (hands, head, fingers).

Triplegia. Paralysis of three limbs.

Verbal chains. Understanding and associating words used for objects.

Withdrawal. Avoidance of facing an annoying or unpleasant situation.

REFERENCES

Banus, B. S. *The developmental therapist: A prototype of the pediatric occupational therapist.* Thorofare, N.J.: Charles B. Slack, 1971.

Brown, D. L. *Developmental handicaps in babies and young children: A guide for parents.* Springfield, Ill.: Charles C Thomas, 1972.

Garrison, D., & Force, D. G. *The psychology of exceptional children.* New York: Ronald Press, 1965.

Grossman, H. J. (Ed.). *Manual on terminology and classification in mental retardation.* Baltimore: American Association on Mental Deficiency, Special Publication Series, No. 2, 1973.

Hunter, M., Schucman, H., & Friedlander, G. *The retarded child from birth to five.* New York: John Day, 1972.

Stedman, T. L. *Medical dictionary.* Baltimore: Williams & Wilkins, 1976.

Vaughan, V. C., McKay, R. J., & Nelson, W. E. *Nelson textbook of pediatrics.* Philadelphia: W. B. Saunders Co., 1975.

Webster's third new international dictionary. Springfield, Mass.: G. & C. Merriam Co., 1971.

The world book dictionary. Chicago: Field Enterprises, Educational Corp., 1971.

About the Authors

Nancy H. Fallen received the Ed.D. degree from the University of Maryland with major fields of interest in special education and child development. She is presently associate professor of education, Department of Special Education, Virginia Commonwealth University. She served as content coordinator for the videotape series *Young Children with Special Needs,* and for the Division of Special Education, Virginia State Department of Education, was coordinator of the task force and author of its report which became the basis for *A Comprehensive State Plan for the Education of Young Handicapped Children Below Age 5 in Virginia.* She initiated a pilot program in team teaching, coordinated a field-based alternative master's degree program in three areas of special education and served as consultant to school divisions and programs throughout Virginia.

Jill E. McGovern received the B.A. in English literature from Northwestern University, the M.A. in early childhood education from Xavier University (New Orleans), and the Ph.D. in special education from the University of New Orleans. Currently, she is assistant professor of education, the College of Charleston, Charleston, South Carolina. Her areas of particular interest are language development and learning disabilities. Jill's teaching experience includes serving as a Peace Corps volunteer in Micronesia, teaching English as a second language, teaching at the preschool and elementary levels in the public schools of New Orleans, serving as a resource person in a reading program, and teaching at the university level. She has also served as a consultant to Head Start and Title I projects as well as to the Educational Diagnostic Center at the College of Charleston and the Charleston County public schools. She has been active in a number of professional organizations and was president of the South Carolina Association for Children with Learning Disabilities during the 1977–78 term.

Elsie H. Blanton, R.N., M.S. Rehabilitation Counseling, is presently chief public health nurse in the Samuel A. Anderson Child Development Clinic in Richmond, Virginia. She specializes in developmental assessment and parental counseling, working with public health nurses in various localities and lecturing at nursing schools, and is involved in volunteer activities with the local Association for Retarded Citizens and Mental Health-Mental Retardation Services Board. The mother of five children, one of whom is mongoloid, she enjoys handwork and reading.

Ellen Bynum is assistant executive director of the Virginia Association for Retarded Citizens and served as staff liaison for the development of the videotape series *Young Children with Special Needs.* She has developed group resource materials for the Youth National Association for Retarded Citizens and received an award from NARC for developing a youth exchange program in Puerto Rico. As an adjunct faculty member at J. Sargeant Reynolds Community College, she teaches sociology, and she also serves as codirector of Skye Pictures, Inc., an educational media organization.

Bonnie S. Carlton, M.Ed., project manager at Lynchburg Training School and Hospital in Lynchburg, Virginia, is part of a developmental training team working with severely and profoundly retarded children. In addition to her love for children, she enjoys music, particularly vocal groups and ensembles.

Bernadine A. Clarke, R.N., MSN, is instructor in maternal child nursing at the Medical College of Virginia, Virginia Commonwealth University. Previously, she taught nursing at Duke University and the Richmond Memorial Hospital School of Nursing. As a professional registered nurse, she gives talks on parenting school-aged children to interested groups and is developing an audiovisual aid demonstrating parenting competencies. In her leisure hours, she plays a mountain dulcimer and enjoys bicycling and camping.

Ardella M. Curtis received her M.Ed. degree in special education from the University of Virginia and is currently coordinator of the Multi-Handicapped Center in Hampton, Virginia. She has been a teacher of the mentally retarded in Eugene, Oregon, and was head teacher at the Children's Rehabilitation Center in Charlottesville, Virginia. She served as assistant supervisor of special education in the Virginia Department of Education and has been a consultant to various programs and clinics throughout Virginia. Presently, she serves on a national committee on legislation for the education of physically handicapped children.

Laura L. Dittman, Ph.D., is a professor at the Institute for Child Study in the College of Education, University of Maryland. Prior to her academic affiliation, she was involved in research in mental retardation and consulting with families of young blind children at Children's Hospital. She was a child development specialist in an interdisciplinary diagnostic clinic for retarded children in Washington, D.C., and is author of the government publication, *The Mentally Retarded Child at Home,* which has been translated into three languages.

David A. Draper, M.D., is associate professor of pediatrics at the Medical College of Virginia, Virginia Commonwealth University. As a practicing pediatrician, he has been involved with high risk infants and their families through the Child Development Study at the National Health Institute. He also initiated and directed the High Risk Intensive Care Nursery and established a parenting program for Richmond, Virginia. He appears regularly on local television as a pediatric consultant for "Ask Your Pediatrician."

Walter Draper, M.D., is a graduate of Richmond College, University of Richmond and the Medical College of Virginia, Virginia Commonwealth University. He received his child psychiatry training at the Virginia Treatment Center for Children where he is currently director. He also serves as chairman and associate professor, Division of Child Psychiatry, the Medical College of Virginia.

Ronald C. Eaves earned his Ph.D. degree in special education at the University of Georgia and is presently associate professor in special education programs at Auburn University. He was previously assistant professor in the Department of Special Education and was coordinator of the CEDAR clinics for one year at Pennsylvania State University. He was also coordinator of identification and diagnosis for the Handicapped Infants and Children Comprehensive Outreach Model Program. His instructional interests center around training school psychologists and teachers of the emotionally disturbed, and he is currently writing the *Teacher Competency Journal,* a performance-based system for training special educators.

Anita S. Fallen received her B.S. degree in mass communications, specializing in broadcast journalism, from Virginia Commonwealth University. She served as production assistant for the videotape series, *Young Children with Special Needs,* and has been a broadcast journalist with public radio in Richmond, Virginia, writing and producing documentaries and feature stories. She is interested in photography and horticulture and enjoys classical music.

Howard G. Garner received his M.Ed. and Ph.D. degrees from the University of Florida. He was the director of education and the director of the junior campus of Starr Commonwealth for Boys in Albion, Michigan for three years, and currently he is assistant professor of special education at Virginia Commonwealth University. In addition to being a member of an infamous musical group called the East Virginia Toadsuckers, he and his family are avid folk dancers.

George A. Giacobbe received his Ph.D. degree in the area of exceptional children from the University of Georgia. Presently he is assistant professor of education in the Department of Special Education, Virginia Commonwealth University. He was a teacher at the Tulsa Boys' Home in Oklahoma, and was at one time a professional violinist. He continues to enjoy playing and listening to music.

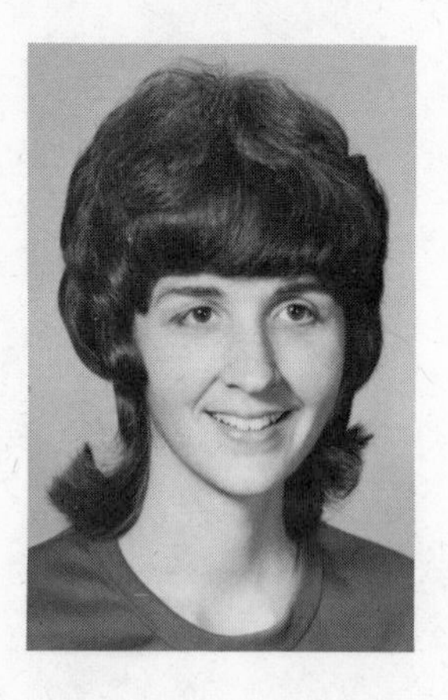

Roberta L. Goodwyn, B.S., OTR, serves as chief of occupational therapy at the Richmond Cerebral Palsy Center. She uses developmental treatment techniques with children and helps parents and teachers with equipment and activities for children with developmental delays. She is chairperson of the Virginia Occupational Therapy Association's Developmental Disabilities Special Interest Group, and serves on the Interprofessional Affairs Committee of the American Academy for Cerebral Palsy and Developmental Medicine. She enjoys outdoor activities and lives on a homestead where she raises animals.

David E. Herr, Ed.D., is associate professor of special education at James Madison University in Harrisonburg, Virginia. Previously, he served on the special education faculty at Pennsylvania State University. His primary interests include teacher training, delineation and evaluation of teaching strategies in various child domains, and the development of behavior management skills in teachers. He has authored numerous articles on teacher training in educational journals.

Sue E. Horn, M.A., CCC, is a speech and language pathologist in the Chesterfield County, Virginia public school system. A graduate of Marshall University, Huntington, West Virginia, she has worked as a speech and language pathologist in Project HEAR and the Powhatan County, Virginia public schools before joining the Early Childhood Handicapped Program in Chesterfield County. As a child development specialist in the program, she deals with language development in the preschool developmentally disabled child.

William A. Horn earned his Ed.D. degree from West Virginia University and is presently assistant professor of special education at Virginia Commonwealth University. He taught primary level EMR students in western Pennsylvania and served on the special education staff at Bloomsburg State College in Pennsylvania and the West Virginia College of Graduate Studies. His present involvement is with development and implementation of competency based teacher-training programs in both on-campus and field-based settings. He is currently president of the Council for Educational Diagnostic Services, a division of the Council for Exceptional Children.

Maureen A. Larkin, Ed.D., is assistant professor of special education at Virginia Commonwealth University. She is director of the University Child Study Center where she coordinates the services of the medical and academic campus for diagnostic evaluations, remediation, and tutoring for the young child through the adolescent age. She is the mother of two daughters and enjoys traveling.

Phillip J. McLaughlin received his Ed.D. degree from the University of Georgia and is currently assistant professor of special education at Virginia Commonwealth University. A member of several professional organizations, including the American Association for the Education of the Severely/Profoundly Handicapped, he also serves as a consultant to public schools on teaching the mentally retarded. He is presently writing *Program Development in Special Education: Designing Individualized Education Programs.*

Robert J. Resnick received his Ph.D. in psychiatry from the University of Tennessee. He is presently assistant professor of psychiatry at the Medical College of Virginia, Virginia Commonwealth University. As a pediatric psychologist, he provides consultative and treatment services to the Department of Pediatrics in addition to conducting a private practice. His research interests are in the areas of psychotherapeutic techniques with children and child-rearing patterns. Advocationally, he tinkers with cars and plays basketball.

Rizpah L. Welch received her M.S. and Ed.D. of Education degrees from Indiana University. She currently serves as professor and chairperson of the Department of Special Education at Virginia Commonwealth University. An experienced classroom teacher, she is a specialist in reading, language development, language arts, mental retardation, and learning disabilities. She has been a consultant/supervisor in special education for the Richmond public schools and served as a consultant in early childhood education in Puerto Rico. She is presently chairperson of the Virginia Developmental Disabilities Planning and Advisory Council.

Paul Wehman earned his Ph.D. from the Department of Studies in Behavioral Disabilities at the University of Wisconsin–Madison. Prior to his appointment as assistant professor of special education at Virginia Commonwealth University, he was a psychologist at the Lincoln Developmental Center in Lincoln, Illinois. His interests focus on teacher training and applied behavior analysis with the severely and profoundly handicapped. His book, *Helping the Mentally Retarded Acquire Play Skills: A Behavioral Approach*, was just recently published.

Richard S. Vacca, Ed.D., is professor and chairman of the Department of Secondary/Post-Secondary Education at Virginia Commonwealth University. A consultant to several public school systems on matters of school law, he is currently state chairman of the National Organization on Legal Problems of Education. Among his most recent credits are a book, coauthored with J. Stephen O'Brien, entitled *The Supreme Court and the Religion-Education Controversy,* and an article in the *University of Richmond Law Review.*

Name Index

Subject Index